THE MULTINATIONAL BANKING INDUSTRY

THE MULTINATIONAL
BANKING INDUSTRY

NEIL COULBECK

NEW YORK UNIVERSITY PRESS

© 1984 N. Coulbeck
New York University Press, Washington Square,
New York, New York, 10003

Library of Congress Cataloging in Publication Data

Coulbeck, Neil, 1952-
    The multinational banking industry.

    Includes index.
    1. Banks and banking, International.   I. Title.
HG3881.C6742   1984   332.1'5   84-11521
ISBN 0-8147-1396-3

Printed and bound in Great Britain

CONTENTS

TABLES

FIGURES

ACKNOWLEDGEMENTS

The research for this book was mostly completed during the author's tenure as Midland Bank Research Fellow in the Department of Management Studies at Loughborough University of Technology. The author is grateful to the Midland Bank for its generous sponsorship of his activities, in the context of their overall support for banking studies at Loughborough. The book remains, of course, entirely the personal work and responsibility of the author.

The author has also received encouragement from Professor John Sizer, Head of the Department of Management Studies, and from Ray Shaw, formerly Senior Lecturer in the Law and Practice of Banking. He has benefited from the excellent facilities at Loughborough, especially the library, and also from collaboration and conversation with colleagues in the Management Studies and Economics Departments of the University.

Thanks are especially due to Mrs Christine Derbyshire and to Miss Margaret McMillan who typed the manuscript.

The author is now employed by National Westminster Bank, Financial Control Division, but this book represents his own views and opinions and is in no way to be taken as expressive of the views of the Bank.

ABBREVIATIONS

ATM	Automated Teller Machine
BIS	Bank for International Settlements
CD	Certificate of Deposit
CHAPS	Clearing House Automated Payments System
CHIPS	Clearing House Interbank Payments System
DFI	Direct Foreign Investment
ECU	European Currency Unit
EFT	Electronic Funds Transfer
FI	Financial Institution (Intermediary)
FRN	Floating Rate Note
GDP	Gross Domestic Product
GNP	Gross National Product
IBF	International Banking Facility
IMF	International Monetary Fund
IT	Information Technology
LCB	London Clearing Bank
LDC	Less Developed Country
LIBOR	London Inter-Bank Offered Rate
MNB	Multinational Bank
MNC	Multinational Corporation
NBFI	Non-Bank Financial Institution (Intermediary)
NIC	Newly Industrialised Country
OECD	Organisation for Economic Cooperation and Development
OPEC	Organisation of Petroleum Exporting Countries
QUACSO	Quasi-Commercial Service Organisation
RO	Representative Office
SDR	Special Drawing Right
SMBs	Small and Medium-sized Businesses
SWIFT	Society for Worldwide International Funds Transfer
T&E	Travel & Entertainment
TSB	Trustee Savings Bank
UMNB	Universal MNB
USP	Unique Selling Proposition
VDU	Visual Display Unit

VRA   Variable Rate Assets
VRL   Variable Rate Liabilities

INTRODUCTION

The problems of international banking and finance are now widely discussed in the media, and in many countries the purpose and function of the national banking system are vigorously debated. It is hoped that this book will provide the general reader and the more serious student of banking with an insight into the operations of large international banks in the major developed economies.

Many studies of banks and banking analyse commercial banks as financial intermediaries in the domestic and international economy. However, the leading banks of the world are first and foremost business enterprises, subject to the common organisational and financial disciplines. This study focuses therefore on universal multinational banks (UMNBs) analysed in terms of their strategic planning, business development and financial constraints. It highlights the market pressures which are causing leading banks in all the developed countries to adopt similar strategic positions, and recognises the fact that a relatively small number of fully diversified UMNBs form a competitive peer group of their own.

The study selects countries and banks which provide the best examples of UMNBs. The survey of each country is inevitably limited in depth, but more detailed case studies are presented to give a better idea of the problems which banks actually face and the ways in which management confronts these problems. Most attention has been devoted to US banks because of their central importance in the world banking system, and because they provide a model for the strategic development of banks in other countries. In later chapters a more broad brush approach is adopted. The analysis concentrates on the development of the banks in the 1960s and 1970s, and in particular on the process of diversification both in the range of activities and in geographical scope.

While much of the analysis is based on financial accounts and statistics, it should not be forgotten that banking is a retail service industry. Bankers work to foster profitable long-term bank-customer relationships, and many aspects of this work are not revealed in mere figures. Banks are also primarily profit-oriented, but have significant social responsibilities to fulfil and certain economic obligations not encountered by other industries.

A major problem in a study of this kind is the collation of data, and many secondary sources have been plundered in an attempt to build up a comprehensive picture of banking in a number of countries. It is hoped that the packaging of information of this kind will be useful to readers and that the references provided will be helpful to further research. In a brief study of this kind the surface has barely been scratched.

The first two chapters of the book provide the conceptual background and some general information on banking markets worldwide. The first chapter outlines the modern banking markets which form the environment for UMNBs, and the nature of bank operations is discussed from the point of view of the general management of the bank. A second chapter discusses multinational banks in particular and their competitive position in the market.

The study of individual countries and banks begins with the USA, thence to Japan whose banks are becoming an ever more powerful force in the world. Then the major European countries are introduced — United Kingdom, France, West Germany. Finally, two briefer chapters look at the Canadian and Swiss multinational banks.

In each of the country studies a similar approach is adopted. Firstly a brief survey is made of the national financial system, looking at the different types of financial institutions and their major activities. Then the regulatory framework is discussed, and the role of the central bank defined. The objects of our study, the major universal multinational banks, are then introduced in context, and their activities briefly described. Finally, an attempt is made to assess the strategic development of these banks in the recent past and foreseeable future. This is illustrated by a detailed case study of one or more banks.

The structure of each chapter is thus:

1. Financial system and regulation.
2. Strategic development of multinational banks.
3. Case study.

For reference, key country statistics are presented below.

Country Key Statistics, 1981

	Population, millions	Area, km² millions	Population density	US$bn GNP	US$ GNP per capita	Multinational banks
USA	230	9.4	25/km²	2,938	12,783	12
Canada	24	10.0	2/km²	274	11,318	5
UK	56	0.2	232/km²	505	9,055	6
France	54	0.6	98/km²	570	10,570	3
West Germany	62	0.3	248/km²	687	11,135	3
Switzerland	6	0.03	25/km²	93	14,470	3
Japan	117	0.4	309/km²	1,128	9,663	6

Note: All figures are rounded.

Source: P. Frazer and D. Vittas, *The Retail Banking Revolution* (Michael Lafferty, London, 1982), IMF and OECD publications, country chapters.

1 MULTINATIONAL BANKING

1.1 Banks and Their Services

Types of Bank

The classification of financial institutions presents some analytical problems since we can use various criteria. Vittas and others in their seminal study of comparative banking (1978) use as their main criterion the function of the bank or financial institution and propose the following scheme:

1. Central bank.
2. Deposit-taking institutions.
3. Medium- and long-term credit institutions.
4. Investing institutions.

Within this scheme they classify organisations further according to the system used by the official statistics of the individual countries. These statistical classifications may have been based either on further functional specialisation, on size, on locality, on type of ownership, on statutory or regulatory provisions.

Certainly function is the most useful general criterion. Central banks are public bodies which in all countries maintain control, by various mechanisms, of the national currency in both domestic and international markets. They also usually have overall responsibility for the banking system and the provision of bank credit. Deposit-taking institutions are empowered to accept deposits from the general public, and they will usually employ these deposits in short- and medium-term lending. They may operate in retail and business sectors, and in domestic, international and retail markets, and the larger deposit-taking institutions may well have developed as commercial enterprises to the extent that they have diversified into numerous other financial services. Since deposit-taking institutions have also progressively extended the volume and maturity of their term lending they have begun to take over many functions of the medium- and long-term credit institutions in many countries. These bodies, many of them created to assist in post-War reconstruction, are often joint ventures of deposit-taking

1

institutions, or are public agencies. They usually borrow by means of notes and debentures from investing institutions and deploy these funds in long-term loans to industry and by taking equity stakes. The investing institutions include insurance companies and pension funds and are not relevant to our discussion of banks, although they do compete in some of the same financial markets.

The present study is primarily concerned with deposit-taking institutions in different countries, and there are numerous sub-groups to consider. The deposit-taking institutions include banks and other types of institution, often known as near-banks. The distinction is usually embodied in statute or regulation. Most deposit banks are also clearing banks since they clear cheques for their customers including other non-clearing banks. They are also described as national banks, because of their nationwide coverage, and money-centre or city banks because they operate from head offices in financial centres. They are also often described as commercial banks to distinguish them from merchant or invest-ment banks. Merchant or investment banks do not normally raise deposits from the public and provide a specialised range of services usually geared to the needs of corporate and international customers.

The form of ownership and organisation is another important method of differentiating between types of bank. Most deposit banks are public companies quoted on the stock exchange of their own and sometimes other countries. Some, however, are under public ownership. Some are privately owned, although this is now virtually extinct. Many merchant or investment banks are still privately owned. Then there are public-sector agencies such as departments of the post office, mutual organisations, trusteeships, cooperative organisations, institutions created by special law or charter, and so on. The remarkable fact is that organisations of such different character compete in the same markets and use much the same methods in order to survive and grow.

The precise nature of the large deposit banks is further compli-cated by the fact that most of them have gone part or all of the way along the road to becoming *universal banks*, banks which offer all types of service, and this has usually meant the acquisition of large numbers of subsidiaries and affiliated companies and the adoption of a holding company structure. Under this arrangement the original deposit bank then becomes one of many subsidiaries, although usually by far the largest, of a commercial company; or is itself the parent holding company of its diverse subsidiary and associated companies.

In the international markets we come across various specialised types of bank, frequently acting as subsidiaries or affiliates of deposit banks. These include Eurobanks, specialising in Euro-currency business, basically a type of merchant bank, and consortium banks which are joint ventures of larger banks acting in concert. The term international bank is usually very loosely used to refer to banks which participate in international banking markets.

It can be seen that a large universal bank can in fact be described by a variety of names, as is shown in the example of German universal banks.

Public limited companies (Aktiengesellschaft, AG)
   quoted on German and other stock exchanges.
Group structure (bank plus subsidiaries and affiliates*).
Bank (Kreditwesengesetz, Banking Act 1961).
Clearing banks.
Deposit banks (public deposits and savings).
National banks (branch networks).
Commercial banks (short-term deposits and lending).
Merchant/investment banks (no division of functions in
   German system).
Mortgage bank subsidiaries.
International banks.
Eurobank subsidiaries.
Consortium bank participations.

*Note that the bank is the holding company. US banks have a separate holding company of which the bank is a subsidiary.

Bank Services

Banks in all countries meet their customers' financial needs by supplying a range of services in convenient locations under the management of qualified staff. There are of course differences in the details of the services offered in different countries, and there are significant differences in the extent of the range of services some banks are permitted to offer or wish to offer. Nevertheless, it is possible to describe in general terms the main types of service offered by commercial banks throughout the world. It would be tedious to present a full list of all the possible bank services, since major universal banks offer hundreds of different facilities, but the following matrices show the basic range offered to customers in the domestic and international markets by a universal bank. In foreign markets a multinational bank merely offers domestic and international services in a different country. The main markets of operation are shown in Figure 1.1.

The matrices also show the main competitors to the commercial banks in each of the market segments. It is notable that in almost every part of the market the universal bank competes against institutions which are specialists in that area, for example savings banks in the personal sector, merchant banks in the corporate sector, finance houses in asset-based finance. Often the universal bank participates in that part of the market by means of a subsidiary specialist institution, and the major management problem then is to integrate the services and operations of the subsidiary effectively with those of the main bank in order to achieve firstly cooperation and then synergy.[1] This process may take years. There are still many mainstream bank services where specialists compete directly with the bank, and this is one of the dangers of offering such a wide range of services. The banks must respond by training staff to very high levels of competence and by placing specialist staff in contact with customers when necessary.

It is also important to bear in mind that although the bank offers services, the customer has only financial needs. Bank services must be adapted to match and satisfy customer needs, and this is why the range of services must evolve continually. Customers have

Figure 1.1: Overview of Financial Markets

Domestic
    Retail markets
    Money markets   } Primary and secondary markets
    Capital markets

International
    International money markets
    (Eurocurrency markets)
    International capital markets   } Primary and secondary markets
    (Eurobond markets)
    Gold and commodity markets including futures markets

Foreign
    Retail markets
    Money markets   } Primary and secondary markets
    Capital markets

---

financial management needs, that is, practical problems to which a solution must be found: for example, how to make payment in a foreign currency to a party in Singapore, or how to finance purchase of a house, or how to invest safely a sum of money. They also have more general needs for a service which in every case offers convenience, security, efficiency, a good price, professional advice if needed, reliable information if needed, and assistance with financial planning. The order of priority of these general needs varies from one segment of the market to another, and from one customer to another. In the third column of the matrices we have attempted to rank these needs for different types of customer, on a purely subjective basis.

MARKET MATRIX FOR TYPICAL UNIVERSAL BANK GROUPS: DOMESTIC MARKETS 1, 2, 3

Domestic Market 1 — Consumer Financial Services (for persons, households, non-profit organisations)

Main Bank Services	*Competitors to Banks*	*Customer Needs*
Current account and associated services including cash cards	Other universal banks Cooperative banks	Convenience
Deposit account	Regional banks	Security
Term deposits	Savings banks	
Investment accounts	Post Office	Efficiency
Overdrafts	Mutual societies/ Building societies/	
Budget accounts	Mortgage banks	
Revolving credits	'Money shops'	Good price
Personal loans	Finance houses	
Credit cards	Insurance companies	
Housing loans (first mortgage)	Stock brokers Accountants	Professional advice
Top-up loans (second mortgage)	Solicitors Insurance brokers	Household financial planning
Stock and share services	Moneylenders	

Investment management	Credit and T&E card companies	Information
Tax management	Retailers	
Executor and Trustee		
Insurance	Travel agents	
Safe deposit		
Instalment credit		
Travel facilities		
Advice and counselling		

Mainly domestic currency business with some foreign exchange

Domestic market 2 — Middle Market and Corporate Financial Services (for sole traders, self-employed, partnerships, private and public companies, public corporations, governments and their agencies)

Main Bank Services	*Competitors to Banks**	*Customer Needs*
Current account and associated services	Other universal banks	Efficiency
Deposit account	Cooperative banks	Security
Term deposits	Regional banks	Good price
Overdraft	Foreign banks	Professional advice
Short and term loans		Convenience
Credit card facilities	Merchant and investment banks	
Hire purchase and instalment credit	Special credit institutions	Corporate planning
Leasing	Finance houses	Information
Factoring	Leasing companies	
Investment management	Factors	
Registrar work	Foreign exchange brokers	

Foreign services	Money brokers
Insurance	Stock brokers/ securities houses
Safe deposit	Accountants
Computer services	Solicitors
Credit references	Travel agents
Merchant banking	Management consultants
Advisory services	Computer bureaux
Import/export finance	Local authorities
Cash management	Credit card and T&E card companies Government departments Public agencies Development agencies

*There is also frequently a good deal of cooperation between banks and these 'competitors' in the area of business finance.

Mainly domestic currency business with some foreign exchange, currency investment and currency lending

Domestic market 3 — Banks and Financial Institutions

Main Bank Services	Competitors to Banks	Customer Needs
Special market for giving and taking of short-term deposits and standby facilities (interbank market)	Central bank	Security
	Discount houses	Efficiency
	Commercial banks	Convenience
Correspondent banking services	Company treasurers	Good price
	Local authorities	
	Moneybrokers	

Domestic and foreign currency business

MARKET MATRIX: INTERNATIONAL MARKETS 1, 2, 3

International Market 1 — Consumer Financial Services

Main Bank Services	Competitors to Banks	Customer Needs
Currency accounts	Foreign international banks	Professional advice
Eurocheques		Information
Travellers cheques	Travel agencies	Security
Credit card	Credit card companies	Good price
Accounts in foreign countries	Savings banks	Convenience
Payment services	Cooperative banks	Travel planning
Insurance	Regional banks	
Foreign exchange	Post Office	
Information		
Passport		
Introductions		

International Market 2 — Middle Market and Corporate Financial Services

Main Bank Services	Competitors to Banks*	Customer Needs
Accounts in foreign countries and currencies	Foreign and international banks	Professional advice
Foreign exchange	Merchant/investment banks	Efficiency
Foreign currency deposits	Multilateral agencies	Convenience
Foreign currency loans	Accountants	Security
Merchant banking	Solicitors	Information
Project finance	Management consultants	Corporate planning

Trade finance	Foreign exchange brokers
Syndicated loans	Stock brokers/ securities houses
Financial packaging	Moneybrokers
Credit information	
Economic intelligence	
Information on markets	
Insurance	
Cash management	
Computer services	
Investment facilities	
Foreign bonds	
Eurobonds	

*Again there is cooperation as well as competition.

Mainly currency business including Eurocurrencies

International Market 3 — Banks and Financial Institutions

Main Bank Services	*Competitors*	*Customer Needs*
Special market for giving and taking of short-term deposits and standby facilities	Central bank Discount houses Commercial banks Company treasurers	Low cost Security Efficiency Good price
Correspondent banking services	Local authorities Moneybrokers	
	Currency business	

Note: In listing competitors and naming services British terminology has been used. Different names are used in different countries but services and types of institution are remarkably similar — see country chapters.

1.2 Universal Multinational Banks

Multinational banking has been described quite simply as 'the ownership of banking facilities in one country by the citizens of another',[1] or as a bank operating in, or conducting banking operations deriving from, 'many different countries and national systems'.[2] These are fairly loose definitions of multinational activities which embrace the international activities of modern commercial banks, with the simple requirement that the bank should have established a physical presence in foreign countries. This physical presence can take the form of a subsidiary or affiliate, a representative office or branch. Mere club or correspondent links do not amount to multinational banking. The key to the activities of a multinational bank is thus *foreign direct investment* (FDI) rather than international lending.

By comparison with some other industries, FDI by banks is not well developed, and has a shorter history, since US banks did not see the same attractions in this process as US manufacturers did in the 1950s and 1960s. Bank FDI is still largely limited to wholesale banking activities (corporate and institutional deposits, lending and advisory services) in recognised financial centres. Very few banks have established foreign retail banking operations which enable them to participate fully in the domestic banking markets of another country. In some cases this is a matter of strategic policy, reflecting a view that a foreign bank can best compete in the wholesale and offshore markets; in others it is a matter of the stage of development reached by a bank. It is also a matter of the limited investment opportunities of this kind available, particularly when the activities of domestic banks are so closely controlled by domestic authorities. In the UK, for example, the acquisition of a domestic banking group by either of two British overseas banks was recently prevented by the authorities.

The sheer size of retail deposit banks in most countries also makes acquisition difficult. For these reasons the greatest attractions and opportunities have arisen in the USA where smaller commercial banks with growth prospects have been acquired by British, Japanese and other foreign banks. In other countries the acquisition of finance houses rather than banks has proved a simpler route and investments of this kind have been made in the UK, Australia and other countries. Acquisition of savings banks and mutual organisations is usually not possible for legal reasons.

Many foreign retail networks are also of colonial vintage. British, Canadian and European banks in particular have retail operations in Africa, Central and Latin America and Asia, acquired when the economic balance of power and terms of trade in the world were quite different.

It is interesting to compare the apparent strategies of two UK banks which have such traditional networks. Lloyds Bank has a large Latin American network but in more recent years has not attempted to increase its retail overseas representation, with the exception of the acquisition of a Californian bank. In fact, it divested from several branches in France, selling them to its rival, Barclays. Barclays Bank by contrast has a very large foreign network of long standing and in recent years has continued to increase its retail overseas representation in the USA, Europe and the Far East.

Banks which choose to specialise in these foreign operations will engage in domestic, international and offshore banking. They will be able to limit FDI to branches or subsidiaries sited in key financial centres to conduct corporate and securities business, funding operations from market deposits and probably borrowing and lending mainly in Eurocurrencies. After a time, such a branch may be able to make some headway in lending to domestic corporates in competition with indigenous banks; and if this business expands further, offices in important provincial centres may be justified. Probably a higher proportion of local staff will be taken on over time, some of them principally engaged in lending to domestic business customers. Over time, the bank may even penetrate the market for medium-sized businesses. In doing this, of course, it begins to take on higher risk credits requiring higher margins, more detailed credit analysis, higher administrative costs and so on. Local currency fundings will also be needed. Some foreign banks, notably American, have reached this stage in their penetration of the UK market.

A further advantage of this selective approach is also the ease with which the bank can divest if progress is unsatisfactory. An office can be closed, staff repatriated, business transferred to another domicile or at worst passed on to a correspondent partner. There is some loss of face but not much financial damage. Divesting from a foreign retail operation is far more difficult since the network must be sold, or closed down at great loss. Large numbers of staff must be redeployed. Prestige is more widely affected. The theory of FDI in banking is discussed more fully in Chapter 2.

The justification for retail FDI and wholesale FDI differs significantly. A bank contemplating retail FDI must be able to apply its management skills and marketing knowledge gained in its domestic market at low marginal cost in the chosen foreign market. This is particularly important since the opportunity to acquire a foreign bank will usually only arise in respect of either a smaller bank which is probably relatively undeveloped in its management practices, or an under-performing bank which requires turning round. The foreign bank must also be successfully integrated into the group's overall activities (synergy). A bank contemplating wholesale FDI has more obvious marketing advantages and does not have the same problems in transferring management expertise, since wholesale branches can effectively be controlled by a few high-quality expatriate staff. In a chosen foreign wholesale market the foreign bank can offer:

— Specialised knowledge of trade and capital markets of home country.
— Specialised knowledge of operations of home country organisations with trade relations or investments in the foreign market.
— Specialisation in wholesale banking with low operating costs which enables foreign bank to offer finest margins.
— Specialisation in wholesale banking and employment of top-quality staff enables foreign bank to offer premium service.

The main advantage lies in the home country base, especially when the home country is an important trading and financial market attractive to foreign traders and investors, and where there are economic or cultural barriers to entry to those markets which a bank of that country can help to overcome.

In considering the activities of multinational corporations in general other factors contributing to multinational status are also considered important besides levels of turnover and investment in foreign markets:

1. Raising of Capital in Foreign Markets

No bank has as yet issued equity in foreign markets or foreign currencies, although several major banks have secured quotation

Table 1.1: Multinational Banks with Share Quotations on Foreign Stock Exchanges

British Banks

Lloyds	New Zealand (1970).
Midland	Paris (1981).
NatWest	Dusseldorf, Frankfurt (1972).

US Bank Holding Companies

Citicorp	London, Amsterdam, Zurich, Geneva, Basel, Tokyo (Japanese Shareholder Service administered by Yasuda Trust).
J P Morgan	London (International Depository Receipts for stock in London and Brussels).
Chase Manhattan	Dusseldorf, Frankfurt, Paris, London, Tokyo.
Bank of America	London, Tokyo.
First Chicago	London, Tokyo.
Bankers Trust	London.
Manufacturers Hanover	London.
Continental Illinois	London.
Wells Fargo	London.
Security Pacific	London.
Chemical	London.

Commonwealth Banks

Royal Bank of Canada	London.
Bank of Montreal	London.
Bank of Nova Scotia	London.
Canadian Imperial Bank of Commerce	London.
Toronto — Dominion Bank	London.
Hong Kong & Shanghai	London.

European Banks

Commerz, Deutsche, Dresdner	London, Antwerp, Brussels, Amsterdam, Vienna, Basle, Berne, Geneva, Lausanne, Zurich, Luxembourg, Paris.
Swiss Bank Corporation	Frankfurt.

Japanese Banks

Dai-Ichi Kangyo	Amsterdam.

Notes

After London, the most popular choices are the Swiss market (Zurich, Geneva, Basel, etc). Tokyo is popular with the American banks. Other European exchanges are also used — Frankfurt, Paris, Amsterdam.

The London and Swiss markets will attract both resident and non-resident investors. German and Japanese markets will attract mainly resident investors. The US market is also mainly resident.

Citicorp is most widely quoted, in both Europe and Japan. Deutsche Bank and Commerzbank are very widely quoted in Europe, but their domestic capital markets lack depth and breadth.

Lloyds, Midland and NatWest have all sought quotations on exchanges of countries in which they had recently acquired subsidiaries, rather than in pursuit of strategic objectives. Commonwealth banks are a special historical case.

Shares of some 120 UK companies are now traded on the New York exchange through the American Depository Receipt (ADR) system, without being listed. Stamp duty and commission costs are low.

of their shares on foreign stock exchanges (see Table 1.1). Many banks have issued foreign bonds in foreign currencies (eg, Barclays and National Westminster in USA, 1981/2) and most large banks have issued Eurobonds and Capital Notes in Eurocurrencies. An element of foreign currency funding of foreign currency banking activities is an essential hedge against foreign exchange risks. Eurobonds and Notes have also been a very cheap, simple and flexible method of raising large sums at either fixed or variable rates.

Banks with foreign branches are also able to arrange short-term local currency borrowing, which may be particularly important in some scarcer currencies — for example, Japanese yen.

Nevertheless, it could be argued that there is in fact as yet no such thing as a multinational bank since no bank has a foreign equity base.

2. Political Independence

Large multinational corporations may have greater economic power and political influence than some of the governments of countries in which they operate, enabling them to act independently of the national interests of those countries and to allocate resources according to their own corporate objectives in spite of the wishes of the foreign government. However, financial markets in all countries are so closely controlled by governments that it is not possible for even a large multinational bank to act independently of governmental interference. Banks are also often looking to government and public sector agencies as potential customers. By comparison with the manufacturing giants, even the largest multinational banks are not in the top size range. As for banks' abilities to influence economic policies of borrowing countries, experience has shown that in practice commercial banks have very little leverage in sovereign risk situations and must rely on the IMF, BIS and other world agencies. Some major banks subscribe to the Guidelines for Multinational Enterprises annexed to the Declaration by Governments of OECD Member Countries on International Investment, which is a code of conduct for acceptable corporate behaviour.

3. Management Outlook

Large multinational corporations require a global approach to business problems with a heavy emphasis on strategic planning, risk management and group-wide strict financial control. Handling of information flows must also be first class. Personnel policies and recruitment must attract, retain and develop the personal and technical skills of sufficient people from a variety of countries. Not all companies are prepared to undertake the inevitable transformation of attitudes and practices necessary to succeed as a multinational in world markets. Banks with large, 'traditionalist' domestic operations have particular problems in this respect. The holding company or parent bank must also successfully promote a group corporate ethos and prevent the outbreak of dysfunctional rivalries between subsidiaries. It is essential to achieve synergic growth of a disparate and dispersed set of group companies. This demands strong established systems and procedures, especially for financial reporting, and the generation of corporate identity and spirit which encourages cooperation. This does not necessarily imply heavy centralisation and in practice different companies have a quite different approach to the question of centralised versus decentralised systems and decision-making. Citicorp, for example, has identified two problems encountered by a growing MNC, namely *bureaucratisation* (staff management and upwards reporting requirements stifling line management and initiative) and *balkanisation* (disintegration of group into separate power blocs). Decentralisation reduces the danger of bureaucratisation, but may lead to loss of control and it increases the danger of balkanisation. In some areas such as treasury management centralisation may be found to be unavoidable and Citicorp, for example, has recently taken some steps to recentralise its asset and liability management to secure global funds management control.

The quality of management information reports available from subsidiaries and divisions is a crucial factor, since if the central executive can rely on accurate monitoring of key figures and developments it may delegate authority but still keep a finger on the pulse and intervene if necessary.

In this study we have accepted the loose definition of multinational banking, which brings in the international operations of the West German, Swiss and Japanese major banks, and of smaller US banks in addition to the more well-established multinational banks (US majors, British, French, Canadian); but special attention is devoted to the activities of multinational banks which have extended their diversified financial service operations into foreign countries, rather than specialising in wholesale operations in foreign countries — in other words, *universal multinational banks* (UMNBs). These large, complex, financial service enterprises, at the centre of whose group operations stands a traditional domestic commercial bank of nineteenth-century origin which steadily diversified in domestic operations, then developed international banking capabilities, and then in certain cases established diversified multinational operations as well, are a fascinating phenomenon.

Very few banks have reached this stage of development and it is possible that even fewer will survive the next round of necessary capital investment in information technology. Banks with global networks are now faced with the prospect of improving communications between overseas offices to accelerate the flow of information and funds. Banks which achieve virtually instantaneous communication by computer-satellite-computer links will be able to offer a superior multinational capability in terms of customer service and their own global funds management. However, the costs and risks of such investment are enormous and will only be undertaken by the very largest and most confident enterprises. Such investment may not even best be undertaken by banks but rather by communications enterprises, or through joint ventures.

A United Nations study of the operations and strategies of transnational (viz. multinational) banks surveyed the position in 1975. They defined banking as being at least the raising of deposits and loans (thus excluding representative offices and agencies) and multinational banking as banking in five or more countries. By this loose definition only 84 banks in the world were classified as multinational in 1975, almost exclusively banks from the major developed countries, namely USA, UK, Switzerland, Japan, West Germany, France, Canada, which are the countries selected for this study. Since then more banks have extended their international activities and would now count as multinational, but still very few banks are universal multinationals in the sense we have discussed.

The United Nations MNBs were (1975) in the size-range \$2 billion total assets–\$40 billion total assets, with branch networks in the range 10–150+, but with most in the middle ranges of \$10–\$40 billion total assets and 10–60 branches. Assets, but not networks, were heavily concentrated with larger banks. One could say that a smaller bank may or may not go multinational as a matter of strategic choice, but a larger bank must go multinational for strategically defensive reasons.[3]

The steady process of diversification and internationalisation of large commercial banks is practically inevitable. It can be traced in various countries, in the context of the historical development of that country's economy and trading operations. The latest major entrants are, of course, Japanese banks, and in due course no doubt Australian banks will begin to make a bigger impact as the economy of the Pacific Basin outgrows other areas. The banks of the Middle East already have a substantial involvement in limited areas of banking (wholesale deposits and development banking).

The inevitable process is *diversification* for offensive reasons (new opportunities) and defensive reasons (protection of existing operations from threats of competition or environmental change). Diversification is both operational (new types of activity) and geographical (new areas for activity). Commercial banks have always been integrated economic units, since they constitute the entire production process for bank services.

Indicators of the degree of geographical multinational diversification include:

Foreign subsidiaries, numbers/size.
Foreign affiliates, numbers/size.
Foreign branches, numbers/size.
Representation in all financial centres.
Representation in all major developed countries.
Representation in selected developing countries.
Foreign *retail* banking acquisitions.
Proportion of foreign liabilities/assets* in group.
Proportion of foreign earnings* in group.
Element of currency loan stock, quotation on foreign stock
    exchanges.
Number of overseas staff.
Practice of global funds management.

*Note that there are various possible definitions of foreign items — foreign currency, foreign domicile, foreign customer relationship — and that international foreign currency business is often done from a *domestic* financial centre.

Indicators of operational multinational diversification include:

Eurocurrency credits, number/size/managerships/agencies.
Eurobonds, issuing/underwriting activity.
Foreign bonds, issuing/underwriting activity.
Foreign local currency lending.
Foreign leasing.
International factoring.
Merchant banking.
Investment management.
Advisory services.
Trade finance.
Interbank borrowing and lending.
Cash management services.

Other indicators of the achievement of multinational capabilities by a bank include:

Innovatory initiatives in world markets.
Market leadership in selected products or markets.
Advanced technological development.
First-class relations with large corporate customers.
First-class relationships with other financial institutions.
First-class relationships with parent and host-country
    authorities.
Prime name in global financial markets.

The major impetus to multinational banking is the wealth maximisation objective of bank management. Multinational banking has been necessary in the first instance to service the needs of multinational customers. And then the development of extensive international money and capital markets since the 1960s has opened up opportunities in wholesale banking for large banks with the requisite skills. Finally, recognition of limited growth opportunities in domestic retail and wholesale markets has driven some banks to make more extensive foreign direct investment in the hope of securing future growth opportunities in foreign markets. Geographical diversification of activities also spreads risk across a number of national economies, reducing exposure to systematic risk in a national market (although none can avoid global systematic risk) and providing countercyclical income streams.

In most cases, banks go multinational for defensive reasons, in order to maintain relationships with existing customers now requiring that level of service, and which they would otherwise have to obtain from local foreign banks or foreign multinationals. The latest banks to adopt this approach are the Japanese, servicing the needs of Japan's MNCs and international traders. There is, however, a danger in the customer service doctrine in banking, since the attempt to provide services beyond its capabilities may lead a bank into unprofitable operations where it never achieves the volume and quality of business necessary to break even. Customer needs are important but cannot be allowed to determine strategic decisions of this importance. The basic aim of a bank is to grow and survive in the interests of its shareholders by operating in selected *profitable* markets, not to follow customers willy-nilly across the world.

These growth/survival needs can be summarised as follows:

Protect or increase domestic/international/foreign market shares.

Ensure or improve future return on assets/equity.

Achieve synergic growth in a complex group.

Achieve economies of scale in operations.

Hedge currency interest rate and country risks.

Attain global funds management benefits.

There are also undoubtedly non-rational reasons for strategic development along these lines in the interests of national prestige, corporate image, or even personal interests of executive management. And historical factors determine many of the present activities of a bank. Nevertheless, whatever the unique historical and cultural position of different banks in different countries, the same rational and irrational reasons tend to push the largest and most progressive along the road to becoming universal multi-national banks.

Figure 1.2 shows in outline the typical structure of a UMNB straddling its various markets and embracing its numerous subsidiaries.

It can also be argued that the growth of multinational banking has welfare effects for national economies. Benefits include:

— Competition in retail and wholesale banking to domestic oligopolies.

— Use of existing capital and management resources at low

Figure 1.2: Universal Multinational Bank Structure

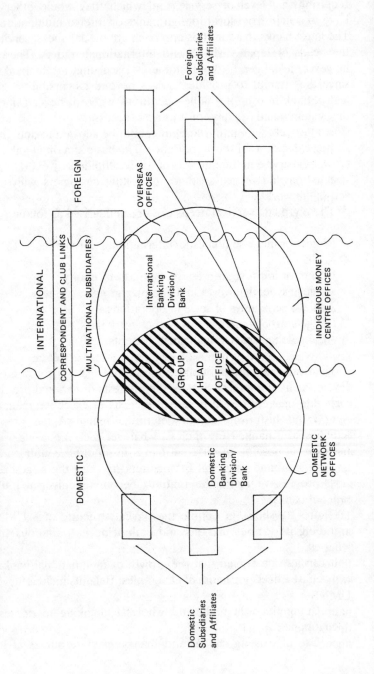

marginal cost when superior skills and financial backing are transferred from one country to another ('technology transfer' in a service industry is equally valid).

— Increased efficiency/lower cost of financial flows between countries, and a higher velocity of circulation of international money.

— Superior financial services available to multinational organisations of all kinds.

— Freer flows of information relating to financial and other markets.

— Political stabilisation effects of cross-investment. Economic and financial considerations can affect political and even military conflicts — for example, the Iranian US hostages and Iranian US bank deposits, and Polish dependence on Western bank lending.

Costs include:

— Banks' partial escape from regulations and controls imposed in domestic markets.

— Destabilising effects on national monetary policies of increased liquidity and circulation of money.

— Weakening of domestic banking industry to the gain of foreign shareholders of foreign banks.

It is possible to identify three basic patterns in the organisation of UMNBs, corresponding to the banks' *strategic structures* — that is, the nature of their business and operations which has derived from previous strategic development, being a mixture of historical factors and active management decisions.

There is a limited number of banks with comprehensive global branch networks and extensive foreign investments (first-tier UMNBs). These banks have long traditions as diversified UMNBs and include the largest US banks, Barclays and possibly Hong Kong and Shanghai. There is a larger number of banks with more limited global branching, concentrated on financial centres and with a smaller portfolio of foreign investments (second-tier UMNBs). Some of these banks have long traditions of multinational banking, while others, such as the Japanese, have entered this phase of development more recently. In view of economic uncertainty, increasing risks, and limited capital resources it seems unlikely that many of these banks will choose to emulate the global branching of the leading UMNBs, although in the longer term the Japanese banks may have the capacity to do so. There is a still larger number of banks with some overseas branches and foreign investments, and membership of clubs and consortia (third-tier UMNBs). These are mostly banks without a long tradition of multinational banking and most of them have ambitions to increase their presence in world markets and become part of the second tier of UMNBs; unless they have chosen to specialise in certain markets.

Another set of banks still reflects very strongly historical origins of global development based on colonial ties. Their networks show distinct regional bias and their worldwide representation has not been fully redistributed in accordance with a multinational banking strategy. Of the British banks, Barclays and Lloyds for example have colonial networks, but have reshaped their organisations to achieve a desired strategic structure; whereas Grindlays or Standard and Chartered have not yet managed so successfully to realign themselves to meet the demands of changing economies and credit markets.

The strategies adopted by different banks are discussed more fully in the country chapters, where account is also taken of historical factors and national economic development processes. In general terms, however, we can say that a MNB faces important decisions in deciding how far to go along the road to diversification, and whether to specialise in terms of services, by concentrating, for example, on wholesale business, or in terms of geographical markets, by concentrating for example on fast-growing economic zones and divesting elsewhere.

1.3 International Financial Intermediation

In order to understand the structure of the multinational banking industry and the operations of UMNBs it is essential to examine the banks' role in the international economy. UMNBs are the most important financial intermediaries in the international markets.

The process is similar to domestic financial intermediation but because there is no sectoral breakdown of the world economy the economic units with which we are concerned are geographical — countries and regions — rather than sectors of the home economy.

Behind the geographical figures the same sectoral redistribution is going on to some extent, but unfortunately the statistics are not designed to show this. Most of the intermediation is of wholesale deposits, so that the personal sector is excluded, and a large part involves deposits given and taken by banks and other financial institutions.

Before discussing the international process it may be useful to consider the theory of financial intermediation in a little more depth. In direct financial markets brokers act as links between borrowers and lenders — for example, stockbrokers. In indirect financial markets an intermediary stands between borrowers and lenders. It takes deposits, offering maturity, price and liquidity features attractive to depositors in that market, and safety; and it makes loans, offering maturity and other features, especially price, attractive to borrowers in that market. The intermediary covers costs and makes a profit by setting an interest margin between rates paid on deposits and charged on advances. It also charges for transactions costs, and may take other fees such as arrangement fees, management or advisory fees. The process is efficient because by pooling deposits and loans the intermediary reduces the uncertainties of direct financial investment for depositors/investors, and the overall systematic level of risk. Pooled depositors' funds will be stable over time in the absence of major financial crisis or the failure of the deposit-holding bank. A large portfolio of loans can be diversified by sectors, borrowers, countries; and this reduces risks. The intermediary also has economies of scale, and builds up considerable expertise in credit assessment and in its own financial management. It can therefore practise maturity transformation, in other words borrow short and lend long. In the long run a commercial bank earns profits from the development and maintenance of a good quality loan portfolio achieved through the skills of its lending officers, although this portfolio must be properly funded in order to ensure optimum, stable profits over time.

International banks operating in the Euromarkets have during the 1970s played a very important role in the process of international financial intermediation by their provision of trade finance, and, more importantly, medium-term currency credits, notably in the form of syndicated loans.[4] They have also been important brokers and underwriters in the international bond markets. It is now evident that commercial banks provided much of the financing required by countries running balance of payments deficits during the period, in addition to their more traditional lending to industrial and commercial customers. This large-scale sovereign lending was a new venture for international banks in the post-War era with which we are concerned, and it has not proved a very happy one since several major borrowing countries encountered debt servicing problems in 1981/2 and there have been frequent reschedulings and rearrangements negotiated with the lending banks.

The need for large-scale borrowing by developing countries in particular arose from international payments imbalances, a large part of which was caused by the surpluses run by OPEC countries, subsequent to oil price rises in 1974 and 1979. These countries have maintained large 'petrodollar' deposits with commercial banks in consequence. Since 1979 the world recession has also obliged industrialised nations of the Group of Ten to finance deficits. The effects of these imbalances are shown in Table 1.2, which portrays the steady increase in the volume of syndicated medium-term Eurocredits, of net new international bank lending of all types, and of net new international bond market finance. Prior to 1977 the smaller developed and non-oil-exporting developing countries financed about one quarter of their total requirements from the banks via the Eurocurrency market, but in 1977 it rose to about one half. Lending continued at high volumes in 1981 (not shown) but in the latter part of 1982 the Euroloan market slumped as banks experienced bad debt problems.

However, credit and country risk analysis practised by the lending banks have insured that they have lent selectively. Lending to developing countries has been almost exclusively to those in the upper income groups, and of the total volume of net floating rate debt in 1982 over 75 per cent was to four borrowers only — Brazil, Mexico, Argentina, South Korea — countries rapidly industrialising, with extensive natural resources, and stable regimes (Table 1.3). Nevertheless, three of these countries have been obliged to reschedule their debts in 1981/2/3.

The figures in Table 1.4 show us in greater detail the geographical sources and uses of Eurocurrency funds during the period 1975–80, which can now be seen as the boom era for Euroloans. These figures are compiled by the Bank for International Settlements (BIS) from information supplied by banks within its reporting area, which now covers most of the developed world. In assessing these flows, it is important to bear in mind the very high volume of inter-

Table 1.2: Indicators of International Payments Imbalances and Their Financing (US$ billions)

	1973	1974	1975	1976	1977	1978	1979	1980
A *Current-account balance of payments*								
1 OPEC	6	67	31	34	26	-2	65	110
2 Group of Ten countries plus Switzerland	12	-13	17	2	4	20	-22	-53
2a (of which the USA)	(7)	(2)	(18)	(5)	(-14)	(-14)	(-1)	(-)
3 Smaller developed economies	—	-16	-19	-23	-24	-29	-10	-24
4 Non-oil developing countries	-6	-23	-32	-19	-13	-24	-39	-66
B *Financing the current-account deficits: smaller developed and developing countries*								
5 Sum of current-account deficits in 3 and 4	-6	-39	-51	-42	-37	-33	-49	-90
6 Capital-market finance	11	27	31	34	33	45	35	62
6a (of which new borrowing from banks in the Eurocurrency market)	n.a.	(10)	(9)	(12)	(17)	(16)	(26)	(32)
7 Other capital flows[a]	6	8	14	12	16	10	24	28
8 Change in reserves (increase = —)	-11	4	6	-4	-12	-23	-10	—
C *International capital markets*								
9 Announced volume of syndicated medium-term Euro-credits	6	28	20	22	37	(51)[b]	(64)[b]	(55)[b]
						58	71	73
10 Average Euro-market spread (per cent)	0.9	1.0	1.7	1.6	1.2	1.0	0.7	0.7
11 Net new international bank lending	n.a.[c]	n.a.	40	70	75	110	130	145
12 Net new international bond market finance	n.a.	n.a.	20	30	31	29	28	29

Notes: a. Includes direct investment and concessional loans. b. Adjusted for approximate refinancing and pre- and repayments. c. n.a. = not available.

Sources: IMF, BIS and Bank of England publications, quoted in R.B. Johnston, *The Economics of the Euro-market* (Macmillan, London, 1983).

Table 1.3: Floating Rate Debt — Major Debtors, 1982

	$ billion	%
Mexico	59	31.6
Brazil	46	24.6
Argentina	21	11.2
South Korea	16	8.5
Other net debtors	45	24.1
Total	187	100.0

Source: *Bank of England Quarterly Bulletin (BEQB)*, March, 1983.

bank borrowing and lending at the core of the Euromarkets, and the role of financial centres in the movement of Eurocurrency deposits.

The figures show that the European area, both banks and non-banks, has been roughly in balance over the period, providing funds in some years and taking funds in other years. The USA has fairly consistently supplied funds to the market, as have the other developed countries. Eastern Europe has been a steady user, as have the developing countries, both of whom were even obliged to withdraw deposits in 1980. The offshore banking countries are of course in balance since they fulfil an entrepot function merely.

The figures in Table 1.5 show the flows which took place in 1981, and the stock position in September 1982. Banks in the BIS area received non-resident deposits totalling US$299 billion. Nearly half these were taken in by banks in Europe, and $79 billion in the United Kingdom alone, reflecting the importance of London as a banking centre. Banks in the USA, Canada, Japan, and various offshore centres accounted for the rest. The sources of these funds were principally banks within the BIS area (US$158 billion), reflecting the importance of the interbank market. A more precise analysis is given in Table 1.6 which shows that the major supplier of funds in the year to September 1982 was the USA (banks and non-banks), with Switzerland a poor second. UK banks took in significant amounts of deposits. The stock positions show large assets held by US banks and non-banks, and by Swiss banks and non-banks, while significant liabilities have been incurred by Canadian, Italian, Japanese and of course UK banks; and by Danish, French, Italian, Japanese, Swedish and especially West German non-banks.

Nearly half the lending to non-residents in 1981 was performed

Table 1.4: Changes in Estimated Net Sources and Uses of Eurocurrency Funds ($ billions)

	Reporting banks	European Area non-banks	USA	Other developed countries[a]	Eastern Europe	Offshore banking countries	Oil-exporting countries	Developing countries	Total[b]
A Uses									
1975	0.8	+ 2.3	− 1.7	+ 7.4	+ 5.8	+ 8.9	+ 1.8	+ 3.8	+ 28.0
1976	+ 4.2	+ 7.9	+ 1.7	+ 8.6	+ 4.9	+ 5.2	+ 4.3	+ 5.2	+ 42.0
1977	+ 5.7	+ 18.4	+ 2.8	+ 6.7	+ 3.0	+ 2.9	+ 6.0	+ 5.3	+ 53.0
1978	+ 11.9	+ 17.2	+ 3.3	+ 9.8	+ 5.7	+ 11.1	+ 8.6	+ 9.8	+ 77.0
1979	+ 15.0	+ 16.8	+ 12.1	+ 14.2	+ 4.6	+ 12.5	+ 6.1	+ 15.0	+ 98.0
1980	+ 12.7	+ 32.4	+ 3.0	+ 24.5	+ 2.9	+ 6.5	+ 3.4	+ 15.9	+ 100.0
Total 1975–80	+ 48.7	+ 95.0	+ 21.2	+ 71.2	+ 26.9	+ 47.1	+ 30.2	+ 55.0	+ 398.0
B Sources									
1975	+ 9.6	+ 2.1	+ 3.5	+ 1.4	+ 0.3	+ 4.0	+ 5.5	+ 0.7	+ 28.0
1976	+ 1.8	+ 6.3	+ 2.6	+ 1.4	+ 1.0	+ 8.3	+ 10.6	+ 5.1	+ 42.0
1977	+ 11.6	+ 9.4	+ 6.1	+ 5.3	—	+ 3.1	+ 8.8	+ 8.2	+ 53.0
1978	+ 13.1	+ 14.1	+ 11.6	+ 7.4	+ 1.8	+ 12.0	+ 0.2	+ 10.2	+ 77.0
1979	+ 6.6	+ 22.9	+ 13.5	+ 5.5	+ 4.2	+ 7.4	+ 26.3	+ 8.0	+ 98.0
1980	+ 5.7	+ 31.3	+ 9.2	+ 8.7	− 0.2	+ 15.2	+ 28.8	− 1.2	+ 100.0
Total 1975–80	+ 48.4	+ 86.1	+ 46.5	+ 36.2	+ 7.1	+ 50.0	+ 80.2	+ 31.0	+ 398.0

Notes: a. Includes Canada and Japan. b. Includes an amount of unallocated funds.

Source: Bank for International Settlements' quarterly press releases, quoted in R.B. Johnston, *The Economics of the Euro-market* (Macmillan, London, 1983).

Table 1.5: International Business of Banks in the BIS Reporting
Area and Offshore Centres, 1981 and 1982 Outstanding ($ billions)[a]

	1981	Outstanding September 1982
Deposits from non-residents		
Total	+ 299	1,814
Placed with banks in:		
Reporting European area	+ 128	1,003
of which, United Kingdom	+ *79*	*484*
United States	+ 38	239
Canada and Japan	+ 40	164
Offshore centres: US banks	+ 33	175
Non-reporting banks	+ 60	234
Source		
Outside reporting area		
Developed countries	+ 3	51
Eastern Europe	—	12
Oil-exporting countries	+ 3	140
Non-oil developing countries	+ 10	98
of which, Latin America	+ *6*	*37*
Sub-total	+ 17	301
Inside reporting area		
Banks	+ 158	1,010
Non-banks	+ 41	227
Unallocated	+ 83	276
Lending to non-residents		
Total	+ 329	1,874
Lent by banks in:		
Reporting European area	+ 136	984
of which, United Kingdom	+ *80*	*460*
United States	+ 76	346
Canada and Japan	+ 24	128
Offshore centres: US banks	+ 32	169
Non-reporting banks[b]	+ 61	248
Direction		
Outside reporting area		
Developed countries	+ 17	106
Eastern Europe	+ 5	52
Oil-exporting countries	+ 4	77
Non-oil developing countries	+ 42	240
of which, Latin America	+ *33*	*169*
Sub-total	+ 66	475
Inside reporting area		
Banks	+ 152	930
Non-banks	+ 31	190
Unallocated	+ 78	279
Foreign currency deposits from residents		
From banks	+ 46	300
From non-banks	+ 8	51

Foreign currency lending to residents

To banks	+ 41	297
To non-banks	+ 30	123

Notes: a. Changes exclude estimated exchange rate effects. b. Partial estimates.

Source: *Bank of England Quarterly Bulletin,* March 1983.

by banks within the European area, and $80 billion was from London (Table 1.5). The banks in the USA have however a greater importance in this lending activity than they do in deposit-taking. Naturally the vast part of this lending is interbank. The size of this market in non-resident deposits is vast compared with the market in resident foreign currency deposits and foreign currency lending, which is the traditional type of international banking.

Tables 1.7, 1.8, 1.9 show in greater detail the business of reporting area banks with different sectors of the world.

The role of commercial banks in funding balance of payments deficits has raised difficult questions for bankers, who are exposed to sovereign risk, and who have also been funding medium-term loans from short-term Eurocurrency deposits although with the protection of interest rate roll-over dates. It has also posed problems for governments and official agencies attempting to achieve order and equilibrium in the financing of surpluses and deficits, since it has been argued that the commercial banks have facilitated the running of excessive deficits, and have also offered credits without the sort of conditions and provisions required by agencies like the IMF.

Commercial banks are in no position to stipulate economic policy guidelines for borrowing countries in the manner of the IMF, and they do not appear to have the same force of moral suasion as the World Bank. Nevertheless, it is interesting to see that during the recent reschedulings central banks and agencies have supported the commercial banks and helped to secure satisfactory agreements with borrowing countries.

In the future it is likely that there will be closer collaboration between commercial banks and official agencies. It is also probable that in the near future banks will prefer to revert to non-sovereign lending direct to economic enterprises, by way of trade finance including leasing, by way of project finance and by asset-based finance of various kinds, in order to reduce their credit risks. It is possible that medium-term finance will be increasingly supplied by

Table 1.6: Net Supply of Funds from Countries within the BIS Reporting Area ($ billions)[a]

Changes (excluding estimated exchange rate effects): increase in net assets (suppliers) +/liabilities (takers) −

	Austria	Belgium	Luxembourg	Canada	Denmark	France	Ireland	Italy	Japan	Netherlands	Sweden	Switzerland	United Kingdom	United States[b]	West Germany	Sub-total	Offshore banking centres[c]	Total (as in Table 1.5)
Year to September 1982																		
Banks	+1.1	−2.7	+1.0	+0.6	+0.2	−1.8	−0.7	+0.4	+1.8	+0.4	+0.8	+4.2	−13.4	+46.5	+3.5	+41.9	+0.1	+42
Non-banks	−0.2	−0.7		+0.1	−0.9	−2.5	−1.3	−4.3	+2.3	+0.2	−2.1	+4.1	−0.6	+24.0	−4.5	+13.6	−2.6	+11
Amounts outstanding at end September 1982: net assets (+)/liabilities (−)																		
Banks	−1.2	−10.2	+5.5	−21.7	+0.4	+4.9	−2.7	−10.6	−14.4	+1.6	−5.3	+19.7	−23.9	+107.2	+3.2	+52.5	+7.5	+60
Non-banks	−1.7	−1.3		−0.8	−9.8	−6.5	−3.9	−16.8	−6.3	—	−8.1	+13.4	−0.3	+100.7	−30.3	+28.3	+8.7	+37
Total	−2.9	−11.5	+5.5	−22.5	−9.4	−1.6	−6.6	−27.4	−20.7	+1.6	−13.4	+33.1	−24.2	+207.9	−27.1	+80.8	+16.2	+97

Notes: a. The figures for banks give the net external lending by banks of the countries shown (ie, total lending to non-residents net of deposits from non-residents, Table 1.5). The figures for non-banks give the net external deposits of non-bank residents of these countries with the BIS reporting banks (ie, deposits from non-banks inside the reporting area net of lending to non-banks inside the reporting area in Table 1.5); business in Swiss francs at banks in Switzerland is excluded. b. The figures for non-banks include deposits with, but not borrowing from, the branches of US banks in offshore banking centres. c. The figures involve a considerable degree of estimation.

Source: *Bank of England Quarterly Bulletin*, March 1983.

Table 1.7: Business of BIS Reporting Area Banks with Non-oil Developing Countries in Latin America, 1981 and 1982 Outstanding ($ billions)

| | Transactions in year to end-September | | Outstanding at end-September |
	1981	1982	1982
Changes exclude estimated exchange rate effects[a]			
Lending			
Total	+23.9	+25.1	169.2
of which, to:			
Argentina	+ 3.4	+ 0.8	22.5
Brazil	+ 4.5	+ 9.5	55.1
Mexico[b]	+12.9	+10.1	60.0
Deposits			
Total	—	+ 2.0	36.9
of which, from:			
Argentina	− 1.9	− 0.5	5.4
Brazil	+ 0.3	− 0.4	4.1
Mexico[b]	+ 2.2	+ 1.1	11.0
Net lendings			
Total	+23.9	+23.1	132.3
of which, to			
Argentina	+ 5.3	+ 1.3	17.1
Brazil	+ 4.2	+ 9.9	51.0
Mexico[b]	+10.7	+ 9.0	49.0

Notes a. The figures for individual countries are adjusted by the Bank of England to exclude the estimated effect of exchange rate movements, but the adjustments are based on incomplete information and should be regarded as approximate. b. By convention, Mexico is included in non-oil developing countries even though it is an exporter of oil.

Source: *Bank of England Quarterly Bulletin*, March 1983.

way of bonds and notes issued by the borrower, a form of direct financing in which the banks act only as brokers, managers and underwriters. The Eurodeposit and loan markets may then become once more, as they were in the 1960s, essentially interbank markets enabling banks to have access to a worldwide market in high quality liquid assets for both borrowing and lending purposes.

Interbank trading in the Euromarkets accounts for about two-thirds of all business and has been said to perform four basic functions:[5]

Table 1.8: Business of BIS Reporting Area Banks with Eastern
Europe, 1981 and 1982 Outstanding ($ billions)

| | Transactions in year to end-September | | Outstanding at end-September |
	1981	1982	1982
Changes exclude estimated exchange rate effects[a]			
Lending			
Total	+ 5.2	− 3.5	52.1
of which, to:			
German Democratic Republic[b]	+ 1.5	− 0.9	8.5
Hungary	+ 0.4	− 0.4	6.3
Poland	+ 0.2	− 1.4	12.9
USSR	+ 4.3	− 1.2	13.7
Deposits			
Total	− 1.4	+ 2.0	12.2
of which, from:			
German Democratic Republic[b]	− 0.2	− 0.6	1.2
Hungary	+ 0.3	− 0.4	0.2
Poland	− 0.1	+ 0.1	0.9
USSR	− 1.7	+ 3.3	7.4
Net Lending			
Total	+ 6.6	− 5.5	39.9
of which, to			
German Democratic Republic[b]	+ 1.7	− 0.3	7.3
Hungary	+ 0.1	−	6.1
Poland	+ 0.3	− 1.5	12.0
USSR	+ 6.0	− 4.5	6.3

Notes a. See footnote a to Table 1.7. b. Excluding the position of banks in West
Germany.

Source: *Bank of England Quarterly Bulletin*, March 1983.

1. Liquidity smoothing — banks can manage their assets and
   liabilities at the margin to meet daily and seasonal fluctuations
   in liquidity requirements.
2. Liquidity transfer — deposits initially placed with certain
   banks can be on-lent to different banks and so on in series,
   often from larger to smaller banks.
3. Currency transfer — banks can adjust deposits and loans in
   order to match up currencies on both sides of the balance
   sheet by buying or selling currency deposits.

Table 1.9: Business of BIS Reporting Area Banks with Oil-exporting
Countries, 1981 and 1982 Outstanding ($ billions)

| | Transactions in year to end-September | | Outstanding at end-September |
	1981	1982	1982
Changes exclude estimated exchange rate effects[a]			
Lending			
Total	+10.6	+10.5	77.2
of which, to:			
Middle East:[b]			
low absorbers	+ 1.2	+ 1.8	9.7
high absorbers	+ 0.9	+4.5	16.6
Nigeria	+ 2.4	+ 1.8	6.0
Venezuela	+ 3.9	+ 2.1	22.5
Other	+ 2.2	+ 0.3	22.4
Deposits			
Total	+29.9	−13.1	140.1
of which, from:			
Middle East:[b]			
low absorbers	+30.6	+ 8.8	72.7
high absorbers	− 2.5	−15.5	30.7
Nigeria	− 3.1	− 0.9	1.6
Venezuela	+ 6.5	− 4.9	13.8
Other	− 1.6	− 0.6	21.3
Net lending			
Total	−19.3	+23.6	−62.9
of which, to:			
Middle East:[b]			
low absorbers	−29.4	− 7.0	−63.0
high absorbers	+ 1.6	+20.0	−14.1
Nigeria	+ 5.5	+ 2.7	+ 4.4
Venezuela	− 2.6	+ 7.0	+ 8.7
Other	+ 5.6	+ 0.9	+ 1.1

Notes a. See footnote a to Table 1.7. b. The split of high and low absorbers
distinguishes countries with higher and lower levels of inward investment.

Source: *Bank of England Quarterly Bulletin*, March 1983.

4. Global liquidity distribution — banks operating in financial
    centres enable funds to be switched around the world from
    markets where there is an excess of liquidity to markets where
    there is a shortage.

These processes are illustrated in Figure 1.3.

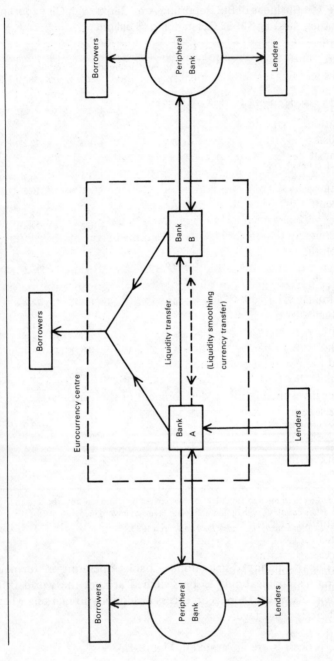

Figure 1.3: Liquidity Distribution Through the Interbank Market

Source: R.B. Johnston, *The Economics of the Euro-market* (Macmillan, London, 1983).

Financial Centres

Although large deposit banks have extensive nationwide networks of offices the Head Office is invariably located in a major financial centre. This is essential in order to maintain close links with other banks and financial institutions, money and capital markets, industrial and commercial companies, government and the media. These centres play an extremely important role in ensuring the efficiency of national and international banking markets.

Historical studies have shown that regional banking and financial centres develop at an early stage in order to meet the needs of a developing economy. A national centre will then usually emerge which links the regional centres and provides a further concentration of banking and financial activities. This national centre will then become the major international financial centre for the country, the chosen location for foreign financial institutions establishing operations in the host country, and the site of the foreign exchange markets. Some international centres may then further develop their range of markets and available services to become clearing centres for international transactions of all kinds conducted by participants from all over the world. In this manner a hierarchy of financial centres is established, providing the means for the global financial markets necessary for the development of world trade and investment to prosper.

Since the post-War boom in international trade and cross-border investment and the development of the Euromarkets these centres have assumed greater importance. It is not possible to understand the activities of the multinational banks without appreciating the role of these centres.

An international financial centre has been defined (Reed, 1981) as

> an urban area which contains a concentration of specialised institutions that possess at least marginally, the international skills and capabilities necessary to facilitate the flow of goods, services, information, and capital between its own national economy and the other national economies of the world. The centre's activities are subject to external influences from other centres and national economies. These centres may serve in some marginal way as satellite centres for the centres further up in the hierarchy.

International centres are invariably also regional centres for their local economy.

An international centre emerges as the host economy becomes an exporter of capital and knowledge to other countries. Foreign banks will establish offices in the capital exporting country in order to attract investment funds and to make use of the host economy's financial markets. The banks of the host economy will in turn establish offices in foreign centres to supervise the foreign investments, service international trade and make use of foreign markets. The cross-border activities of the major banks are soon supplemented by those of other types of financial institution, and by smaller banks. Nevertheless, the relative importance of an international financial centre is best indicated by: the number of large internationally active banks headquartered in the centre; the volume of foreign financial liabilities held in the centre; and the extent of the foreign network of offices controlled by banks headquartered there.

Reed (1981) studied a large number of international centres and classified them as host centres (centres which had attracted foreign banks to open offices) and true centres (centres which had attracted foreign banks but whose own banks had significant international operations). The true international centres he identified were:

Bahrain, Basel, Beirut, Bogotá, Brussels, Buenos Aires, Caracas, Dusseldorf, Jakarta, Johannesburg, Kobe, Kuala Lumpur, Los Angeles, Luxembourg, Madrid, Melbourne, Mexico City, Milan, Montreal, Moscow, Osaka, Panama City, Rio de Janeiro, Rome, São Paulo, Seoul, Singapore, Sydney, Toronto.

Some of these centres (for example, Luxembourg, Brussels, Toronto, Montreal, Basel) manage substantial volumes of foreign liabilities and assets, but do not have the depth and breadth of business conducted via the relatively select number of supranational centres. A supranational centre is defined by Reed as

> an international financial centre which has an institutional infrastructure that permits it to coordinate its sourcing (gathering and assimilating) and marketing (disseminating) of capital and information to achieve desired degrees of customisation for an individual country, region, institution, or individual without

sacrificing economies of scale and specialisation of its sourcing and marketing activities. Computers and data banks central to the highly integrated global systems of financial and commodity markets, investments, trade, production, and economic and political intelligence are pre-eminent in this centre. In addition, many of the centre's activities transcend the authority and control of any single nation-state, including its home country.

The only centre to be accorded full supranational status is London, closely followed by New York and then Tokyo. Other major centres with supranational features identified by Reed were: Amsterdam, Chicago, Frankfurt, Hamburg, Hong Kong, Paris, San Francisco and Zurich. The hallmark of these centres, located in the major industrial areas of the world — USA, Northern Europe, Pacific basin — is their importance as communications centres as well as simply financial markets, and the concentration there of corporate and individual expertise.

It may appear surprising that London is still ranked as the pre-eminent centre, in spite of the relatively small size and poor growth of the UK economy in the post-War period compared to USA, Japan and West Germany. The main reason for this is the development of the Euromarkets, powered by the London branches of US banks using London as an offshore centre. There are other significant advantages in London's favour:

1. Long tradition of international financing and extensive Commonwealth links.
2. Accumulated expertise and established facilities.
3. Convenient geographical location.
4. Absence of regulations affecting flows of international investment, and favourable tax environment.
5. Politically acceptable location for OPEC and other depositors.

The single most important factor which has led to the use of London as the world centre for Eurocurrency financing has been the attitude of the UK authorities and their ability to nurture healthy financial markets without resorting to fiat controls. Nevertheless, international financing can be conducted in many centres, and nothing guarantees London's future pre-eminence. Significant steps have been taken to liberalise both New York and Tokyo as Eurocurrency centres in recent years.

Multinational banks also make use of offshore banking centres for certain purposes. These offshore centres have extremely favourable tax regimes and may be used for the taking and placing of large volumes of funds. Leading offshore centres and their regulatory features are shown in Table 1.10.

The distribution of international banking business across the world's centres is shown in Table 1.11, which reinforces the importance of the leading supranational centres. The full picture only emerges when equity and bond markets are also assessed, as in Table 1.12, which shows the importance of the New York capital markets and the relative weakness of London in this respect. The strength of the Swiss and Japanese markets are also shown.

Payment Systems

Our analysis so far has emphasised the economic role of money as a store of value (financial asset), but money has equally important functions as unit of account and medium of exchange. It is the means by which settlement of debts is achieved in a developed economy.

The business of money transmission is a core business for deposit banks. For a large multinational bank its capabilities in domestic and international funds transfer are an essential element of its services; indeed, in many cases the transactions business (current account and associated services) is still the starting point of banker-customer relationships with all types of customer. Nevertheless, banks worldwide have adopted a pricing policy which means that they often only partially recover from customers the cost of money transmission services from direct service charges, and in effect subsidise loss-making transmission services from net interest income (income earned from borrowing and lending). Many banks are now attempting to reduce the level of cross-subsidisation, which is particularly pronounced in the case of personal customer accounts where recovery of costs is very low, because of pressures on net interest margins.

A payment system has been defined as the instruments, rules and procedures that enable users to meet payment obligations. In a developed country several instruments of payment are available to users, but the system as a whole is an integrated system capable of handling all types of instruments. Types of instruments have developed over time, starting with cash media (coin, bank notes), then paper media (bills of exchange, promissory notes, cheques, drafts, giros), then plastic cards (charge and credit cards), and finally electronic funds transfer (EFT) methods which are still in the early stages of development (direct debits/credits, point-of-sale systems, debit cards, home/office banking, international message switching, automated clearing houses).

In selecting an instrument, users are much influenced by historic commercial practice and by the availability of a well-established, efficient mechanism for the processing of particular instruments. In different countries quite different payment methods have gained national acceptance over time — notably cheques in UK, USA and Canada, and giros in some Continental European countries. Relative dependence on cash also differs, being higher in Japan, for example, than in other developed countries. The relative importance of banks and post offices as operators of money transmission services also differs significantly, although cheque-based systems tend to be bank-dominated. Given institutional and behavioural rigidities of this kind, the user is free to choose the instrument which is most convenient, secure, quick, reliable and cheap for him. These are the factors which a financial institution must bear in mind when providing transmission services to customers.

Users will choose different instruments for different purposes, and in some cases will be required by their creditor to make payment in a certain manner. Cash is still relatively cheap, quick and convenient for small payments. Cheques or giros tend to be used for the great mass of middle-range payments by personal and business customers. Large transactions are often settled by draft, banker's payment, telegraphic transfer, bill or other special method which provides greater speed and security. International payments are made by transfers between bank accounts originated by telex or other instruction, or by remittance and collection of paper.

Banks play a crucial role in the execution of payments. They provide customers with cash which is still the only legal tender, and by various methods facilitate settlement by means of transfer between bank accounts.

Major banks in all countries are now devoting considerable resources to the further development of EFT systems in the interests of customer convenience and reduced operating costs. EFT systems embrace various methods in various stages of development in different countries:

Table 1.10: A Comparison of Some Offshore Banking Centres, 1980

	Ease of entry	Local capital requirements	Taxes and levies	Annual licence fees	Number of offshore banks	Total offshore assets (US$m)
Anguilla	Until now unregulated.	None	None	EC$1,350	100	—
Bahamas	Relatively easy even where establishment of new banks is concerned.	None	None	$300–45,000	263	116 (Mar. 1980)
Bahrain	Generally limited to branches of major international banks.	None	None	$25,000	54 (Oct. 1980)	33 (June 1980)
Cayman Islands	Relatively easy even where establishment of new banks is concerned.	None	None	CI$15,000 (Class A) CI$ 5,000 (Class B)	260	38 (Mar. 1980) US banks only
Hong Kong	Foreign banks are now being licensed after a 13-year moratorium. For the most part only one branch of large international banks will be allowed.	None	A proposal has been made that offshore profits be taxed at 17%. It is not yet clear how this will be applied. In addition, there is a 10% withholding tax on interest paid.	—	394 (Banks and deposit takers)	28 (Mar. 1980)
Jersey	Only large, reputable international banks have been admitted.	None	£300 per annum corporate tax companies.	—	33	2
Lebanon	Foreign banks must deposit L£7.5 million with the Treasury. Other new banks must have 50% Lebanese	L£15 million	None	—	78	3 (Dec. 1979)

Table 1.10: continued

			ownership and deposit L£4.5 million.			
Luxembourg	Only large, reputable international banks have been admitted.	Lux f250 million	40% corporate tax 40% municipal business tax 30% liquidity ratio	—	92	57 (Mar. 1980)
Netherlands Antilles	Extremely easy.	None	3–6% profit tax. No liquidity requirements.	—	43	4 (Sept. 1979)
New Hebrides	Extremely easy.	None	None	$A1,000	13	—
Panama	Relatively easy for branches or subsidiaries of international banks.	$250,000	None	None	66	18.6 (Mar. 1979)
Philippines	Limited entry until profitability of existing operations has been assured. Major international banks favoured.	$1 million	None (5% tax abolished Feb. 1981)	$20,000	17 OBUs	2 (Mar. 1980)
Seychelles	Limited to branches or subsidiaries of major international banks.	None	None	$20,000	1	—
Singapore	Relatively easy, preference for major international banks.	S$3 million	A 10% profit tax is levied on offshore operations.	S$50,000	115 ACUs (Dec. 1980)	46 (Jan. 1980)
United Arab Emirates	Restricted licences are limited, in theory, to reputable international banks.	None	None (at least not in Sharjah)		55	4 (Mar. 1980)

Source: G. Ta, lecture given at Loughborough University, 1983.

Table 1.11: International Banking Analysed by Centre ($ billions; *percentage share of total market in italics*)

	Gross lending	Of which: United Kingdom	United States	Japan	France	Bahamas	Singapore	Luxembourg[a]	Swiss trustee accounts	Belgium[a]	Netherlands	Switzerland	West Germany	Canada	Bahrain	Cayman Islands[b]	Hong Kong	Italy	Panama
End-Sept. 1980																			
Foreign currency lending to non-residents	1,086	309	3	45	104	126		89	..	50	50	31	22	32	..	32	31	19	33
Domestic currency lending to non-residents	327	21	162	15	25			2	..	3	11	30	50	1	..		2	1	
Foreign currency lending to residents	297	129	..	47	31			18	..	17	6	6	2	12				17	..
Total[c]	1,778	459	165	107	160	126	51	108	68	70	66	67	74	45	34	32	33	37	33
		25.8	*9.3*	*6.0*	*9.0*	*7.1*	*2.9*	*6.1*	*3.8*	*3.9*	*3.7*	*3.8*	*4.2*	*2.5*	*1.9*	*1.8*	*1.9*	*2.1*	*1.9*
End-Sept. 1981																			
Foreign currency lending to non-residents	1,276	379	4	64	110	155		84	..	56	52	29	21	37	..	39	39	23	38
Domestic currency lending to non-residents	370	21	210	19	23			1	..	3	12	29	44	1	..		2	1	
Foreign currency lending to residents	360	159	..	67	33			16	..	18	7	5	2	21				17	..
Total[c]	2,094	559	214	149	165	155	77	101	88	77	71	63	66	59	46	39	41	41	38
		26.7	*10.2*	*7.1*	*7.9*	*7.4*	*3.7*	*4.8*	*4.2*	*3.7*	*3.4*	*3.0*	*3.2*	*2.8*	*2.2*	*1.9*	*2.0*	*2.0*	*1.8*
End-Sept. 1982																			
Foreign currency lending to non-residents	1,369	434	7	70	113	134		84	..	55	49	30	20	36	..	45	41	24	39[d]
Domestic currency lending to non-residents	506	25	339	21	21			1	..	2	12	31	43	2	..		2	1	
Foreign currency lending to residents	420	183	..	90	37			17	..	21	8	6	2	25				16	..
Total[c]	2,387	642	346	180	172	134	103	102	92	78	69	67	66	63	60	45	43	40	39[d]
		26.9	*14.5*	*7.5*	*7.2*	*5.6*	*4.3*	*4.3*	*3.9*	*3.3*	*2.9*	*2.8*	*2.8*	*2.6*	*2.5*	*1.9*	*1.8*	*1.7*	*1.6*

.. = not available.

Notes: a. Lending by banks in Belgium to Luxembourg and *vice versa* is classified as lending to residents and is therefore excluded. Similarly, lending by these banks both in Belgian and Luxembourg francs is classified as domestic currency lending. b. Foreign assets of US banks only. c. The three components do not sum to the total because of the inclusion in the total of Swiss trustee accounts. The role of the Swiss banks in operating these accounts is formally that of an agent, but to the extent that they advise clients where the funds should be placed they can be said to be performing virtually a banking function. d. Data for end-March 1982.

Sources: BIS, IMF, and various national sources, quoted in *Bank of England Quarterly Bulletin*, March 1983.

Table 1.12: International Comparison of Estimated Value of Listed Securities (Shares and bonds at market prices unless otherwise indicated; average figures, end of 1979 and 1980)

	Shares	Bonds	Private domestic	Of which: Government	International	Total
				(US$ billion)		
New York	1,075	485	153	321	11	1,560
Tokyo	334	210	8	195	7	544
Association of German Stock Exchanges[a]	75	324	214	68	42	399
London	177	189	15	151	24	365
Paris	55	118	22	96	0	173
Milan[a]	18	106	2	104	0	124
Johannesburg	82	26	1	25	0	108
Toronto[b]	107	—	—	—	—	107
Zurich[c]	43	55	26	14	15	98
Copenhagen[a]	5	70	56	14	0	75
Amsterdam	30	32	17	12	3	62
Brussels	11	49	3	45	1	60
Luxembourg[a]	3	48	—	—	—	51

Notes: a. Bonds at par value. b. No figures for bonds available c. Excluding foreign shares.

Estimate of Trading Volumes on Some International Stock Exchanges (Index Zurich = 100%)

1979/80	Shares	Bonds	Total
New York	1,408	33	880
London	798	230	580
Tokyo	726	169	512
Zurich	100	100	100
Paris	55	93	70
Toronto	91	—	56
Frankfurt[a]	32	85	52
Düsseldorf	24	59	38
Amsterdam	22	43	30
Johannesburg	17	35	24

Note: a. In Frankfurt, most of the trading in bonds is done on the OTC market and not included in the turnover figures shown here.

Source: H.B. Meier, *Swiss Capital Markets* (*Euromoney* for Handelsbank NW, 1983).

— Automated cash dispensers/teller machines (common in most countries, based on plastic card).
— Direct debit and credit (based on bank-customer exchange of computer tapes, well-established in some countries, especially UK, France and West Germany).

— Point of sale (POS) systems (based on bank-retailer exchange of computer tapes or direct computer exchange link between retailer and bank, operated by customer's plastic card, at pilot stage in US and Europe).

— Point of residence (POR) or point of work (POW) systems (based on direct computer link between customer and bank, operated by customer terminal, at experimental stage in US and Europe; experiments have also made use of videotex systems in this context, and cable television circuits).

— Automated clearing houses (ACH) (designed to make inter-bank and money market settlements by electronic means with same-day settlement, based on bank-to-bank computer links).

It should also be stressed that a great deal of the processing of paper instruments is now automated to a high degree. Instruments in standard form in debit and credit clearing systems are read and sorted by machine, and all postings to customer accounts are made automatically by the bank's main computer accounting system which is fed with the clearing system information. Still the paper itself is transported at great cost from collecting bank to paying bank, and each document is handled and sorted several times. Banks are also devoting considerable resources to research and development in this area, exploring methods of making settlement on the basis of paper collected or instructions given, without actually moving the paper itself.

A likely outcome of this work is a system of truncated pay-ments. In cheque truncation, a cheque collected by one bank is processed and held at the collecting bank. Only the information on the cheque is transmitted electronically to the paying bank. Possibly a photograph of the cheque could be transmitted too by the method known as image processing. In credit truncation, the paying bank processes and holds the credit transfer/giro and trans-mits electronic information to the payee's bank (collecting bank).

Other developments in consumer payments include the paying of bills by telephone touch-tone instructions, and the memory card — a plastic card incorporating a microchip which records trans-actions made with the card — being developed in France.

In international payments a degree of automation has existed for many years because telex has traditionally been used to pass instructions between banks to debit and credit accounts, with confirmation by post. Mail transfers are still used for smaller transactions. In recent years a highly successful computer-based message-switching system known as SWIFT has also been developed to enable banks to pass instructions quickly and safely. Banks are also working on development of photofacsimile transmission methods for documents ('docfax').

Until recently, the quickest possible method of volume information transfer has been by direct computer links down cable lines. The efficiency of these links, and the efficiency of the computers themselves, is constantly being improved, the latest development being fibre-optic cables. However, a further step-up in capacity is possible if satellite-routed beams replace cable links. Satellite links could transform international communications and payments, and major banks are investing in this area. Startling examples of satellite communications in operation are the VISA and American Express card operations. Satellite links to the main computers in the USA enable retailers worldwide to gain almost instantaneous authorisation for payments by cards presented at their counters.

A crucial function of major banks is to act as clearing agents by operating as bankers for smaller banks, other financial institutions and foreign banks, enabling them to make settlements by means of debits and credits to their accounts with the major banks. The major banks in their turn make settlement through debits and credits to their accounts with the central bank, which is their banker. A major deposit bank will thus process its own customer's transactions, and also indirectly the transactions of other institutions' customers. The large transfers of funds involved between institutions and also large customers have always required a special clearing system in the main financial centre, facilitating same-day settlement of large transactions. In both New York and London the traditional paper-based systems of settlement are now being replaced by electronic systems which link the major banks' computers together. New York's Clearing House Interbank Payments System (CHIPS) was established in 1970 but has only recently achieved same-day settlement. CHIPS links over 100 banks to a central computer in the New York Clearing House, but only 14 major banks are settling members through accounts maintained at the Federal Reserve Bank of New York. CHIPS not only caters for US domestic settlements but also for Eurodollar settlements which are transfers between accounts at US banks.

London's Clearing House Automated Payments System (CHAPS) dates from 1984 to permit same-day settlement between banks through 13 CHAPS settlement banks, being existing clearing house members. CHAPS links the computer systems of the settling banks to each other via the Post Office Packet Switching Service (PSS) and 'gateway' computers. There is no central organisation to operate CHAPS and joint development is minimal.

In all bank EFT systems, problems arise as well as opportunities. Major difficulties include:

1. Reliability of systems. Technological progress is defeating this problem — for example dual systems, new materials, improved circuit design.
2. Security. This is a huge future problem in all major data-processing operations.
3. Law. Legal basis of EFT transactions is not well established in statute or case law.
4. Economics. High volumes are required to achieve break-even on massive outlays.
5. Cooperation and competition. Cost considerations demand some joint development but banks cannot afford to sacrifice competitive opportunities.
6. Customer acceptance. Information technology education is defeating this problem.
7. Transactions balances. Same-day settlement eliminates bank float, that is, the money in the bank's hands between collection and final settlement, usually a minimum of two days' interest-free balances and very valuable to the bank. Efficient funds transfer enables customers to minimise transactions balances and reduces the volume of current account balances, which are very valuable to the bank. These are serious losses of income to the banks.

A study by a group of computer experts of the Bank for International Settlements attempted to compare use of different payments instruments in different countries, and the institutional structure of the system. The group had great difficulty in obtaining satisfactory data even for the largest countries and only broad conclusions could be drawn about volumes of transactions:

USA — heavy emphasis on cheques processed by commercial banks, with extensive reliance on correspondent banking networks.

Canada — also cheque-based.

UK — also cheque and bank-based but with a significant volume of other types of payment, eg, direct debits/credits.

France — cheque and bank-based, but also a very large volume of postal cheques, and significant volumes of other types of payment.

West Germany — paper giros and direct debits much more widely used than cheques.

Switzerland — also giro-based.

Japan — data not available but system is dominated by bank cheques, with heavy use of cash.

It is clear that, in spite of technological developments, payment systems are still paper-based to a large extent for the mass of ordinary transactions. Banks or other institutions which undertake money transmission have to run large computer systems, develop extensive branch networks and/or correspondent banking networks, employ large numbers of staff and instal expensive processing machinery. This investment represents a massive virtually fixed cost at the heart of a retail deposit bank's operations.

The development of EFT systems which will be centralised and capital-intensive may change the cost structure of money transmission business, possibly making it attractive to new entrants — non-bank financial institutions, processing/communications companies and others. For the banks themselves, such radical changes at the core of their business may force them to reconsider the nature of their business altogether. If customers are effectively able to initiate their own transactions from their own computer terminals, the need for a financial intermediary for transactions purposes disappears, and the bank becomes merely a provider of the necessary technology. One major US bank has taken this approach seriously. In its 1981 report Citicorp develops the theme of a bank as merely one of many providers of information, financial transaction details being merely a special form of information. This means that non-banks can get into the business of financial intermediation, and that banks can get into other types of information or communications business. The essential expertise is in *information technology*, not in any particular type of information or range of services. Not all banks would accept such a radical view, but it is beyond question that data processing systems of various kinds are now at the very centre of all banking operations.

1.4 International Banking Markets

The major participants in international retail markets are personal customers who require travel facilities or may wish to make use of international and offshore deposit and investment opportunities, and middle market business customers needing to make payments and arrange finance in connection with international trade.

Personal Customers

The international financial needs of the mass market are limited to the occasional need to make international payments and to use foreign currencies. Wealthier customers may make extensive use of investment management services. The main providers of services in this area are:

Commercial deposit banks.
Investment/merchant banks.
Credit card companies.
Savings banks.

Savings banks and other providers of retail financial services have begun to provide foreign services competitive with those of the commercial banks.

Services are provided through worldwide branch networks where available, through correspondent banking links, and through special links arranged between banks for mutual encashment of cheques, and so on. There are also various global organisations running payment systems based on plastic cards.

The overall size of this market is rapidly growing, although it is not large by comparison with domestic retail markets. The largest element is the world market for travellers cheques which is of considerable size and highly profitable.

This market is largely beyond regulatory control.

Business Customers

All types of business customer may engage in importing and exporting, and need to use international banking services. Corporate and institutional customers may also make use of routine retail services as well as services available on the wholesale markets.

The major providers of these services are:

Commercial deposit banks.
Investment/merchant banks (including foreign banks).
Finance houses.
Public sector agencies.

The commercial banks and merchant banks dominate this market, although finance houses may supply some specialist services.

The main instruments are domestic and foreign currency current and deposit accounts; overdrafts, loans, advances against collections, negotiations, produce loans, documentary credit facilities, leases, hire purchase, and factoring. Banks also make payments and provide extensive advisory services to their customers, generating some fee income.

Services are provided through international branch networks, correspondent links, and link arrangements with banks and financial institutions in other countries.

Prices are set by competitive forces, although in many countries public-sector export-import banks offer on their own account or in collaboration with banks finance for exports at subsidised rates. The degree of subsidy permitted is now controlled by an agreement between OECD countries.

This is an important market for commercial banks, and also for investment banks and foreign banks who may have the advantage of greater specialisation by type of service or geographically.

International Money and Capital Markets

In the international markets the distinction between money and capital markets is less important than in domestic markets. The major market is the Eurocurrency market in short-term bank deposits, but this market also forms the basis of a medium- and long-term capital market when the short-term deposits are used to finance longer-term borrowing by means of roll-over Eurocredits. The Eurocredit market was far larger in volume than the market for international bonds (Eurobonds) which strictly speaking constitutes the international capital market. Eurobonds are to be distinguished from foreign bonds which are merely sales of foreign corporation bonds to investors in another country. Cross-border trading in equities is now increasing and may be an important future development.

It is possible for foreign residents to participate in the national financial markets of different countries, as borrowers, lenders and even as intermediaries. This is common enough, although the activity is often limited by exchange control and other regulations imposed by national governments. Since the abolition of UK Exchange Control, for example, we have seen UK investing institutions putting large volumes of funds into the US capital markets. OPEC countries have long been major investors in US money market instruments, especially bank deposits. Bonds and equities of foreign companies have traditionally been quoted on major stock exchanges, and bonds have also been placed privately.

In all these cases the financial market itself is a domestic market, and the currency which the investor uses is the domestic currency. These are not international financial markets in the now generally accepted sense. A fully-fledged international financial market transcends national boundaries by enabling borrowers and lenders from different countries to conduct transactions in currencies other than their own domestic currencies, and usually with complete freedom from the regulations affecting particular domestic markets. They are perhaps best described as external markets, separate from but linked to national financial markets. The different categories of bank lending and the current terminology is shown in Figure 1.4.

Figure 1.4: Categories of Bank Lending

	Bank loans to:	
	Residents	Non-residents
In:		
Domestic currency	A	B
Foreign currency	C	D

A — 'domestic' lending
B — 'traditional' foreign lending
C + D — 'Eurocurrency' lending
B + D — 'International' lending
B + C + D — 'International banking operations'
D — Entrepot business

Source: R.B. Johnston, *The Economics of the Euro-market* (Macmillan, London, 1983).

By far the most important market is the Eurocurrency market, which is largely a Eurodollar market since the US$ counts for about three-quarters of all Eurocurrencies. Other significant currencies are Deutschemarks, Swiss Francs, Japanese Yen, Pound Sterling, and French Francs. A Eurocurrency is simply defined as a currency sum in the form of a bank deposit which is not subject to control by the domestic monetary authorities of the currency concerned. Usually the bank deposit will be held in a bank in a different country from that of the currency's origin, such as US dollars held on deposit in London or the Bahamas; but US monetary authorities now allow external deposits to be held in specially controlled units inside the USA — known as International Banking Facilities (IBFs).

Clearly the starting point for a Eurocurrency is a bank deposit in the domestic currency, which is then transferred to an external location. The original transaction may be based on payment for goods or services (eg, a US importer pays for West German imports in dollars by transfer to a German bank in Frankfurt), or a foreign exchange transaction (eg, the US importer pays in Deutschemarks, requesting his bank to buy Deutschemarks from a German bank which receives dollars in exchange and remits them to Head Office in Frankfurt), or on a simple transfer, perhaps to take advantage of better interest rates offered by Eurobanks in London compared with domestic banks in New York or Frankfurt (arbitrage).

The Eurocurrency markets are wholesale markets, the typical minimum deposit being $100,000. The initial depositors and final borrowers may be public agencies, corporations or financial institutions. Banks, as well as being important depositors and end-users, also make large volumes of transactions between themselves. A single Eurocurrency deposit may pass through several banks before finally leaving the Euromarket, each bank taking a small margin in the process. The major instruments in the market are deposits in Eurocurrencies, more recently in currency cocktails such as SDRs or ECUs, and Eurobonds.

Deposits. Bank time deposits are the heart of the market. Deposits may be placed at call or for fixed periods up to 12 months for most currencies but as long as 5 years for US dollars and sterling. Deposits can be placed with commercial banks and their branches in the world's financial centres, the major ones being:

London.
New York.
Tokyo.
Singapore.
Bahrain.

Banks also issue certificates of deposit (CDs) although these are not available in such a wide range of currencies. US dollar CDs are a very important source of funds for London Eurobanks. There are various types of CD:

Tap or straight CDs with a fixed rate of interest, with maturities 1–12 months.
Floating rate CDs with maturities up to 3 years.
Tranche CDs with a fixed rate of interest and maturities up to 5 years, placed directly with investors.
Discount CDs issued at a discount to par value (a recent innovation).

Most CDs are fully negotiable instruments which can be freely traded in a secondary market.

Currency Cocktail Deposits. These are bank deposits on standard terms, but denominated in a basket of different currencies. The most usual denominations are IMF Special Drawing Rights (SDRs) which are composed of:

US dollars	app. 40%
Deutschemark	app. 20%
Japanese yen	app. 13%
French franc	app. 13%
Pound sterling	app. 13%

and European Currency Units (ECUs) which are composed of the currencies of EEC member countries weighted according to the Gross National Products of the countries concerned. SDRs and ECUs do not exist as media of exchange, they are merely units of account. The actual deposit is made in a Eurocurrency at the prevailing rate of exchange against the notional unit.

There have now also been some issues of Euro-commercial paper and this market may grow.

Eurobonds. These are international bonds issued or guaranteed by first-class borrowers (multinational corporations, international agencies or sovereign states). They are managed, underwritten and placed by leading banks acting in syndicate. Placements may be to the public and are then quoted on a major stock exchange. There is an active secondary market. Private placements with financial institutions are not quoted and there is only a limited secondary market. There are various types of bond:

Straight fixed-rate bonds, with maturities usually about 15 years, although shortening more recently.

Floating rate bonds, usually known as floating rate notes (FRNs), since their maturities are generally 5–7 years. They are usually linked to LIBOR for six-month interbank deposits, and the investor is often protected by an agreement that if rates fall below a certain level he is paid a minimum rate of interest, sometimes fixed for the remainder of the life of the issue.

Convertible Eurobonds are similar to domestic convertible bonds, giving the investor the right to convert to equity or common stock in the corporation. Most are issued with maturities of 10–15 years.

Bonds with warrants allow the investor to purchase shares in the issuing corporation at a pre-set price. The warrant is detachable and can be traded.

The interest on bonds is paid annually or semi-annually. Currency option bonds have been developed which allow the investor to take payment of interest or capital in a currency other than that of the bond's issue.

Foreign bonds are, as previously noted, not part of the Euro-markets, but they are a traditional feature of the international capital markets. Foreign bonds are issued and traded in a chosen foreign market, subject to the laws and regulations of that country. Major countries of issue have been the USA, Switzerland, Japan, West Germany, Saudi Arabia, and the Netherlands. The foreign bond market enables foreign borrowers to tap the domestic bond market of other countries, particularly the USA and Switzerland. Switzerland's importance stems from the fact that Swiss banks have large investment management portfolios to invest and the Swiss authorities have not allowed the issue of Swiss franc Euro-bonds.

We have concentrated so far on sources of Euromarket funds, but we can now consider in more detail the use of these funds. This is the Eurocredit market in Eurocurrency bank loans to international borrowers. It is a market made by large commercial banks, and a comparatively small number of such banks exert an enormous influence on the market because of their size, their ability to attract deposits, their range of outlets, skills and reputation.

The major users of funds are other banks, large private-sector corporations, governments and public agencies. The only criteria for borrowers are their size and creditworthiness. Larger loans are always syndicated, with one or more major bank acting as lead manager, and the same or another bank acting as agent for the participating banks. The lead manager negotiates with the borrower to agree amounts, terms and rates, and invites other banks to participate in the loan by circulating a memorandum containing information about the loan and the borrower. It may also participate, but the attraction of lead managing lies in the special fee the manager earns for arranging the deal. Merchant banks with only limited lending capabilities are very active as lead managers. The syndication fee is shared with participating banks in proportion to their contributions. The responsibilities of the manager do not usually involve underwriting as such, but a successful manager must be able to ensure that credits he takes on are funded. The large commercial bank has an advantage over the merchant bank here, since it can in difficult cases lend more from its own resources. It is understood that each participating bank makes its own credit assessment of the proposition, but the manager is in an exposed position since he provides some accounting information and is also showing his own positive attitude to the loan by taking on the manager's role. There may be a tendency then for participating banks to follow the leader.

The agent's role is to collect and monitor repayments of principal and interest, and to administer security arrangements (collateral). In case of default the agent bank takes on a very important role in coordinating syndicate response to events.

Most Eurodollars are used in the private sector, particularly in the financing of international trade at favourable interest rates. However, commercial banks also make considerable use of Eurodollars and other Eurocurrencies to provide project finance for major production ventures, to engage in arbitrage operations, to make currency swaps to improve their liquidity position, to finance a country's general domestic credit needs, to finance foreign direct investment by company customers or portfolio investment by individuals, pension funds and other forms of trust.

The main types of Euroloan are:

Fixed rate loans, medium-term, at a predetermined rate of interest, according to market conditions and the lender's view on future interest rates.

Roll-over loans are far more common. The lending bank raises short-term deposits on a fixed basis, and lends these on to the borrower, with an agreement to renegotiate rates at preset intervals when the deposits are renewed, usually every 3 or 6 months. The cost to the borrower is linked to the market rate and usually quoted as LIBOR + x per cent. Roll-over loans can include multi-currency option clauses. The final commitment may be over several years.

Standby credits are similar to overdraft facilities. The bank gives a commitment to provide funds at an agreed rate. A fee is charged for undrawn funds.

In such a large and free market prices are set by forces of supply and demand for different currencies. Major factors influencing supply and demand are: domestic interest rates; domestic monetary policy and reserve requirements; domestic government regulations; and relative strength on foreign exchange markets.

Euro-rates must be competitive with domestic rates in order to attract borrowers and lenders, so that domestic deposit and loan rates act as floor and ceiling to Euro-deposit and loan rates.

The key interest rate is LIBOR (London Inter-bank Offered Rate) since this represents the marginal cost of funds in a given currency. The offered rate is the rate at which a bank will lend funds to another bank, whereas the bid rate is the rate banks will pay for deposits.

In pricing Eurocredits and bonds the credit standing of the borrower also plays an important part. Eurocredits are priced at a margin above LIBOR, and Eurobonds are priced according to the issuer's perception of market opinion on its bonds. The bond rating agencies play an important role here.

There is no central mechanism for controlling the Euromarkets although central banks of the developed countries have recognised their responsibilities in this area and gone some way towards establishing a coordinated response to problems in the market. A good deal of concern has been expressed that the markets are a cause of inflation, and that banks operating in the market are subject to high levels of operating risk because of their exposure to sovereign borrowers, and to funding risks, country risks and exchange rate risks. Since the markets are external to any single financial system no central bank acts as lender of last resort in any liquidity shortage, or has responsibility for managing a general liquidity crisis.

Nevertheless, banks did weather a liquidity crisis in 1974 and are now coping with bad and doubtful debts. The markets continue to thrive and grow. In general, the central banks of major countries have agreed that the central bank of the country of origin (parent) of a Eurobank has the main responsibility for supervising a Eurobank, and not the host country authorities. There is a standing Committee on Banking Regulation and Supervisory Practices of central bankers which keeps the market under review.

The very rapid growth of the Euromarket during the 1970s can be explained by reference to the internal dynamics of the market and to external factors affecting the market. The rate of growth of lending is shown in Table 1.13, which distinguishes gross lending from lending net of interbank deposits and loans.

In 1957/8 the major European currencies became once more convertible into other major currencies in the foreign exchange markets, and relaxed many of their foreign exchange controls. This and the creation of the EEC in 1958 signalled the re-emergence of Europe in international trading. At this time the USA was running a large and persistent deficit on balance of payments which the US authorities financed by transfers of dollars rather than gold. Substantial dollar balances thus accumulated abroad, providing the Eurodollar deposit base, and the foundation of a money and capital market.

During the 1960s, as the importance of international trade and investment increased, a real need arose for a market able to accommodate the borrowing needs of large US and European corporations, and banks responded by making Eurodollars available. External factors helped again, as the US authorities tried to reduce the payments deficits and took various measures:

1. 1963, Interest Equalisation Tax (IET) imposed additional taxes on US investment in foreign securities, thus encouraging

US multinationals to make direct investments overseas, and to retain funds abroad.

2. 1965, Voluntary Foreign Credit Restraints (VFCR) discouraged US banks from making advances to US companies for overseas investment purposes, and to foreign borrowers. The US companies sought accommodation from foreign branches of US banks with Eurodollars available, and from foreign banks.

3. 1965, Office of Foreign Direct Investment Guidelines discouraged US-based financing of foreign direct investment.

4. Various domestic credit squeezes in the US drove up domestic interest rates and made Eurodollar borrowing cheaper at times. Regulation Q persistently held New York deposit rates lower than Eurodollar rates. Eurodollars were sometimes used as an additional source of funds by the parent domestic bank.

During this period the quality of services provided by banks, and the range of facilities available in financial centres throughout the world, grew quickly. This process of consolidation has continued to take place in the 1970s, enabling the market to withstand significant changes and shocks.

In 1973/4 the OPEC-inspired oil crisis enormously increased the volume of Eurodollar deposits. The subsequent recession meant that many governments needed to finance deficits in their balance of payments and sovereign borrowers came to the markets in large numbers, together with state and international agencies, and central banks.

By 1976 the market was no longer totally reliant on US dollars and made greater use of the yen, Deutschemark and Swiss franc.

In the last few years the market has continued to grow but problems have arisen because of excessive competition between a large number of Eurobanks with an excess supply of Eurocurrency deposits lending to borrowers who, in generally difficult economic conditions, are now finding that they are overborrowed.

The efficiency of the market has arguably been its strongest reason for growth. The Eurobanks have consistently been able to offer better rates to depositors and finer rates to borrowers than domestic banks. A well-managed Eurobank benefits from:

1. Freedom for regulations, especially reserve requirements.
2. Ability to specialise in wholesale operations and restrain overheads.

Table 1.13: Estimates of International Bank lending and the Size of the Eurocurrency Market (US $ billions)

End-years	1 International bank lending[a, b]	2 International lending by banks in the USA	3 Domestic currency lending by other reporting banks to non-residents	4 Foreign currency lending by reporting banks to residents	5 Broadly defined *gross* measures of the Eurocurrency market $5 = 1 - 2 - 3 + 4$
1970	117.1	13.9	10.0	10.1	103.3
1971	142.7	16.9	11.9	10.6	124.5
1972	184.1	20.7	13.4	14.2	164.2
1973	289.4	26.7	23.0	24.5	264.2
1974	359.3	46.2	33.4	43.1	322.8
1975	442.4	59.8	41.2	109.3	450.7
1976	548.0	81.1	50.3	123.3	539.9
1977	698.7	92.6	85.2	151.2	663.1
1978	904.7	130.8	117.7	188.4	844.6
1979	1,110.7	136.0	148.2	242.1	1,068.6
1980	1,321.9	176.8	169.3	318.9	1,294.7

Table 1.13: continued

End-years	6 Lending by offshore branches of US banks[b]	7 Foreign currency lending by banks in Japan and Canada	8 Narrowly-defined (European area) *gross* measure of the Eurocurrency currency market 8 = 5 − 6 − 7	9 Estimated *net* size of narrowly-defined (European area) Eurocurrency market	10 Annual growth rate of the narrowly-defined *net* size of the Eurocurrency market
1970	—	19.0	84.3	57.0	29.5
1971	—	18.4	106.1	71.0	24.6
1972	—	24.2	140.0	92.0	29.6
1973	23.8	50.1	190.3	132.0	43.5
1974	31.7	51.2	239.9	177.0	34.1
1975	51.1	52.1	347.5	205.0	15.8
1976	74.9	58.1	406.9	247.0	20.5
1977	91.1	59.9	512.1	300.0	21.4
1978	106.5	82.6	655.5	375.0	25.0
1979	127.6	105.0	836.0	475.0	26.0
1980	141.0	147.5	1,006.2	575.0	21.0

Notes: a. External assets of banks in the Group of Ten countries and Switzerland and from end-1977 of banks in Austria, Denmark and Ireland also. b. External positions of foreign branches of US banks are included for the Bahamas and Cayman Islands from 1973 and in Panama, Lebanon, Hong Kong and Singapore since 1975 as well. Columns 3 and 4 include estimates of lending by banks in Canada and Japan not included in the press releases.

Source: BIS quarterly press releases, quoted in R. B. Johnston, *The Economics of the Euro-market* (Macmillan, London, 1983).

3. Until recently, relatively low risk lending, with a lower ratio of bad debts to advances, and the need for only modest provisions.

Other important operational factors encouraging the successful growth of the markets in the 1970s have been the emergence of extensive interbank deposit and foreign exchange markets in key financial centres allowing 24-hour global bank funding, and the rapid sophistication of information and communication technology allowing fast transfer of funds and data (telematics). Although the markets have not been subject to direct controls, the central banks of the developed countries and the official international agencies have monitored their progress closely and tried to promote their orderly expansion. This has been particularly evident in their activities in guiding commercial banks' responses to the bad debt crises of 1981/2/3.

The development of bank lending markets since the oil price rises of 1974 is shown in Table 1.14, under various categories:

1. Growth in gross foreign currency lending by Euro-banks (row 1).
2. Even stronger growth in international lending in domestic currencies by banks in USA (row 4) and in other countries (row 5).
3. Equally strong growth in international lending in foreign currencies by offshore branches of US banks (row 3).
4. Net international bank lending volumes.

Clearly US banks play a dominant role, and the US dollar is the key currency, but the importance of lending by other international banks such as Canadians and Japanese is increasing.

Foreign exchange markets complement the money and capital markets in financial centres, facilitating the flow of currencies between countries. They are an essential adjunct to the Eurocurrency markets where borrowers and lenders are frequently dealing in foreign currencies. In terms of volume, the foreign exchange markets are much smaller than the bank deposit markets which form the basis of the Euromarkets, and so interest rates in the money markets will tend to influence exchange rates, rather than the other way round.

Banks are the only direct participants in the foreign exchange markets, most importantly the commercial banks and the central banks. Commercial banks act on behalf of their customers, personal and business, to supply their foreign currency needs, and also need to satisfy their own foreign currency funding requirements. They may also deal in the market to earn dealing profits through arbitrage and speculation. Central banks intervene in order to maintain orderly markets and to protect the value of the national currency. Banks of all kinds deal directly with each other or through brokers, by means of telephone and telex communications, and via computer links.

The instruments in this market are simply cash or bank deposits in the currency concerned, deliverable at agreed rates either after two days (spot market) or a longer predetermined period. In a spot contract, currency is bought or sold at a price agreed at the moment the deal is concluded, for delivery two days later to allow time for the transfer of funds. In the forward market, currency is bought or sold at a price agreed at the moment the deal is concluded, for delivery at some future date. When the contract term expires the seller must deliver the currency, and the buyer must either accept it, close out the contract, or extend the term. The purpose of forward exchange contracts is to enable a participant to hedge his exchange risk. Commonly, spot and forward contracts are combined in swap deals undertaken for protection against exchange risks.

Prices in the market are now largely determined by supply and demand since the abandonment of fixed exchange rates for the major currencies. Consequently, exchange rates have shown great volatility in recent years, and the importance of hedging to all participants has increased. Still, few governments and central banks are prepared to let their currencies float in total freedom, and many of the European currencies are linked to the 'snake' values of the European Monetary System.

Foreign exchange markets are often closely regulated by governments concerned to insulate their currency from the forces of supply and demand. Strict systems of exchange control have been applied from time to time which provide for the vetting of every proposed foreign exchange transaction. Some form of exchange control is still common in many countries. Controls can only be applied to the domestic currency, and to transactions in and out of that currency, so that in this respect again the Eurocurrency markets are free markets. Other methods of control are the

Table 1.14: International Bank Lending, 1974–80

	Amounts outstanding end-1973	1974	1975	1976	1977	1978	1979	1980	1974/80	Amounts outstanding end-1980
		Changes, in billions of US dollars and in percentages								
Foreign currency lending by:										
(1) Banks in the narrowly defined Euro-currency market[a]										
$ billion	187.6	27.6	42.9	47.2	68.5	117.2	137.9	111.5	552.8[e]	751.2
percentage		14.7	19.9	18.3	22.4	30.5	27.5	17.4	294.7	
(2) Canadian and Japanese banks										
$ billion	28.2	4.6	− 0.6	4.2	− 0.5	11.7	11.5	24.4	55.3	83.5
percentage		16.3	− 1.8	13.0	− 1.4	32.6	24.2	41.2	196.1	
(3) Offshore branches of US banks[b]										
$ billion	23.8	9.4	17.9	23.8	16.2	15.4	21.2	14.4	118.3	142.1
percentage		39.5	53.9	46.6	21.6	16.9	19.9	11.3	497.1	
Lending in domestic currencies by:										
(4) Banks in the USA										
$ billion	26.7	19.5	13.6	21.3	11.5	36.7	17.1	40.9	150.6	176.9
percentage		73.0	29.4	35.6	14.2	39.6	14.4	30.1	564.0	
(5) Banks in reporting countries other than the USA[c]										
$ billion	23.0	10.3	7.9	9.1	13.4	32.5	36.2	21.1	130.5[e]	169.3
percentage		44.8	23.7	22.1	26.6	38.1	30.7	14.2	567.4	

Table 1.14: continued

Overall gross international lending[d]										
(6) = (1) + (2) + (3) + (4) + (5)										
$ billion	289.3	71.4	81.7	105.6	109.1	214.6	218.1	212.3	1012.8[d]	1323.1
percentage		24.7	22.7	23.9	19.9	31.0	24.2	19.1	350.4	
Overall net international bank lending[f]										
(7) $ billion	170	50	40	70	75	110	130	145.0	620[e]	819
percentage		29.4	18.2	26.9	22.7	25.6	24.1	21.8	304.7	

Notes: a. Banks in Belgium–Luxembourg, France, West Germany, Italy, the Netherlands, Sweden, Switzerland, the United Kingdom and since end-1977 Austria, Denmark and Ireland. b. Branches of US banks in the Bahamas, Caymans and (since end-1974) in Panama and (since end-1975) in Hong Kong and Singapore. c. Banks in Belgium–Luxembourg, Canada, France, West Germany, Italy, Japan, the Netherlands, Sweden, Switzerland, the United Kingdom and since end-1977, in Austria, Denmark and Ireland, as well as certain trade-related items for the United Kingdom and France, which had been previously excluded from the statistics. d. External assets in domestic and foreign currency of banks in Group of Ten countries, Luxembourg and Switzerland. of the branches of US banks in the offshore centres listed in note 2 and, since end-1977, of banks in Austria, Denmark and Ireland. e. Owing to the inclusion, since end-1977, of data reported by banks in Austria, Denmark and Ireland and also slight changes in the coverage of the statistics, these totals do not always correspond to the differences between the amounts outstanding at end-1980 and end-1973. f. After making an adjustment for double-counting from redepositing of funds between banks in the interbank market.

Source: BIS Annual Reports, quoted in R.B. Johnston, *The Economics of the Euro-Market* (Macmillan, London, 1983).

fixed exchange rate, and central bank intervention in the markets to support a currency under pressure.

The major currencies traded in the foreign exchange markets are those of the world's major free economies — the US and Canadian dollars, the pound sterling, the Japanese yen, the German mark, the Swiss franc, the French franc. The crucial importance of the foreign exchange market lies in the fact that the market for each national currency is the main financial link between the domestic economy and the world economy. It is also the medium through which overseas interest rates impact on domestic rates. With the large volumes of short-term capital flows (so-called 'hot money') now found, all sensitive to relatively small differentials in interest rates in different financial centres, this is now an important factor for domestic money markets and for the monetary authorities. Speculators will engage in international arbitrage when significant interest rate differentials appear, that is, they will transfer funds from one centre and/or currency to another. However, the speculator must in doing so accept an exchange risk relating to the new currency, whose value may appreciate or depreciate over time. Normally he will protect himself against this risk by means of a swap contract, dealing in the forward market. To take forward cover in this way costs him a premium, and clearly the actions of arbitrageurs will tend to establish a new equilibrium between currencies where the interest rate on the first currency equates to the interest rate less the cost of forward cover on the second currency.[6]

The forward exchange rate is thus the key rate in the determination of short-term capital flows, since it embodies the market's view of likely future changes in the exchange rate. It is this rate, as well as the spot rate, which the authorities must manipulate if they intend to intervene in the foreign exchange markets. It is this rate which holders of currency deposits need to consider when choosing between different currencies.

1.5 Structure of the Multinational Banking Industry

It is the argument of this book that UMNBs have similar strategic structures and face similar problems in their development. In spite of their particular histories and the peculiarities of their national financial systems, there is more in common between Citicorp,

Barclays, Deutsche, Société Générale, and Mitsubishi (to quote examples of the case studies chosen for each country) than there is between, say, Citicorp and a US regional bank, or Barclays and the Trustee Savings Banks (TSB), or Soc. Gén. and Crédit Agricole, or Mitsubishi and one of the Japanese cooperative banks. In the restricted and highly competitive market for multinational banking the similar pressures encountered by the banks lead to a convergence of organisational structures, and use of similar management techniques, especially in business development and financial control.

It is also true to say that this process of convergence is taking place within domestic markets, and that pressures of competition mean that institutions which were previously specialised have diversified and adopted planned development strategies. The TSB is becoming more like a clearing bank's domestic banking operation, Crédit Agricole more like a commercial bank, and so on. In many countries non-banks, including non-commercial organisations, are becoming indistinguishable from commercial banks.

It is possible to identify UMNBs in most of the major OECD countries, namely USA, UK, France, West Germany, Japan, Switzerland, Canada, Italy, the Netherlands. There are one or two instances of UMNBs from other countries (eg, Sweden) but the largest and most important banks come from the above-mentioned countries and are the focus of our study. Particular attention has been devoted to banks from the five largest economies (USA, UK, France, West Germany, Japan), since these are inevitably the largest banks, and also hold key positions in the largest financial centres and make the markets in the leading currencies.

The Swiss banks occupy a special position in the multinational banking industry since although its domestic economy is small and the balance sheet sizes of the Swiss banks do not put them in the Top 20 or so world banks, nevertheless Zurich, Basel and Geneva are prime financial centres, the Swiss franc is a leading currency, and the balance sheet sizes of the Swiss banks do not reflect their importance in world banking markets since they are massive deployers of trust funds on behalf of their clients, and massive placers of bonds with clients. Even their limited branch networks are deceptive since a presence in the main financial centre is all that is required for that type of business.

The Canadian banks also occupy a special position, since the Canadian economy is small (but growing) and the Canadian dollar and Canadian financial centres have historically been dominated by New York and the US dollar (although this is changing). Nevertheless, the Canadian banks do have very extensive overseas networks, and they do have direct investments in foreign retail banking. The Canadians are also a significant presence in the Euromarkets, but lack Swiss strength in the capital markets.

Italian, Dutch and other European banks have varying and significant strengths in the multinational industry but it was not felt that a detailed study of their operations would add very much of import to observations made on the other leading Western banks.

Table 1.15 identifies the major banks in each selected country and gives brief details of their diversification in terms of international subsidiaries and affiliates, and overseas offices of the parent bank. Such figures give no indication of the nature of activities undertaken by the subsidiaries and affiliates, or the date of their acquisition and size. They are thus only a crude indicator of real strength in the multinational markets.

An indication of relative strength in two of the important wholesale markets for multinational banks, Eurocredits and Eurobonds, can be gained from the published details of syndicated loans and bond issues which show the borrower, amount and terms of issue, lead managers, participating banks and agents. Table 1.16 shows the performance of some of our selected MNBs within the Top 50 banks in syndicated loans and Top 40 in bonds, on the basis of the number of issues for which the bank acted as lead manager. The lead manager advises the issuer, coordinates the syndication, introduces the issue to the market, takes part of the lending and earns a good fee. It is a skilled, prestige business in which merchant/investment banks play a significant role as managers, although because of their size they are often unable to participate fully as leaders.

In the Eurocredit markets our selected MNBs dominate the scene, particularly the large US banks, and some way behind them the British. This is a commercial lending business demanding standard banking skills of negotiation and credit analysis, coupled with substantial lending capacity, mostly in US dollars, and consequently one would expect the commercial banks to play a leading role. Business development in this market has been a priority for many MNBs during the 1970s.

The Swiss banks have not shown the same interest in these markets, regarding their distinctive competence as the capital

Table 1.15: Summary of Subsidiaries, Affiliates and Overseas Offices of Selected Multinational Banks, 1980

	International subsidiaries	International affiliates	Branches	Representative offices
USA				
Bank of America	23	25	105	15
Citibank	46	8	151	12
Chase Manhattan		42	83	21
Manufacturers Hanover	7	9	17	25
Morgan Guaranty	8	26	18	8
Chemical Bank	11	9	15	22
Continental Illinois	9	16	18	12
Bankers Trust	11	5	12	27
UK				
Barclays	23	17	211	
Lloyds	16	6	24	11
Midland	9	10	16	
National Westminster	5	6	10	7
Standard Chartered	27	12	16	8
Hong Kong & Shanghai[a]	41	11	86	7
France				
Banque Nationale de Paris	21	24	34	23
Crédit Lyonnais	5	28	25	21
Société Générale	5	25	13	25
West Germany				
Deutsche	8	28	12	18
Dresdner	3	15	8	14
Commerz	3	16	9	19
Switzerland				
Swiss Bank Corporation	12	5	8	21
Union Bank of Switzerland	5	11	6	20
Crédit Suisse	7	12	10	22
Japan				
Dai-Ichi Kangyo	5	13	7	13
Fuji	6	12	6	12
Mitsubishi	4	14	6	12
Sumitomo	4	8	8	10
Mitsui	3	15	8	12
Sanwa	3	15	9	10
Canada				
Royal Bank of Canada	23	11	86	10
Bank of Montreal	9	5	12	16
Bank of Nova Scotia	19	12	81	14
Canadian Imperial Bank of Commerce	14	6	46	15
Toronto-Dominion Bank	10	2	10	16

Note: a. Strictly, a Hong Kong bank.

Source: Bankers Almanac.

Table 1.16: Syndicated Eurocredits — Top 50 Lead Managers, 1979–82

	1982			% share of MNB business	1981			1980			1979		
	Rank	No. of issues	Amount $m		Rank	No. of issues	Amount $m	Rank	No. of issues	Amount $m	Rank	No. of issues	Amount $m
USA													
Citibank	1	151	8,535	12.0	2	157	14,440	1	89	4,111	1	78	5,077
Bank of America	2	132	6,245	8.8	3	140	10,895	4	70	2,737	4	69	3,856
Chase Manhattan	3	125	4,079	5.8	1	140	22,082	2	101	4,090	3	71	4,001
Manufacturers Hanover	7	93	3,066	4.3	6	116	4,895	7	51	2,264	9	31	2,237
Morgan Guaranty	6	84	3,136	4.4	4	78	10,168	9	42	1,986	8	33	2,512
Chemical Bank	10	67	2,575	3.6	22	56	1,548	32	26	793	10	34	1,990
Continental Illinois	14	58	2,349	3.3	16	54	1,966	38	26	555	36	16	612
Bankers Trust	17	62	1,989	2.4	8	57	4,175	27	23	886	12	31	1,730
UK													
Barclays	11	70	2,537	3.8	13	77	2,442	26	43	938	22	18	992
Lloyds	9	113	2,667	3.8	9	109	3,371	11	74	1,712	6	39	2,624
Midland	18	95	1,946	2.7	10	159	3,236	18	57	1,309	19	31	1,114
National Westminster	5	129	3,354	4.7	5	102	5,856	5	63	2,630	14	33	1,574
Standard Chartered	19	71	1,858	2.6	36	68	1,154	—	—	—	50	13	446
Hong Kong & Shanghai	34	51	1,192	1.7	30	57	1,243	—	—	—	—	—	—
France													
Banque Nationale de Paris	29	67	1,407	2.0	18	55	1,696	20	38	1,169	—	—	—
Crédit Lyonnais	31	60	1,298	1.8	17	75	1,841	6	91	2,292	11	34	1,960
Société Générale	49	40	807	1.1	32	50	1,233	13	48	1,556	21	12	1,069
West Germany													
Deutsche	24	21	1,616	2.3	37	32	1,151	29	26	861	7	29	2,550
Dresdner	40	36	1,002	1.4	41	38	965	14	46	1,508	23	14	915
Commerz	44	38	900	1.3	—	—	—	40	19	551	27	17	863

Table 1.16: continued

Switzerland													
Swiss Bank Corporation	—	—	—	—	—	—	—	41	19	510	40	12	570
Union Bank of Switzerland	—	—	—	—	—	—	—	—	—	—	—	—	—
Crédit Suisse First Boston[a]	28	26	1,442	2.0	15	21	2,002	15	20	1,497	37	14	582
Japan													
Dai-Ichi Kangyo	25	84	1,583	2.2	49	40	703	45	15	471	—	—	—
Fuji	16	120	1,990	2.8	34	68	1,190	49	18	466	—	—	—
Mitsubishi	26	83	1,552	2.2	50	38	666	—	—	—	47	16	470
Sumitomo	20	111	1,845	2.6	27	72	1,300	—	—	—	34	23	626
Mitsui	—	—	—	—	—	—	—	—	—	—	—	—	—
Sanwa	39	71	1,074	1.5	45	46	746	—	—	—	31	15	673
Canada													
Royal Bank of Canada	12	90	2,397	3.4	11	103	3,119	17	48	1,389	24	31	904
Bank of Montreal	15	55	2,019	2.8	7	65	4,413	3	62	2,748	5	57	3,680
Bank of Nova Scotia	22	51	1,758	2.5	12	81	2,490	21	26	1,150	43	10	528
Canadian Imperial Bank of Commerce	8	49	2,682	3.8	26	53	1,403	8	40	2,114	30	13	719
Total MNBs	2,303		70,900	100									
Top 50 Total	3,353		97,060										

Note: a. Crédit Suisse is a partner with First National Bank of Boston in Crédit Suisse First Boston.

Source: *Euromoney.*

Table 1.16 continued: Eurobonds and Notes — Top 40 Lead Managers. 1979–82

	1982				1981			1980			1979		
	Rank	No. of issues	Amount $m	% share of MNB business	Rank	No. of issues	Amount $m	Rank	No. of issues	Amount $m	Rank	No. of issues	Amount $m
USA													
Citibank	17	14	644	2.7	28	8	265	12	8	364	17	4	310
Bank of America	26	7	527	2.2									
Chase Manhattan													
Manufacturers Hanover	19	8	607	2.6	27	7	268	18	6	127	18	10	303
Morgan Guaranty	4	42	1,814	7.7	11	17	668	40	5	138	40	2	113
Chemical Bank					37	4	195						
Continental Illinois					34	4	211						
Bankers Trust													
UK													
Barclays (BBI)	35	7	303	1.3	31	2	223	35	2	211	35	2	126
Lloyds (LBI)									4	239			
Midland													
National Westminster													
Standard Chartered													
Hong Kong & Shanghai													
France													
Banque Nationale de Paris	28	14	487	2.1	16	11	514	13	10	351	12	14	431
Crédit Lyonnais	18	13	609	2.6	38	6	192	24	8	202	15	12	317
Société Générale	10	25	997	4.2	12	11	663	8	10	621	7	15	564
West Germany													
Deutsche	2	71	5,356	22.8	2	32	2,016	2	29	1,713	2	23	1,345
Dresdner	12	19	754	3.2	7	6	270	7	14	663	9	10	476
Commerz	13	21	734	3.1	18	5	209	18	8	316	27	6	182

Table 1.16: continued

Switzerland													
Swiss Bank Corporation	7	23	1,687	7.2	19	8	20	330	7	298	31	3	138
Union Bank of Switzerland	11	15	775	3.3	15	10	17	550	6	322	13	6	401
Crédit Suisse First Boston	1	92	7,196	30.6	1	61	1	3,580	38	1,860	1	36	1,723
Japan													
Dai-Ichi Kangyo													
Fuji													
Mitsubishi													
Sumitomo (SFI)					40	5	31	171	6	158			
Mitsui													
Sanwa													
Canada													
Royal Bank of Canada	16	16	682	2.9									
Bank of Montreal													
Bank of Nova Scotia													
Canadian Imperial	33	4	345	1.5									
Bank of Commerce													
Total MNBs		391	23,517	100									
Top 40 Total		821	42,217										

Source: *Euromoney.*

markets and investment management, rather than commercial lending, and preferring to avoid the risks inherent in a large portfolio of commercial advances. The Japanese city banks compete with other specialised Japanese industrial banks. Table 1.17 shows some examples of other important participants in the Eurocredit markets: the Japanese specialist banks, especially Bank of Tokyo; the US investment banks such as Lazard; the British merchant banks such as Morgan Grenfell; and the recently established Arab Eurobanks.

Table 1.18 gives an indication of the direction in which the various country banks lend in the Eurocredit market. The US banks have been massive lenders in North America, Latin America and Europe, but have also been major lenders in all areas except Eastern Europe and Africa. The Canadian banks' portfolio has a similar profile. The UK banks have lent proportionately more in the Far East, Africa and Eastern Europe, and less in North America (USA and Canada). French banks have similar strengths in the Far East and Eastern Europe, and even less success in North America. Most of the West German banks' lending is in Europe, while the Swiss banks are not major lenders in this market. The

Table 1.17: Some Other Institutions with Significant Eurocredit and Eurobond Business, 1982

	Eurocredits			Eurobonds		
	Rank	No. of issues	Amount $m	Rank	No. of issues	Amount $m
Industrial Bank of Japan	13	94	2,389			
Long Term Credit Bank of Japan	27	68	1,467			
Lazard Bros.	30	33	1,312			
Gulf International Bank	32	84	1,290			
Arab Banking Corporation	33	68	1,216			
Morgan Grenfell	36	27	1,100			
Banque Paribas	23	71	1,752			
Bank of Tokyo	4	187	3,453			
Morgan Stanley				3	63	3,688
Salomon Bros.				5	40	1,773
Merrill Lynch				6	36	1,714
Nomura Securities				14	21	733
Westdeutsche Landesbank				20	17	599
SG Warburg				8	36	1,548

Source: *Euromoney.*

Japanese banks have recently lent heavily in Latin America, the Middle and Far East, and Western Europe.

The Eurocredit market can basically be split into private sector and public sector lending and some banks have greater strengths in the private sector area, either as a result of a policy to restrict

Table 1.18: Eurocredits: Direction of Lending by Major Banks of Different Countries, 1980–2

	US	Canada	UK	France	West Germany	Switzer- land	Japan
			LATIN AMERICA				
1980	7,044	2,469	2,677	3,024	1,598	613	1,638
1981	15,523	2,518	4,560	2,430	667	516	5,093
1982	9,098	2,220	5,103	2,463	682	442	7,459
			EASTERN EUROPE				
1980	565	131	1,084	543	924	132	195
1981	188	42	540	271	463	75	556
1982	123	20	288	195	1,167	0	300
			OPEC				
1980	3,556	582	1,211	935	837	123	552
1981	3,987	607	1,909	1,276	230	356	1,648
1982	2,300	768	3,130	951	94	137	3,188
			FAR EAST				
1980	2,739	729	2,527	690	489	33	680
1981	4,469	824	4,232	1,308	185	180	1,956
1982	3,708	1,256	6,289	1,048	497	387	4,223
			AFRICA				
1980	263	26	251	433	58	0	0
1981	237	114	406	471	10	6	179
1982	195	1	293	443	0	29	110
			WESTERN EUROPE				
1980	3,954	2,246	5,300	2,719	2,396	392	1,516
1981	5,074	2,121	7,229	3,211	501	290	4,574
1982	5,706	1,485	7,154	2,821	868	125	6,764
			NORTH AMERICA				
1980	6,033	4,815	1,191	132	140	70	14
1981	53,259	8,478	5,805	1,035	898	277	40
1982	20,542	4,630	2,469	486	204	420	977

Source: *Euromoney.*

sovereign lending, or as a result of special advantages they enjoy because of their customer base. In 1982, for example, Continental Illinois, First National Bank of Chicago and some other US regionals with important US corporate customers figured much more prominently in private sector lending than in public sector lending. Bankers Trust and Crédit Suisse First Boston also show up much better in the corporate market, as does Barclays amongst the British.

Over two-thirds of the amount and volume of Eurocredits are still denominated in US dollars, the rest being split between sterling, yen, Canadian dollars, Deutschemarks and other currencies. The majority of credits are completed and signed in New York and London, the other important signing centres being Paris, Hong Kong and Frankfurt.

Looking at trends over the years, we can see that our MNBs have come to play a more important role in the markets in 1981 and 1982, not so much because of successful marketing but because many other institutions have withdrawn from increasingly

Table 1.19: Eurobonds and Notes: Top 20 Countries of Issuer, 1982

Country	No. of issues	Amount $ m	Public sector amount $ m	Private sector amount $ m
1. USA	159	13,656	—	13,656
2. Canada	79	6,679	4,544	2,135
3. France	65	6,428	5,181	1,247
4. Supranational agencies	50	4,331	N/A	N/A
5. Japan	48	2,062	125	1,937
6. Netherlands	22	942	—	942
7. Austria	19	991	711	280
8. Mexico	17	1,327	777	550
9. Sweden	15	1,454	1,025	429
10. UK	15	941	—	941
11. Denmark	14	846	751	95
12. West Germany	11	1,370	—	1,370
13. Australia	11	1,074	374	700
14. Italy	11	740	565	175
15. Ireland	9	558	383	175
16. Finland	9	406	264	143
17. Norway	7	319	143	175
18. New Zealand	6	694	503	191
19. Switzerland	5	600	—	600
20. Spain	4	259	259	—

Source: *Euromoney.*

unattractive markets, leaving the core lenders in the field, mainly engaged in 1982 in rescheduling past debts.

In the Eurobond markets the picture is very different indeed. Investment and merchant banks play a much more important role, as one would expect in this type of business which is the work of issuing houses demanding skills in judging the market, coupled with substantial placing power in US dollars and other currencies. Not all MNBs have devoted the necessary resources to establish a significant presence in this market, recognising that it is not necessarily their distinctive competence. The exceptions to this are the Swiss, German and French banks which have always been strong in these markets, and which also have placing power with their home markets, and in the Swiss case, with their investment clients. Placing power has enabled one of the German regional banks to establish a powerful presence in this market. The French banks suffer competition from their investment banks (banques d'affaires) but still have a substantial presence.

In the USA the commercial banks must give way to the investment banks with their specialised skills, with the exception of Morgan which itself specialises in wholesale business. US investment banks also compete with Canadian commercial banks. In the UK similarly the clearers yield pride of place to the merchant banks and have had very little success in the bond markets, although this is partly a reflection of the lack of placing power in the UK, scarcity of sterling bonds, and low borrowing requirements of British industry. In Japan the securities houses lead the banks.

In the private and public sector areas of the market there does not appear to be such a major split of business for the banks, although the US investment banks are more successful in the private sector than in the public sector, where borrowers appear to favour the large banks. British merchant banks also do better in the private sector.

The private sector of the market is bigger than the public sector overall, mainly because the public sector agencies of the major countries and especially the USA make very limited use of Eurobonds, although France is an exception here because of its extensive nationalised industries. US issuers accounted for about one third of total borrowing, in 1982, and other major borrowers were Canada, France and Japan, together with supranational agencies. Then there are various borrowers from most industrial and many developing countries (see Table 1.19).

As in Eurocredits the major currency is US dollars, followed by Deutschemarks, Canadian dollars and a sprinkling of other major currencies. Trends in recent years show little change in the relative strengths of different participants, reflecting the fact that it is more difficult to establish a presence in the bond markets than in the Eurocredits markets if a bank does not have any particular skills.

In discussing the Eurocredit and Eurobond markets it is clear that our MNBs as defined are not the only significant participants, and not the only organisations with international networks and foreign investments. There are in fact very many financial service enterprises operating in particular parts of the multinational banking markets which compete, and sometimes cooperate, with the commercial banks. Commercial banks now have their own merchant banking capabilities, but the merchant bank specialists are important competitors, including:

1. *US investment banks* — a select group of New York houses, most of which are still partnerships rather than companies, dominates the North American and Eurobond markets, and is active in other markets:
    securities sales, brokerage, investment management
    corporate finance
    mergers and take-overs
    issuing house activities
    commodities
    underwriting.
    Their activities are centred in New York, where they employ about 1,500 staff in total, mostly top graduate recruits nowadays, but they also have some overseas offices in financial centres, and some have extensive provincial brokerage networks. Several houses have now been acquired by banks or other financial institutions keen to acquire their investment banking skills and branch networks.
    Because of regulations commercial banks are unable to compete for bond, issuing house and brokerage business in the USA, but can do so in the Euromarkets and can compete on corporate advisory services. Recently the investment banks competed with commercial banks by offering money market mutual funds and limited cheque-book facilities.
2. *British merchant banks* — a select group of London houses, mostly partnerships, with strength in the British and Eurobond

markets and active over a similar range of activities to the US houses. They also employ small numbers of highly-qualified staff. Merchant banks do not engage in brokerage business. Some merchant banks have been acquired by commercial banks but most have retained their independence and the British commercial banks have not been restricted in their merchant banking activities, except for the need to foster the right staff and skills.

Some of the larger houses have overseas offices and a few have UK provincial offices. Merchant banks engage in some commercial banking including term loans, equity participations, trade finance, project finance.

3. *Japanese securities firms* — a select group of Tokyo houses engaged in the same range of activities as the US investment banks and not yet suffering such competition from the Japanese city banks.

Another important class of bank which tends to specialise in syndicated credits is the consortium banks. These are simply joint venture international Eurobanks whose shareholders are commercial banks. They were popular with emerging MNBs in the early 1970s, but parental interest has since waned as they have developed the ability to operate on a multinational scale themselves. Consortia still offer a useful way for a bank to gain experience in international banking, or to cultivate a specialised market. Arab banks have, for example, initiated several consortia in recent years, as have Japanese banks. Private banks and investing institutions have also participated. Table 1.20 shows some examples of typical consortium banks and indicates their main purpose and their shareholders. Many are located in London for access to the Euromarkets, but consortia have been established elsewhere.

There are numerous other participants in the multinational banking industry whose importance is continually increasing and who offer competition to the major banks. Briefly these include:

— financial service organisations such as American Express and VISA with international strength in retail banking and other areas;
— other financial organisations such as stockbrokers, money brokers, investment houses;
— communications and data processing companies who are

Table 1.20: Selected Consortium Banks, 1981

BANK	SPECIALISATION	SHAREHOLDERS
Anglo-Romanian Bank Ltd, London	Trade with Eastern Europe	Romanian Bank for Foreign Trade (50%), Barclays Bank International (30%), Manufacturers Hanover Holding (Delaware) Inc. (20%)
Arab Banking Corp., Bahrain	Placement of OPEC funds	Kuwait Ministry of Finance (33.3%), Libya Secretariat of Treasury (33.3%), UAE Abu Dhabi Investment Authority (33.3%)
Australian-European Finance Corp., Sydney	Corporate lending and financial services	Commonwealth Trading Bank (23%), Banque Nationale de Paris (23%), Algemene Bank Nederland (18%), Banca Nazionale del Lavoro (18%), Dresdner Bank (18%)
Banque Européenne de Crédit, Brussels	Eurocurrency lending	Amsterdam-Rotterdam Bank, Banca Commerciale Italiana, Creditanstalt Bankverein, Deutsche Bank, Société Générale, Midland Bank, Société Générale de Banque (14% each)
European Banking Co., London	Eurocurrency lending	as for BEC above
International Energy Bank, London	Finance and advice to energy related industries	Bank of Scotland (15%), Banque Worms (10%), Barclays Bank International (15%), Canadian Imperial Bank of Commerce (20%), Republic National Bank of Dallas (20%), Société Financière Européenne (20%)
International Mexican Bank, London	Merchant banking to Mexican customers	Banco Nacional de Mexico (25%), Bank of America (20%), Banco Nacional de Comercia Exterior (13%), Nacional Financiera (13%), Union Bank of Switzerland (12%), Deutsche Bank (12%), Dai-Ichi Kangyo Bank (5%)
Singapore International Merchant Bankers, Singapore	Merchant banking	Oversea-Chinese Banking (50%), Continental Illinois (25%), Schroders (25%), Great Eastern Life Assurance (1%)

Source: Investors Chronicle, *World Banking Survey* (1982).

major systems suppliers to banks and may in future choose to compete in certain markets.

Banking is an information industry and depends for its success on good flows of up-to-date information and advice. Suppliers of these services include:

— press and information organisations such as the *Wall Street Journal, Financial Times,* Reuters and so on; journalists, observers, academics;
— accountants, solicitors, management consultants, and other professional advisers;
— official statistical and information services run by governments, central banks and other agencies;
— telecommunications and data processing systems suppliers.

Other important participants in international markets with whom multinational banks cooperate are:

— export credit agencies of different countries supplying subsidised credit and providing export insurance;
— supranational agencies such as the World Bank and its affiliates, the International Monetary Fund, and the Bank for International Settlements;
— international bodies such as the International Accounting Standards Committee, Unidroit, International Chamber of Commerce, and so on;
— courts of individual countries. In international transactions disputes often arise as to the proper law and jurisdiction to be applied, but the commercial courts in London and New York are the most widely used by international banks.

1.6 Regulation and Supervision

The global networks of multinational banks pose several supervisory problems. In the past few years the supervisory bodies of different countries have become aware of the similar problems they face within each financial system, and of the need for a cooperative approach to the supervision of international markets. The degree of interdependence in modern financial markets means

that it is in everybody's interests to work towards mutually acceptable arrangements.

A major area of concern is international lending and in particular the danger of default on large-scale sovereign borrowing
undertaken during the 1970s. It is now proposed to establish an
information exchange on credit and country risk to assist bankers
making cross-border lending decisions. In addition, many authorities, notably the US, are requiring banks to disclose the proportion
of lending to different areas and to limit exposure to individual
countries.

The regulatory provisions of different countries differ significantly, and banks with foreign operations come under the control
of the authorities of the host country. Since 1974, the countries of
the G10 group together with Switzerland and Luxembourg have
collaborated by way of the Basel Committee on Banking Regulations and Supervisory Practices under the chairmanship of Peter
Cooke of the Bank of England's Banking Supervision Division
to set guidelines for mutual responsibilities in the control of foreign
operations. The original 1975 Basel Concordat has now been
updated (1983) as a set of statements of principle covering contact
and cooperation between national supervisory bodies and the
division of responsibility. The general aims are to ensure that all
banking activities are supervised, and that standards of supervision
are adequate.

The present guidelines are as follows:

1. Where the foreign operation is recognised as a bank or similar
   institution in the host country it is subject to host country
   supervision. The host authorities should however inform the
   parent authorities of serious problems which arise in a parent
   bank's foreign establishment.
2. When the foreign operation is not an autonomous operation
   then the parent authorities have primary responsibility and
   must decide whether they can delegate this responsibility to
   the host authority. If they have no faith in the host authority
   they should supervise the foreign operation themselves, or prevent its establishment.
3. Conversely, host authorities should prevent the establishment
   of operations whose parents are in their view inadequately
   supervised.
4. When a parent holding company establishes non-bank opera-

tions, the host authority should liaise with the parent authorities responsible for monitoring diversification of activities.

5. Solvency, liquidity, and foreign exchange regulation are a joint responsibility of host and parent authorities, the parent authorities supervising the parent and group as a whole, while the host authorities supervise the foreign operation and the host country markets.

These guidelines attempt to coordinate national regulations, and to provide for the fact that the quality of regulation varies between different financial systems. They effectively exclude poorly-regulated parent banks and their authorities from the world banking scene. This is necessary in view of the proliferation of loosely-regulated offshore banking centres in recent years which can act as homes for unsound institutions and permit unsafe practices.

The safety and soundness of banks and markets still devolve inevitably on the authorities of each financial system. The major areas to be controlled are:

1. *Market entry* — licensing and legal provisions, competence, guarantees of parents, justification.
2. *Capital adequacy* — minimum capital, capital to deposits and risk asset ratios.
3. *Liquidity control* — practices vary significantly between different authorities. Some set balance sheet ratios, others monitor the internal management controls of banks themselves.
4. *Permissible business activities* — regulations vary from country to country. Some authorities allow almost total freedom, others impose severe regulations, although generally speaking tightly-regulated systems are being liberalised.
5. *Loan concentration and country risk* — many regulatory authorities control loan concentration, and after recent difficulties attempts are being made to monitor country exposure.
6. *Foreign currency exposure* — as with liquidity controls, practices vary considerably, from percentage limits to general supervision of internal controls.
7. *Bank inspection* — surveillance methods vary from detailed inspection audits to arm's-length control through regular reports and discussions with senior management.
8. *Deposit insurance* — most countries have now introduced

schemes to protect retail depositors from bank failure.

9. *Emergency measures* — central banks provide temporary
    assistance to banks with short-term liquidity problems as a
    lender of last resort on a routine basis. They also in emergen-
    cies act, usually in concert with commercial banks, to assist
    banks in severe difficulties by recycling deposits and/or by
    providing for capital restructuring of the business.

It has been argued that the scope of multinational banking
activities is now such that an international agreement of greater
power than the Basle Concordat is necessary to secure consistency
between national supervisors, and to formalise arrangements for
liquidity and solvency regulation in international markets. At present much depends on the goodwill and cooperation of central
bankers, and their willingness to devise solutions to problems as
and when they arise. This approach has nevertheless been successful in averting crises in the markets in recent years.

Notes

1. See Grubel (1977).
2. See Robinson (1972).
3. 'The study undertaken by the Centre on Transnational Corporations found
that the very largest Transnational Banks in many countries have tended towards
universal banking. The intermediate and small TNBs — immense in comparison
with many national banks — generally choose to specialise often in wholesale
banking services.' — United Nations (1981).
4. For more detailed analysis see Johnston (1983), ch. 6. He shows how
efficiently the banks have undertaken this role: 'In the international economy,
international banks and, more narrowly, the Euro-currency markets can ... be
regarded as ... an international financial intermediary: they take deposits from
surplus economies and lend them to deficit countries: they specialise in evaluating
international lending risks; they are largely outside direct interference by national
governments, and, because international banking is based on global networks of
branches and subsidiaries, it might be viewed as a world branch banking system.
Moreover, since the overwhelming majority of deposits and loans are denominated
in the main international reserve currency — the dollar — international
intermediation need not involve the taking of exchange risks' (p. 146).
5. See Johnston (1983), pp. 98–100.
6. For greater detail see Llewellyn (1980).

References

Bain, A.D., *The Economics of the Financial System*, (Martin Robertson, Oxford, 1981).

BIS, *Payment Systems in Eleven Developed Countries* (BIS, Basel, 1980).

Crockett, A., *International Money* (Nelson, London, 1977).

Donaldson, J.A. and Donaldson, T.H., *The Medium-Term Loan Market* (Macmillan, London, 1983).

Drake, P.J., *Money, Finance and Development* (Martin Robertson, Oxford, 1980).

Dufey, G. and Giddy, I.H., *The International Money Market* (Prentice-Hall, New Jersey, 1978).

Frazer, P. and Vittas, D., *The Retail Banking Revolution* (M. Lafferty Publications, London, 1982).

Goldsmith, R.W., *Financial Structure and Development* (Yale University, New Haven, 1969).

Hudson, N.R., *Money and Exchange Dealing in International Banking* (Macmillan, London, 1979).

Johnston, R.B., *The Economics of the Euro-market* (Macmillan, London 1983).

Kemp, L.J., *A Guide to World Money and Capital Markets* (McGraw-Hill, Maidenhead, 1981).

Lees, F.A. and Eng, M., *International Financial Markets* (Praeger, New York, 1975).

Lindon, W., *Inside the Money Market* (Random House, New York, 1972).

Llewellyn, D.T., *International Financial Integration* (Macmillan, London, 1980).

Mendelsohn, M., *Money on the Move* (McGraw-Hill, New York, 1980).

Reed, H.C., *The Preeminence of Financial Centres* (Praeger, New York, 1981).

Revell, J., *Costs and Margins in Banking* (OECD, Paris, 1980).

Shaw, E.R., *The London Money Market* (Heinemann, London, 1981).

Tew, B., *The Evolution of the International Monetary System, 1945–81* (Hutchinson, London, 1981).

Vittas, D. (*ed.*), *Banking Systems Abroad* (Inter-Bank Research Organisation, London, 1978).

Watson, A., *The Finance of International Trade* (Institute of Bankers, London, 1980).

Wood, D. and Byrne, J., *International Buisiness Finance* (Macmillan, London, 1981).

Specialised Reading on Multinational Banks

Baker, J. and Bradford, M.G., *American Banks Abroad* (Praeger, New York 1974).

Baum, J.D., *The Banks of Canada in the Commonwealth Caribbean* (Praeger, New York, 1974).

Born, K.E., *International Banking in the Nineteenth and Twentieth Centuries* (Berg, Leamington Spa, 1983).

Crouch, G.J., *Transnational Banking and the World Economy* (Transnational Corporation Research Project, University of Sydney, Sydney, 1979).

Dale, R., *Bank Supervision Around the World* (Group of Thirty, New York, 1982).

Grubel, H.G., 'A Theory of Multinational Banking', *Banca Nazionale del Lavoro Quarterly Review*, December 1977.

Robinson, S.W., *Multinational Banking* (A.W. Sijthoff, Leiden, 1972).

United Nations, *Transnational Banks: Operations, Strategies, and their Effects in*

Developing Countries (United Nations Centre on Transnational Corporations, New York, 1981).

Weston, R., *Domestic and Multinational Banking* (Croom Helm, London, 1980).

Specialised Reading on Euromarkets

Angelini, A., Eng, M. and Lees, F.A., *International Lending Risk and the Euromarkets* (Macmillan, London, 1979).

Bell, G., *The Eurodollar Market and the International Financial System* (Macmillan, London, 1973).

Brown, B., *The Forward Market in Foreign Exchange* (Croom Helm, London, 1983).

Clendenning, W.E., *The Euro-dollar Market* (Clarendon, Oxford, 1970).

Coninx, R.F.G., *Foreign Exchange Today* (Woodhead Faulkner, Cambridge, 1980).

Davis, S.I., *The Euro-bank: its Origins, Management and Outlook* (Macmillan, London, 1977).

Einzig, P. and Quinn, B.S., *The Euro-dollar System* (Macmillan, London, 1977).

Ellis, J.G., 'Eurobanks and the Inter-bank Market', *Bank of England Quarterly Bulletin*, September, 1981.

'Foreign Exchange Market in London', *Bank of England Quarterly Bulletin*, December, 1980.

Kane, D.R., *The Eurodollar Market and the Years of Crisis* (Croom Helm, London, 1983).

Lomax, D. and Guttmann, P., *the Euromarket and International Financial Policies* (Macmillan, London, 1981).

McKenzie, G., *The Economics of the Eurocurrency System* (Macmillan, London, 1976).

McKinnon, R.I., *The Eurocurrency Market* (Essays in International Finance, No. 125, Princeton University Press, Princeton, 1977).

Data Sources

Bank for International Settlements (BIS) in Basel, Switzerland, Annual Reports and Press Releases.

Bank of England Quarterly Bulletin (*BEQB*) statistical annex and feature articles, especially the new annual International Banking Markets survey in the March edition, reviewing the previous year's developments.

Euromoney, especially February editions containing Syndicated Loan Rankings, and the March Annual Financing Report.

Federal Reserve Board, Federal Reserve Bulletins.

International Monetary fund (IMF) in Washington, USA, *International Financial Statistics*.

Morgan Guaranty, New York, *World Financial Markets*.

World Bank in Washington, USA, annual Reports and Development Reports.

Information on the external business of banks in their country is also published by the Deutsche Bank (Monthly report), the Swiss National Bank (the Swiss Banks Annual Report), the Netherlands Bank (Quarterly Statistics), and the Austrian National Bank. Statistics are also available on currency business of banks in the offshore centres of Hong Kong and Bahrain.

For a full discussion of statistics and their interpretation see R.B. Johnston, *The Economics of the Euro-Market* (Macmillan, London, 1983), ch. 3, and *BEQB*, March, 1983, p.52.

Further useful sources have been:

Banker Research Unit, *The Top 100* (Financial Times, London, 1981).

Bank Annual Reports.

2 COMMERCIAL BANK OPERATIONS

The commercial banks in this study are large public companies quoted on the world's major stock exchanges. With the exception of the publicly owned French banks their shares are widely held by a large number of investors including resident and non-resident individuals, investing institutions and businesses. They are 'household names' in their own country, and are often well known in foreign countries. Their activities are closely watched by regulatory authorities, competitors, depositors, shareholders, loan stock holders, and scrutinised in detail by investment analysts and the financial press. They are also the legitimate concern of employees.

They operate, as we have seen, in diverse markets, offering an extensive range of services to all types of customers. These banks must, then, be all things to all men, and so manage their operations as to satisfy the demands of many parties. Nevertheless, as commercial banks, their overriding concern must be to survive in the long term, which means earning sufficient profit from operations to avoid failure, and to satisfy investors with a decent return, after meeting all necessary expenses. In this they do not differ from any other commercial enterprise, or public enterprise which, like the French banks, is required to operate by 'commercial' criteria — in other words, to earn sufficient surpluses to cover all investment needs and give a return on the original investment, in order in the long run to maximise the wealth of the shareholders/investors.[1]

The peculiar status of these banks as 'national' banks also means that they are sometimes expected to act in disregard of purely commercial criteria in the national interest. This fact, and the banks' commitment to social responsibility, means that in some ways they are best regarded as quasi-commercial service organisations (QUACSO), where profit is not considered as a primary objective but merely as an inevitable constraint.

It has also been argued that the banks' evident desire for continuous growth in all aspects of their business and repeated expansion into new areas suggests that their primary object is often to maximise volume of business (assets and turnover) subject to a residual profit constraint, rather than maximise return on assets or return on investment.

With these qualifications in mind, however, we shall in our analysis adopt the conventional model of profit maximisation as that which best explains bank behaviour. Certainly staff in the banks are now profit-conscious in a way that they may not have been 20 years ago, when the QUACSO ethos was considerably stronger. It is also evident that many banks are now eschewing continuous growth in favour of quality business and profitability.

2.1 Management Policies

Banks are probably unique in their responsibilities to a number of constituencies. As suggested in the previous discussion, their basic commitment is to investors. Investors who purchase shares in large deposit banks are normally expecting steady but unspectacular returns, stable over long periods,[2] and good capital growth in line with general trends in the stock market. Bank stock is not a glamour stock. Most large banks have at present a low price/earnings ratio, suggesting that the market does not expect high levels of profits from the banks in the foreseeable future, and are quoted at a discount to net asset value, suggesting that investors are unsure about quality of earnings and assets. These factors reflect the problems encountered by commercial banks in their domestic markets, where they are suffering cost pressures, excessive competition and from the effects of the recession on industry; and in their international markets where there is excessive competition and where the effects of recession are also felt.

In some cases banks are able to avoid disclosing true levels of profit by making internal transfers to reserve accounts. All banks certainly attempt to maintain a smooth flow of dividends by varying the proportion of profit retained.

Disclosure requirements and accounting standards vary from country to country but there is now a general trend towards greater disclosure. Shareholders and investment analysts are increasingly keen to know how profits are earned, where money is lent, what sort of bad debt provisions are being made. They also want to know about management and operating expenses, about community activities and grants made, and about the bank's plans, objectives and philosophy.

The bank's only commitment to loan stock holders is to meet the interest payments due and to redeem the stock at the proper time. In this respect loan stock holders do not differ from depositors.

Banks have important obligations to government and governmental agencies including central banks and regulatory bodies. Many of these obligations will be specified in laws and rules, and compliance will be monitored by the responsible supervisory office. Nevertheless, the banks have a positive duty to know, understand and act in accordance with any relevant legislation or body of rules. In some cases, for example exchange control, the banks themselves administer and control the application of rules; in others it seems to be commonly accepted that banks act to the letter of the law and may make every attempt to avoid the consequences of regulatory rules without actually transgressing. The regulatory body must then resort to moral suasion or to new ordinances in order to maintain control. However, in view of the wide powers held by central banks and regulatory bodies it will never be in the banks' interests to prejudice long-term relationships and goodwill, since in the final analysis the central bank holds greatest power in the financial markets, and the regulatory body (which may also be the central bank) has powers to make investigations, and to wind up unsatisfactory banks.

Large banks and central banks in fact share a mutual responsibility towards the financial markets themselves and to the institutions which operate in them. The central bank is charged with such a responsiblity, but it is in the large banks' interest to see order and stability maintained in order to ensure their own long-term survival. It is common to see central banks and large banks acting in concert to resolve difficulties which have occurred within one financial institution, or with a major bank depositor or borrower.

All banks have contractual obligations to their depositors who must be assured that their deposits will be repaid in accordance with the contractual terms (on demand, or after an agreed term) and that they will receive the declared rate of interest. If depositors lose confidence in the bank then rapid withdrawal of deposits could lead to bank failure. Since the failure of one bank may adversely affect all financial institutions, unless remedial measures are quickly taken, it is often argued that the responsibility to depositors is enveloped in a wider responsibility to the financial system and to all depositors in general — a form of public duty. In many countries depositors of individual banks are given limited protection by deposit insurance or emergency fund schemes, established by the banks themselves or a public agency.

Banks also have responsibilities to borrowers, who will expect funds to be made available in agreed sums over the stated periods. Borrowers also expect their bank to respond helpfully to changed circumstances of the borrower wherever possible, and to accommodate reasonable demands for additional or renewed finance. In practice, the management of long-term relationships above and beyond the limits of contractual agreements with borrowing customers is one of the banker's greatest skills.

Customers also expect other services offered by the bank to be of high quality. They will rightly demand that transactions be handled promptly, courteously and accurately, and that the bank account in detail to the customer. They demand ease and convenience, and a satisfactory scale of charges. They expect to have access to a full range of financial services, and they also increasingly demand professional advice and consultancy on all aspects of financial affairs

Employees of the bank also have an interest in the survival of the bank over the long term and in its ability to pay salaries and pensions at competitive rates. Human resources are one of the banks' most important resources, and they now recognise that in order to get best use of these resources at all levels in the organisation they must provide not only financial rewards but also the opportunity for personal and career development. The banks also have responsibilities to the employment market in general, as do all major employers in modern society. They are therefore expected to participate in training and secondment programmes, and to employ all types of people on fair terms.

Large banks have operating units in many parts of the world and in each case their presence has an impact on the local community. Most banks now recognise that they have a duty towards that community, and a general imperative to act as a good corporate citizen. In their own domestic communities most major banks recognise special responsiblities towards the economic and cultural development of their country, and therefore run active social responsibility programmes embracing for example assistance to environmental protection groups, educational institutions, neighbourhood projects, cultural organisations, housing and redevelopment associations. Of course, there is an element of self-interest in such programmes because they are effectively also part of the bank's public relations activities designed to counter hostile criticism and to help to improve the bank's image with existing and potential customers. It is also in the interests of the banks to promote economic progress, since they benefit from any upturn in activity. Each bank develops its own philosophy in this area, and its approach will be affected by its particular historical development, role in society, and by the personal views of senior management and ordinary staff. Some bankers would argue that a bank fulfils its social role merely by acting in its own best commercial interests in an environment of free competition; others would still say that a bank must earn its franchise, its corporate right to exist, by contributing to society as a whole.[3]

While the bank has responsibilities to its constituencies, constituency members also have responsibilities for the bank and its operations. Shareholders have basic powers which they express by way of votes at shareholders' meetings, and include appointment of directors and their reappointment, approval of capital restructuring, appointment of auditors, and so on. The shareholders can also wind the company up. In practice, many smaller investors play little part in the determination of the company's progress, although representatives of institutional investors with larger shareholdings may take a more active interest in company affairs. Shareholders can also have a significant impact on directors and senior management by their actions in buying and selling shares, voting with their feet, since share price is a vital market measure of performance. In general, management must always seek to act in the interests of shareholders.

The board of directors has primary responsibility for the bank's operations and directors are accountable to the shareholders for the bank's actions and financial results. They must also act in accordance with the stated objects of the company, and ensure that the bank acts within the parameters of current laws and regulations. They must determine the scope and purpose of the group's activities, define its overall objectives, set policies, and appoint suitable senior management to ensure achievement of objectives. In many cases, boards also give final approval to large customer credits.

Typical bank boards are of substantial size and include representatives of senior management, representatives of commerce and industry, and prominent people from other fields. In the group set-up common to most banks there will, of course, be a hierarchy of boards of directors, with separate boards for the group, the main bank, and other group companies. Of course, the precise legal responsibilities and defined structure of boards varies from country to country according to differences in company law, but the above description is broadly accurate for the banks in this study. The major exception is the West German system, where there is an additional supervisory board which includes representatives of staff and outsiders, is not involved in the decision-making processes described above, and is not accountable for results.

In practice, the balance of power between board of directors and executive management is delicate. In many cases, executive management effectively controls the bank and reports to the board in order to seek ratification only.

2.2 Planning and Development

In this section we shall consider how the bank or bank group manages its operations in general terms, and in particular how senior management provides for the future growth and progress of the organisation in a changing environment. It is essential that the large, diversified corporation maintains a common sense of purpose and direction, and that it is able to make full use of human, physical and financial resources.

Corporate Planning

Planning has long been recognised as the key management responsibility, but it is only in the last twenty years or so that large organisations have developed comprehensive planning procedures permeating all levels of operations. Banks were late-comers to corporate planning of this type with its formalised reporting systems, although bankers have of course always directed their activities with an eye to future progress and maintained control of their budgets. All types of organisation are now also obliged to spend more time on top-level strategic planning, because the social and economic environment, commercial markets and technological domain within which they operate are changing more rapidly all the while.[4] All detailed operational plans must be worked out within the framework of a careful and continuous review of changing conditions, and in the knowledge that unpredictable 'shock' events will occur from time to time.

The board of directors and executive management must first

determine the general aims of the group, sometimes called the corporate mission, comprising a few corporate objectives. These are very broad qualitative statements of intent and might include for example a determination to:

1. Maintain a position as a leading domestic and international bank.
2. Maintain growth in assets and an adequate level of profitability.
3. Pursue standards of excellence in the provision of a full range of financial services.
4. Act as a good corporate citizen.

It is then the job of executive management to establish specific aims for different business sectors of the bank in order to ensure achievement of the corporate mission. In a large multi-divisional bank or complex group of companies this will involve consultation with the responsible divisional management or board of directors. This type of consultation to establish agreed objectives is essential at all stages in the planning process. Some of these aims will be qualitative and concerned with, say, the presentation of an effective corporate image, the maintenance of independence from governmental interference, or the pursuit of personnel policies designed to promote development of individuals and their careers. Others will be broadly quantified — for example, attainment of a desired business mix in terms of geographical diversification, market segments, types of services, and currencies of deposits, capital and loans; or increased market share in certain market segments, with a general aim of improving penetration in segments where the bank has a weak presence and asserting market leadership where it is strong; or an insistent drive to restrain growth in overhead costs in high-cost areas such as domestic branch banking. Then there are financial objectives which can be quantified more precisely by reference to the performance of peer group competitors and the judgment of the market:

1. Maintain position in bank earnings league against competitors.
2. Achieve satisfactory rate of return on assets compared with competitors.
3. Achieve satisfactory rate of return on equity compared with competitors, and maintain real growth in earnings per share.

4. Maintain satisfactory level of dividend cover and achieve stability in dividend payments.
5. Secure stability of share price, long-term price appreciation, and an optimal price/earnings ratio.
6. Maintain adequate capital to fund necessary capital expenditure, absorb expected and unpredictable loan losses, and to satisfy regulators, investors and depositors. Again, comparison may be made with capital positions of competitors.
7. Minimise corporate tax liabilities by legitimate means.

Obviously, the corporation's ability to achieve certain financial results depends not only on internal efforts (endogenous factors) but also on external events (exogenous factors). External events should generally have an equal impact on competitors, so that the corporation's relative performance is not affected, and many external events affect industry and commerce as a whole, so that performance relative to the stock market as a whole may be unaffected too. Nevertheless, absolute levels of earnings are significantly affected by major exogenous variables such as:

1. The US dollar-domestic currency exchange rate.
2. Changes in national gross domestic product (GDP).
3. Changes in the retail price index (inflation).
4. Changes in major banks' lending rates to corporate customers.
5. Changes in interbank, domestic money market, and Eurocurrency market rates.

It is possible to plan ahead for such changes by means of sensitivity analysis, by exploring what would happen to the bank if certain changes in selected exogenous variables did take place. This process is greatly aided by computer modelling of forecast balance sheets and profit and loss accounts. By this method the bank can consider what its earnings would be if, say, interest rates fell by a given number of percentage points, or the US dollar depreciated by a given amount.

Another approach to this problem is the use of scenarios in forecasting. In this system an attempt is made to envisage several possible future sets of circumstances and to assess the bank's performance in each case. Usually a best, worst and mediocre outcome for bank earnings are forecast on the basis of foreseeable likely trends in the economy and in banking markets.

It is not, of course, possible to plan ahead for political, military and national happenings which impact on the bank — new laws controlling credit, a military invasion affecting a creditor or debtor nation, a sudden rise in commodity prices (all of which have occurred more than once in recent years). It has been suggested that such environmental turbulence, and the extreme difficulty of accurately predicting variables such as interest rates, exchange rates and rates of inflation or economic growth, mean that long-range planning is a futile activity.

Certainly elaborate forecasting over a time horizon beyond the coming year is unlikely to be worth while in terms of costs and benefits to the bank. However, the fact that forecasts are doomed to be wrong, and have often been wrong by orders of magnitude in recent years, does not vitiate the entire planning process. It does not even have any bearing at all on one of the most important features of corporate planning, which is the educational benefit to managers, who are obliged to think critically about their business, and to consider all aspects of business development.

Most large banks now consider the planning process to be of central importance to management at all levels, since it enables managers with responsibility for profit centres to decide answers to three fundamental questions:

Where are we now?
Where do we want to be?
How shall we get there?

It enables management to act creatively and positively to achieve given objectives, rather than merely to continue on existing paths and respond to crisis and change as they arise. It enables management to achieve consistency of purpose in the myriad business decisions made each day in different parts of the bank. It enables management to obtain improved performance through specific agreed actions, to relate available temporal, human, physical and financial resources to planned objectives, and to take corrective action when performance is found to be inadequate. It improves the level of management and clerical communication, participation and commitment. For these reasons, many banks expect the planning process to continue to grow in importance in the future and to occupy more of the time of senior and middle management.

It is now necessary to trace further the activity of planning within the bank and to discuss how goals, strategies and tactics are established. We should first note, however, that the bank will also need to establish certain policies or guidelines, which in many organisations will take the form of an unwritten code of conduct, governing management in their decisions, and embracing such things as the acceptance of fees, gifts and rewards by bank officers, the use of insider information for the benefit of self or a customer, the professional principle of always acting in the customer's best interests, fair dealings, the avoidance of abnormal credit or other banking risks. The bank will also have established banking practices which management will normally be expected to observe, covering for example lending procedures and the taking of security, disclosure of customer's affairs, provision of advice on financial affairs, and so on. Correct practice must be observed even at the level of collection of individual cheques and other minor transactions, in order to protect the customer's interests and the reputation of the bank. These procedures are laid down in the bank's written rules and books of instruction, and reinforced by informal training efforts.

Corporate planning is coordinated at group level, and this is where mission and objectives are set. However, earnings are generated by operational divisions or subsidiaries, and in the next stage of the planning process it is necessary to establish specific goals for market share and performance targets in each individual business sector, and to devise strategies and tactics to achieve those goals. This is the heart of the planning process as performed by senior and middle management. Each business sector is expected to produce an annual overall strategic plan with a 5-year time horizon, and an annual one-year operating plan.[5] These are submitted to the group planners and are eventually approved by the board of directors. Typical business sectors include the domestic branch bank network, the international division, the trust division, other significant bank profit centres, and major subsidiaries such as finance houses, foreign banks, merchant/investment banks, and so on. Clearly the planning mechanism is closely linked to the organisational structure and decision-making hierarchy of the corporation since it is the major medium for communication, and the embodiment of management accountability.

What then is the typical content of the strategic plans produced by business sectors? A great deal of attention has been devoted to the practice of strategic planning by businessmen and by academics, and there is now a fair consensus on both the theory and practice of this art.[6] Still, each organisation must work out its own solution to certain problems:

1. To what extent should planning be top-down, or bottom-up, and how should downgoing and upcoming streams of ideas be reconciled in a typical mixed system?
2. To what extent should management and clerical staff be involved in planning and setting objectives in a consultative and participative manner? Current trends are towards greater involvement and greater decentralisation of accountability.
3. To what extent are specific absolute targets set (profit planning) for financial returns; and to what degree is security of employment linked to achievement, or financial incentives?
4. To what extent are the corporate plan and its possible outcomes modelled and computer forecasts made?

The five-year plan for a business sector is generally agreed to be a provisional, flexible plan, whose main purpose is probably educational for the managers concerned in its production. It should consider:

1. *Environmental conditions.* Population and social trends, projected inflation rates, projected levels of economic activity and personal disposable income, interest rate and exchange rate assumptions, expected government action on key areas such as monetary policy and public expenditure; consumer movements, and social responsiblity concerns. The bank's economics department will often provide all business sectors with standard forecasts of major economic variables. In highly-regulated banking systems account must also be taken of expected changes in legislation and rules affecting bank operations. Consequences of technological change must also be considered.
2. *Competitive circumstances.* Analysis of market trends and market shares, profile of significant competitors, discussion of expected changes in customer behaviour. One common form of analysis is in terms of the bank's existing *strengths* in certain markets, and its *weaknesses*; and then in terms of future market *opportunities*, and the *threats* posed by competitors (SWOT analysis).
3. *Review of past performance.* The last year's operations must be assessed against planned performance and the reasons for

variances identified. Specific successes and failures of strategies and tactics must be highlighted and lessons learned. On this basis a detailed present position audit can be rendered.

4. *Objectives and goals.* Objectives for the business sector are described in general terms, consonant with objectives already specified at group level. Goals for market shares, volumes of deposit and loan business, numbers of accounts and sales of related services can then be determined by projecting current figures in the light of expected trends and intended efforts. Targets for return on assets, return on investment, contribution and so on can be set — ratios and figures used will vary according to each bank's management accounting system. Skeleton projected balance sheets and profit and loss accounts for the five-year period will be produced.

5. *Key strategies.* Central initiatives required to achieve objectives and goals must then be stated. These embody active management decisions[7] and disposition of resources — for example, concentration of effort on selected market segments, introduction of new services, provision of improved facilities to customers or in back-up operations, acquisition of subsidiaries or participations in new ventures, withdrawal from unprofitable areas, creation of a new organisational unit, new promotional ventures. A typical domestic branch banking business sector may for example have taken the following initiatives in, say, 1982:

1. Concentrate on personal customers and small businesses.
2. Introduce new loan schemes for businesses and savings schemes for personal customers.
3. Open new branches in growing areas and close some in declining areas.
4. Provide more ATMs and conduct pilot experiments in EFT.
5. Invest in counter terminals and new branch processors (office automation).
6. Participate in public sector economic aids to small businesses.
7. Create head office small business advisory and information unit, and increase promotional support to branches in this area.

6. *Resources.* Implementation of strategies involves deployment of resources, and requirements must be stated in terms of financial needs (capital budget, and working capital) and personnel needs (new staff, specialist recruitments, training and redeployment of existing staff).

7. *Profit forecasts.* The type of forecasting undertaken and the use of techniques such as sensitivity analysis and scenarios will vary widely, as will the degree of emphasis on profit planning within the wider process of corporate planning.

Strategic planning is a fascinating process but it must act as an aid to actual management decisions and practice. For this reason, the additional and harsher discipline of one-year operating plans is required. The one-year plans also provide the basis for strict review of current performance against plan by a monthly/quarterly review system. The operating plan will include the following items:

8. *Financial projections.* Forecasts are made of expected balance sheets and profit and loss to the level of detail found in the bank's management accounting system. These are monthly/quarterly projections providing for quarterly review of key earnings factors. They are made in the light of a careful assessment of expected business conditions including environmental factors and competitive factors and based on economics and marketing department input, and expectations of line management in contact with the market place and dealing with customers.

9. *Tactics/action programmes.* Specific activities are delegated to responsible line management to ensure that strategies are realised. It is at this stage that various operating units will be charged with specific tasks — network regions to achieve volume of business targets, marketing and premises departments to deal with branch location, marketing department to arrange promotional support, computer division to purchase supplies of equipment, and so on. But the emphasis will be on the key volume of business targets assigned to managers directly responsible for relationships with particular market segments/customers.

10. *Resources.* Annual requirements for personnel and financial support must be spelled out in accordance with the detailed balance sheet and profit and loss projections.

The vital planning document at this stage becomes the one-year operating statement which is regularly reviewed and which forms part of the bank's budgetary control system, coming under the wing of financial controllers as well as planners, since financial controllers have responsiblity for management accounting and management information systems.

In practice, there is a possible conflict here since management accounting systems were often installed before planning systems arrived and in some banks there are both management accounting budgets and operating statements for planning purposes. Furthermore, the older management accounting systems may be linked to a management by objectives (M by O) scheme which is analogous to but not in fact part of the corporate planning hierarchy of objectives. These conflicts reflect the problem of managing change in very large organisations, and the difficulty of achieving perfect consistency at all levels. However, goodwill, good communications, consultation and experienced judgement of managers go a long way to resolving such difficulties in the real world.

Within a large business sector the planning process must devolve further. At this stage there is again strong emphasis on bottom-up planning and management participation. Just as the business sector retains autonomy and submits plans to the group management, so regional and unit heads prepare their own plans and submit them. Senior management may of course insist on adjustments before giving approval. Eventually the manager in charge of each profit centre will produce his own five-year and one-year plans in consultation with the senior management to whom he reports and by reference to bank objectives. Some banks now hold large annual planning conferences at which all managers are addressed by group executives so that a consistent approach is maintained.

Each manager relies to a large extent on his own staff to assist him in the achievement of planned objectives and he must ensure that they are aware of these objectives, that they understand the need for such attempts to improve performance, and that they in their turn are given goals which are:

Specific,
Ambitious,
Attainable.

Provision must also be made for rewarding successful achievers. In practice these individual staff members or small teams of staff will be expected to sell certain numbers of new services, generate a certain volume of new business, and so on. This is the end-result of the planning process — personal targets for individual members of staff who thus participate, each at his own level and according to his own competence and opportunities, in the bank and group strategic development. Staff may regard this additional responsibility as an imposed burden. On the other hand, if communication has been effective and employee relations are good, then they are given the chance to determine their own destiny and to link their own personal goals and objectives to corporate goals and objectives. That would be a perfect world; but, in fact, to many bankers the planning process does give a new sense of involvement and interest in their banking life.

Eventually the performance targets achieved by the bank in its operations are designed to satisfy the various constituencies to which the bank has responsibilities. We return then full-circle to the board of directors and its accountability for the satisfactory progress of the bank and its strategic development.

In the country and case studies of the second part of this study it is the strategic development of the bank group in this broad sense that is traced, in the belief that this is the best way in which to gain a picture of the real purpose and direction of the bank as a financial services enterprise. A model of the corporate planning process as discussed above is presented in Figure 2.1.

There has been some general discussion of approaches to strategic development by banks. One analyst has described three main banking strategies at corporate level:

1. *Strategies of self-determination.* The bank should identify its own particular proprietary skills, that is to say, its ability to perform certain services in a superior way because of unique resources, lower unit costs, and strategic initiatives. The bank can also manage its operations in order to assert market leadership and retain an oligopolistic position if it is so privileged. As will become clear in the country studies, most multinational banks do have an oligopolistic market in their domestic banking. In more technical terms, Mason (1979) has related strategies to business development and particularly to growth in lending business by describing strategic planning as a 'process of determining the bank's future customer base and risk class', while Edmister (1980) has described strategies of financial institutions in more general terms as 'institutional specialisations for making profit by recognising (potential) sources and borrowers, selecting profitable investment transactions, and effectively utilising labour and capital in transactions'.
2. *Strategies of drift.* These are flexible strategies which allow for

Figure 2.1: Corporate Planning Model

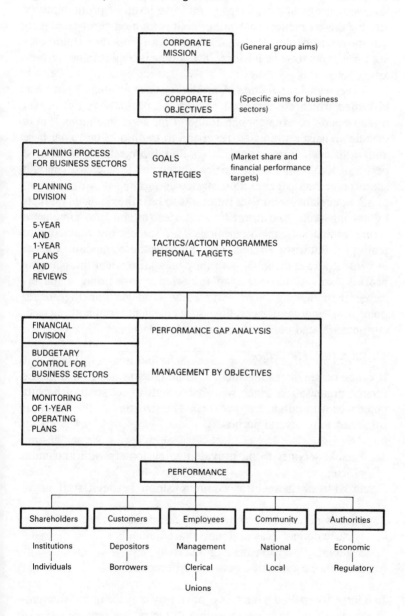

rapid response to changing circumstances and can be run in tandem with a central strategy of self-determination. They do not involve major, conscious steps to improve levels of profitability by altering basic practices, but rather concentrate on short-term tactical moves to exploit the weaknesses of a competitor ('outflanking') or simply to seize business development opportunities as they arise ('fortuitous').

3. *Strategies of retardation.* Various types of strategy have been identified which are intended to improve profitability but in fact often impede it, even though founded on good intentions. These include archaistic strategies (reversion to traditional customer base and practices), pure strategies (notional projections of desired performance), militant strategies (attempts to increase market share regardless), contraction strategies (scaling-down of operations), speculative strategies (attempts to beat the financial markets by dealing skill), and futuristic strategies (attempts to envisage a future model of bank operations and force-grow the bank to realise it). Futuristic strategies are perhaps the commonest danger in bank strategic planning, and they may arise when the planning process assumes too great an importance, overriding managers rather than helping them. Ultimately, strategic thinking should poise the minds of operating staff to make optimal tactical, customer-related decisions in the market place.

Organisational Structure

It is one of senior management's prime tasks to design a structure for the organisation which will enable staff to set about achieving objectives with minimal impedance. The structure of the organisation must fulfil several purposes:

1. Enable services to be provided to customers with maximum efficiency.
2. Provide a channel for communication between staff at all levels.
3. Clearly define areas of delegated responsibility.
4. Clearly define areas of financial accountability.
5. Establish a decision-making hierarchy.
6. Facilitate cooperation between different units.

In a large diversified bank this is obviously a major task. Structures differ from bank to bank according to the philosophy and style of senior management, and the historical business mix of the bank. Furthermore, much of the organisational structure of the bank is determined by the existing nature of its operations in existing locations, leaving limited scope for significant modifications. Nevertheless, it is possible to establish some general principles.

We have previously discussed some of the problems of group structure. At this level the organisational form is moulded largely by legal considerations. Each separate company must have the type of board required by law and acceptable to the regulatory authorities. One main group or parent bank board will have overall responsibility and must ensure that subsidiary and affiliated companies are properly controlled by bank executives. The group executives report to the main board and are responsible for all aspects of group performance, by subsidiaries and operating divisions.

It is in the creation of the divisional and sub-divisional structure that management has scope to shape the organisation to its own ends. There are three basic methods that can be used to define areas of responsibility:

1. Functional criteria. The division is designed to perform certain types of activity, for example computer operations, trust services, international banking.
2. Geographical criteria. The division is designed to provide banking services in certain locations, for example international banking in Europe, or the Pacific Basin.
3. Market criteria. The division is designed to provide banking services to certain types of customer, for example large corporations, consumers.

In practice banks use all these methods as and when appropriate, at all different levels within the organisation. For certain specialised support units the functional criteria are appropriate. In international banking, and also in domestic branch banking at a lower level, regional categories make sense. For certain identifiable market segments special units can be created.

There has, in recent years, been some move to adopt market criteria where possible, in order to improve customer service. In a market-oriented unit the customer will find specialist staff able to meet his needs, and will also only need to go to one office of the bank to gain access to all services. Within such a unit, bank staff can be delegated responsibility for individual customer accounts so that the customer will be able to deal on personal terms with a known bank officer. Account responsibility can also be adopted in primarily geographical units such as branches.

The corporate planning and budgetary control procedures which are fitted to the organisational structure ensure that there is effective communication upwards and downwards, that responsibilities are defined, and that accountability subsists. The decision-making hierarchy generally corresponds to the planning hierarchy, although certain types of decision, notably lending, may go through a different route for review by specialist senior managers or management committees. The individual decision-making power of each bank officer must be clearly established, in terms of staff authority, budgetary spending limits, and lending discretion. Cooperation between units must generally be achieved informally. In most banks a line manager is only accountable to his immediate superior and not to management, however senior, in parallel units. In real life rivalries do exist between units which in theory should always cooperate for the good of the bank or group as a whole.

It is evident that, as multinational banks grow and diversify, their organisational structure becomes more and more complex, and administration problems may inhibit performance. Some major banks have identified the particular problems arising from expansion and have adopted a policy of limited decentralisation to avoid the dangers of bureaucratic stultification. The progressive decentralisation of management responsibility to market-oriented units or regional units is a trend which can be observed in many multinational banks who are beginning to experience problems with:

1. Bureaucratisation — overextended lines of decision-making authority, and excessive overlay of staff departments.
2. Balkanisation — disintegration of group into companies and divisions with separate objectives and dysfunctional rivalries.
3. Dispersal — attenuation of management control and dilution of corporate identity.

These tendencies represent the opposite of the synergy effect sought by group management of conglomerates — mutual benefits from intra-group transfers of resources.

A major problem for a larger, diversified organisation is to promote a group-wide spirit of enthusiasm and cooperation which will surmount the inevitable difficulties raised by the administrative structure. A positive approach to cooperation within the group, in the interests of customer service and bank profits, will override merely technical distinctions between different operating divisions or bank subsidiaries. If truly multinational banks are to emerge then this positive approach by staff will be needed.

Premises and Equipment

The bank's premises serve a dual function as work locations for bank staff and their back-up equipment, and also often act as contact points for customers. In this capacity they are playing an important part in the creation of the bank's image in the eye of the public. Since financial services themselves are intangible the customer relies for visual information about the bank on the appearance of bank staff and buildings.

Head office buildings normally house a mixture of central administrative and functional departments. They are invariably located in the prime financial districts of the major financial centre of the bank's home region, which is usually also the capital city. Functional departments such as treasury must of necessity be located close to the actual financial markets, and the same usually applies to the international banking division which must be close to the offices of other banks and corporate customers, and to the Euromarkets. Administrative departments do not need to be centrally located and some banks have devolved administrative support units to provincial centres in order to avoid the high occupancy costs of city locations and to ease staff residential problems.

Head office buildings also carry prestige, and impressive sites and premises help to assert the bank's image of strength and its presence in the financial centre.

Buildings designed to house processing operations (eg, computer centres) do not need to be located at the financial centre, but they must be geographically at the hub of the bank's operations in order to minimise the costs of transporting data to and from the centres, and to shorten telecommunication links. Suitable provincial sites are often chosen, although some processing must usually be done in the main financial centre.

In the provision of services to customers the bank's network of offices, nationally and worldwide, is its main delivery system and most important marketing aid. Only through strategically sited offices of subsidiaries, representative offices and branches can the bank satisfy the demands of customers for quick access to top-quality personal service.

In the post-War period most large banks have consolidated their national domestic branch networks, the exception being the US banks who have not yet been given freedom to open branches nationwide. In most countries the offices of all types of bank and other financial institutions have proliferated to the point where overpopulation has been reached and there is a danger of over-banking and diminished profitability. Some comparative figures are shown in Table 2.1, which shows that France and West Germany are especially heavy banked, because of the extensive networks of savings banks in those countries, directly competing with commercial banks for retail business.

Smaller banks and non-banks may still be expanding but for most large banks it is a case of making marginal adjustments to their national networks, closing unprofitable branches and opening branches in areas where the bank is poorly represented, or where above-average growth and activity are expected.

In considering where to locate domestic branches a bank must first decide whether it intends to achieve national coverage or to be more selective and go for major population centres or particular regions in depth. Most large banks will attempt national coverage in order to gain economies of scale from operations, and to assert market leadership. This is one reason why oligopolies of large banks tend to emerge as the banking market matures over time and larger banks extend their networks and take over smaller competitors.

Table 2.1: Branch and ATM Networks, 1981 (inhabitants per branch or ATM)

	Bank and other deposit-taking institution branches	ATMs	Proportion of adult population with bank account (%)
France	1,576	18,000	90-100
West Germany	1,432	200,000	100
Japan	2,880	7,900	N/A
UK	2,609	19,500	60
US	2,083	8,800	80

Source: P. Frazer and D. Vittas, The Retail Banking Revolution (Michael Lafferty, London, 1982).

For historical reasons individual banks often have strengths in certain regions, usually the region of origin before the bank became a national bank. It is still important for banks to take into account differences in growth and activity between regions when opening and closing branches, since these can be substantial especially if structural changes are taking place within the national economy leading to rapid decline of some traditional industries. Regional factors to consider include:

1. Population and its profile — density, socio-economic class, age, level of employment/unemployment, types of employment, levels of income.
2. Industry and commerce — types of activity, long-term trends of growth/decline, rate of birth and death of new firms, degree of public sector assistance, inward investment.
3. Housing — quality of housing stock, extent of home-ownership.
4. Banking habits — degree of penetration of banking market, regional savings performance, historical loyalties to financial institutions, use of lending and other facilities.
5. Economic infrastructure — roads and transport services, water, electricity and other power, communications, national/geographic hindrances.

When a region has been approved as suitable for bank representation, bearing in mind that investment in bank premises is costly and that the outlay can only be recouped from several years' activity, a specific location within the region can be selected. Locational factors to consider include:

1. Population and profile — as above, but density of population is a key factor, and the catchment area of the location must be determined.
2. Industry and commerce — as above, but individual large firms can be identified and specific policies/plans of public authorities assessed.
3. Housing — as above.
4. Banking habits — particular emphasis on the presence of competitors and their strength in the market.
5. Retailing activity — turnover and trade of shopping centres is a vital indicator of area prosperity and spending power.

6. Professional firms — their number and variety are another good indicator of local activity.

When a location has been approved as suitable for bank representation, then a specific site can be selected. Here, cost becomes an overriding factor. Bank premises are costly because they must generally be in central locations where purchase prices or lease rentals are high, and because they must be built to high standards consonant with the bank's image. The need to install safes in a full-service branch adds significantly to costs.
Site factors to consider include:

1. Cost of freehold acquisition or leasehold acquisition/rentals.
2. Proximity of site to retailing centre, or to major activity centres such as factories, offices, hospitals.
3. Proximity of site to professional firms and representatives of commerce and industry.
4. Ease of access to site by customers.

Strategies for international networks vary widely from bank to bank, but most large banks have determined to establish worldwide networks in order to service the needs of other bank customers and large corporate or sovereign borrowers. Mere correspondent links are inadequate to support modern international banking activities. Banks can adopt various approaches to improving their representation:

1. Representative offices — cheap and simple, avoiding regulatory problems, but activities are limited.
2. Joint venture participation (affiliates) — low risk, and gains access to local knowledge and skills, avoiding regulatory problems, but only part share in returns.
3. Subsidiary — closer control of operations, greater share.
4. Full branch — full control of operations and full permitted range of activities. Regulatory approval will be required.

International offices are usually opened in three types of location, for obvious strategic reasons:

1. Major financial centres.
2. Offshore financial centres.
3. Major industrial and commercial centres.

A few banks also run foreign retail networks in which case they would apply the same criteria for judgement as they do in the determination of their national networks. They would, however, first need to assess trends in the national economy, levels of competition in the banking industry as a whole, expected profitability of operations, political risks and so on associated with direct foreign investment (DFI) of this kind. The costs and benefits of direct foreign investment need careful consideration as part of the bank's multinational strategy.

In theory, investment of £Xm overseas in portfolio form (ie, securities) should be more efficient than investment of £Xm direct since it is cheaper to perform and commitment is less extensive. The direct foreign investor must have special motives, or there must be special factors which detract from the efficiency of portfolio investment and promote the efficiency of direct investment.

Studies and research have shown that in most direct foreign investment decisions *strategic, market* and *behavioural* factors are dominant. Precise evaluation of economic and financial risks and returns is extremely difficult to achieve for substantial DFI projects and frequently play a small part in the decision-making process.

1. *Strategy.* From the strategic point of view, MNCs making DFIs have been categorised as:

1. Market seekers, looking for expansion in new markets.
2. Raw-material seekers, looking to secure sources of supplies.
3. Production-efficiency seekers, looking to establish more efficient operations than at home.
4. Knowledge seekers, looking to gain technological or other skills by acquisition.

In the case of the multinational banks, category 1. would seem applicable as the banks' domestic market is highly competitive. If raw materials are interpreted as foreign currency deposits then 2. is also applicable as the banks seek a firm deposit and capital base for international banking activities. 3. does not seem applicable as there is little evidence to suggest that banking operations in foreign countries are more production-efficient. 4. is applicable as the banks seek to acquire marketing and organisational skills of foreign, especially US banks; and to gain knowledge of local financial markets and customers.

2. *Markets*. During the 1970s, many banks felt that the banking markets in their home country were saturated and that with a slow-growing economy there was little room for domestic expansion. The faster growing and prosperous US economy was obviously attractive for investment, and, because of the low concentration of US banks, remarkably easy to enter. The rapidly-growing international banking markets were also attractive and prompted the investment by many banks in branches in money centres throughout the world. It could be said that in many respects it was necessary during these early years of the expansion of international financial intermediation for major banks to 'grow and survive' in a market dominated by US banking giants.

3. *Behaviour*. Such a need for growth may have been compounded by organisational and behavioural factors. For many large corporations growth in size tends to become a goal in itself, associated with prestige, progress, power and other attributes.

Growth may also offer the only opportunity for full deployment and utilisation of corporate resources — staff and management skills, lending capacity, capital strength and ability to mobilise capital. It is also fair to say that many corporations have an explicit or implicit doctrine of 'pursuit of excellence' and expansion abroad may have appeared the next challenge in this pursuit.

From the behavioural point of view, studies of US firms have shown that foreign investment is frequently on an ad hoc basis — a response to a specific perceived opportunity, rather than the fruit of a planned search programme. Many non-US banks have seized opportunities to acquire under-performing US banks in this way.

Studies have also shown that DFI decisions may be taken for non-managerial reasons of prestige, glamour, by individual executives in the interests of personal advancement, or by dint of pressure from interested departments. Simple emulation and even envy may also be present.

Although strategic and behavioural motives may dominate DFI decisions there are important special economic and financial factors which may contribute to the bold decision to invest abroad. The important factors affecting bank investments have been market imperfections, oligopolistic competition and risk diversification.

1. *Market imperfections*. Investment by foreign banks of many nationalities in the USA by means of direct acquisition is a basic

example of market imperfections causing DFI. There is no reason why, by the classical theory of comparative advantages leading to international trade and investment under conditions of free competition, the US banks should have been at any comparative disadvantage. However, strict regulation and control over many years have prevented concentration in the US banking industry and resulted in the existence of many small and medium-sized banks which are ripe for acquisition by foreign banks.

Domestic market imperfections may have led to more aggressive overseas expansion than would have occurred otherwise. In many countries it is now clear that no bank can significantly increase its domestic market share in the foreseeable future by means of acquisition or growth, except in the very long term by consistently outperforming its peers.

2. *Oligopolistic competition.* Many large deposit banks have maintained an oligopoly for years now in their domestic operations. It is also arguable that an extensive oligopoly has been established by the principal international banks of the world in their international operations. Successful oligopolists are able to maintain profits through administration of prices which may be formally fixed in a cartel arrangement or informally fixed by the forces of competition.

Oligopolists are usually considered to benefit from the following advantages within their own markets, besides their ability to make rather than take prices:

a.   economies of scale,
b.   accumulated managerial and staff expertise,
c.   knowledge of markets,
d.   technological investment and advancement,
e.   research and development,
f.   financial strength,
g.   stable market share,
h.   product/service quality,
i.   corporate name and image.

Most of these advantages are transferable to foreign markets and may well enable a company to make a successful foreign direct investment and overcome the difficulties of operating in a strange environment.

In the case of the banks they have benefited from their strong position in their domestic markets in the following ways especially:

— Long experience in running a nationwide branch and money transmission network.
— Long experience in money market and international banking in their main financial centre.

As regards oligopolistic competition in international markets the banks have also benefited in the following special ways:

— Experience of running overseas networks and of international banking based on the leading financial centres
— Establishment of corporate names, images and reputations over many years.

3. *International diversification of risks.* Portfolio theory has also been applied to the array of direct investments made by corporations, using the same basic criteria of risk and return. This is particularly suitable for analysis of banking investments because of the essentially risky nature of all banking assets. Diversification of holdings of banking assets over several countries should in theory lead to a reduction in risk over the assets of the bank as a whole and a consequent improvement in the risk/return ratio. The potential for this improvement has increased in many banks as the performance of the domestic economy has declined and the riskiness of their domestic assets increased correspondingly — especially the riskiness of domestic corporate lending. In order to offset this increasing level of risk in corporate lending, two markets have appeared attractive:

— International corporate and government lending, where losses have been less than in domestic lending, until very recently.
— Foreign retail markets, since consumer lending is traditionally safe business.

International diversification should also provide improved performance of the corporate portfolio of activities in the face of other risks besides pure banking or credit risks:

— Political risk due to instability, government interference, etc.

— Interest rate risk due to fluctuations in domestic levels of interest.

— Exchange rate risk due to fluctuations in exchange rates and their effect on valuation of corporate total assets and on the money value of international banking claims and obligations — viz. translation and transaction losses/gains, which may be reduced by matching or hedging.

So far we have concentrated on the theoretical reasons in support of foreign direct investment and on highlighting the circumstances and conditions which have made DFI appropriate for multinational banks in the 1970s. There are, however, difficulties associated with DFI and not all such investments are successful. Several of the medium-sized and smaller US regional banks who moved into international banking centres during the late-1960s were not successful, and some have since divested. There is perhaps a particular danger in banking, in as much as initial set-up costs may be low for new branches, and acquisition of established businesses may be fairly easy, while integration into group activities may appear deceptively simple. The apparent ease with which new investments can be made may lead to overeagerness for new ventures and acquisitions; and questions of prestige and reputation may delay divestment from failed ventures.

General difficulties that may arise with DFIs are:

— Problems of integrating foreign investments into existing group activities.

— Problems of management control and organisational changes.

— Exposure to new risks in new markets, and in new categories, eg, political, foreign exchange, and other risks.

The banks have certainly been exposed to such difficulties and have been obliged to learn the necessary skills to cope. In this process of learning and adaptation the non-US banks may have had certain special disadvantages compared to the major US banks engaged in a similar process. These are:

— Traditional and conservative management practices in the domestic bank.

— Lack of staff exposure to severe competition and lack of skills in marketing and sales.

— Weakness of domestic economy and slow growth of domestic business.

The vital importance of this learning and adaptation process for the corporation, and the enormous consequences for the corporation which has made substantial foreign investments, have been emphasised by the senior executive of a company which diversified internationally during the 1960s:

> For a company ... which has already realised a good share of its potential in the (domestic) market place ... the case for world wide marketing seems almost irresistible. To have competitors to enjoy the growth potentialities abroad would be to concede to them substantial earnings which they can use to compete more effectively everywhere, including the domestic market. For such a company, a beginning is made with exports. But more importantly, the company will inevitably be drawn to make direct investment, first in marketing facilities, sales offices and warehouses and then as necessary with plants ... In these circumstances, the company finds it has not just grown — it has been transformed. In making direct investments abroad it has become multinational ... it must be organised as a world enterprise. The company's assets and efforts must be managed multinationally, in accordance with market opportunities wherever they may be.*

Equipment costs are now a significant part of the bank's capital budget, annual operating costs and depreciation costs. Forces of competition, customer demand and technological advance mean that a major bank must stay at the forefront of information technology (IT). Banks are one of the major users of IT in the world economy, for:

— *Central data processing*. High capacity, speedy and reliable machinery is required to deal with large volumes of transactions. Banks are purchasers of the very largest processors for these purposes.

* Speech delivered by President of Chas. Pfizer & Co. in 1967, quoted in Henning, Pigott and Scott (1978), p. 286. For 'exports, marketing facilities, sales offices, warehouses, plants' read 'finance of foreign trade, correspondents, representative offices, money-centre branches, retail branch networks', respectively.

— *Distributed data processing.* Smaller capacity, speedy, reliable, cheap and flexible machinery is required for intermediate handling of mainstream customer transactions, and for processing of special types of transaction.

— *Management information.* Banks have more recently begun to find uses for microcomputers as aids to management at operating level.

In all cases care must be taken to ensure that suitable systems are purchased and that their use is cost-effective. It must be remembered that the rate of depreciation of this type of equipment is very rapid and that obsolescence rapidly occurs. Installation of new machinery may also take considerable time, cause disruption, and involve significant development costs in the creation of suitable software systems.

Banks are also heavy users of all types of communication equipment, from typewriters, through telephone and telex up to modern developments such as facsimile transmission, videotext — viewdata, and so on — direct computer links, and satellite-assisted communications. In all these areas continuous investment in research, development and new equipment is required.

Another significant area of investment is in the various forms of electronic funds transfer — cash dispensers, ATMs, counter terminals, customer home or office terminals, point of sale systems and so on.

Gradually banking is becoming a much more capital-intensive, high technology industry. It is clearly in the banks' interests to reduce the enormous and ever-increasing burden of staff costs wherever possible by automation. In the process it can offer customers greater control over their financial transactions, and a new range of efficient services. However, certain risks are also incurred, common to all high-technology investment:

— Strategic errors and misguided investment can lead to significant losses.

— High volumes of business are required to recoup costs and ensure profitability with such a large element of fixed equipment costs. On the other hand, it has been argued that staff costs are also effectively fixed costs at present.

— Customer acceptance of new technology is difficult to assess.

— Security, confidentiality, and reliability are additional problems with computer systems.
— Changes in commercial practice may give rise to untested legal difficulty.

None of these problems is insurmountable and the level of investment in equipment will no doubt continue to rise as techniques are refined and new areas of banking automated. It is still difficult to predict how radically the banks' cost structures will be affected because the effect on bank employment is uncertain. At present, most major banks expect improved productivity of staff due to automation of operational procedures to enable existing staff to cope with larger volumes of business, and to facilitate redeployment of staff to customer-related marketing activities. In other words, technological change will lead to changes in job content rather than job numbers. However, more radical developments such as customer terminals, where customers take over responsibility for transactions, could lead to a permanent reduction in the load of work for the banks and a need for staff reductions.

2.3 Financial Control

Since the purpose of banking activity is wealth maximisation, the ultimate measure of all operations is financial. Monitoring and control of financial performance is a vital function. Surprisingly, it was an area to which major banks devoted relatively few resources until recently. However, since the adoption of corporate planning objectives the need for an accurate and comprehensive system of financial control has become evident.

Bank Finances

In order to understand the process of financial control in a large multinational bank it is necessary to analyse the structure of the bank's balance sheet and to see how profits are earned and how the financial position changes during the year. The consolidated financial statements of the group are best used for this purpose, since they represent the activities of all types of operation, and in particular both domestic and international business. Their aggregate nature means that details are lost but this does not prevent us from gaining a broad view of the bank's affairs. In considering a bank balance sheet many special factors should be borne in mind, since a bank's financial flows differ significantly from those of other businesses.

The balance sheet is highly geared. A small capital base, consisting of shareholder's funds plus reserves and long-term loan capital, supports a much larger volume of deposits, which are then able to fund large volumes of customer loans. The bank's capital is needed to fund fixed assets (premises and equipment), to provide for future investment needs, and to absorb future losses. Both investors and regulators are concerned to see that the bank has an amount of capital adequate to meet these needs. If the bank cannot build up adequate capital from retained earnings then it must either dispose of assets to raise cash, issue new shares, or raise term loans, provided that these are of sufficient maturity to count as capital. Assets can also be revalued and a credit taken to reserves. Investors and regulators commonly measure the capital ratio of shareholders' funds to customers' deposits to assess the adequacy of capital. Regulators who obtain detailed information from the banks are able to calculate a risk asset ratio of shareholders' funds to advances. In this calculation different categories of advances are weighted according to their level of expected risk. Riskier assets such as commercial advances are weighted more heavily, so that a bank with a riskier portfolio will need to maintain more capital to satisfy the regulators that it can meet unexpected losses.

There has been some dispute over the eligibility of loan capital as true bank capital and regulators will usually only allow longer-term loans, and those which are subordinated to ordinary creditors. This has caused difficulties, since banks have increasingly resorted to medium-term loans and notes rather than to share issues in recent years, largely because of the market's poor view of bank shares on many stock markets, and the high cost of raising equity capital.

In the two balance sheet abstracts presented in Table 2.2 (Citicorp and National Westminster) shareholders' funds represent only 3–5 per cent of total liabilities, and loan capital a further 1–3 per cent. In fact, the US bank relies more on loan capital than the British bank, but the proportion of total capital (shareholders' funds plus loan capital to total liabilities) is similar — 6.6 per cent for Citicorp, 6.5 per cent for National Westminster.

Deposits are mainly composed of interest bearing liabilities,

Table 2.2: Multinational Bank Consolidated Balance Sheet Abstracts: Average Balances and Interest Rates

	Citicorp, 1981			NatWest, 1981			
	Average volume	Average	% of total	Average volume	Average	1981 % of	(1979) % of
Interest earning assets	$m	rate	assets	£m	rate	total assets	
Market placings							
Domestic	2,555	17.3	2.2	4,021	14.2	10.3	(11.2)
International	13,067	15.3	/11.3	9,397	15.0	24.1	(19.4)
Lendings to customers							
Domestic	30,193	15.8	26.1	9,903	14.8	25.4	(27.7)
International	41,833	19.2	36.1	8,081	18.3	20.7	(20.4)
Investment securities							
Domestic	6,932	12.0	6.0	622	12.2	1.6	(2.4)
International	2,591	12.8	2.2	520	11.3	1.3	(1.6)
Other earnings assets							
Domestic	1,851	18.4	1.6	2,155	11.4	5.5	(5.1)
International				633	15.6	1.6	(1.3)
Total earning assets	99,022	16.9	85.4	35,322	15.3	90.7	(89.1)
Non-interest earning assets							
	16,873		14.6	3,604		9.3	(10.9)
Total assets	115,895		100.0	38,936		100.0	(100.0)
Interest bearing liabilities							
Deposits							
Savings							
Domestic	1,983	5.0	1.7	4,807	9.9	12.3	(11.9)
International[a]				852	5.4	2.2	(2.2)
Time							
Domestic	20,337	15.3	17.5	6,336	12.7	16.3	(16.2)
International[a]	52,132	15.5	50.0	15,439	16.4	39.6	(34.2)
Short-term borrowings							
Domestic	6,779	16.0	5.8	506	13.8	1.3	(2.1)
International	7,713	17.1	6.6	547	14.6	1.4	(0.9)
Loan capital	3,576	12.6	3.1	493	12.6	1.3	(1.1)
Total interest bearing liabilities	92,520	15.3	79.8	28,980	14.1	74.4	(68.6)
Non-interest bearing liabilities							
Demand deposits	8,615		7.4	6.351		16.3	(22.9)
Other	10,733		9.3	1,588		4.1	(2.8)
Total liabilities	111,868		96.5	36,919		94.8	(94.4)
Shareholders' funds	4,027		3.5	2,017		5.2	(5.6)

Total liabilities and shareholders' funds	115,895	100.0	38,936	100.0 (100.0)

Citicorp:
Spread   1.6
Net Interest Margin   2.60 — domestic 3.56
                               — international 1.96

NatWest:
Spread   1.3
Net Interest Margin   3.80 — domestic 5.83
                               — international 1.98

Note: a. Two categories amalgamated.

although the British bank still has a significant proportion of non-interest bearing demand deposits on current account. These include domestic and foreign currency deposits, although mainly domestic, and are derived from all market segments — individuals, other financial institutions, corporate and middle market.

Interest bearing deposits have been broken down into savings and time deposits and short-term borrowings, and in each case into domestic and international. The two banks show significant differences in their sources of deposits which are discussed in detail later.

Non-interest earning assets include holdings of cash (notes and coin), items in collection, and current accounts with other banks. For obvious reasons banks try to minimise these holdings but need to hold cash to service customers' needs, and require balances for operational purposes. Central banks also require commercial banks to hold a certain amount of non-interest bearing balances.

A very significant proportion of loans is in the form of domestic and international market placings. These include interbank loans, and holdings of other money market instruments. Banks need to hold substantial volumes of these safe, shorter-term assets in order to ensure that they have a buffer of liquidity to meet expected and unforeseeable cash demands. Regulators also require commercial banks to hold certain amounts of approved types of asset, namely first-class money market liquid assets, in order to provide the banking system as a whole with a sizeable pool of liquidity, and to set prudential guidelines for the liquidity management of each bank. Some regulators apply liquidity ratios in conjunction with capital ratios, but often the control of commercial banks' liquidity is more flexible.

Central banks also often require commercial banks to hold certain liquid *reserve* assets as part of their overall control of the level of credit and the rate of expansion of the money supply. Although the purpose of reserve assets is entirely different, in practice reserve assets are also first-class money market liquid assets.

One reason why regulators have become more flexible on liquidity ratios is that a large bank does not have to rely on its buffer stock of liquid assets to meet liquidity needs by, for example, selling Treasury bills. It can instead simply borrow on the money market, increasing its liabilities rather than decreasing its assets to achieve its funding aims. In practice, sophisticated banks now use both methods, both asset management and liability management.

Investment securities form a larger part of the US bank balance sheet than the British bank balance sheet, but most commercial banks do have sizeable investment portfolios. Some short-dated government bonds in fact count as liquid and reserve assets for banks. In addition, the banks may carry large volumes of stock on behalf of customers, and on their own account. From their own holdings of government bonds and first-class corporate stock the bank will hope to earn income and also to make profits by dealing.

The most important category of assets is lendings to customers (excluding other financial institutions) amounting to about one half of total assets. These are the major source of earnings because of the amounts involved and the high returns (average rate of interest earned). In both banks, the very significant volume of international lending earns the highest rate of return of all categories. Lendings to customers include advances to individuals, and to the corporate and middle market by all available methods and for a wide variety of purposes, as previously discussed in Chapter 1. The key to successful and stable growth in bank earnings is the progressive building of a diversified portfolio of customer advances (by geographical location, by type of customer, by currency) which earn a satisfactory rate of interest and whose level of risk is commensurate with the rate of return, so that bad debt losses are acceptable. A more accurate description of the return on categories of advances than the simple rate of interest shown in Table 2.2 is the *yield* expressed as the average rate of return less an allowance for bad debt provisions. Allowance should also be made for the fact that the central bank will require the bank to hold certain reserve assets in proportion to advances made, and these reduce the yield on advances further since they are low-earning assets. Of course the actual rate of return on assets must take into account the cost of funds (interest expense) and then the operating costs of the bank and the provision for bad debt losses.

The process of arriving at a statement of profit from banking operations is shown in Table 2.3 for Citicorp and National Westminster. Interest revenue from all sources including customer advances is the prime source of income. From this is deducted interest expense from all liabilities, to give *net interest income,* the crucial determinant of bank profits. This figure derives from the spread between rates of interest charged on assets and rates of

Table 2.3: Consolidated Income Statements: Citicorp and NatWest

Income	Citicorp 1981 $m	% of total income	NatWest 1981 £m	% of total income	1979 £m	% of total income
Interest revenue	16,658		5,278		2,724	
Interest expense — deposits	13,844		4,010		1,776	
— loan capital	335		62		30	
	14,179		4,072		1,806	
Net interest income	2,479	61	1,206	70	918	73
Investment income	(5)	(—)	113	7	78	6
Commission and foreign exchange	1,354	33	351	20	231	18
Other revenue	263	6	55	3	29	3
Total	1,617	39	406	23	260	27
Total income	4,091	100	1,725	100	1,256	100
Operating expenses:						
Personnel	1,489	36	809	47	534	42
Premises	268	7 }	201	12	134	11
Equipment	225	6 }				
Other	954	23	199	12	120	10
Total expenditure	2,936	72	1,209	70	788	63
Bad and doubtful debts	305	7	42	2	40	3
Income before taxes	850	21	474	27	428	34
Associated companies	—	—	20	1	20	1
Taxation	319	8	57	3	92	7
Net income	531	13	437	25	356	28

Net income after adjustment for minority interests, etc. is attributable to shareholders.

interest paid on liabilities. Other sources of income are relatively unimportant, although Citicorp has a larger share of its total income deriving from commission, fees and foreign exchange (33 per cent against 18 per cent). This is extremely high by international banking standards, although most banks are now attempting to boost their fee income as spreads on lending narrow down. Fee income also has the virtue of insulation from interest rate movements.

From total income are deducted firstly operating expenses of which the biggest part is personnel (salaries, pensions, profit sharing allocation) representing about 40 per cent of total income, or over half of all expenses. National Westminster with its larger branch network has significantly higher proportionate staff costs. Premises and equipment are also important items. Then there are other general and administrative expenses.

Before arriving at a profit figure before tax we must deduct a charge for bad and doubtful debts and add the profit contribution from any associated companies. Finally, deduction of tax and amounts due to minority interests gives us the net income/net profit figure from the bank's operations. This profit is attributable to shareholders. The bank's directors will distribute a certain amount by way of dividend, and a certain proportion will be retained to finance future growth.

The balance sheet and profit and loss accounts reviewed above do not show us the movement of funds through the bank during the year. Table 2.4 represents sources and uses of funds. Clearly the major use of funds in both banks is, as one would expect, giving loans to customers, although National Westminster has also accumulated liquid assets. This reflects a fundamental difference between a bank in an underlent position which has to place its funds in lower earning liquid assets, and a bank in a fully lent position which runs down liquid assets to fund its loans. Other applications of funds are cash payments to cover dividends and taxation, and capital expenditure on premises, equipment and other assets. Sources of funds include new deposits, loan capital and medium-term borrowed funds, running down of liquid asset holdings, sale of securities and other disposals. In 1981 Citicorp clearly preferred to avoid the need to raise fresh deposits if at all possible and made extensive use of other sources. Since it has only limited access to cheap retail deposits and had to pay 15–17 per cent for other types of deposit with an average rate of return on assets of

Table 2.4: Consolidated Statements of Sources and Uses of Funds: Citicorp and NatWest

	1981 Citicorp		1981 NatWest		1979	
	$m	%	£m	%	£m	%
Sources						
Funds from operations	850	10	534	6	469	7
Increase in:						
Deposits + borrowed funds	581	7	7,992	90	6,390	92
Loan capital + term debt	2,505	29	323	4	54	1
Share capital	—	—	4	—	5	—
Decrease in:						
Liquid banking assets	3,844	44	—	—	—	—
Securities	860	10	—	—	—	—
Disposals	—	—	21	—	15	—
Total	8,640	100	8,874	100	6,933	100
Uses						
Taxation	319	4	148	2	14	—
Dividends	198	2	53	1	34	1
Premises and equipment	146	2	141	2	124	2
Other	718	8	3	—	89	1
Increase in:						
Loans to customers	7,259	84	7,387	83	4,596	66
Liquid banking assets	—	—	1,142	13	2,076	30
Total	8,640	100	8,874	100	6,933	100

only 16.9 per cent, this was clearly designed to limit costs of funds. Other possible sources of funds are share capital (new issues); and of course cash flows from profitable operations are available.

It is in fact by working on both sides of the balance sheet, on assets and liabilities, that a bank seeks to optimise the earnings it generates from the net interest margin — the difference between its earnings and its cost of funds. This challenging task is known as funds management.

Funds Management

Funds management has become an increasingly important function in recent years as the banks' business mix has diversified, and as the environment has become more difficult. Specific changes which have demanded more skilful funds management are:

— High and volatile interest rates.
— New sources of deposits and loss of some old sources, in

particular increased reliance on funds purchased on the money markets rather than retail deposits.
— Impact of monetary controls.
— New lending activities.
— Problems in maintaining capital adequacy.
— Need for performance measurement to improve competitiveness.

In funds management the bank must be viewed as a whole — as an interactive system, operating within wider economic and social systems. Funds management is directly concerned with the financial consequences of very broad issues of strategy, structure and business development over long time spans; these are the province of top-level strategic planning of such elements as organisation, customer base, earnings retention and capital structure, mergers and acquisition, types of business, and changes in the broad categories of assets and liabilities. An example of this type of strategic planning would be, say, a decision to build up mortgage lending to a larger proportion of total advances, from previously lower levels. This would involve commitment of resources over several years. Funds management is also concerned with *short-to-intermediate term* decisions affecting the way in which a bank obtains funds and disposes of them; in other words, the management of categories of assets and liabilities in a dynamic environment, and in the context of the bank's strategic development.

Clearly the objectives of such funds management must coincide with the objectives of the bank as a whole — namely wealth maximisation, defined as the maximisation of the present value of future cash flows accruing to shareholders. They will also be subordinate to specific strategies and policies of the bank. For example, the decision to increase the level of mortgage lending has certain consequences for funds management and it is the funds manager's job to provide for those consequences in the short and medium terms, so that the overriding market strategy can be achieved. Legal, regulatory and other constraints must of course be observed.

Funds management concentrates most effectively on the disposition of categories of assets and liabilities over which management has full discretionary control — ideally money market instruments which can be traded in wholesale financial markets. But it extends to other areas where direct management is more problematical, for example pricing policy for retail deposits or customer loans.

The key variables affecting wealth maximisation have been identified as:

1. Spread, interest margin and asset/liability management;
2. Liquidity management;
3. Capital management;
4. Overhead cost control.

The most important aspect of asset/liability management is undoubtedly management of spread, interest margin and funds gap. It suffices here to state briefly the principles, which are not complicated, although achievement of goals in practice can be exceedingly complicated.

Spread (average rate earned − average rate paid) is the difference between returns on interest bearing assets and costs of interest bearing liabilities. Clearly, a high positive spread is desirable, but policy should aim to maintain and stabilise the spread over time. In particular, spread management must pay attention to interest rate cycles, to risk and return on the bank's portfolio of assets, and to the impact of assets and liabilities acquired on overhead costs.

Net interest margin (Interest income − interest expense/Earning assets) is the net return on interest bearing financial assets, allowing for costs of all deposit-type liabilities. It thus accounts for the value to the bank of any non-interest bearing deposits (current accounts), and the cost to the bank of holding cash and other non-earning assets. Effective management of the net interest margin is the key to long-term stable growth in bank earnings since it is, as has been shown, by far the largest source of income.

Another important factor is the proportion of fixed to variable rate assets, and fixed to variable rate liabilities, and the interactions between these categories. Management of these relationships has become increasingly important with the advent of liability management and increased volatility of interest rates.

The ratio of rate-sensitive (variable rate) assets (VRA) to rate-sensitive (variable rate) liabilities (VRL) can be used to assess the exposure of a bank's balance sheet and its earnings to fluctuations in interest rates. The desired ratio is that which smoothes out fluctuations in earnings in spite of fluctuating interest rates. A ratio of 1:1 may not necessarily achieve this because changes in interest rate do not affect categories of liability and asset at the same time or to the same extent — in other words, categories of liability and asset have varying degrees of interest rate sensitivity. However, we can say that if a ratio is greater than 1:1 then an *increase in interest rates should increase earnings* because of the larger amount of variable rate assets which will be repriced ... and so on for all possibilities:

VRA:VRL	*Interest Rates*	*Effect on Earnings*
> 1	+ Rising	+ Increase
> 1	− Falling	− Decrease
< 1	+ Rising	− Decrease
< 1	− Falling	+ Increase

Most British banks have VRA:VRL in excess of 1:1, which means they are susceptible to loss of earnings if interest rates fall. However, the *size* of this ratio, and the underlying gap between VRA and VRL which it represents, can be varied — a process known as gap-management — in order to minimise the effects of falling rates and maximise gains from rising rates. If the gap is increased (by offering depositors fixed rate liabilities and encouraging borrowers to take variable rate lending) when interest rates are expected to rise then the bank will be best placed to benefit from a rise when it comes; similarly the gap should be decreased by reducing fixed rate liabilities and/or encouraging fixed-rate lending when rates are expected to fall.

In general terms, of course, the larger the gap the more significant is the impact of changing interest rates on earnings. In the case of the sterling business of British retail deposit banks, a very large gap exists because of the current account base and the typically low levels of fixed rate lending — so that a decline in interest rates will have a large adverse impact on earnings. On the other hand, there are severe constraints on the management response to this, in terms of what the market will bear. Fixed rate lending is rare for short-term bank loans and overdrafts, being restricted largely to instalment finance and leasing in the UK; and fixed rate liabilities are not usually issued by UK deposit banks. In effect, by pursuing variable rate policies on both sides of the balance sheet the British deposit banks have eliminated many of the problems of gap management as expounded by the theorists; but they are left with their exposure to a fall in interest rates which reduces the endowment effect of current account balances. Of course, if a bank has undertaken a significant amount of fixed-rate lending by way of mortgage advances, instalment credit to customers or businesses, or leasing agreements, while still relying on variable rate liabilities, then it is exposed to a *rise* in interest rates as funding costs increase. American money centre banks are exposed this way (see country chapters), as are the large West German banks.

In order to assess its exposure properly, the bank needs to know not only whether certain classes of assets and liabilities are fixed or variable rate, but also the original maturities and more importantly actual durations of each class. Only this information will reveal the degree of sensitivity of the bank's balance sheet to changes in interest rates. Essentially, the bank must know how long it will be before it can replace existing deposits with new deposits at new interest rates and make new loans at new rates — or, more technically, the time-scale for repricing particular classes of assets and liabilities. It is in fact possible to construct an accurate picture of this by charting the degree of maturity mismatching between classes of asset and liability (term deposits and term loans), classifying by way of maturity bands. Where a term loan is matched by a term deposit of equal maturity so that both will be repriced at the same time, there is no exposure to interest rate changes, since they run in tandem. In practice, a good deal of large corporate lending and in particular Eurocurrency lending is funded on a strictly matched book to avoid exposure. If currencies are also matched, then exchange rate exposure is eliminated too. However, banks also practice maturity transformation and run mismatched books. Typically they will borrow shorter-term funds than they lend. Retail deposit banks do this because they take current (demand) account and retail deposit (time/savings) account balances and use them to fund longer-term loans, and this exposes them to a fall in interest rates because assets at variable rates will be repriced more quickly than deposits — since demand deposits are effectively fixed rate liabilities, their cost being the cost of administration and overheads. Wholesale banks borrow short on the money markets and lend longer-term when short-term money market rates are lower than long-term lending rates. If they do this, profiting by the turn, they are exposed to an increase in interest rates since their cost of funds will rise when liabilities are repriced more quickly than assets. This is one classic recipe for banking disaster. It is also possible that money market rates for long-term funds will be cheaper than those for short-term funds, but this will only occur when the market clearly expects interest rates to rise and consequently discounts the cost of long-term funds. A bank will then borrow longer and lend shorter in order to benefit when rates rise. The problem is, of course, that any customer who takes a similar view will want to borrow over a fixed long term at present low rates — the opposite to the bank.

Generally, any type of mismatching of assets and liabilities creates an interest rate exposure one way or the other, which a bank must monitor and strictly control, but may also exploit to improve earnings.

A further problem arises for the bank when interest rates rise through the effect this has on borrowing customers whose debt servicing commitments are increased. This extra burden may cause an increase in defaults on repayment, with adverse consequences for bank cash flow, and even increased bad debts with adverse consequences for earnings. It may also mean that the bank has to set higher lending rates to compensate for the additional risk.

Movements in interest rates also have an important effect on investments held by the bank (usually government stock in the main) because they affect the market price and consequently the market value of the bank's investment portfolio. The bank can suffer significant capital losses on its bond portfolio if interest rates rise sharply and the market price of old issues of stock falls. Accounting rules normally require that investments are carried in the books at the lower of cost or market value and a prudent bank must readjust its valuation every year and write off capital losses annually. Conversely, at a time of falling interest rates the market value of the bank's portfolio will rise and capital gains can be made by selling stock. This is one of the standard methods by which deposit banks offset the detrimental effects of falling interest rates.

A bank's ability to adjust to interest rate changes, which constitute the major threat to bank earnings, is constrained not only by the countervailing preferences of customers but also by competitive forces in the market place. A bank which needs deposits cannot bid at rates lower than those offered by competitors, otherwise depositors will withdraw funds on maturity and new deposits will not be forthcoming. Similarly, a bank cannot afford to set lending rates significantly out of line with competitors. The relative efficiency of financial markets and the mobility of both depositors and borrowers between banks and between banks and other financial institutions severely limit a bank's room for manoeuvre because of the impact on cash flow and liquidity. As well as transferring deposits customers may also choose to draw down borrowing facilities more quickly in anticipation of interest rate changes, or conversely to repay borrowing more quickly. When numbers of corporate borrowers take a similar view and act in concert the aggregate effect on the bank is very significant.

On the other hand, it should be noted that financial markets are far from perfectly efficient and that a bank and its customers may react inadequately to interest rate changes because of imperfect information mediated by market prices and by commentators, because of insufficient options offered by the market, because of institutional ignorance of the implications of market information, or because of transaction costs involved in making adjustments.

In a large diversified bank with both retail deposit banking operations and wholesale operations, and access to domestic and international funding sources, there are many offsetting effects since a movement in rates one way affects different parts of the group differently. In the domestic operations, for example, a fall in interest rates may lead to a decline in retail bank earnings (where there is no large volume of fixed rate lending) but to an improvement in finance house and mortgage subsidiary earnings (where there is a large volume of fixed rate lending). The finance house has a countercyclical effect.[8]

These earnings fluctuations caused by *changes* in interest rates must be distinguished from differences in earnings generated by the bank at different *static levels* of rates. For a wholesale bank, if rates stabilise, it does not matter at what level since it works on spread and has low overheads. For a retail bank, if rates stabilise, it is better for the bank if they stabilise at higher levels since it works on net interest margin and has high overheads. In other words, a retail bank with large volumes of non-interest bearing current accounts benefits from a larger gap between the cost of those accounts and the price it charges for loans. This *endowment effect* has however become less and less important for even the largest deposit banks because:

— Rising overheads mean that the fixed costs of running current accounts are substantial. For example, UK clearing banks reckon they pay equivalent to 9–10 per cent interest on current accounts.

— The proportion of current accounts in group funds is diminishing all the time as personal and corporate customers seek a better return on their financial assets.

— Many banks credit customers with a notional allowance for credit interest on current account balances at a rate below deposit/savings account rate. This allowance is never paid over to the customer, but it can be offset against charges and therefore reduces the bank's commission earnings and total income, thus reducing commission income when rates rise.

Much of the business of the international division is on a matched basis because the risks would otherwise become unacceptably high, but still adjustments can be made to the bank's money market positions.

In order to achieve the best results from funds management in a universal bank, it is essential to centralise this function and to manage liabilities and assets on a global basis — quite literally, since funds can be raised from branches and subsidiaries in financial centres throughout the world. The world's leading banks have only very recently started to work to achieve this kind of integration and control of funding operations, but as interest rates and exchange rates continue to deviate alarmingly from predictable patterns it is becoming clear that optimal funds management can have a tremendous impact on earnings.

The need for global management is reinforced by the fact that foreign currency exposure also has an impact on earnings in a multinational bank. In their banking business banks strictly control their exposure to movements in exchange rates and are prepared to take only limited risk positions in their dealings. Dealing rooms undoubtedly make significant contributions to profit, and occasionally in a badly managed bank they also record significant losses. But no soundly managed bank can rely on beating the exchange rate to make long-term profits. On the other hand, a bank with a substantial volume of foreign currency business, which can fully protect all its dealing transactions from exchange rate losses, cannot protect itself from translation gains and losses. These occur when items in foreign currency are translated into the domestic currency for final accounting for the bank's annual report. Amounts will normally be converted at the rate prevailing on the date of the balance sheet and movements in exchange rates will affect the amount of profit recorded from foreign currency operations. It will also affect the stated value of assets and liabilities, and of costs allocated to foreign currency operating units. It is in fact only a nominal or paper loss unless sums are actually remitted to the parent bank and used to purchase domestic currency; but nevertheless it affects the figures presented to shareholders, analysts and others. Since many international banks now have foreign subsidiaries and conduct very large volumes of business in US dollars in particular, translation gains and losses arising from fluctuations in the US dollar exchange rate and other rates are very important. Each bank must devise its own policies for dealing with this problem since there are no international accounting standards here.[9] The most common types of translation gain/loss are those caused by foreign currency profits, and those caused by foreign currency liabilities (loan capital and deposits) whose value and interest charges vary with exchange rates.

We shall now focus more closely on the actual decision-making process. Line management must continually attempt to make optimal decisions with limited knowledge of the past and present situation, and in uncertainty about the future. The quality of these decisions will depend to a large extent on the availability of relevant, accurate and up-to-date information on the past and present, derived from management information systems. Nevertheless, a judgement must be made, since the future cannot be known.

A problem which continually faces management is the pricing of loans, the costing of funds and the setting of the spread on new business undertaken. As we have seen, the bank derives funds from different sources at different rates and lends all over the place. In the financial accounts net income is derived from the difference between average rates charged and average rates paid. However, such average costing of funds is not appropriate when assessing new lending and the funding required because the bank must (if it is fully lent) raise new funds for new loans. The correct cost of funds to finance new lending is the marginal cost of funds to the bank, which is usually the cost of raising wholesale deposits in the appropriate currency on the money markets. For a British bank, for example, the marginal cost of funds will normally be the cost of 3-month or other interbank deposits in London, and this will be applied to all new lending. This system is based on the concept of a bank and group pool of funds, so that no attempt is made to allocate certain types of deposit to certain types of loan. All types of deposit are pooled centrally at head office and then made available to operating units who need to fund lending. Lending units are charged a common rate for funds used. Inevitably, some units are net suppliers of deposits to the pool, while others are net takers of deposits from the pool. Deposits supplied to the pool earn interest from head office at a common rate, so that some units will earn profits from the deposits they bring into the bank, and others from the advances they make. In addition to customer deposits flowing into the pool from operating units, the bank and group treasurer's office will resort to the money markets on a daily basis to maintain the necessary flow of wholesale deposits required to balance the bank's books. The deposits raised by the treasurer's department are of course the largest volume of deposits by far.

The treasurer's department will also deal on the money markets in order to maintain the bank's liquidity and money position to cope not only with demand for new loans, but also other demands on cash flow — customers drawing down balances, deposits maturing, tax, dividend payments, capital expenditure by the bank, and so on. Management must forecast these cash flows as accurately as possible on the basis of known requirements (eg, maturity of fixed term deposits) and experience of usual trends (eg, seasonal deposit fluctuations). It must also bear in mind the requirements of the regulatory authorities in terms of liquid assets the bank must hold on a daily basis. Then each day the bank must balance its books by dealing on the money markets — selling liquid assets or, more commonly, borrowing funds on the interbank markets as and when required.

Clearly, the bank cannot countenance illiquidity for that means failure and disaster. Daily liquidity is essential, and so a certain prudence is required to give the bank sufficient room to manoeuvre in the event of the unexpected. However, holding excessive liquid assets, which are low earning assets, or borrowing excessive funds at expensive money market rates which, if not required, must simply be lent out to the market again with only a small turn on the deal, both reduce the bank's earning power by diluting the average return on assets. The art of liquidity management then is to balance the imperative need for adequate liquidity at all times against the need to keep up the level of bank earnings.

Capital management does not have the same daily urgency as liquidity management. One mistake in liquidity management may cause a bank to fail through technical insolvency (inability to meet its debts as and when due) even though it is solvent in the broader sense (assets exceed liabilities, and there is a positive net worth). A capital buffer is no good to a bank treasurer who must meet a cash payment by the end of the business day. Banking failures are always liquidity failures, and financial system failures occur when liquidity problems at one institution cause the market in liquid assets to dry up and hence create liquidity problems for other institutions.[10] Nevertheless, adequate capital must be maintained by a commercial bank, not least in order to promote general confidence in the resilience of the institutions participating in the financial markets. The problem then for management is to raise expensive capital on the best terms and in the amounts required to satisfy the different criteria applied by regulators, investors, depositors and others. The principal methods of raising capital (apart from merely adding to reserves by property revaluations), are to retain earnings, to issue shares, or to borrow loan capital. Major banks use all these methods but are increasingly making use of loan capital issued on the international capital markets, notably floating rate notes. A foreign currency component of capital is necessary to a multinational bank lending and conducting operations in foreign currencies, since it will have to cover bad debts and make capital outlays in foreign currency.

International banks have had to cope with the impact of inflation on their balance sheets. Inflation swells the size of balance sheet totals and therefore forces the bank to increase its capital in order to maintain the same capital ratios. If earnings are inadequate to do this the bank will have to resort to other methods of raising capital externally.

Financial capital is an expensive resource. It is raised centrally, but there then occurs the problem of allocation of cost of capital. In theory, a portion of capital should be assigned to all assets and the true yield calculated on earning assets should include a charge for capital. All operating units should also in theory be allocated a portion of capital to fund their operations. Such a system allows senior management to measure the actual return on investment from earning assets and from profit centres. However, few banks have achieved such depth and precision in their management accounting. Many banks have consciously rejected a capital allocation system because it is so difficult to set reliable criteria for allocation, and because the heavy charge over which they have no control has a demotivating effect on the managers of profit centres.

Nevertheless, the theoretical appeal of such a system remains, and some banks have devised methods of providing reasonably accurate measurement of return on investment by allocating capital.

Overhead cost control is an unglamorous but essential part of financial control in banking. In large, growing organisations it is an essential discipline, particularly in times of high inflation which continually pushes up staff costs. Banks have also had to devote more attention to cost control since they have begun to feel the effects of continuous squeeze on their interest margins due to competitive pressures.

Cost control is a particularly difficult problem for a deposit bank with an extensive branch network and large numbers of staff in branches and in head office support units. A retail banking operation carries a heavy burden of effectively fixed costs, since it is not possible quickly to reduce numbers of staff or dispose of premises. Table 2.5 shows the overriding importance of staff costs in a typical retail banking operation which characterises the domestic banking operations of most banks.

When faced with the need to cut costs a bank which wishes to avoid industrial relations problems that may blow up if it attempts to restrain salaries or initiate redundancies will probably first move to stop all new recruitment. Since there is a continuous stream of

Table 2.5: Typical Cost Structure: Retail Banking

		% of total costs	% of total income
Personnel —	Salaries	50	34
	Pensions	15	10
	Concessionary loans	5	3
	Total staff costs	70	47
	Occupancy (leasehold premises)	5	3
	Notional rental (freehold premises)	3	2
	Equipment	3	2
	Depreciation	5	3
	Communications	5	3
	Miscellaneous	4	3
	Bad and doubtful debts	5	3
	Total costs	100	66
	Total income	150	100

staff retiring or leaving the bank's service for other reasons, failure to replace these people will soon reduce numbers by natural wastage. Another course is to redeploy staff in unproductive units to areas of new business which are generating profits, provided that such units exist in the bank and that staff are prepared to move. Effective control of staff numbers is the key to bank productivity. The greater volume of business a bank can support from a given number of staff the greater its profits and return on investment. It becomes necessary then for the bank to establish systems for determining the number of staff of given experience needed to cope with given volumes of business. This involves a comprehensive approach to work measurement for all staff activities, and adherence to job specifications devised by responsible management. In effect, every existing member of staff's activities must be fully justified, and a case made for any new posts created.

The bank also has some room for manoeuvre with premises, especially prestige head office locations, since it can shift operations to cheaper premises without radically affecting the bank's performance capability. In the modern environment expenditure on new equipment is essential, and depreciation is a standard accounting charge. Attempts to restrain communications and other costs (eg, restraining telephone usage, or reducing expense allowances) may have a salutary effect on staff attitudes but will not make much impact on actual costs.

The charge for bad and doubtful debts is not really a part of overhead costs since it can be directly related to particular loans and affects the rate of return on those loans. Decisions on debt provisions are perhaps better considered as part of credit policy. However, it is useful to consider the mechanics of the accounting process at this stage. The annual charge against profits consists of various elements:

1. Specific bad debts written off, *less* recoveries of debts previously provided for.
2. Specific provisions for doubtful debts, those which are thought to be beyond recovery, and which the bank wants to cover in advance in order to spread the burden of charge-offs over several years.
3. General provisions for unidentified and unexpected future losses.

It is a matter of judgement for the bank as to when it makes provisions and in what amounts, although regulatory authorities may impose rules. Generally there are recognised to be two stages in a loan 'going bad' — failure to repay capital, and failure to repay interest.

Failure to repay interest is considered far more serious and such debts are usually considered doubtful and beyond recovery, so that a prudent bank will make a specific provision against that loan in the current year. When the bank is satisfied that there is no hope of recovery, the full amount will be written off. If recovery is later made an amount will be recredited in that year.

All the major banks have had to cope with the effects of persistent inflation on their operations, although rates of inflation have varied significantly between the different nations. Inflation is an excessive growth in the supply of money, which in a developed economy means rapid growth in bank deposits. A bank conducting its business in an inflationary economy will find the volume of its deposits rising continually. The general rise in the level of prices caused by inflation will lead to an increase in loan demand from customers too, since they are conducting their affairs in the same inflationary conditions. The banks' balance sheets will then grow roughly in line with the level of inflation, regardless of any real growth in deposits or loan demand. Of course, most governments attempt to restrain inflation by the imposition of some form of monetary control, usually involving limited acceptable growth of bank deposits.

The immediate repercussion of inflation for a commercial bank will be some form of restriction on the rate of growth of its deposits and/or advances, in addition to the normal reserve requirements imposed in order to restrain credit creation. Different policies have been pursued in practice but the main options open to the authorities are:

— Control of the size of the base of 'hard' money on which banking operations are founded, namely cash and deposits with the central bank.
— Ceilings on bank advances.
— Penal reserve requirements on excessive growth in bank deposits or advances.
— Open market operations in the sale of government securities and short-term money market instruments, which affect banks'

liquidity and influence interest rates.
— More direct control of interest rates.

When the authorities desire to deflate for any reason, they will resort to a selection of the above methods, and the banks will have to cope with them.

However, inflation also causes direct problems for banks. The increase in balance sheet footings requires a proportional increase in capital if capital adequacy is to be maintained. If retained profits are insufficient, the bank will have to resort to expensive new capital (share issues or loan capital) or see its capital adequacy fall. Of course, high inflation brings with it high interest rates, and for a retail deposit bank with access to current account funds this should mean higher profits because of a wider interest margin due to the endowment effect. But high inflation also brings cost pressures, and in particular salary increases, which will diminish profitability. Most banks in highly inflationary economies have had to accept a fall in their capital ratios as capital has been steadily eroded.

Inflation also has a direct impact on the bank's financial position as shown in the financial statements, because it affects different items in the accounts in a different manner. Banks in an inflationary economy now generally produce inflation-adjusted balance sheets and profit and loss accounts which show a more accurate position than historic cost accounts. The treatment of inflation in accounts is a very vexed question, but in simple terms a bank must make allowances for the following effects:

1. Fixed asset values will rise in line with the general level of prices and so the bank should revalue its properties regularly to show the true market value, and credit a capital reserve account. Many banks do still, however, maintain substantial hidden reserves by undervaluing their fixed assets.
2. The value of financial assets declines under inflation because they are future claims on another party and inflation reduces the future purchasing power of money. Banks are massive holders of financial assets whose value is eroded by inflation. This effect is offset by the opposite effect on financial liabilities which are future promises to pay, whose value is eroded by inflation. Banks are massive holders of liabilities too. However, it is in the nature of the banking business that the maturity of advances will exceed that of deposits, so that inflation

will have a greater impact on bank advances, to the bank's detriment. An annual adjustment should then be made to allow for this loss, and if deducted from profits will have a substantial impact on bank earnings.
3. If the bank is borrowing loan capital it benefits from the effect of inflation on this type of liability and can adjust accordingly.

For these reasons banks do not welcome inflation. It is unfortunate for them in terms of public relations that to customers and to the general public banks would appear to profit from inflation, because they charge high nominal rates to borrowers, grow in nominal size, and record high historic cost profits. In fact, the only beneficiaries of inflation are borrowers of funds, including many of the bank's customers.

2.4 Marketing

Banks operate in increasingly competitive markets. They have therefore been obliged to devote considerable attention to the marketing of their services in order to maintain their share of the market and to improve profitability. We have seen how market considerations are an important factor in the planning process, and how specific volume of business targets are built into the corporate plan. We now need to look in greater detail at some of the practical problems of marketing the services of a large, diversified bank.

In many ways marketing-oriented companies are companies whose staff have a certain attitude of mind — that the customer is important, and that the company provides goods or services to meet the customer's needs. It is easy for staff in a large company like a bank to become introverted and more concerned with bank internal procedures than with the customers. This is encouraged by the quasi-public-service nature of some banking activities.

Promoting a marketing orientation is a long-term process involving:

— Management control — the planning system and objectives.
— Leadership — example and inspiration given by all levels of management.

— Communication — reinforcement of the idea through internal newspapers, training, briefing.
— Incentives — bonuses for superior performance.

No member of staff in a bank can avoid the marketing responsibility. Every contact with the customer is important — the telephonist, the receptionist, every letter, every statement sent. When the service itself is intangible the customer can only judge quality by the people who provide the service.

Financial Services

Bank marketing has been described as:

— Identifying the most profitable markets now and in the future.
— Assessing the present and future needs of customers.
— Setting business development goals and making plans to meet them.
— Managing the various services and promoting them to achieve the plans.[11]

These tasks must be undertaken in a competitive and dynamic environment. An organisation which is marketing-oriented will have to engage in certain types of activity, including:

— Studying attitudes and needs of different categories of customer.
— Identifying customer needs which it can satisfy from its present or obtainable resources.
— Seeking the best way of satisfying those needs while making a profit.
— Seeking to anticipate and adapt to changes in society and in the market.
— Recognising moral and legal standards of the community to which it belongs.

These activities are not only the responsibility of a marketing department and specialist staff. They form part of the general duties of all line management and clerical staff, throughout the organisation which is truly marketing-oriented.

Banks were late-comers to marketing, but during the 1970s they

have transformed their approach. Planning and marketing departments have been established and extensive use is made of market
research. Business development has become a major responsibility
of all line managers, and staff throughout the banks are accus-
tomed to working to achieve targets for sales of various services. It
has been something of a revolution and has involved significant
changes in the behaviour and attitudes of bank staff. It has proved
to be a problem in many countries that bank staff have previously
perceived their jobs as 'professional', and seen their role as
responding to customer requests rather than initiating new business. A more active selling role is now necessary for bankers who
want to continue making profits.

Other important aspects of bank marketing today are public
relations, the management of the banks' relationships with government, the media, and through them the general public, and advertising. Advertising is only a part of overall marketing activity but it
is important because of its enormous effect on the bank's image in
the eyes of the world. The basic functions of a typical marketing
department are listed in Table 2.6.

There are special difficulties in marketing bank services which
are not encountered in the marketing of, say, groceries. When the
bank lends money to a customer, or advises on business policy, or
gives financial advice, or merely accepts a customer's deposit, it

Table 2.6: Typical Market Planning Department Functions:
Domestic Deposit Bank

Research and information — commissioning of regular reports and special studies,
  analysis and presentation of results, profiles of customers.

Product/services development — feasibility studies, introduction of new services, pilot
  tests, launches. Maintains Service Manual. Observes competitors' services, and
  pricing.

Branch support — services to assist managers and branch staff. Studies on methods of
  distribution of services. Closing and opening branches.

Business development — promotion of particular services, eg, student campaigns,
  employee recruitment campaigns (the unbanked), conversion of wage earners to
  monthly payment, cash cards, direct debits and credits. Representation at shows
  and exhibitions.

Education and training — seminars for customers, staff training in marketing ideas and
  product knowledge, bank brochures and other publications.

Technical services — exploration of new possibilities raised by technological
  developments.

---

undertakes a heavy responsibility. The limits of this responsibility have been defined in part by the Courts in terms of the rights and duties of the banker-customer relationship, and the concepts of fiduciary care and undue influence in British law for example. But every good banker knows that he must carefully weigh the effects of his actions on the customer's general welfare.

The banks also have special responsibilities in assisting in the implementation of economic policy. These responsibilities some-times conflict with marketing activities — for example, credit controls may inhibit planned expansion of customer advances or set priorities in lending to different sectors; prudential controls may limit lending and prevent diversification into some activities; exchange controls may require extensive administration. It has also been argued that banks have wider economic/social responsi-bilities to assist in the promotion of economic development and to ensure that ethnic minorities are properly catered for. For these reasons, profitability, although the major measure of bank success, cannot be counted the only measure.

There are special difficulties with the marketing of all types of services as opposed to goods. These stem from the fact that a service is an intangible, contractual arrangement. It is provided by one person or persons to another, and hence the quality of the interpersonal relationships established are important. The service may be consumed over a long period of time so that good rela-tionships must be maintained over many years.

As far as sales and promotion go, the difficulty comes in description and packaging. The customer cannot see and inspect a financial service, although he may see and form judgements on people and premises. A lot depends on communication through brochures and advertisements, and on the public image of the provider of services — the name of the bank.

A particular difficulty with financial services is the sensitivity of money and financial affairs as a subject, and the very high levels of service expected by users of such services. The large banks have an additional problem here, since they have to ensure that customers are happy to entrust their personal financial affairs to a massive organisation such as a modern multinational bank.

It must always be remembered that a financial service is a definite set of solutions to a definite set of problems encountered by a specific group of people at a certain point in time — in other words it satisfies a particular customer's needs.

Banks offer many services to many types of customer but at the centre of each transaction is the service contract. The aim in bank marketing is to build on the original contract and to both lengthen it and broaden it. This means developing a growing relationship with the customer — an art known as relationship banking. It can only be effectively achieved by taking personal care over customers and their needs, although the level of care will vary according to the type of customer.

In dealing with business customers the element of personal care is vital to the relationship. The bank must put highly-skilled and personable staff in contact with existing and potential customers, and provide them with full back-up facilities. It is the corporate banker's responsibility to use his skill and time to nurture relationships and bring to bear as many of the bank's services as possible to meet the customer's needs. The customer may not always be aware of his needs, in the area of financial planning, for example; or may have judged his needs wrongly, for example when calculating overdraft requirements.

In dealing with personal customers in the mass market the same amount of skill and time cannot be devoted to relationships for cost reasons — except in the case of wealthy individuals, or where specific fees are charged, as in trust work. The problem for the bank here is to ensure that more junior staff who are available to devote time to personal customers, have a full grasp of customer needs and bank services. This is basically a training problem, educating staff in product knowledge and improving their understanding of personal financial planning.

It is necessary for a bank to decide on the range of services it wishes to offer and the extent of the markets it wants to approach. A universal bank may decide that it can offer virtually every kind of financial service to all segments of the market — being 'all things to all men'. A multinational bank may decide that it will invest in any profitable financial services operation anywhere in the world. The only limits to the activities of banks with such policies are their available resources in capital and staff, and the opportunities for profitable growth.

In practice, most banks recognise limits on their own areas of managerial competence, and rather than attempting total coverage of all markets concentrate on exploiting their existing strengths. They attempt to identify a 'niche' in the market — a particular part of the market and set of services in which they specialise and where they attempt to offer a superior service. As the pressure of competition grows in financial services it becomes more important for banks to identify 'niches' in the markets in which they operate.

Establishing a niche requires adequate market research, the setting up of a competitive product range, and the creation of a differentiated corporate style and image. It requires careful training of staff to be able to offer the superior service.

Business Development

Any business development programme in banking must be approached carefully, and short-term gains must be balanced against long-term growth. There are several conflicting forces:

Short term	*Long term*
Competitive pricing	Adequate profit margins
Direct selling effort	Customer goodwill
Profit goals	Non-profit goals
Growth	Stability
Risk and reward	Safety and survival

The banker must also consider whether he is to direct his major efforts towards greater penetration of existing markets, or towards development of new markets; and towards improvement of existing services, or towards development of entirely new services and lines of business.

It is extemely important in an industry like banking which deals with such a wide range of customers to study the needs of different categories of customer. The process of defining relevant categories is known as market segmentation. The market can be segmented by various criteria, and in varying levels of detail, but a typical scheme suitable for the branch banking division is shown below, based on segmentation by customer type; and for the international banking division, based on customer type and geographical factors (Figures 2.2 and 2.3).

The important thing is that each segment, however defined, will require a different marketing approach and quite possibly an entirely different range of services.

Segmentation should enable the bank to identify strategic markets, select particular business development opportunities, design appropriate services, allocate the necessary marketing efforts and direct promotional activity. Division of the market into segments

Figure 2.2: Market Segmentation — Domestic Banking

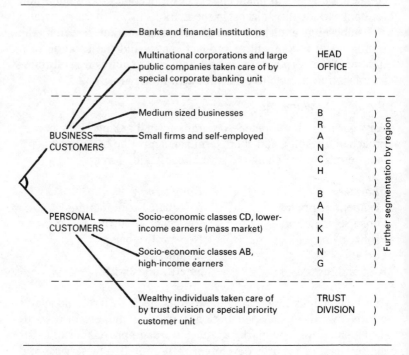

also enables the bank to see more clearly trends in different parts of the market.

Segmentation is normally according to basic categories of customer, but more sophisticated and detailed classification is possible according to various criteria:

Consumers	geographical (location of customer)
	demographic (socio-economic class, age, etc.)
	psychographic (attitudes and preferences)
	behaviour (habits in use of services)
Businesses	geographical (location(s))
	legal (incorporated, private or public)
	size (turnover, employees)
	industrial classification
	business profile

The practical result of market planning as far as line managers and

Figure 2.3: Market Segmentation — International Banking

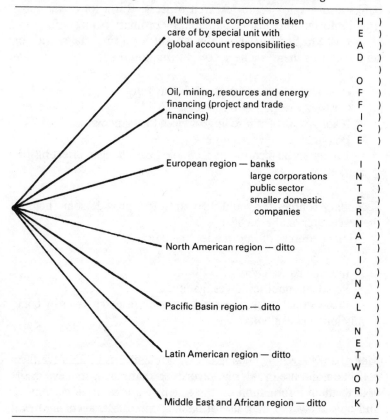

Multinational corporations taken care of by special unit with global account responsibilities	H) E) A) D)
	O)
Oil, mining, resources and energy financing (project and trade financing)	F) F) I) C) E)
European region — banks large corporations public sector smaller domestic companies	I) N) T) E) R) N) A)
North American region — ditto	T) I) O) N) A)
Pacific Basin region — ditto	L)
	N) E)
Latin American region — ditto	T) W) O) R)
Middle East and African region — ditto	K)

their staff are concerned is the setting of targets for the selling of services to different types of customer.

In the preparation of strategic plans a survey of the market is essential. Study of the markets is also required when developing new products, planning sales and promotion techniques, and setting prices. It is a mistake to assume that bankers have a 'feel' for the markets and can work on experience and hunches in arriving at marketing decisions. Any individual's experience is limited and there is no substitute for objective information. Having said that, it is true that all statistical information needs to be treated with care, and can only give an approximate picture, so that experienced judgement is important.

There are market research consultants which the banks use. The banks also employ some research officers. But a lot of the most useful information must be gathered by ordinary bank staff.

In order to find out about the market for a financial service or set of services there is a need for information on:

— Customer characteristics and behaviour.
— Customer response to services.
— Likely profits from selling services to segments.
— Potential for new customers.
— Likely social/economic/technological changes affecting the market.

Secondary sources (eg, published statistics) provide some help to the researcher, and are cheap.

Primary sources of information include:

— Internal bank records.
— Personal enquiries/investigations.
— Professional market research by bank researchers or by commissioned consultants.

Many banks are now making considerable efforts to improve their collection and use of internal records so that managers have available to them information on the salient features of all customers, and on the level of their use of bank services. Managers are being encouraged to become more active in personal efforts to seek out new business and to develop contacts. Professional research must be sparingly used because of cost, but consumer panels are a useful device to find out about consumer attitudes to banks and their services.

In a mature market such as the financial services market in advanced countries, every bank has limited scope to gain new customers. This compels the banks to look closely at their existing customers and to endeavour to sell more services to them. In order to achieve this, however, managers require far more information than they currently have available. The race is on for banks to establish on their computers a viable management information database for marketing purposes.

The significant facts about all customers can be stored on the computer. This not only gives the manager quick access to vital facts when preparing to meet a customer; more importantly, it enables the manager to identify different types of customer (eg, businesses of different sizes, personal customers of different ages), and the extent to which different customers are making use of bank services.

The bank has to maintain an attractive and profitable range of services. Some staple bank services such as current accounts have been available for many years, but they are continually refined and improved — recent examples being the provision of cheque cards and the use of cash dispensers and ATMs.

It is useful to bear in mind the product life-cycle theory commonly used in marketing. This holds that particular services are introduced, grow in popularity, and then their profitability declines as competitors enter the market. In banking, many services have a very long life, but for most of their life the market in which they sell is mature or even saturated, because of the very high level of competition between the providers of financial services.

A bank can make major extensions to its range of services by acquiring a subsidiary, as the deposit banks in many countries did in order to move into instalment finance via acquisitions of finance houses. Or it can develop its own in-house services, as the same banks did when moving into the house mortgage market. Or it can make its own use of an existing service under licence, as many banks have done with credit cards.

Innovation of specific services is a risky business. Imitation is the simplest way, and in the financial services industry many services can be quickly copied from competitors. New types of deposit and loan may only require a few months or even weeks to introduce. Some newer services based on sophisticated computer systems may require a longer lead time and the bank which gains a lead in this field has an opportunity to license its service to others.

Finally, there is genuine invention, where a new service is simply created to fill a perceived need. These are comparatively rare, but examples include some of the recent business loan schemes, the revolving credit account and the recent premium credit cards, and money market funds.

Even apparently minor alterations to services must be carefully thought out in advance. In a first screening, obvious drawbacks must be identified — the service may be outside the law, outside the competence of the bank, or contrary to some established bank policy. Services which appear viable must then be subjected to a close scrutiny of the possible profits to be generated and of the practical methods of operation. Before launching a new service, line managers and specialists such as inspectors/auditors must be consulted, and ideally there should be some kind of test marketing of the service.

Services that have been developed must be brought to the customer. The first requirement is a means of reaching the customer — the delivery system. For banks this is primarily the branch network, domestic and international, and the staff on location. However, there are many supplements to this:

— Offices of subsidiaries/affiliates (eg, finance houses).
— Correspondent banks for international business.
— Travelling representatives for sale of specific services, eg. unit trusts, insurance, credit cards to merchants.
— Services sold through direct response to newspaper adverts or in reply to mail shots.
— Services sold through non-branch locations (eg, ATMs in department stores), and in the future possibly home/office computer terminals.

The mechanical side of selling provides logistical problems in ensuring that the services can be provided on the terms and at the times expected by customers. Branches must be open, computer systems up, staff informed, forms and other documents available.

Selling financial services is a difficult art, even when logistical problems are fully overcome. Indirect methods of selling are only partially successful and real success must be through personal selling. High-pressure selling is likely to be counter-productive. In selling banking services in particular the approach must be consultative and empathic, eliciting from the customer his problems and needs and offering services to meet the needs. The chances of succeeding in a face-to-face encounter with the customer are considerably improved if the banker prepares himself well — refamiliarising himself with the likely bank services, and more importantly researching as much as possible about the customer and his financial circumstances. In working up to approach a large business for a new account such research may take weeks; with personal customers in 'off the street', a minute only may be available to scan the customer's file. The kind of attention given to a customer after the interview is also important — prompt performance of actions promised, in particular, and maintaining contact to ensure satisfaction, to cope with complaints and problems, and to offer new services.

A large part of banking is selling of the bank in the person of the banker, so that standards of personal presentation, courtesy and so on must be very high. This extends to all staff with whom the customer has contact. It also extends to bank premises, and literature — brochures, statements, and most importantly, letters.

The selling approach in banking has been described as *consultative* and based on empathy; as 'soft' rather than 'hard'. Customers will react against pressure and bombardment. The technique is to draw out from the customer in conversation the financial problem with which he is faced, and then to suggest a positive solution through the provision of an appropriate bank service. This requires considerable skill in listening, and in probing by careful questioning. This can only be done if a good rapport is established with the customer, at a personal level. Good product knowledge enables the members of staff to respond quickly to customer enquiries and requests, and also to take the opportunity to *cross-sell* services.

However, the personal selling approach can be supplemented by recognised retailing techniques to encourage customers to make purchases:

— Branch layout.
— Attractive promotional material.
— Service reminders in statements and other correspondence.
— Branch location to catch passing trade.

Another important techique is packaging or merchanidising — that is, presenting the service to the customer in an attractive and convenient form.

Packaging can also refer to the offer of a combination of services. For example, the current account package includes cheque book, cash card, cheque card, statements, and so on. That is a ready-made package. For business customers, tailor-made packages of a variety of suitable services are more appropriate.

In order to sell bank services management must effectively inform the customer about the services, and persuade him to obtain them from the bank rather than a competitor. This requires a long-term programme of customer education, continually talking with customers and potential customers, ascertaining their needs and showing them how the bank can help; providing explanatory guides on financial planning and on bank services; speaking in seminars and to other groups; discussing changes and innovations in national and local media. The public is taking an increasing interest in the activities of banks and the banks have an excellent opportunity to inform the public about their activities and plans.

Besides this long-term programme the bank must communicate specific messages to existing and potential customers about its services — for example, when introducing a loan guarantee scheme, or when introducing house mortgage schemes.

Messages must be clear and simple, aimed at a target audience, using appropriate media. The target audience will be the market segment for whom the service was designed, but within this audience there will be decision-makers and opinion-formers who have great influence over that audience as a whole. For example, in the business sector financial managers and directors are decision-makers, solicitors and accountants are vital opinion-formers. These are the key people. In the personal sector heads of households (usually mature males) are decision-makers, but women are vital opinion-formers; although social trends in this and other areas are changing, and must be monitored. The chosen message must gain the attention of the audience, suggest a benefit the customer can obtain from the service, a reason why he should believe the bank can offer that benefit, and a reason why he should approach the bank for it. It has also been said that the message should contain a 'unique selling proposition' (USP) — a feature which distinguishes this service from any other — and in most cases instructions as to how the customer should proceed and obtain the service, — for example, fill in the coupon, or contact the nearest branch, or dial a number.

The available media include:

National — newspapers
        — magazines
        — TV
        — radio
  Local — newspapers
        — magazines
        — TV

— radio
— cinemas
— billboards and other displays
— promotional materials at point of sale.

Banks can also communicate their presence and image through a variety of activities such as sponsorship of cultural, sporting and educational events; participation by staff in local events; comment by staff on economic and industrial affairs in various media. Specific messages can rarely be delivered through these media.

There has been a significant growth in all countries of bank advertising on TV in recent years and this is an important part of a bank's publicity effort because of the high visibility, and the large costs involved. The first step in a TV campaign is to establish the bank's image and to monitor audience recall of the image. When a firm image has been established then the bank can proceed to run adverts describing different services, aimed at specific target audiences. The image established through TV can also be effectively used in other contexts. For example, business services are most effectively advertised to decision-makers and opinion-formers through newspapers and journals; but the same public image can be used to good effect.

The precise nature of a bank's advertising and promotional campaign will vary greatly according to the cultural environment of the host society and the expectations of customers. The type of packages, incentives and general hard selling appropriate to the Californian retail market will not be well received in Japan or other less consumer-oriented societies. Style must also be appropriate to the particular market segment, so that a different image and message is conveyed to finance directors from that conveyed to home-buyers.

There are two basic methods of pricing a product or service. Management can look at the customers and their needs, assess what they are prepared to pay for a service bearing in mind other calls on their expenditure and the prices for substitute services offered by competitors, and then decide whether the bank can supply a service at that price to cover costs and give an adequate return in view of the risks involved. This is market-based pricing. Or management can assess the costs of offering a certain service, add the required mark-up for profits, and see if it is acceptable to the market at that price. This is cost-plus pricing. In practice, the two methods are not mutually exclusive. The bank must look both to the market and the prices it will bear for certain products, and also to its own costs. In this respect we must remember that the vast majority of bank costs are fixed costs and that the unit costs once a service is established are low. This may be a temptation to offer a lot of services whose profitability is doubtful.

Commercial banks earn most of their income from their interest margin, and interest rates are the key to profits. The general level of interest rates is beyond the banks' control, being determined by economic forces and government actions. Base lending rates are also virtually beyond the banks' control because the force of competition in wholesale markets is so strong that no bank can move far from its competitors or from other money market rates. Rates for wholesale deposits and certificates of deposit must be closely tied to money market rates, and rates for large borrowers must be closely competitive with other available sources of borrowing. In the market for retail deposits, again close attention must be paid to competitors' rates, including non-bank institutions. In the market for business lending (middle market) competitive forces are a little less strong than for large corporate lending and the strength of established relationships may allow some variation of prices by negotiation. Consumer credit and housing loans must be priced against bank and non-bank competitors. Pricing of service charges and other fees present different problems. In the past, banks have tended to rely on income from interest margins and not to bother too much about other income, in many cases running associated services at a loss. Under the pressures of competition, and in view of falling interest rates, this policy is being revised. Banks now want to achieve better recovery of costs on current accounts, and have raised charges and free banking thresholds to achieve this.

This move towards cost recovery can be expected to extend to other services. American banks recently started to charge substantial fees for credit cards, for example. Customers may expect to pay more for services such as safe deposit, and for managerial time in interview. It is worth noting that some services, for example stock and share transaction, and trustee work, have always been based on full recovery, and that use of these services tends to have been limited to wealthier customers. The move towards cost recovery in the mass market will have to be carefully handled if the banks are not to lose customers.

In corporate and international markets too banks are making every effort to secure management fees when possible in order to boost income from lending which, because of competitive pressures, is at very low spreads.

A local manager has only limited control over prices, usually only when negotiating with a business customer where he will be expected to use his judgement to offer a package price for lending and other services which will prove attractive in view of the competition. Even here the bank has firm guidelines.

Centrally determined prices	*Negotiable prices (within guidelines)*
Personal current accounts	Business current accounts
Deposit and investment	Overdrafts
accounts	Merchant banking
Trustee work	International services
Transmission services	Business loans, leasing, factoring
Personal loans	

Business development in international banking is based on the same principles as those applied in domestic banking. The emphasis is, however, rather different because of the different nature of the markets. Since the bulk of business is wholesale banking, the international banker must devote his efforts to identifying potential individual target customers — a large corporation, or major international bank. He must then attempt to fathom the financial problems faced by the potential customer and devise creative solutions which can be offered in a highly competitive market at attractive prices. Since all customers at this level are multi-banked, there is not the same opportunity to develop customer loyalty and the bank will be judged on price and performance by comparison with competitors.

In such wide and dispersed markets one of the bank's biggest assets is its name. It is the desire to establish name which is responsible for the tendency of some major banks to countenance expansion at the expense of profitability. Mere presence in *all* major markets may be essential to a bank's name and image in its existing markets.

In wholesale markets mass advertising and promotion are inappropriate. The bank must establish its image and secure its reputation by influencing the judgement of opinion-leaders and decision-makers. Advertising will be restricted almost entirely to selected prestige newspapers and magazines perused by senior businessmen. The bank may also enhance its image by sponsorship of cultural and sporting events, and by publication of economic and financial reports. Otherwise, the responsibility for business development rests in the hands of individual bankers in the field. Important activities include calling on prospective customers, and maintaining relationships with existing customers on an account management basis. In such an exposed and competitive market the successful development of the bank's business depends absolutely on the personal skills of individual members of staff. Effective business development becomes a function of personal motivation and ability.

2.5 Personnel Management

The personnel policy of the bank is designed to develop methods and procedures to promote the most efficient organisation and management of manpower. The bank's human resources of competent and motivated staff are arguably its most important corporate resources, and the area in which it is most realistically possible to achieve superior performance over a number of years. Interest and fee income is generated by the active personal skills of lending bankers and other customer-serving staff. On the other hand, in a retail bank up to three-quarters of operating expenses will be staff expenses including salaries, pensions and other benefits. The productivity and real earning power of the staff is obviously a crucial issue for large banks.

Personnel policy aims to achieve productivity by ensuring that staff are managed in accordance with overall objectives and current strategies. This will involve careful management of the following areas:

— Selection and recruitment of staff for all areas of business.
— Manpower planning for the entire organisation and succession planning for senior staff.
— Training in technical skills, general business skills, and internal procedures.
— Career and personal development of staff, especially those with management potential.
— Appraisal and monitoring of staff in specific terms (work

measurement) and general terms (personal qualities).

— Salary policy and other benefits such as pensions, insurance, staff cars, staff advances, profit sharing, holiday entitlement, and so on.

— Staff relations including negotiations with unions or other representative bodies, suggestions schemes, internal communication of objectives and initiatives, general concern for staff welfare.

— Legal compliance with current rules on contracts of employment, dismissal, redundancy, discrimination (race, sex, creed), staff representation, health and safety at work.

The core relationship between bank and staff is the contract of employment, the minimal requirements for which are laid out in law. In very general terms an employee undertakes:

— To serve as required and according to trade custom.
— To provide competence he/she has warranted.
— To take reasonable care in performance of duties.
— To act in good faith.
— To avoid conflicts of interest.
— To maintain confidentiality.

An employer undertakes:

— To remunerate the employee in accordance with contract.
— To ensure adequate health and safety conditions.
— To avoid discrimination.
— To provide a contract of employment.

Of course, employer and employee are free to contract on other matters, and frequently do, especially where senior staff are concerned.

It is beyond our scope to describe in detail personnel management practice in banks, particularly in view of the differences in national cultures. However, large organisations do have some similar problems. Banks are massive employers of a very varied workforce, as Table 2.7 shows, although the number of employees in relation to assets and profits varies considerably according to the business mix of the bank. Retail and wholesale banking have quite different characteristics in this respect, and the nature of employment also differs significantly.

Employment in the banking industry has been growing steadily in all the advanced countries in the post-War period, as has employment in the services sector as a whole. New staff have been necessary to cope with rapidly increasing volumes of business. Increased automation of transactions processing has improved productivity enormously, but has still not coped with increased volumes. In addition, the expanding range of bank services and improved quality of customer provision have meant additional staff requirements in customer-oriented activities. Some observers forecast a peak in bank employment in the 1980s, as the impact of EFT is felt and as competition in retail markets puts a cost squeeze on the large deposit banks. At present, it is predicted that any necessary reductions in numbers can be achieved by natural wastage, but this assumes that bank profits are adequate to allow for a fairly relaxed period of readjustment as parts of the banking business change from labour-intensive to capital-intensive.

The personnel problem in wholesale banking is relatively

Table 2.7: Employees and Assets: Selected Banks, 1980

	Employees	Assets (US$ m)	Assets per employee
USA			
Citicorp	52,700	109,581	2,040
Bank of America	83,700	106,803	1,276
Chase Manhattan	33,500	75,772	2,260
UK			
Barclays	120,300	88,474	735
Lloyds	63,300	47,379	748
Midland	77,900	60,440	776
NatWest	80,700	82,447	1,022
France			
BNP	57,000	105,584	1,852
Crédit Lyonnais	46,000	98,833	2,149
Société Générale	44,400	90,794	2,045
Germany			
Deutsche	44,100	88,242	2,000
Dresdner	31,400	62,841	2,001
Commerz	27,500	50,737	4,793

Source: Bank Annual Reports.

simple. Here are typically a limited number of operating units, a smaller range of services, no massive transactions volumes, a select clientele. A small cadre of highly-skilled staff is required, some of whom will be heavily specialised to cater for small market segments, backed by a small support staff and using sophisticated technology where this can be justified by turnover. A small management hierarchy suffices to give adequate control, and much work is conducted on a team or project basis, where personal relations tend to usurp to some extent the formal relations of corporate authority. Career development and rewards can be tailored to a large extent to fit individuals and their own abilities/performance. Staff representative bodies have no function to perform in a world of individualism, high levels of skill and motivation, fast career progression, and survival of the fittest.

Increasingly, new recruits to wholesale banking are either top-quality university graduates, MBA/business school graduates, or mature individuals with specialist skills or head-hunted from rival organisations. Career development is largely in the hands of the individual, and skills are acquired on the job rather than by formal examination and training. Much depends on the personal ability, motivation and eventually range of contacts of the individual.

Ultimately of course the same qualities will lead to success in retail banking or in any other career for that matter. But the problems of personnel policy in retail banking are much more complex, because there are large numbers of diverse and dispersed operating units, a large range of services, massive transaction volumes, a huge and variegated customer base, and consequently enormous numbers of staff engaged in quite different activities and with quite different aspirations and abilities.

Management of such a complex organisation and its successful development must be based firstly on manpower planning, requiring close study of key areas:

— The profile of the existing workforce in terms of age, length of service, levels, skills, experience, qualifications, sex.
— The dynamics of the workforce in terms of frequency and types of promotion, recruitment, retirement, wastage.
— The objectives and current strategies of the business and the consequent staff needs, expressed in a coherent long-range plan for the guidance of recruitment and staff development activities.

In a large deposit bank the objectives of the business will require adequate staffing in a variety of functions:

— Senior and middle management of operating divisions and units.
— Support functions for operating units, such as personnel, financial control, marketing, public relations, and so on.
— Junior management and clerical staff of operating units and support units.

The great bulk of staff will consist of clerical staff of operating units, including branches and the data processing centres serving the branch network. In most large banks about half these junior employees are female, many are in their teens, and most will not expect to progress towards a management career. Their professional training is therefore limited and their motivations and aspirations inevitably different from those interested in a long-term banking career. Nevertheless, the contribution of the bank's junior staff is crucial to successful operations and management must show considerable qualities of leadership to ensure best efforts are maintained. The opportunity is open to any member of staff to progress towards a management career at any time, by securing the necessary qualifications and displaying superior performance on the job. Outside the data processing centres even junior staff are increasingly expected to participate in servicing customers and must develop the necessary general business skills, in particular the skills of marketing and public relations.

Most large banks now recruit at three levels — firstly, school leavers of good quality who are taken on as apprentices, gaining experience in clerical tasks, receiving in-house training and with the option of taking professional qualifications. The policy of banks on in-house versus external professional examination varies from country to country, and bank to bank, but certainly the level of external examinations is not comparable with the traditional professions, and the power of the professional associations is not the same as the equivalent bodies for lawyers, accountants, medical doctors and so on. Many first-class banks rely entirely on in-house training, although retail banks increasingly resort to external qualifications to promote the professional competence of their large numbers of staff. Secondly, the banks recruit quality graduates who are taken on to a special accelerated training programme and will be expected to show the personal skills and motivation to enable them to progress to middle or senior management. The nature of these programmes varies from bank to bank, but they usually involve a period of mixed training and on-the-job experience lasting anything from one to four years leading to a first junior managerial appointment, after which the graduate is merged into the mainstream of the bank's management. Thirdly, the banks recruit small numbers of mature individuals with specialist skills, such as lawyers, accountants, marketing specialists, systems analysts, programmers and so on. These specialists are usually recruited at or near management level and are immediately merged into the mainstream of management, although their ability to progress in their career may be limited by their very specialisation.

Many large banks still pursue to a remarkable extent a policy of 'generalist' management development. Mainstream managers are given a variety of experience in different functions over an extended period and are expected to master a number of skills as and when required. Such a policy stresses managerial qualities such as:

— Commitment and loyalty to the bank.
— Long-term drive and ambition to achieve a senior managerial position.
— Ability to manage staff, including specialists with superior technical skills.
— General problem-solving ability and pragmatism, including business planning.
— Ability to work in a team and collaborate in consensus decision-making.

These policies produce widely-experienced senior managers whose commitment to the bank has been proven in several different tasks, able to call on specialist expertise as and when required. In a branch banking network such managers are essential to head up effectively the large numbers of diverse operating units.

Even in branch banking the need for very high levels of specialist skills is, however, continually increasing and banks are forced to recruit outsiders and to persuade some of their generalist managers to specialise. Where the requirements of retail banking have not shaped the bank's organisation and ethos, for example in the US money-centre banks, this process of specialisation of staff by function has been taken much further. Under such a policy, young managers with exceptional ability can achieve senior positions within their specialisation more quickly. They can then be trained in general management skills in order to equip them for responsibilities relating to other specialisations.

In a multinational group, career development of senior management is complicated by the existence of subsidiaries and the need for group planning and control functions. Even managers within subsidiary operating units need to understand the scope of group activities as a whole, and to call on the resources of other operating units in order to be fully effective. Senior managers in fully integrated groups will need experience in various subsidiaries, and career paths of group management will cover all subsidiaries. Inevitably, however, conflicts of loyalty and problems of identity may arise since in most cases subsidiaries recruit on their own initiative, subject to the constraints of group corporate planning for human resources. A manager's early training and experience will be orientated towards the particular company or division into which he was recruited and he must grow out of this to achieve a group perspective.

The skills required of bankers are continually changing but a core of subjects can be identified which contains elements essential to an understanding of bank operations:

— Financial management and accounting.
— Commercial law and law of banking.
— Economics of financial institutions and managerial economics.
— Business planning and control, marketing and personnel management.
— Credit analysis and bank operations.

Increasingly managers also need skills in systems work, and a very high degree of competence in the handling of public relations. These do not have to be formally taught, they can be learned by an intelligent, adaptive mind through experience in banking and contact with financial markets. However, the higher levels of skill required in present competitive conditions means that formal disciplines are becoming more important to the banker.

Banks invest massively in the training and development of their staff in order to improve their competitive position in terms of customer service and efficiency. There is also an important motivational factor in training, since intelligent and capable staff will only achieve job satisfaction and build long-term careers with the bank if they feel that they are being given sufficient opportunities for personal development. Ideally, the employee's aims of personal achievement should be synchronised with the employer's aims of corporate achievement, but achieving that for several thousand different employees is no easy task.

Notes

1. 'Wealth maximisation is defined as the maximisation of the present value of future cash flows accruing to the common stockholders. For a particular stockholder, these cash flows can represent dividends and/or capital appreciation.' — J.A. Haslem, 'Bank Portfolio Management', *US Bankers Magazine*, June 1982, pp. 92–7.

2. There have been notable exceptions to the banks' record of earnings growth in recent years — notably two of the Big Three German banks, one or two of the US majors, and the UK clearing banks in 1974.

3. This view was held by the notable commercial banker David Rockefeller while Chairman of Chase Manhatten Bank — see D. Rockefeller, *Creative Bank Management* (McGraw-Hill, New York, 1964). It is also noticeable that in many countries senior management of commercial banks, central banks and official agencies are able to move from one type of organisation to another apparently without encountering great ethical problems of finding radically different sets of objectives.

4. For further discussion of this point and of strategic planning in general see H.I. Ansoff, *Corporate Strategy* (Allen Lane, London, 1965). Various articles have appeared in the leading journal *Long Range Planning* (Journal of the Long Range Planning Society) in recent years specifically discussing bank planning procedures.

5. The system described here is commonly found in large banks but there are obviously significant differences in practices between banks.

6. The judgemental aspects of strategic planning persuade most commentators that this is an art rather than a science, even though attempts are made to quantify where possible.

7. There is of course a strong gaming element in strategic decision-making since one is uncertain of the outcome of decisions made, and one also knows that competitors will make similar strategic decisions based on similar thinking. In fact, the strategy statements of major banks in both domestic and international markets are remarkably similar — but then they are similar organisations faced by similar problems. For proof of this see country chapters and especially case studies of individual banks.

8. This describes the situation for a typical British bank with a large retail deposit base and variable rate lending. Large US banks with fixed rate consumer lending funded from wholesale deposits are the opposite case — exposure to an increase in rates.

9. For a further discussion of the problems faced by multinational firms with exchange rate exposure see Eiteman, D.K. and Stonehill, A.J., *Multinational Business Finance* (Addison-Wesley, New York, 1981).

10. For further discussion of banking crises and their lessons for bank management see Revell, J., *Solvency and Regulation of Banks* (University of Wales Press, Cardiff, 1975). There is now a considerable literature in this area, with notable theoretical contributions from Maisel and others.

11. See McIver, C. and Naylor, G., *Marketing of Financial Services* (Institute of Bankers, London, 1980).

References

Ansoff, H.I., *Corporate Strategy* (Allen Lane, London, 1965).

Arthur Andersen & Co. and Bank Administration Institute, *New Dimensions in Banking: Managing the Strategic Position* (A. Anderson and BAI, Illinois, 1983).

Bradley, S.P. and Crane, D.B., *Management of Bank Portfolios* (J. Wiley, New York, 1975).

Compton, E.N., *Inside Commercial Banking* (J. Wiley, New York, 1981).

Crosse, H.D. and Hempel, G.H., *Management Policies for Commercial Banks* (Prentice-Hall, Englewood Cliffs, 1979).

Davis, S.I., *The Management Function in International Banking* (Macmillan, London, 1979).

Edmister, R.O., *Financial Institutions: Markets and Management* (McGraw-Hill, New York, 1980).

Eiteman, D.K. and Stonehill, A.I., *Multinational Business Finance* (Addison-Wesley, New York, 1981).

P. Frazer and D. Vittas, *The Retail Banking Revolution* (Michael Lafferty, London, 1982).

Hayes, D.A., *Bank Funds Management,* (University of Michigan, Michigan, 1980).

Hempel, G.H. and Yawitz, J.B., *Financial Management of Financial Institutions* (Prentice-Hall, Englewood Cliffs, 1977).

Henning, C.N., Piggott, W.M. and Scott. R.H., *International Financial Management* (McGraw-Hill, New York, 1978).

Herrick, T.G., *Bank Analyst's Handbook* (J.Wiley, New York, 1979).

Maisel, S.D. (*ed.*), *Risk and Capital Adequacy in Commercial Banks* (University of Chicago Press, Chicago, National Bureau of Economic Research, 1981).

Mason, J.M., *Financial Management of Commercial Banks* (Warren, Gorham & Lamont, Boston, 1979).

Pezzullo, M.A., *Marketing for Bankers* (American Bankers Association, Washington, 1982).

Revell, J., *Solvency and Regulation of Banks* (University of Wales Press, Cardiff, 1975).

Roussakis, E.N., *Managing Commercial Bank Funds* (Praeger, New York, 1976).

Stigum, M.L. and Branch, R.O., *Managing Bank Assets and Liabilities* (Dow Jones Irwin, Homewood, Illinois, 1983).

Thompson, T.W. *et al.*, *Banking Tomorrow: Managing Markets Through Planning* (Van Nostrand Reinhold, New York, 1978).

3 US BANKS

3.1 Financial System

The US system of financial institutions is large and complicated. There are many different types of institution, and there is a thick layer of interweaving regulations. The main participants are shown in Figure 3.1. Banking and non-banking organisations have been split into depository and non-depository institutions because the ability to take deposits from the public is closely controlled in the US.

Figure 3.1: US Financial System

Federal Reserve System
> Federal Reserve Board
> 12 regional banks

Depository Institutions
> Commercial banks
> > national banks
> > state member banks
> > other state banks
>
> Foreign banks
> Mutual savings banks
> Savings and loan associations
> Credit unions

Non-depository Institutions
> Finance companies
> Insurance companies
> > life insurance
> > general insurance
>
> Investment banking and brokerage firms
> Mortgage banking companies
> Pension funds
> Open end investment companies

Bank Regulatory Bodies
> Federal Reserve Board of Governors
> Federal Deposit Insurance Corporation (FDIC)
> Comptroller of the Currency
> State bank regulators

Commercial Banks

Commercial banks in the USA number over 14,000, operating more than 36,000 offices throughout the country. The size and activity of different banks vary enormously, but all are free to take deposits and to lend to persons, business firms, governmental and non-profit institutions. Their powers of investment are, however, severely limited, to public sector securities. The commercial banks offer demand and time deposits and operate a country-wide money transmission service. They tend to specialise in corporate business (wholesale banking), and they have diversified into trust and other activities. All commercial banks are owned by stockholders and raise capital by selling common or preferred stock, by issuing medium- or long-term debt, and by retained earnings. They must be chartered either by the Comptroller of the Currency (national banks) or by their home state (state banks). State banks may also elect to become members of the Federal Reserve System for operational purposes (state member banks). All but a few commercial banks have their deposits fully insured with the Federal Deposit Insurance Corporation (FDIC — see Table 3.1). The nature of the banks' activities is affected by laws which prohibit the establishment of branches outside the home state (interstate banking). Some states also have laws which prohibit statewide branching, and permit only limited branching (16 states) or even unit banking (12 states) (see Table 3.2).

The position is complicated by the fact that many banks are in fact wholly-owned subsidiaries of bank holding companies. The holding companies were created to enable banks to acquire subsidiaries engaged in related financial activities such as leasing, mortgage banking, credit cards, data processing. The type of business which the holding companies can acquire is now regulated by the Federal Reserve Board with the aim of preventing banks from diversifying into unrelated activities through the device of a holding company. The control of the holding company is substantially the same as that of the bank, which is by far the largest asset of the holding company. The holding company does not usually engage in any activities of its own, although it is sometimes used as a funding vehicle for the bank group. All the major banks are now structured in this way. It is possible for a holding company to own more than one bank, and frequently a holding company will own a string of unit banks within a state, thus defeating to a certain extent the

Table 3.1: Numbers of US Commercial Banks and Offices by Class of Bank, 1940, 1950, 1960, 1970–80

Year	National Banks			State Federal Reserve Member Banks			Non-member Insured Banks			Non-insured Banks		
	Banks	Branches[b]	Total offices	Banks	Branches[b]	Total offices	Banks	Branches[b]	Total offices	Banks	Branches[b]	Total offices
1940	5,144	1,542	6,686	1,342	1,003	2,345	6,952	941	7,893	923	52	975
1950	4,958	2,230	7,188	1,912	1,359	3,271	6,562	1,204	7,768	689	52	741
1960	4,529	5,507	10,036	1,641	2,624	4,265	6,948	2,305	9,253	353	47	400
1970	4,620	12,522	17,142	1,147	3,651	4,798	7,735	5,424	13,159	184	47	231
1971	4,599	13,272	17,871	1,128	3,819	4,947	7,875	5,989	13,864	181	40	221
1972	4,612	13,959	18,571	1,092	3,981	5,073	8,017	6,626	14,643	206	45	251
1973	4,659	14,908	19,567	1,076	4,051	5,127	8,229	7,444	15,673	207	46	253
1974	4,708	15,729	20,437	1,072	4,209	5,281	8,438	8,446	16,884	240	48	288
1975	4,741	16,269	21,010	1,046	4,406	5,452	8,586	9,254	17,840	257	50	307
1976	4,735	16,667	21,402	1,023	4,672	5,695	8,639	9,729	18,368	276	54	330
1977	4,654	17,578	22,232	1,015	4,595	5,610	8,734	10,663	19,397	307	54	361
1978	4,564	18,107	22,671	1,000	4,721	5,721	8,814	11,696	20,510	333	51	384
1979	4,448	18,798	23,246	977	4,879	5,856	8,926	12,844	21,770	357	51	408
1980	4,425	19,738	24,163	997	4,771	5,768	9,000	13,949	22,949	414	39	453

1980 Total banks of all types 14,836 (main offices)
Total domestic branches 38,497
Total offices 53,333

	National	SFRMB	NMIB	NIB
1980 Percentage shares of all deposits	55.0	16.0	28.8	0.1

Notes: a. 50 States and D.C. b. Includes domestic branches only.

Source: FDIC, *Annual Report*, 1940, 1950, 1960, and 1970–1979; FDIC, *Changes Among Operating Banks and Branches*, 1980, quoted in Golembe (1981).

Table 3.2: US State Branching Laws

	Statewide branching	Limited area branching	Unit banking
	Alaska	Alabama	Colorado
	Arizona	Arkansas	Illinois
	California	Florida	Kansas
	Connecticut	Georgia	Missouri
	Delaware	Indiana	Montana
	Columbia	Iowa	Nebraska
	Hawaii	Kentucky	N. Dakota
	Idaho	Louisiana	Oklahoma
	Maine	Massachusetts	Texas
	Maryland	Michigan	W. Virginia
	Nevada	Minnesota	Wyoming
	New Jersey	Mississippi	
	New York	New Hampshire	
	N. Carolina	New Mexico	
	Ohio	Pennsylvania	
	Oregon	Tennessee	
	Rhode Island	Wisconsin	
	S. Carolina		
	S. Dakota		
	Utah		
	Vermont		
	Virginia		
	Washington		
Number:	23	17	11
1980 Deposits per bank ($m)	273.2	68.8	39.0
1980 Deposits per office ($m)	24.7	16.6	27.8

Source: C.H. Golembe and D.S. Holland, *Federal Regulation of Banking* (Golembe Associates and ABA, Washington, 1981).

restrictions on branching in unit banking states. Holding companies can acquire non-bank subsidiaries in more than one state, but the type of activity is closely controlled to prevent the deterioration of the principle of restricted interstate banking. Some holding companies which owned bank subsidiaries in more than one state prior to the 1956 legislation were allowed to continue in that fashion.

The activities of the banks vary according to size and location. The smaller banks rely for funds more on retail demand and time deposits, and also do a good deal of lending to the personal sector and to the agricultural community. Larger banks rely for funds more on interbank deposits, money market instruments and corporate deposits, and do a good deal of lending to other financial institutions and to the industrial and commercial sector. The very largest banks have massive international banking operations, raising and lending large sums abroad. Some of the largest banks have no involvement at all with retail banking as a matter of policy.

Foreign banks have become a significant force in US banking, by obtaining ownership and control of domestic banks, and by mounting their own operations in the wholesale banking area. The activities of foreign banks are now regulated by the International Banking Act of 1978, which allows freedom of entry to foreign banks on the basis of reciprocity. Foreign banks have made substantial acquisitions in recent years, culminating in the takeover by Midland Bank of Crocker National Bank, then the thirteenth largest bank in the USA. Japanese and British banks in particular have shown a keen determination to establish a foothold in both retail and wholesale banking in New York, California and Illinois.

The extent of this involvement is shown in Table 3.3. The total assets of $236.5 billion were equivalent to over 15 per cent of total US commercial bank domestic assets in 1980. Both domestic and foreign banks make use of Edge Act Corporations and Agreement Corporations. 'Edges' were authorised by the Edge Act of 1919 to finance and promote US foreign commerce. Banks may establish Edge Act subsidiaries outside their home state and these subsidiaries, which are regulated by the Federal Reserve Board, may accept deposits and make loans or investments which must be directly related to international trade. The major banks have sited

Table 3.3: Foreign Banking in the USA, 1980

Type of bank	Number	US assets $ billion
US chartered insured commercial banks owned or invested in by:		
Foreign individuals	62 banks	32.5
Foreign bank holding companies	51 banks	49.1
Other foreign bodies	8 banks	6.6
Edge and Agreement Corporations	16 corporations	0.5
US branches of foreign banks	169 branches	89.7
US agencies of foreign banks	177 agencies	58.1
		236.5

Source: Federal Reserve Board, 'Foreign Investment in US Banking Institutions', 1980, quoted in Golembe (1981).

'Edges' in the main money centres to perform standard international banking functions — international time deposits, foreign exchange, trade financing, currency loans, and so on. Since 1979 'Edges' have been allowed to operate interstate branches. In 1980 there were 57 'banking Edges' with 42 domestic branches and 12 foreign branches, and 54 'investment Edges' with 4 domestic branches.

The Thrift Institutions

Mutual savings banks originated in the nineteenth century in similar fashion to building societies and the TSBs in the UK, as vehicles for household savings and housing finance. They exist only in 17 states, mainly in the North East (Alaska, Connecticut, Delaware, Indiana, Maine, Maryland, Massachusetts, Minnesota, New Hampshire, New Jersey, New York, Oregon, Pennsylvania, Rhode Island, Vermont, Washington and Wisconsin) and with particular strength in New England.

Their sources of funds are almost entirely time deposits, although they can now offer negotiable order of withdrawal (NOW) facilities to give a quasi-current account service, and in two states simple demand deposit accounts are allowed. Their uses of funds are also straightforward: investment in securities including equity investments in some cases, consumer credit, and residential mortgage loans. Some of the larger savings banks are active in giving government insured or guaranteed real estate loans, and in commercial property investment. The mutuals have no capital structure and no commercial function. They are nevertheless a serious competitive threat to the banks in some states.

Savings and loan associations perform similar functions to the mutual savings banks and have a similar asset and liability structure. Like commercial banks, however, they are prohibited from making equity investments. Their lending is almost entirely long-term mortgage loans. Savings and loans are either depositor-owned or stock corporations and may be federally or state chartered.

Credit unions are not a powerful force in terms of absolute size, but they are growing rapidly and in the field of consumer credit in metropolitan areas they provide competition to banks because they are able to offer lower rates of interest. They are also expanding their range of financial services.

The relative importance of the various depository institutions is shown in Table 3.4. Commercial banks still dominate the demand deposit market but they have only a half share in the more important time deposit sector.

Other Financial Institutions

Non-depository institutions must rely for their sources of funds on money market instruments such as commercial paper or debentures. Insurance companies and pension funds have a steady stream of premium income.

Finance companies are important sources of consumer credit by direct lending and by indirect lending through dealer point of sale finance. Other companies specialise in commercial credit by way of revolving credits to finance inventory (stock) and receivables (debtors), instalment credit for purchase of equipment, factoring and leasing.

Approximately one third of total finance company assets is accounted for by the two captive houses belonging to General Motors and Ford. In total there are over 3,000 companies and some of the largest are subsidiaries of bank holding companies.

Insurance companies usually engage in both life and general

Table 3.4: Deposits of Major US Depository Institutions by Type of Institution, 1979 ($ billions)

		Percentage of total	Percentage of time deposits
Commercial banks[a] — demand deposits	435.0	24.4	
— time deposits	673.8	37.9	50.2
Mutual savings banks[b]	142.0	8.0	10.6
Savings and loan associations[b]	470.2	26.4	35.0
Credit unions[b]	56.2	3.3	4.2
Total deposits	1,777.2	100.0	100.0
Total time deposits	1,339.5		

Notes: Since 1970 commercial banks have maintained their market share of time deposits at about 50%, but their share of total deposits has slipped gradually from 67.5% to 62.3%. This reflects the more rapid growth in time deposits than demand deposits as consumers show greater interest-rate sensitivity and since NOW accounts have been available. a. Domestic offices only. b. No demand deposits.

Source: C.H. Golembe and D.S. Holland, *Federal Regulation of Banking* (Golembe Associates and ABA, Washington, 1981).

insurance underwriting, although the two activities are of course quite distinct. They may be organised as either mutual or stock companies and are far more heavily capitalised than banks. They invest their funds largely in corporate bonds and other securities including some equity investments. Life companies are also heavily involved in mortgage lending, especially on commercial property.

Investment banking and brokerage firms are generally partnerships. There are over 4,000 reporting to the Securities and Exchange Commission (SEC), and they may be involved in buying and selling securities for customers, trading on their own account, underwriting and distributing new issues, conducting research, providing corporate advisory services relating to investments, mergers, and acquisitions. They may also operate mutual funds and deal in futures markets. In recent years some of the leading houses have been taken over by other financial institutions including banks.

Mortgage banking companies buy and sell both residential and commercial real estate mortgages. They are also frequently involved in property management and land development. Many bank holding companies have acquired mortgage banking subsidiaries.

Pension funds have become major participants in the US banking system as in all the developed countries in the post-War period. It is important to note that although pension funds and life insurance companies compete for the total savings of the personal sector, there is a difference between these forms of committed, contractual savings and the uncommitted or discretionary savings which flow into bank deposits.

Open End Investment Companies or mutual funds provide for the pooling of investors' funds and their investment in equities, money market deposits, and so on. The explosive growth of money market mutual funds in recent years has been the most important single change in the deposit market. In 1982 banks were permitted to operate such funds and have already started to claw back some of the deposits they had lost to non-bank fund managers, the biggest of which was the brokerage firm of Merrill Lynch.

The banking industry in the USA has been highly regulated for a considerable period. Regulatory constraints have had a major impact on the strategic development of major US banks in both their domestic and international operations.

The establishment of a banking business is closely controlled because all banks must obtain the relevant state or national charter from the state banking regulators or the Comptroller of the Currency. Applicants are required to present a feasibility study, to raise a minimum amount of capital and to show that the new bank will meet the needs and convenience of the local community, or offer certain advantages. For national banks, approval by the Comptroller gives automatic entry to the Federal Reserve System and to the Federal Deposit Insurance Corporation (FDIC) deposit insurance scheme.

National and state banks are regulated by the National Bank Act 1864, which gives 'competitive equality' to both types of bank, and laid reserve requirements on national banks.

In 1913 the Federal Reserve System was created. Twelve regional Federal Reserve Banks were established with powers to issue notes, to hold reserves of member banks, to meet their liquidity needs, and to promote and facilitate members' clearing operations. The Federal Reserve Board was established in Washington, and over time the 'Fed' has assumed wide powers in the field of monetary policy.[1]

After the multiple bank failures of the early 1930s the Glass-Steagall Act (Banking Act of 1933) was passed to establish the FDIC, and to divorce investment banking from commercial banking.[2] The Banking Act of 1935 increased the powers and responsibilities of the Federal Reserve Board. These Acts also prohibited payment of interest on demand deposits and gave to the FDIC and Federal Reserve System authority to set maximum rates paid on savings and time deposits.[3]

The provisions with regard to interstate and intrastate branching have already been discussed. The McFadden Act of 1927 permitted branching for national banks but required them to obey state branching regulations.

Both the Glass-Steagall Act and McFadden Act have been subject to continuous lobbying by the large national banks eager to diversify their activities and extend their geographical coverage. Bank diversification is also monitored by the Department of Justice under the Bank Merger Act of 1960 as amended in 1966, which allows the Department to file suit to block mergers for antitrust reasons,[4] and by the Federal Reserve Board and Comptroller of Currency under the Bank Holding Company Act of 1956, amended in 1966 and 1970. Mergers must be approved by the Fed or Comptroller. The Fed has sole power to regulate holding company activities, their formation and their subsequent acquisitions. The Fed has to apply competitive tests to all acquisitions, and can only approve activities closely related to banking or a proper incident thereto.[5]

There are numerous detailed regulations affecting commercial banks' sources and uses of funds applied by federal and state bodies. These include minimum amounts of capital, controls on non-deposit liabilities, rates of interest on liabilities and sometimes on loans. There are statutory reserve requirements on demand and time deposits. There are important lending limits — for example, no more than 10 per cent of the bank's capital may be lent to any one person. Concentration of lending and country risk exposure are also now monitored by the Fed.

Banks are also subject to regular examination by federal and state bodies, and examiners have power to insist on changes. They look closely at capital adequacy, liquidity, quality of management and systems, volume and quality of loan portfolio, maturity of loans and investments, and security provisions. Large banks will be examined by the FDIC, the Fed, and the Comptroller of Currency, all with differing approaches.

The most important recent development on the regulatory front has been the passage of the Depository Institutions Deregulation and Monetary Control Act of 1980, which brought all institutions under the Federal Reserve System for the purposes of reserve requirements and also gave all institutions access to the Fed's discount window. Moreover, the Depository Institutions Deregulation Committee was established to phase out all rate ceilings on deposits over a period of six years. The Act also allowed banks to operate zero-balance demand deposit accounts automatically funded from savings accounts, and allowed all banks to operate negotiable order of withdrawal (NOW) accounts. Powers of savings and loan associations were expanded to allow them to offer consumer credit, credit card and trust services. The act has liberalised retail banking to a considerable extent.

There are also laws governing consumer credit and advertising through the Truth-in-Lending Act of 1968 and these were simplified by the 1980 act. In 1978 an Electronic Funds Transfer (EFT) Act provided a framework for establishing the rights, liabilities and responsibilities of participants in EFT systems.

In their foreign activities banks are required to seek permission to open branches. The activities of subsidiaries and affiliates are also closely controlled. Banks themselves may only invest in foreign banks, but holding companies and Edge Act corporations can invest in financial activities such as leasing, fiduciary/trust business, advisory services, insurance, data processing, management of mutual funds, dealing in securities. It is noticeable that holding companies have much wider powers to diversify outside the USA than inside.

The Federal Reserve Board has now passed a resolution permitting the establishment of International Banking Facilities (IBFs) to promote the development of 'offshore' financial centres in the USA. IBFs can be established by banks to accept foreign deposits and make foreign loans without reserve requirements or interest rate ceilings being applied, provided that transactions are of minimum size $100,000. Host states may also offer favourable corporate tax arrangements to attract US and foreign banks. IBFs are now well-established in New York.

3.2 Strategic Development of Multinational Banks

The Federal Reserve has identified 176 commercial banks as large money-centre banks for statistical purposes. These banks provide correspondent facilities to smaller commercial banks and also act as reserve banks to non-members of the Federal Reserve System. The correspondent banking link is vital to smaller banks.

Of these money-centre banks, a few of the largest may be identified in terms of the size and the scope of their international operations as multinational banks. They are all based in New York, California (San Francisco/Los Angeles) or Chicago and the group of 13[6] may be likened to the 13 Japanese city banks which are based in Tokyo, Osaka, and other centres. All these banks rank in the largest 100 banks in the world by asset size, have significant international business (deposits and lending) and some representation overseas. They are listed in Table 3.5.

We can further identify the three US majors, Bank of America, Citibank, and Chase Manhattan, as market leaders; and of these three Bank of America and Citibank are the two dominant rivals, and the two largest commercial banks in the world.[7]

Not all these banks are universal banks, and most of them have severely limited domestic branch networks. Morgan Guaranty, Bankers Trust, and Irving Trust have specialised in corporate

Table 3.5: US Multinational Bank Holding Companies, 1980

Holding company	Bank	Head office	Assets $ billion	Deposits $ billion
Citicorp	Citibank (formerly First National City Bank)	New York	115	72
Bank America Corp.	Bank of America	San Francisco	112	88
Chase Manhattan Corp.	Chase Manhattan Bank	New York	76	57
Manufacturers Hanover Corp.	Manufacturers Trust Hanover	New York	56	42
J.P. Morgan & Co. Inc.	Morgan Guaranty Trust	New York	52	36
Continental Illinois Corp.	Continental Illinois	Chicago	42	27
Chemical New York Corp.	Chemical Bank	New York	41	30
Bankers Trust New York Corp.	Bankers Trust	New York	34	24
Western Bancorporation	Various	Los Angeles	32	25
First Chicago Corp.	First National Bank of Chicago	Chicago	29	21
Security Pacific Corp.	Security Pacific	Los Angeles	28	21
Wells Fargo & Co.	Wells Fargo	San Francisco	24	16
Irving Bank Corp.	Irving Trust	New York	18	14

Source: Banker Research Unit, *The Top 100* (Financial Times, London, 1981).

wholesale banking, but the others have shown commitment to the retail market in spite of the limitations on their branching due to regulations.

The profile of the domestic liabilities and assets of all large commercial banks is shown in Table 3.6, and gives a fair picture of the purely domestic activities of the money-centre banks. It is evident that the banks rely to a very large extent on corporate time deposits for their funding, and also make extensive use of borrowed funds (federal funds purchased from other banks and securities sold to other banks under agreement to repurchase ('repos') and other liabilities including subordinated notes and debentures). Less than a quarter of these banks' demand deposits are estimated to be consumer deposits, and the only major source of retail deposits is savings deposits.

The banks' major use of funds is in loans to the commercial and industrial sector and for real estate. There is also significant lending to individuals and to other financial institutions, and extensive

Table 3.6: Large Weekly Reporting Commercial Banks with Domestic Assets of $1 billion or More, 1981 ($000 millions)

Liabilities		Assets	
Demand deposits	174[a]	Cash items	93
Savings deposits	71[b]	US Treasury securities	34
Time deposits	268[c]	Other securities	74
Borrowed funds	141	Fed funds sold	32
Other liabilities	71	Loans	
Residual	50	Commercial and industrial	186
		Real estate	117
		Individuals	65
		Financial institutions, etc.	50
		Agriculture	6
		Other	14
		less provisions	(11)
		Leasing	10
		Other assets	105
Total	775	Total	775

Notes: a. Of which individuals, partnerships, corporations 130 – after adjustment. b. Of which individuals and nonprofit organisations 68. c. Of which individuals, partnerships, corporations 236 – the bulk of these being deposits in excess of $100,000 in the form of negotiable CDs (178) and ordinary time deposits (47).

Source: *Federal Reserve Bulletin*, Tables 1.27 and 1.29.

dealing in government and municipal securities. Table 3.7 shows the broad spread of commercial sector lending.

To gain a fair picture of the activities of the larger multinational banks we must take into account their international operations. This is best achieved by a study of individual bank balance sheets, but a general picture of the scope and nature of operations can be gained from the figures presented in Table 3.8. The table shows that the major part of the US banks' foreign liabilities derives from their own foreign branches, but there are also significant non-resident deposits, demand and time, domiciled in the USA, principally in New York. The banks are also custodians of large volumes of funds, most of which are placed in short-term government securities in the New York money market. The banks are very selective in their deployment of funds abroad. Large volumes are channelled to branches in the Bahamas, British West Indies, and Panama where many loans arranged in the USA are booked for convenience. Large volumes are lent to various Latin American countries, especially Brazil and Mexico. Most of the European funds go to London branches which will lend them on in Europe and the Middle East. There are significant flows to the Far East,

Table 3.7: Large Weekly Reporting Commercial Banks' Domestic Classified Commercial and Industrial Loans, 1981 ($000 millions)

Manufacturing (durables)	27
Food, drink, tobacco	4
Textiles	4
Petroleum refining	5
Chemicals	4
Other non-durable goods	4
Mining, gas, petroleum	24
Commodity dealers	2
Wholesale trade	13
Retail trade	13
Transportation	9
Communication	4
Public utilities	11
Construction	7
Services	26
All other	17
Total domestic loans	174[a]

Note: a. Of which term loans of maturity more than 1 year, 85.

Source: *Federal Reserve Bulletin*, Table 1.30.

especially to Japan, which is an eager taker of dollar loans. The US banks' reliance on foreign offices, especially those in offshore centres in the Caribbean, has been significantly modified by the

Table 3.8: Liabilities to and Claims on Foreigners Reported by Banks in the USA, Payable in US Dollars ($000 millions)

LIABILITIES	1978	1979	1980	1981
Holder and type of liability				
Banks' own liabilities	*79*	*117*	*125*	*162*
Demand deposits	19	23	23	20
Time deposits	13	14	15	29
Other	10	17	18	17
Own foreign offices	37	64	69	96
Banks' custody liabilities	*88*	*70*	*81*	*80*
US Treasury bills, etc.	68	49	58	55
Other instruments	17	20	20	19
Other	3	3	3	6
Total	*167*	*187*	*206*	*242*
CLAIMS				
Area and selected countries				
Europe	*24*	*28*	*32*	*48*
Belgium-Luxembourg	1	1	2	3
France	4	3	3	4
Italy	2	2	3	5
UK	10	14	15	23
Canada	*5*	*4*	*5*	*9*
Latin America and Caribbean	*58*	*68*	*93*	*137*
Argentina	2	4	6	8
Bahamas	22	19	29	43
Brazil	6	8	10	17
British West Indies	10	10	16	21
Chile	1	1	2	4
Mexico	5	9	13	22
Panama	3	6	5	7
Venezuela	3	5	5	7
Asia	*25*	*31*	*39*	*50*
Hong Kong	1	2	2	4
Japan	13	17	21	27
Korea	2	4	6	7
Africa	*2*	*2*	*2*	*4*
Australia	*1*	*1*	*1*	*1*
Total	*116*	*134*	*173*	*249*

Source: *Federal Reserve Bulletin.*

recent provisions for the establishment of International Banking Facilities in certain states.

The New York banks are still the most powerful and influential group of banks in the world, because of their size and traditional international reach, and because of the central importance of New York in the US and world monetary systems. Table 3.9 shows that Citicorp and Chase Manhattan have by far the largest overseas network, as signified by numbers of international subsidiaries and affiliates, and numbers of overseas branches, because of their long-standing commitment to international banking. Citicorp, Chase Manhattan Corp, Manufacturers Hanover Corp and Chemical New York Corp have all developed as fully diversified financial service organisations within the considerable constraints of the regulatory framework. New York State has permitted statewide branching since 1977, and most of the banks have extensive metropolitan networks of a few dozen branches. The banks have

Table 3.9: New York, Chicago and California Banks, 1979

	Major domestic subsidiaries and affiliates	Major international subsidiaries and affiliates	Overseas branches	Other overseas offices
Citicorp	18	54	150	12
Chase Manhattan Corp.	11	42	83	21
Manufacturers Hanover Corp.	6	16	17	25
J.P. Morgan & Co. Inc.	9	34	18	8
Chemical New York Corp.	9	20	15	22
Bankers Trust New York Corp.	14	16	12	27
Irving Bank Corp.	21	9	7	14
Chicago Banks, 1979				
Continental Illinois Corp.	12	25	18	12
First Chicago Corp.	18	28	26	14
California Banks, 1979				
Bank America Corp.	17	49	110	15
Western Bancorp	24	6	7	14
Security Pacific Corp.	14	12	7	10
Wells Fargo & Co.	9	16	4	16

Source: Banker Research Unit, *The Top 100* (Financial Times, London, 1981).

extended their activities nationwide as far as possible through Edge Act corporations, finance house operations and so on, and have lobbied vigorously to achieve deregulation. They perform vital clearing functions for dollar transactions in New York and are all members of CHIPS.

The Chicago banks operate under very strict state unit bank branching laws, and consequently have limited involvement in retail banking. Their corporate and international portfolios are extensive, and they are of course major suppliers of finance to the industries of the American Mid-west. Chicago is also the prime commodities market in the USA, and the site of the most important financial futures market.

The California banks have benefited from the rapid post-War growth in the economy of the area. The state also has liberal branching laws and all these banks have become considerably involved in retail banking through extensive branch networks which are larger than those of their New York peers. For this reason they bear most resemblance to European banks. Bank of America has traditional strengths in the international area but the others have been late starters by comparison. Bank of America and the others maintain a significant presence in New York, because San Francisco and Los Angeles are important domestic money centres but have only a limited international role.

In the post-War period the major US banks have expanded rapidly, have developed full-service banking at home and overseas, and have refined bank management techniques to a high degree. They have benefited from the dominant position of US industry and of the dollar in the world economy, and from the worldwide extension of US multinational enterprises. They have been restrained by wide-ranging regulations and controls.

All the major banks have organised themselves in similar fashion as one-bank holding companies[8] with numerous domestic subsidiaries, and international subsidiaries and affiliates. The great range of activities undertaken by domestic subsidiaries clearly shows that every opportunity has been taken to diversify, subject to the Federal regulations (see note 5, p. 211). On the international scene, merchant and offshore banking including fiduciary activities are important, and the major banks have subsidiaries in most of the important financial centres. The larger banks have also made selective strategic investments in many countries, usually by means of participations in commercial banks, finance houses and occasionally consortium banks. A typical range of subsidiaries and affiliates is shown in Figure 3.2.

These operations are of course complementary to the branch networks and activities of the principal banks. Domestic branch networks are severely constrained by regulation, while the extent of overseas branching is related to the history of each individual bank's involvement in international banking. For US banks in general, the 1979 position is shown in Table 3.10. However, of these 789 branches, 372 were operated by the three largest banks, 200 by Citibank alone. There is a heavy concentration of branches

Figure 3.2: Typical US Bank Corporation — Holding Company, US Bank Corp ('USB')

Domestic subsidiaries (mainly wholly-owned)

    US Bank (main bank)
    USB Capital Corporation (funds raising in New York)
    US Bank Leasing (domestic and international leasing)
    US Bank Commercial Finance (hire purchase, factoring)
    US Bank Realty (mortgage banking)
    US Bank Consumer Finance (consumer credit)
    US Bank Data Processing (management services to other banks)
    USB International — Texas
                       Florida
                       Chicago   } (Edge Act Corporations)
                       California
    Brokers Co. (discount brokerage firm)
    S & L (savings and loan association)

International subsidiaries (mainly wholly-owned)

    US Bank Asia Ltd. Hong Kong (merchant bank)
    US Bank Middle East (commercial bank)
    US Bank Ltd. London (merchant bank)
    US Bank, Channel Islands (offshore banking)
    US Bank of Canada, Ltd. (commercial bank)
    US Bank Suisse, SA, Zurich (merchant bank)
    US Banque de Paris, SA (merchant bank)
    US Bank Overseas Finance, Netherlands Antilles (funding vehicle)

International affiliates (participations 5–50%)

    Bank (Spain)
    Bank (Indonesia)
    Bank (Brazil)
    Bank (Singapore)
    Bank (West Indies)
    Finance House (Australia)
    Finance House (Hong Kong)
    Consortium Bank (London)

---

in Central and Latin America, the Caribbean, and the financial centres of Europe, and the Far East, with the bulk of assets held in London, the Bahamas and Cayman Islands.

Broadly speaking, the present structure of the domestic banking industry was established in the late-1950s and early-1960s, which

Table 3.10: US Federal Reserve Member Bank Foreign Branches, 31 December 1979

Argentina	41	Mariana Islands	1
Austria	1	Marshall Islands	1
Bahamas	77	Mauritius	1
Bahrain	7	Mexico	5
Belgium	9	Monaco	1
Bolivia	6	Netherlands	6
Brazil	20	Netherlands Antilles	4
Brunei	3	Nicaragua	1
Caroline Islands	1	Oman	2
Cayman Islands	73	Pakistan	6
Chile	6	Panama	32
Denmark	3	Paraguay	9
Dominican Rep.	18	Peru	3
Ecuador	13	Philippines	12
Egypt	6	Puerto Rico	25
El Salvador	2	Qatar	1
France	13	Romania	1
Gabon	1	Saudi Arabia	2
Germany	27	Senegal	1
Greece	16	Seychelles	1
Guam	4	Singapore	22
Guatemala	3	Spain	4
Guyana	1	Sri Lanka	1
Haiti	5	Sudan	1
Honduras	3	Switzerland	9
Hong Kong	46	Taiwan	7
India	10	Thailand	2
Indonesia	5	Trinidad and Tobago	5
Ireland	4	Tunisia	2
Italy	14	United Arab Emirates	9
Ivory Coast	2	United Kingdom	60
Jamaica	5	Uruguay	9
Japan	29	Venezuela	1
Jordan	3	Viet Nam	1
Kenya	2	Virgin Islands (U.S.)	24
Korea	11	Virgin Islands (Br.)	2
Lebanon	4	Yemen Arab Republic	1
Liberia	4	Other (West Indies)	4
Luxembourg	4		
Malaysia	5	Total	789

Source: Board of Governors of the Federal Reserve System, quoted in Guenther (1981).

period saw significant New York mergers leading to the creation of Chase Manhattan (from Chase National and Bank of Manhattan), Chemical Bank (from Chemical Bank and Trust, and Corn Exchange Bank and Trust) and Manufacturers Hanover (from Hanover Bank and Manufacturers Trust). This period also saw the banks develop the idea of full-service banking including leasing, instalment credit, factoring, mortgage banking, and so on. Credit cards were introduced and became an important mode of consumer payments and credit.

It was during the 1960s that the larger commercial banks began to segment their domestic market and to take a professional approach to product development, promotion and personal selling. They also became concerned with their corporate image and their role in their community. A more competitive mood was established through rigorous competition in quality of service — leading for example to Personal Bankers,[9] drive-in banks, and in the corporate sector to vigorous calling programmes by business development officers.

During the 1970s competitive pressures in the home market increased. Deposits were sought by savings banks, and by nonbanks through money market mutual funds. Advances were sought by US banks, finance companies and foreign banks. The first radical changes in technology occurred as new delivery systems were introduced — ATMs, point of sale systems, and other forms of electronic funds transfer.

The 1960s also saw the remarkable growth in international banking activities of the major banks. In 1956 US banks operated 123 branches abroad. Between 1960 and 1970 the number of foreign branches increased from 124 to over 500 and short-term liabilities to foreigners from US banks rose from $21 billion to $42 billion. During the 1970s this expansion continued apace, and by 1975 there were over 700 overseas branches and short-term liabilities of $94 billion. US banks had previously been involved in international banking, their influence growing steadily from the late nineteenth century until by 1920 they operated 181 branches abroad, but most of this activity died away during the Great Depression. The post-War international banking boom is closely linked to the spread of US multinational enterprises in the aftermath of the Marshall plan, and to the emergence of the Eurodollar markets whose history was briefly described in Chapter 1.

A clearer picture of the process of diversification and internationalisation can be gained by examining two individual cases where information has been published. Between 1971 and 1979 Chase Manhattan Corporation made the following investments in financial businesses:

1971: Chase Econometrics Assoc. (100%); Inversiones Atlantida SA (22%)
1972: Alliance Holdings Ltd. (33%); Alliance Acceptance Co. Ltd. (33%); Chase Bank (CI) Ltd. (57%); Chase Manhattan Asia Ltd. (100%); Banco de Investimentos lar Brasileiro SA (100%); Libra Bank Ltd. (24%); Philippine American Investment Corp (20%)
1973: Orion Leasing Ltd. (20%); Chase Bank AG (100%)
1974: Banque de Réescompte et de Placement (20%); Interactive Data Corp (100%)
1976: Orion Pacific Holdings Ltd (20%)
1977: Saudi Investments Banking Corp (20%)
1978: Orion Finance Ltd (20%); Managistics (100%)
1979: Orion Caribbean Ltd (20%); Chase NBA Group Dispository (22%); Computer Power Inc (100%).

Here we see diversification into data processing and into merchant and offshore banking in various financial centres. The rate of investment slows down after 1974. If we look at figures for Manufacturers Hanover Corporation we see a process of domestic diversification into consumer banking and finance including mortgage banking.

1972: First National Bank of Bay Shore (100%)
1973: Citizens Mortgage Corp (100%); Fidelity Bank of Colonie (100%); State Bank of Ontario (100%); Citizens Bank of Monroe (100%)
1974: Ritter Financial Corp (100%).

It is also interesting to examine the rate at which foreign branches and representative offices have been opened in recent years. Figures for a selection of the smaller banks are presented in Table 3.11 which shows that the rate of expansion is fairly slow, perhaps 2 or 3 a year in most cases.

If we look at the development of the balance sheets of these same four banks over the period 1970–9 the growth of total assets

Table 3.11: Growth of Foreign Networks, Selected US Banks, 1970-9

Bank	Year									
	1970	1971	1972	1973	1974	1975	1976	1977	1978	1979
Manufacturers Hanover										
Branches	—	1	—	1	3	2	1	2	2	4
Rep. offices/agencies	1	—	—	1	3	3	4	—	1	4
J.P. Morgan										
Branches	—	1	1	—	—	—	—	—	3	1
Rep. offices/agencies	—	1	—	—	—	—	—	2	—	—
Continental Illinois										
Branches	—	1	1	5	1	—	—	—	2	—
Rep. offices/agencies	—	—	—	—	—	—	—	—	—	—
Chemical										
Branches	—	3	1	—	3	—	1	—	4	—
Rep. offices/agencies	—	2	1	1	1	4	2	—	2	3

has ranged from 241% (Chemical) to 301% (Continental Illinois). Citicorp has enjoyed the fastest growth (310%), and others have grown a little more slowly (around 200%). In all cases the ratio of profits to assets (return on assets) has declined over the period, but the ratio of profits to shareholders' funds (return on equity) has usually remained steady or increased as the proportion of shareholders' funds to assets (capital ratio) has declined. These are very crude measures of performance. The proportion of advances to assets has stabilised somewhere between 50 and 60 per cent for these banks, with the exception of Continental Illinois whose rapid growth in assets has resulted in a larger lending ratio. Figures are presented in Table 3.12.

It is difficult to generalise about the organisational structure of the large US banks because these structures are subject to frequent change, and each bank tends to favour its own particular methods. However, at the senior level most banks have a number of general managers with specialised staff responsibilities such as company secretary, auditing, corporate communications, legal affairs and regulations, corporate planning. A chief executive officer will preside over the bank's identified operational divisions, which typically include consumer banking, corporate sector, international banking, institutional banking, financial services, operations and management services. Increasingly, the banks identify market seg-

Table 3.12: Financial Ratios for Selected US Banks, 1970–9

Bank		1970 %	1979 %	Deposit growth 1970–9 %	Advances growth 1970–9 %
Citicorp					
1. Profits/assets		0.6	0.5		
2. Profits/shareholders' funds		11.1	15.0		
3. Shareholders' funds/assets		5.1	3.4		
4. Advances/assets		58.7	60.9	234.5	197.6
Bank of America					
1. Profits/assets		1.3	0.9		
2. Profits/shareholders' funds		30.0	27.4		
3. Shareholders' funds/assets		4.2	3.3		
4. Advances/assets		53.6	54.9	231.4	257.9
Chase Manhattan					
1. Profits/assets		0.6	0.5		
2. Profits/shareholders' funds		12.6	13.5		
3. Shareholders' funds/assets		4.5	3.6		
4. Advances/assets		57.7	63.3	127.5	187.0
Manufacturers Hanover					
1. Profits/assets	1971	1.1	0.7		
2. Profits/shareholders' funds	1971	21.5	22.0		
3. Shareholder's funds/assets	1971	5.0	3.4		
4. Advances/assets	1971	57.1	59.5	244.6	284.6
Chemical					
1. Profits/assets		1.2	0.6		
2. Profits/shareholders' funds		20.2	18.4		
3. Shareholders' funds/assets		5.7	3.4		
4. Advances/assets		56.0	53.9	223.1	228.6
Continental Illinois					
1. Profits/assets		1.1	0.7		
2. Profits/shareholders' funds		18.1	18.1		
3. Shareholders' funds/assets		6.2	3.9		
4. Advances/assets		51.2	66.8	235.6	422.8
Bankers Trust					
1. Profits/assets		1.0	0.8		
2. Profits/shareholders' funds		19.0	21.5		
3. Shareholders' funds/assets		5.3	3.7		
4. Advances/assets		52.4	54.3	161.1	212.1
First Chicago					
1. Profits/assets		1.2	0.5		
2. Profits/shareholders' funds		15.8	12.2		
3. Shareholders' funds/assets		7.4	4.1		
4. Advances/assets		56.8	53.3	235.6	243.8

Source: Banker Research Unit, *The Top 100* (Financial Times, London, 1981).

ments and create organisational units designed to meet the needs of that market segment. This is even more frequent within the large operating divisions where specialised units may be created to deal with export finance, multinational industries by sector, real estate finance and so on.

Figures 3.3 and 3.4 show typical management/organisational structures based on bank organograms. They show that functional and geographical criteria are now subordinated to market segmentation in the creation of an appropriate management structure.

Figure 3.3: Typical US Bank General Management Structure

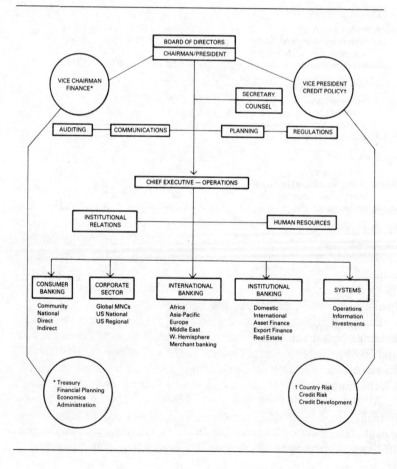

Figure 3.4: Typical US Bank Divisional Structure Based on Market Segmentation

---

Home state banking division — consumer and middle market banking through community branches.

Corporate banking division — commercial banking services for multinational firms, large and medium-sized enterprises.

International division — international commercial banking, merchant banking and foreign trade services through overseas network, subdivided by regions, and through Edge Act offices.

Commercial division — asset-based financing in the domestic and international market.

Financial services division — treasury, foreign exchange, and funds transfer for corporations and financial institutions.

Real estate division — nationwide finance on a regional basis for investors, property developers, mortgage bankers.

Trust division — investment management and advice for worldwide fiduciary funds.

3.3 Case Studies

Bank America Corporation

Bank of America has its roots in the Bank of Italy founded in 1904 by A.P. Giannini 'to serve all classes throughout California' from its base in San Francisco. The bank grew rapidly under Giannini's guidance through an expanding branch network and through bold acquisitions, some of which were subsequently disallowed by the 1933 Banking Act. It had an early involvement in international banking, especially in Central and Latin America.

Bank America Corporation (BA) was incorporated as a bank holding company in Delaware in 1968, with B of A National Trust and Savings Association (so named in 1930) as its principal asset. Its stock is traded in New York, San Francisco, Los Angeles, and Chicago; and is also listed in London and Tokyo.

At the end of 1981 BA had 1,207 domestic and foreign branches, and 26 corporate banking and representative offices. It was also represented by over 800 offices of major subsidiaries and affiliates. The unique feature of BA is its California domestic banking division with a network of 1,092 branches, most of which at present are local full-service branches. The bank used to boast 'A branch within a mile and a half of almost every Californian' and it still has a network larger than that of the four largest New York retail banking operations combined, and larger than that of its two largest Californian competitors combined.

It services 4.2 million customers with 10–11 million accounts, amounting to about 35 per cent of all banking transactions in California, although this market share has declined from about 40 per cent in 1970. Domestic banking accounts for over half of BA's loan portfolio and over half of its earnings. Overseas, the bank has a network of 115 branches and 17 representative offices and is a major borrower and lender.

In order to understand the Bank's operations it is necessary to analyse its different activities, complicated as they are:

BA is highly diversified, both geographically and in the types of business it conducts, including retail banking for consumers, domestic wholesale banking for businesses, foreign lending, foreign exchange activities, and a variety of fee services. Each of these lines of business contributes a different combination of revenue types, operating expenses, and a degree of risk to the corporation, producing distinct effects on the income statement and distinct levels of profitability.

Thus, shifts in BA's mix of business — affected by business cycles, exchange rates, interest rates, government policies, and corporate strategies — have a dominant effect on earnings progress. (*Annual Report*, 1980.)

BA manages its highly diverse operations through four separate principal profit centres:

1. *Retail Banking, Data Services, Premises*, comprising three divisions — California Division, Electronic Banking and Data Services, and Centralised Services. These divisions handle consumer and middle market banking in California, including Bank Americard/Visa and Mastercard operations, and also the necessary systems support. Each division is a profit accounting operating division.
2. *World Banking*, comprising six divisions — Asia Division,

Europe Middle East and Africa Division, Latin America/ Caribbean Division, North America Division, Financial Services Division, Global Systems Services. The Divisions serve major corporate clients, financial institutions worldwide and consumers in international markets. Financial Services Division supplements traditional commercial banking services with the capabilities of the BankAmerilease Group, the Merchant Banking Group specialising in loan syndications and corporate advisory services and Bank Advisory Services. Global Systems cover payment services for major customers, including cash management.

3. *Non-bank activities*, comprising various subsidiaries offering related services, the main elements being Finance America Corporation which engages in consumer and small business lending throughout the US and Canada, and has embarked on a programme of acquiring subsidiary thrift institutions in various states where legislation permits; Decimus Corporation which specialises in computer leasing and provides data processing services to banks and other financial institutions; BA Mortgage and International Realty Corporation; and BA Cheque Corporation which markets BA travellers cheques and just recently a series of consumer information reports and videotraining films.

4. *Capital, Administrative, and Investment Management*, comprising Bank Investment Securities Division which manages the Bank's substantial portfolio; Trust Department which provides financial planning, investment management, custody and trust administration services to individual and institutional clients throughout the world; and Money and Capital Management which includes the corporation's accounting functions and the highly important Money Manager and Capital Management units concerned with domestic interest rate exposure. The Administration section contains various central staff units such as Cashier's, Personnel, Legal, Legislative, Bank Tax, Corporate Communications and Productivity Management.

The work of the Money Manager Unit is essential to an understanding of the Bank's overall profitability. The unit acts as an internal clearing house for domestic sources and uses of funds, buying in all deposits and other liabilities from branches and other centres at notional market rates, and selling funds for loans and investments to profit centres on a matched maturity basis. The unit absorbs the full costs of any aggregate mismatching and carries the entire corporation's interest rate exposure.

The relative performance of the major centres is shown in Table 3.13. The contrast between Retail Banking and World Banking is striking. World Banking has shown great consistency over recent years and a respectable return on equity and assets. Retail Banking has shown a strong increase in performance, but very large funding losses on domestic operations are being absorbed by the Money Manager Unit. During the mid-1970s BA rapidly increased its portfolio of fixed rate mortgage loans and consumer credit, and in recent years has been forced to fund these with short-term liabilities bought at prevailing higher interest rates, which has resulted in significant reductions in earnings. The Bank describes its method of constructing overall profit figures as a Building Block system, designed to reveal the true performance of various sectors of the Bank in the light of strategic objectives — for example, the objective of a long-term commitment to consumer banking in the home area of California. The poor performance of the California Division is being tackled by management which has created Area Management Groups of branches to focus marketing efforts, and has pushed ahead with the instalment of ATMs. Personnel numbers and costs have been held back. Falling interest rates during 1982 helped to relieve the pressure on funding costs, but domestic net interest revenue was still further reduced because of a reduced net interest margin due to the continued movement of consumer deposits out of demand deposits into higher-yielding instruments. Like all major deposit banks, BA is faced with a dilemma, since if it does not offer personal customers a decent return on savings it will lose the deposits to competitors such as mutual funds, but in offering a decent return it drives up its own cost of funds and reduces the benefit of the endowment effect of demand deposits.

The balance sheet summary and analyses of types of loan outstanding and deposits presented in Tables 3.14, 3.15 and 3.16, reveal these developments in detail. BA relies for its sources of funds on domestic interest-bearing deposits (one third), foreign interest bearing deposits (one third), non-interest bearing deposits including demand deposits (one fifth), and short-, medium- and long-term debt and equity. However, there have been significant changes between 1976 and 1981, all leading to a higher cost of funds:

1. Reduction in percentage of non-interest bearing liabilities

from 24.5% of total to 22.1% (−2.4%) including a reduction in demand deposits from 18.6% to 13.4% (−5.2%).

2. Reduction in percentage of regulated consumer savings from 12.1% to 6.0% (−6.1%), and increase in percentage of market-related time and savings deposits from 9.8% to 18.1% (+8.3%).

3. Significant increases in average rates paid on domestic market-related deposits from about 6% to 12–14%; on foreign interest bearing deposits from about $6\frac{1}{2}$% to about 15%; and also on other borrowings, resulting in an overall increase in the average rate paid from 6.07% to 13.64% (+7.57%). Over the same period the average rate on interest earning assets has only increased from 8.30% to 15.18% (+6.88%), and the spread has consequently deteriorated from 2.23% to 1.54% (−0.69%).

These changes occurred progressively over the five-year period.

There have been significant changes on the asset side, showing an increased emphasis on domestic lending:

Table 3.13: Bank of America Performance by Major Profit Centres, 1981

	Average total assets $ billion	Average total net loans $ billion	Income before securities transactions $ million	Return on average total assets %	Return on average equity capital %
1. Retail banking, etc.					
1981	33.5	29.1	541	1.62	47.3
1977	20.2	15.6	210	1.04	30.2
2. World banking					
1981	65.6	33.0	385	0.59	17.5
1977	40.1	20.8	239	0.60	17.4
3. Non-bank activities					
1981	2.1	1.7	48	2.33	17.4
1977	1.1	0.8	16	1.49	17.3
4. Capital, etc.					
1981	11.7	2.3	(529)	(4.57)	(142.7)
1977	10.2	0.3	(71)	(0.69)	(18.8)
TOTAL BA					
1981	112.9	66.0	445	0.39	11.2
1977	71.6	37.5	395	0.55	15.5

Source: *Annual Report* (1981).

Table 3.14: Bank of America Corporation Balance Sheet Summary, 1976, 1981 (Dollar amounts in millions)

	1981 Average Balance	1981 Average Rate[a]	1981 % of total assets	1976 Average Balance	1976 Average Rate[a]	1976 % of total assets
Interest-earning deposits	$16,546	14.78%	14.6	$10,103	6.91%	15.5
State, county, and municipal securities	1,555	9.22	1.4	2,416	8.02	3.7
Other securities	5,722	9.83	6.1	6,003	6.61	9.3
Total securities	7,277	9.70	7.5	8,419	7.01	13.0
Funds sold	3,267	16.27	2.9	2,457	5.19	3.8
Real estate loans	16,645	11.69	14.7	6,468	8.12	10.0
Consumer loans	9,141	15.73	8.1	3,257	13.59	5.0
Other loans	15,668	17.15	13.8	9,981	7.63	15.4
Total domestic loans	41,454	14.64	36.7	19,706	8.92	30.4
Foreign loans	25,080	16.66	22.2	13,688	8.60	21.2
Allowance for loan losses	(565)			(287)		
Total net loans	65,969	15.54	58.4	33,107	9.23	51.2
Lease financing	1,739	10.07	1.5	688	11.50	1.1
Other real estate owned	26			32		
Total earning assets	94,823	15.18%	84.0	54,806	8.30%	84.8
Nonearning assets	18,079		16.0	9,804		15.2
TOTAL ASSETS	$112,902		100.0	$64,610		100.0
Interest-bearing transaction accounts	$ 1,670	5.29%	1.5	$ —	— %	
Consumer savings	6,807	5.22	6.0	7,844	4.98	12.1
Consumer time	7,330	12.30	6.5	4,096	6.25	6.3
Public savings and time	813	14.08	0.7	1,976	5.90	3.1

Table 3.14: continued

	31 Dec 1981		% of total loans	31 Dec 1978		% of total loans
Other savings and time	20,501	14.58	18.1	6,318	6.08	9.8
Total domestic interest-bearing deposits	37,120	11.99	32.9	20,234	5.67	31.3
Foreign interest-bearing deposits	37,611	15.12	33.3	22,278	6.49	34.5
Funds purchased/borrowed	5,995	14.57	5.3	2,597	5.27	4.0
Commercial paper	1,965	16.34	1.7	503	5.19	0.8
Intermediate-term debt	437	11.30	0.4	—	—	
Long-term debt and subordinated capital notes	823	8.45	0.7	1,014	7.52	1.6
Total interest-bearing liabilities	83,953	13.64%	74.3	46,626	6.07%	72.2
Demand deposits	15,126		13.4	12,007		18.6
Other noninterest-bearing liabilities	9,831		8.7	3,818		5.9
Total liabilities	108,909		96.5	62,451		96.7
Equity capital	3,993		3.5	2,159		3.3
TOTAL LIABILITIES AND EQUITY CAPITAL	$112,902		100.0	$64,610		100.0

Net interest revenue as a percentage of earning assets 3.11%

a. Taxable-equivalent

LOAN OUTSTANDINGS BY TYPE (Net of unearned income) (in millions)

	31 Dec 1981	% of total loans	31 Dec 1978	% of total loans
Real estate — construction	$ 2,775	3.9	$ 1,095	2.2
Real estate — mortgage	14,839	20.8	10,047	20.4
Credit card	2,333	3.3	1,524	3.1
Consumer instalment	6,841	9.6	4,223	8.6
Other consumer	529	0.7	504	1.0
Commercial and industrial	13,412	18.8	8,857	18.0
Agriculture	1,699	2.4	954	1.9
Other loans	1,956	2.7	1,720	3.5

Table 3.14: continued

	31 Dec 1981	% of total deposits	31 Dec 1978	% of total deposits
Total domestic loans	44,384	62.3	28,924	58.7
Foreign loans	27,466	38.6	20,818	42.2
Total loans	71,850		49,742	
Less: allowance for loan losses	(614)	(0.9)	(429)	(0.9)
TOTAL NET LOANS	$71,236	100.0	$49,313	100.0

DEPOSITS (in millions)	31 Dec 1981	% of total deposits	31 Dec 1978	% of total deposits
Demand deposits				
Domestic bank	$13,075	13.9	$13,108	17.2
Overseas branches	1,696	1.8	1,437	1.9
Overseas and Edge Act subsidiaries[a]	2,682	2.8	4,545	6.0
Total demand deposits	17,453	18.5	19,090	25.2
Savings and Time deposits				
Domestic bank				
Interest-bearing transaction accounts	1,952	2.1	213	0.3
Other	39,452	41.8	27,194	35.9
Overseas branches	29,581	31.3	25,821	34.1
Domestic subsidiaries	12	—	—	—
Overseas and Edge Act subsidiaries[a]	5,919	7.7	3,510	4.6
Total savings and time deposits	76,916	81.5	56,738	74.8
TOTAL DEPOSITS	$94,369	100.0	$75,828	100.0

a. Includes international banking facilities.

Source: *Annual Report* (1981).

Table 3.15: Bank of America: Global Loans and Securities by Currency, 1981 (Percentages)

US dollars	83.2
British pounds	2.4
Italian lira	2.4
Deutsche mark	2.0
Japanese yen	1.6
Swiss francs	0.9
Canadian dollars	0.9
Other currencies	6.6
	100.0

Table 3.16: Bank of America: Total Loans and Securities — Non-US Borrowers by Domicile of Borrowers, 1981

	$ millions	% of total
Industrialised countries	15,857	51.7
Centrally-planned economies	600	2.0
Oil-exporting (OPEC) countries	2,774	9.1
Developing countries:		
High income	621	2.0
Upper middle income	4,316	14.1
Intermediate middle income	4,603	15.0
Lower middle income	1,313	4.3
Low income	557	1.8
	30,641	100.0

1. Reduction in the investment portfolio from 13% of total to 7.5% (−5.5%).
2. Increase in domestic real estate loans from 10.0% to 14.7% (+4.7%), and in consumer loans from 5.0% to 8.1% (+3.1%). This means a significant increase in fixed rate loans outstanding, some of which are long-term loans. Total domestic loans have increased from 30.4% to 36.7% (+6.3%), and total net loans from 51.2% to 58.4% (+7.2%). Clearly the relative importance of foreign loans has diminished. In contrast to the progressive changes in the domestic portfolio this reduction in foreign loans, which were otherwise increasing just as rapidly as domestic loans, occurred between 1978 and 1979. This was a point when many major banks decided that their exposure in foreign markets was sufficient and that the balance between risk and return was better in domestic mar-

kets: 'The global banking environment in 1979 had two dominant elements: intense competition and abundant liquidity. In
many areas, this combination led to unrealistically low interest
margins and caused World Banking Division management to
restrain loan growth.' (*Annual Report*, 1979.)

Since 1979 bad debt problems in Eastern Europe and Latin
America have strengthened this argument, and led BA and other
banks to emphasise quality loans to first-class borrowers, trade
financing, and fee-earning advisory services. Nevertheless, steady
growth in the foreign loan portfolio has been resumed.

Earnings from international activities have not been subject to
the same fluctuations as domestic earnings because there are no
interest rate mismatching problems. Eurobanking activities are
largely on a strictly matched basis. Nor does BA suffer from currency exposure problems because over 83 per cent of its global
loans and securities are in US dollars, with the remainder well
spread amongst other world currencies (see Table 3.15). Geographical exposure is shown in Table 3.16 and reveals that the
Bank's commitment to Eastern Europe and developing countries is
high but that over half of total foreign loans and securities are to
borrowers in industrialised countries, mainly Europe and Japan.
Very little lending has gone to the poorer developing countries, the
largest amounts going to Brazil and Mexico.

The Bank emphasises its control of asset quality through credit
analysis, rigorous loan documentation, periodic review and follow-
up procedures. Its exposure to loss is minimised by diversification
of its portfolio amongst countries, industries and types of borrower, and it has developed extensive country risk analysis of a
nation's cash flow position, foreign exchange reserves, collateral,
external guarantees, and socio-economic factors. BA is not as
heavily exposed to 'problem' countries as some New York banks,
but its commitments are nevertheless substantial.

Our analysis so far has stressed the problems incurred by BA in
the latter half of the 1970s. It is fascinating to see how this massive
organisation has taken measures to cope with change and adver-
sity. Some of its problems have been caused by internal factors and
past management decisions, some have been caused by external
factors in the environment largely beyond management control
and often unpredictable. Both must be met by adaptive management.

The process of adaptation began in 1979 when a new strategic planning effort and a major productivity programme were mounted throughout the bank in preparation for 'Moving into the 80s' — the theme of the 1979 Annual Report. Since then themes have been 'The Spectrum of Change' (1980), and 'Extending Our Reach' (1981). Top management at the Bank has also changed as A.W. Clausen has been replaced by S.H. Armacost, on Clausen's departure to the World Bank presidency. In the 1981 report there is a corporate overview and discussion of markets included in management's discussion of operations, and the following points from that review reveal much about BA's approach to the 1980s:

1. There is a focus on primary market segments, and strategic initiatives have been taken to improve and extend its service to these rapidly-changing markets, building on the Bank's strengths as an experienced provider of global and diverse financial services to all types of customer.

2. In the consumer market the aim is to improve quality and cost-effectiveness of services for the mass market, and provide specialised help for customers with more complex financial needs. The Bank has started to improve delivery of services by rationalising the branch network, installing ATMs in branches and free-standing, and by experimenting with banking by phone and home banking. The Bank foresees further development of Finance America Thrift Corporation in other states, and has also acquired C. Schwab & Co. a nationwide firm of brokers. It has brought in new liability products such as Individual Retirement Accounts, Interest Bearing Transactions Accounts, Money Market Certificates, and in 1982 Money Market Deposit Accounts. Foreign currency travellers' cheques have been introduced, and the Bank has also started to make available adjustable-rate home mortgages and other housing finance, linked to market rates. The Bank has also attacked profitability by cutting out some cheque account products and by increasing service charges. It has identified related financial services as a growth area, segmenting the market into middle market, consumers and priority customers. It has boosted credit cards through promotions, and acquired a 60-branch bank in Argentina.

3. In the business, financial institutions and governments sector the aim is to concentrate on key geographic areas, selected

markets; and to provide high quality, innovative services. The Bank has increased its representation in major US cities, and in Canada, Gibraltar, Kenya and China. It has extended its offshore banking capabilities through establishment of Edge Act offices and International Banking Facilities. It has devoted resources to improvements in telematics. In its lending policy, the Bank will develop its existing strengths in managing large loan syndications, and in lending to governments; in its Californian middle market (especially small businesses); in agribusiness; in correspondent banking; and in leasing. It also plans to increase its expertise and marketing efforts in identified growth industries such as construction, shipping, energy, telecommunications and other high-technology areas. The Bank also has competence in underwriting of municipal debt and Eurobonds. The Bank must also meet service needs of customers and has improved its capabilities in cash management for large corporations, payroll and tax reporting for small and medium-sized businesses, and correspondent bank services. BA became the first non-New York member of CHIPS, the automated clearing system operated by the New York Clearing House Association, and has made special arrangements to settle CHIPS balances from its Federal Reserve Bank of San Francisco reserve account. The Bank has also devoted resources to improving its trust, investment and advisory services.

The problems faced by BA are typical of those faced by many major deposit banks which are squeezed by pressures of competition and rising costs in their domestic market, and by competition and narrow margins in their international market. The solutions BA has adopted are also similar to programmes adopted by other US banks and by similar banks in other countries. The central importance of strategic market planning in helping with adaptation to change has been stressed, and the crucial role of funds management in maintaining profitability.

Citicorp

The City Bank of New York, later to become First National City Bank, was chartered by New York State in 1812. It became National City Bank of New York in 1864. National City started a foreign department in 1897 to provide foreign exchange and trade finance, and in 1914 was the first US national bank to open a foreign branch, in Buenos Aires. It subsequently expanded its foreign network in South America, and acquired International Banking Corporation.

National City was the first major commercial bank to open a personal credit department in 1928, the first to make consumer mortgage loans, and the first to offer special checking accounts. In 1929 National City merged with the Farmer's Loan and Trust Company and subsequently built up the world's largest trust business to complement the world's largest international banking business.

In 1955 a merger with First National Bank of New York led to the creation of First National City Bank of New York, reduced to First National City Bank in 1962, and subsequently to Citibank. The Bank occupied new headquarters on Park Avenue in 1961 and built a new operations centre on Wall Street in 1968.

The Bank continually widened the frontiers of traditional banking, always among the leaders in such developments as equipment leasing, travellers cheques, credit cards, investment trusts, negotiable certificates of deposit,[10] Eurodollar certificates of deposit, overseas branching, retail bank banking abroad and so on.

In 1968 First National City Corporation was created as a one-bank holding company, subsequent to a major planning review. The Bank was the first to act on the principle that a market economy should be served by a market-oriented bank, and it set about creating organisational units which could identify profitable market opportunities, allocate necessary resources to exploit them, and provide rewarding jobs to talented people. It also installed an account management system, with bank officers responsible for individual customers. The creation of new opportunities was a vital element of this plan, since the Bank was determined to improve its earnings per share performance and build its capital base, and considered that prospective growth in traditional banking activities was insufficient to generate this improvement. At the same time, the Bank recognised a genuine commitment to its metropolitan community and to the US economy,[11] even though the Chairman was bold enough to claim in 1970: 'Our purpose is to provide any worthwhile financial services anyplace in the world permitted by law.'

The 1968 reorganisation led to the creation of six major groups:

1. Personal Banking Group providing banking and financial services to consumers and small businesses in the Metropolitan New York Area, through a network of 181 branches, and through the Master Charge credit card.
2. Investment Management Group providing asset management services to individuals and institutions, and full financial services to high net worth individuals. Market-oriented divisions were established (Institutional Investment, Custodian Services, Personal Investment) and a Securities Operations Division.
3. Corporate Banking Group serving large corporate customers, financial institutions and government bodies with US headquarters. The Group had market-oriented divisions to cover financial institutions, energy related industries, capital goods and other industries, consumer goods and services, Wall Street banking, and general corporate services. Each division was further segmented (see Figure 3.5)
4. Commercial Banking Group serving medium-sized businesses in the Bank's catchment area with a full range of financial services. The Bank recognised its low market share in this sector, which it determined to increase by providing financial advice to owner-managers. There was also a separate Real Estate and Construction Industries Division.

In the creation of corporate banking and commercial banking groups the existence of overlap was recognised.

5. International Banking Group managing all the Bank's overseas activities and US-based international banking activities, through a network of 264 offices in 65 countries, including 175 branches and various subsidiary operations. The Bank expected to increase its use of subsidiaries because the branch network already effectively covered the major trade routes and financial centres of the world. The Group was organised on both geographical and functional lines. In New York were group functional managers and also heads of six geographical divisions. Each of these divisions had a functional management in New York, and also Senior Officers in each country of operation. The Group was also responsible for overseas investment services and international leasing.
6. Operating Group providing operational and systems support

Figure 3.5: Citicorp: Corporate Banking Group Organisation, 1970

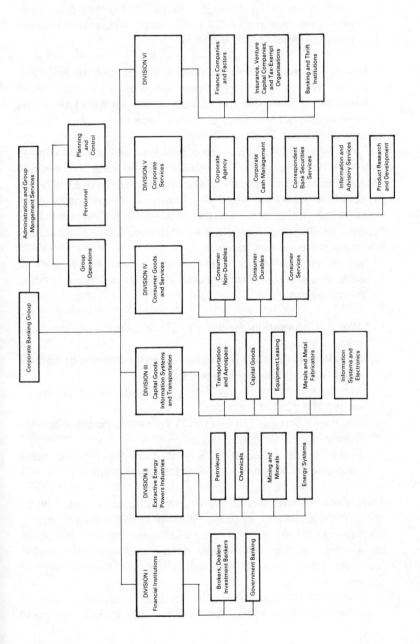

in four functional areas — paper processing (cheques and collections), management support (management information, computers, loan accounting), premises and corporate services, and operations connected with some Corporate Banking Group activities (funds transfer).

Citicorp's top management operated sometimes on an individual basis, but frequently through committees, especially in the financial area where the Asset and Liability Committee held sway, and in overall policy. There were also staff departments such as Economics, Personnel, Public Relations.

The 1968 reorganisation also enabled the holding company to overcome some geographic constraints on business by acquiring related financial businesses in other states and overseas. The reorganisation boldly envisaged devolution of all operational functions to the six groups, but this was not achieved until 1977 because of the mushrooming cost and complexity of computer systems installed in that period.

During the 1970s the Bank made certain adjustments to improve its service to certain special markets, creating additional organisational units:

1. World Corporation Group (1973) to service multinational corporations.
2. Section of Investment Management Group devoted to high net worth individuals (1973) worldwide.
3. Merchant Banking Group (1974) to provide corporate capital-raising and advisory services.
4. Consumer Services Group (1975) to develop personal banking worldwide.
5. Financial and Information Services Group (1979) providing services to governments and financial institutions.

The Bank also elaborated its management information and control system, and improved its technical skills in the areas of treasury management, credit policy, personnel, financial control and auditing, aiming always to establish the systems and procedures, and to foster the personal skills, required by a global financial services enterprise.

In 1979 the Bank again reorganised, after reviewing its strategic plans for the 1980s, taking the view that the United States and other developed countries would continue to evolve into post-industrial, service-based economies. Service industries are labour-intensive, and customers participate in and partly control the inter-mediation process, implying that the Bank must create new delivery/distribution systems convenient to the user, and also create decision-making authority and operational flexibility near the point of service.

The Bank also assumed that it would continue to operate under severe regulatory constraints, a difficulty it would tackle by lobby-ing for legal reforms, and by taking whatever avoidance measures it could. It also foresaw problems in coping with further diversifi-cation and globalisation under its existing management structure, especially in view of the dangers of bureaucratisation and Balkani-sation. The Bank's solutions to these problems involved the con-solidation of its core business approach, and the promotion of decentralised team management. The Bank also devoted further resources to a new Office of Corporate Strategy and Development. Like many other banks, Citicorp recognised that in the 1960s and 1970s the momentum of earnings growth came from international banking to corporate customers, but that in the 1980s growth must come from consumer services, merchant banking, electronic bank-ing and services for financial institutions.

In 1981 the Bank summarised the position:

In order to meet the challenges of today's and tomorrow's marketplace, Citicorp has organised its activities around customer-oriented core businesses. These organisational units, the two largest of which relate to the corporation's business with institutions and individuals, are structured to provide manager-ial initiative, and to place the human and financial resources of the corporation as close as possible to the marketplace served. (*Annual Report*, 1981.)

These core businesses are now:

1. Institutional Banking
2. Individual Banking
3. Financial and Information Services Group (FISG)
4. Financial Markets Group (FMG)
5. Investment Management Group (IMG)
6. Merchant Banking Group (MBG).

There is a further Legal and External Affairs Group (LEAG) which coordinates resources. However, the Bank has also recognised that developments in communications technology mean that in future competition may come from any type of business enterprise which decides to enter the field of financial services, and that the key to success for financial intermediaries in the future will be the mastery of electronic systems. The Bank claimed to have invested $500 million in systems development by 1981.

Citicorp is a very different organisation from Bank of America. In 1980 it had a total of 2,096 offices worldwide, but its domestic branch network numbered only about 200 branches and total US offices 796. It employed a staff of 53,700, 26,800 in domestic offices and 26,900 overseas.

The balance sheet totals are nearly the same, but the different business mix results in a different balance sheet structure, and different funds management concerns. The balance sheet is presented in Table 3.17. On the liabilities side Citicorp has a higher percentage of interest bearing liabilities, due to a lower level of demand deposits in domestic offices. It has a far lower percentage of domestic interest bearing deposits (9.8% against BA's 32.9%, a difference of $25,736 million) and its consumer deposits are negligible. It relies massively on foreign deposits (45% against BA's 33.3%, a difference of $14,521 million) and also has recourse to funds borrowed in the New York money markets, especially Fed funds and repos from other banks, and in foreign money markets.

In sum, Citicorp is far more of a money centre bank than BA. The consequences of this are a significantly higher average cost of funds, the average rate paid being 15.33% against BA's 13.64% (difference of 1.69%), and on a larger volume of interest bearing liabilities. On the assets side however Citicorp achieves an average rate of 16.92% against 15.18% (difference 1.74%), and on a larger volume of interest earning assets. Nevertheless, BA's funding advantages have enabled it to show a better net interest margin (net interest revenue as a percentage of earning assets) in recent years. Citicorp's assets include a higher percentage of foreign loans (36.0% against 22.2%), enabling it to achieve a slightly higher percentage of total loans to assets.

If we look at the changes over a period of time we can see that Citicorp's percentage of deposits to assets has declined from 62.8% to 54.8% (−8%), mainly due to a 6% decline in the percentage of domestic deposits, especially negotiable CDs. Clearly

Table 3.17: Citicorp Balance Sheet Summary, 1976, 1981: Average
Balances and Interest Rates (taxable equivalent basis)

In millions of dollars	Average volume	1981 % Average rate	% of total assets
INTEREST REVENUE			
Loans (Net of Unearned Discount)			
Commercial Loans			
In Domestic Offices			
Commercial and Industrial	$ 14,755	17.32	12.7
Mortgate and Real Estate	2,385	15.49	2.1
Loans to Financial Institutions	1,254	15.00	1.1
In Overseas Offices	36,924	19.26	31.8
Total Commercial Loans	$ 55,318	18.48	47.7
Consumer Loans			
In Domestic Offices	$ 11,799	14.16	10.2
In Overseas Offices	4,909	18.67	4.2
Total Consumer Loans	$ 16,708	15.48	14.4
Total Loans	$ 72,026	17.79	62.1
Funds Sold and Resale Agreements	$ 2,555	17.26	2.2
Investment Securities			
In Domestic Offices			
U.S. Treasury and Federal Agencies	$ 3,901	10.89	3.4
State and Municipal	683	13.53	0.6
Other	397	10.09	0.3
In Overseas Offices (Principally local government issues)	1,946	11.79	1.7
Total	$ 6,927	11.36	6.0
Trading Account Securities			
U.S. Treasury and Federal Agencies	$ 1,804	13.93	1.6
State and Municipal	147	15.74	0.1
Other (Principally in overseas offices)	645	15.90	0.6
Total	$ 2,596	14.52	2.2
Lease Financing	$ 1,851	18.36	1.6
Interest-Bearing Deposits (Principally in overseas offices)	$ 13,067	15.28	11.2
Total Interest-Earning Assets	$ 99,022	16.92	85.4
Other Non-Interest Earning Assets	16,873		14.6
TOTAL ASSETS	$115,895		100.0
INTEREST EXPENSE			
Deposits			
In Domestic Offices			
Savings Deposits	$ 1,983	5.01	1.7
Negotiable Certificates of Deposit	2,762	15.49	2.4
Other Time Deposits	6,639	14.34	5.7
Total Domestic Interest-Bearing Deposits	$ 11,384	13.00	9.8

Table 3.17: continued

In Overseas Offices	52,132	15.56	45.0
Total	$ 63,516	15.10	54.8
Funds Borrowed			
In Domestic Offices			
Purchased Funds and Other			
Borrowings			
Federal Funds Purchased and			
Securities Sold Under Agreements			
to Repurchase	$ 10,936	15.89	9.4
Commercial Paper	4,867	16.51	4.2
Other Purchased Funds	1,912	14.63	1.6
Intermediate-Term Debt	922	15.51	0.8
Long-Term Debt and Convertible Notes	2,654	11.63	2.3
Total in Domestic Offices	$ 21,291	15.37	18.4
In Overseas Offices	7,713	17.05	6.7
Total	$ 29,004	15.82	25.0
Total Interest-Bearing Liabilities	$ 92,520	15.33	79.8
Demand Deposits in Domestic Offices	8,615		7.4
Other Non-Interest Bearing Liabilities	10,733		9.3
Common Stockholders' Equity	4,027		3.5
TOTAL LIABILITIES AND STOCKHOLDERS' EQUITY	$115,895		100.0
NET INTEREST REVENUE AS A PERCENTAGE OF AVERAGE INTEREST EARNING ASSETS (NET INTEREST MARGIN)		2.60	

	Average volume	1976 % Average rate	% of total assets
INTEREST REVENUE			
Interest-Bearing Deposits (Principally in Overseas Offices)	$ 7,093	6.51	12.1
Loans (Net of Unearned Discount)			
In Domestic Offices			
Commercial and Industrial	$ 8,162	8.32	14.0
Mortgage and Real Estate*	2,199	6.54	3.8
Loans to Financial Institutions	1,414	5.10	2.4
Loans for Purchasing or carrying securities	500	5.86	0.9
Other Loans*	2,699	10.70	4.6
Total Loans in Domestic Offices	$ 14,974	8.10	25.6
In Overseas Offices*	21,966	10.14	37.5
Total Loans	$ 36,940	9.32	63.1
Funds Sold	377	6.05	0.6
Total	$ 37,317	9.28	63.7
Investment Securities			
In Domestic Offices			
U.S. Treasury and Federal Agencies	$ 1,128	7.07	1.9

Table 3.17: continued

State and Municipal		1,099	11.90	1.9
Other		153	6.60	0.3
In Overseas Offices (Principally local government issues)		1,208	12.14	2.1
Total	$	3,588	10.23	6.1
Trading Account Securities				
U.S. Treasury and Federal Agencies, Net.	$	374	6.12	0.6
State and Municipal		77	15.06	0.1
Other (Principally in Overseas Offices)		289	8.24	0.6
Total	$	740	7.88	1.3
Direct Lease Financing		1,096	13.47	1.9
Total Interest Revenue	$	49,834	9.03	85.2
Other Assets		8,616		14.8
Total Assets	$	58,450		100.0
INTEREST EXPENSE				
Deposits				
In Domestic Offices				
Savings Deposits	$	1,652	4.50	2.8
Negotiable Certificates of Deposit		4,969	5.90	8.5
Other Time Deposits		2,604	5.02	4.4
Total Domestic Interest-Bearing Deposits	$	9,225	5.40	15.8
In Overseas Offices		27,500	5.84	47.0
Total	$	36,725	5.73	62.8
Funds Borrowed				
In Domestic Offices				
Purchased Funds and Other Borrowings				
Federal Funds Purchased and Securities Sold Under Agreements to Repurchase	$	2,535	5.12	4.3
Commercial paper		1,213	5.47	2.1
Other Purchased Funds		212	5.33	0.4
Intermediate-Term Debt		714	6.43	1.2
Long-Term Debt and Convertible Notes		364	5.69	0.6
Total in Domestic offices	$	5,038	5.44	8.6
In Overseas Offices		2,159	10.63	3.7
Total	$	7,197	7.00	12.3
Other, Non-Interest Bearing	$	5,912		10.1
Total Interest Expense	$	49,834	5.23	85.2
Net Interest Revenue			3.80	
Other Liabilities		8,616		14.8
Total Liabilities	$	58,450		100.0

*Consumer loans are included in these captions.

Source: *Annual Report.*

the bank now prefers to use other money market sources of US borrowed funds, notably Fed funds and commercial paper, and to raise funds abroad. Overall, a higher percentage of the Bank's total liabilities were interest-bearing in 1981, 79.8% against 75.2% in 1976. On the assets side there are few significant observable changes, although the proportion of foreign loans has decreased slightly from 37.5% of total assets to 36% in 1981, as part of an overall decrease in the proportion of loans made.

Figures in Table 3.18 show that there has been a significant shift of emphasis within the portfolio towards domestic consumer lending, both mortgage finance and consumer credit, in recent years, and that the volume of foreign consumer lending has also increased. Commercial loans, especially from overseas offices, have been held back by comparison although they are still the most important form of lending. Nearly half of this portfolio is in the form of local currency loans which are funded by local borrowing, thus eliminating exchange risk. The bulk is to industrial countries and to major exporters of manufactures among the developing countries (see Tables 3.19 and 3.20). Nevertheless, Citicorp is heavily exposed to 'problem' countries.

Since it lacks a significant retail deposit base, Citicorp does not encounter quite the same interest rate exposure problems as BA, although it too suffered reduced earnings on its fixed-rate consumer portfolio when interest rates rose in 1979 and 1980. Nor does it have such a costly branch network. However, the lack of a solid domestic retail base means that the Bank is continually driven to explore new markets and develop new techniques. Without its rigorous and imaginative strategic planning, Citicorp and other banks in a similar position would not progress in their highly competitive markets. This situation could be transformed if banks of this type were able to extend their services nationwide within the USA. Their constant fear is that non-bank organisations which are not subject to the banking regulations may clean up the retail banking market, especially with the help of new technology.

In the consumer credit and credit card field, the retail chain of Sears Roebuck is already the market leader. Insurance companies are diversifying into other financial services, as have travel firms such as American Express which has now combined with a large brokers' firm, and computer companies such as Control Data. Banks in many countries are acutely aware of these problems for the future. Citi's strategy for the future thus concentrates heavily on mastery of data processing and communications technology as the key to successful financial intermediation, as the following extract from the 1981 *Annual Report* makes clear:

> Citibank uses electronic funds transfer, the combination of bank computers, communications lines, and terminal equipment to reach out and get closer to our customers. We lease lines to

Table 3.18: Citicorp: Loans Outstanding 1977–81

In millions of dollars at year end	1981	1980	1979	1978	1977
Commercial					
In domestic offices					
Commercial and industrial[a]	$16,442	$14,548	$13,243	$ 9,810	$ 9,440
Mortgage and real estate[b]	2,635	2,057	1,436	1,155	1,146
Loans to financial institutions	1,287	1,425	1,369	1,201	2,060
	$20,364	$18,030	$16,048	$12,166	$12,646
In overseas offices	39,254	37,000	33,739	30,941	26,892
	$59,618	$55,030	$49,787	$43,107	$39,538
Unearned discount	(434)	(420)	(270)	(205)	(164)
Allowance for possible losses on commercial loans	(400)	(359)	(328)	(304)	(242)
Commercial loans, net	$58,784	$54,251	$49,189	$42,598	$39,132
Consumer					
In domestic offices					
Mortgage and real estate[b]	$ 5,925	$ 4,317	$ 3,195	$ 1,896$	$1,161
Instalment, revolving credit and other	9,556	8,435	7,542	5,372	2,714
	$15,481	$12,752	$10,737	$ 7,268	$ 3,875
In overseas offices	6,806	6,116	5,188	4,018	3,192
	$22,287	$18,868	$15,925	$11,286	$ 7,067
Unearned discount	(3,759)	(3,057)	(2,448)	(1,482)	(989)
Allowance for consumer credit losses	(173)	(147)	(129)	(103)	(77)
Consumer loans, net	$18,355	$15,664	$13,348	$ 9,701	$ 6,001
TOTAL LOANS, NET	$77,139	$69,915	$62,537	$52,299	$45,133

Notes: a. Includes loans not otherwise separately categorised. b. Includes only loans secured primarily by real estate.

Source: *Annual Report.*

Table 3.19: Citicorp: Local Currency Loans in Overseas Offices[a], Net of Unearned Discount, as of 31 December, 1981

By domicile of borrower[b] in millions of dollars	Local currency loans
Industrial countries	$11,933
Oil-exporting developing countries	498
Non-oil developing countries	
Net oil exporters	430
Major exporters of manufactures	4,452
Other net oil importers	1,083
Low income	155
Total	$18,551

Notes: a. Not including Puerto Rico, Guam and US Virgin Islands. b. Country classifications are based on International Monetary Fund definitions.

Source: *Annual Report.*

Table 3.20: Citicorp: Foreign Currency Loans in Overseas Offices[a], Net of Unearned Discount, as of 31 December, 1981

By domicile of borrower[b] In millions of dollars	Guaranteed foreign currency loans[c]	Other foreign currency loans			
		Due within 1 year	Due within 1-5 years	Due after 5 years	Total
Industrial countries	$ —	$ 4,652	$2,858	$1,312	$ 8,822
Centrally-planned economies	32	192	205	19	416
Oil-exporting developing countries	200	1,466	625	156	2,247
Non-oil developing countries					
Net oil exporters	58	1,633	985	327	2,945
Major exporters of manufactures	359	2,188	2,686	929	5,803
Other net oil importers	122	1,471	1,064	479	3,014
Low income	53	148	75	21	244
Total	$824	$11,750	$8,498	$3,243	$23,491

Notes: a. Not including Puerto Rico, Guam and US Virgin Islands. b. Country classifications are based on International Monetary Fund definitions. c. Foreign currency guaranteed loans are guaranteed by governments, government agencies, banks or corporations whose principal domicile is in an industrialised country.

Source: *Annual Report.*

ensure that customers can bank any time and almost anywhere. We have devoted millions of dollars to the research and development of special hardware and software programs to provide customers with new tools and, equally important, to differentiate our own services from those of other service providers. In a real sense, the delivery mechanism has become an essential part of the service — our link to customers. Banking networks are proliferating, and innovative services are emerging almost monthly: from automated teller machines to payment of bills by telephone, to home banking, to home financial management programs. Each service and each system is different and customers find it increasingly easy to choose. These systems will grow in scope and function and ultimately link with other types of services. They will compete with similar systems provided by brokerage houses, data processors, and even communications carriers, making the financial services industry more competitive in the decade ahead than it has been at any time in modern history.

Notes

1. The functions of the Federal Reserve System are now:
— To regulate US money supply.
— To hold legal reserves of members.
— To meet currency needs of members, government and public.
— To effect nationwide telegraphic transfers ('Fed wire').
— To promote and facilitate clearance and collection of cheques for all banks.
— To examine and supervise state member banks.
— To collect and interpret economic data.
— To act as banker to government and government agencies.
These are fairly typical central bank functions.

2. Specifically, the securities activities of commercial banks were limited to underwriting and dealing in government and municipal debt. Interlocking directorships or offices between commercial banks and securities firms were also prohibited.

3. 1981 maximum interest rates payable by commercial banks on time and savings deposits — Federal Reserve Board Regulation: Savings — $5\frac{1}{4}$%; Time — $5\frac{1}{4}$% — $7\frac{1}{4}$% increasing with maturity; Individual Retirement Accounts — 8% maturity less than 18 months. Money market time deposit rates are linked to Treasury bill rates. These restrictions are being phased out by 1986 — Depository Institutions Deregulation Committee.

4. The Department has generally prevented mergers between local competitors, but allowed banks to enter markets in different cities if they open a new branch or expand the existing activities of a small local bank.

5. By 1981 the Fed has permitted acquisitions of the following types of

activity by commercial banks under the Bank Holding Company Act S.4(c)(8) ('laundry list'):

1. Mortgage banks, finance companies, credit cards, factoring, leasing, industrial banks, servicing of loans
2. Fiduciary/trust business
3. Financial advice
4. Investments to promote community welfare
5. Accounting and data processing services
6. Credit related insurance broking and underwriting
7. Management consultancy for banks only
8. Trading in gold and silver
9. Travellers cheques and money orders
10. Futures trading
11. Underwriting public sector securities
12. Cheque verification
13. Consumer oriented financial courses
14. Real estate appraisal
15. General and life insurance underwriting in small communities.

Disallowed activities have included:

1. Linked life assurance, mortgage guarantee insurance
2. Underwriting ordinary life insurance
3. Real estate brokerage and syndication, property management
4. Land development
5. Management consultancy broadly defined
6. Operating a travel agency
7. Operating a savings and loan association
8. Offering key punching services.

The US Treasury Department has recently considered whether to allow bank holding companies to go into real estate, insurance and bond dealing/underwriting.

6. Two other large international banks, Crocker National Bank and Marine Midland, have been excluded as they are now subsidiaries of Midland Bank and Hong Kong and Shanghai Banking Corporation respectively. Other banks recently categorised as multinational by the Comptroller of Currency are First National Bank of Boston, First Interstate, and Mellon.

7. The largest banking organisation in the world is the French Crédit Agricole, a conglomeration of regional credit cooperatives, and an almost entirely domestic concern.

8. The exception is Western Bancorporation, which is a multi-bank holding company with banks in eleven Western states.

9. A Personal Banker is appointed with direct responsibility for certain personal customer accounts. Personal customers can contact their Personal Banker on any matter. The technique has been adopted by banks in many countries.

10. The CD is a money market instrument which revolutionised banking by allowing banks to compete for money market funds. It was a necessary preliminary to the practice of liability management which has made effective funds management possible for banks.

11. Citibank encountered severe public relations problems at this time, and was attacked by the Nader consumer lobby. This doubtless stimulated its thinking on corporate responsibility.

References

American Bankers Association, *Bank Fact Book* (ABA, Washington, 1981).

Compton, E.N., *Inside Commercial Banking* (Wiley, New York, 1981)

Golembe, C.H. and Holland, D.S., *Federal Regulation of Banking* (Golembe Associates and ABA, Washington, 1981).

Guenther, Dr. H., *Banking and Finance in North America* (Financial Times Business Publishing, London, 1981).

Peat, Marwick, Mitchell & Co., *Banking in the United States* (Peat, Marwick, Mitchell & Co., New York, 1980).

Robichek, A.A. *et al.*, *Management of Financial Institutions* (Dryden Press, Hinsdale, 1976).

Teplitz, P.V., *Trends Affecting the US Banking System*, (Cambridge Research Institute, Ballinger, Cambridge, Mass., 1976).

Wood, O.G., *Commercial Banking — Practice and Policy* (D. Van Nostrand, New York, 1980).

4 JAPANESE BANKS

4.1 Financial System

The Japanese financial system has a fairly simple structure, but it is subject to peculiar pressures due to the unique nature of Japan's economic development during the twentieth century. There is a considerable degree of government intervention, and the quality of Japanese business culture means that relations between financial institutions, regulatory bodies and customers are sometimes different from those in the West.

For analytical purposes it is useful to divide Japanese financial institutions into those in the private sector and those in the government sector (see Figure 4.1). In the private sector we have commercial banks, a wide variety of specialised financial institutions covering long-term credit, small business, and agribusiness, and other financial institutions including insurance companies, securities houses and dealers. In the government sector we have the Export-Import Bank and Development Bank, various public finance corporations, and the Post Office which plays a very significant role in Japanese retail banking.

Commercial banks include the 12 city banks based in Tokyo, Osaka, Nagoya and Kobe which hold nearly 20 per cent of all deposits and loans and exert a powerful influence in the Japanese economy because of their special role in the area of corporate finance and international banking. These banks have nationwide branch networks of average size 213 branches in 1981 and are full-service banks catering for the middle and consumer markets. They have also recently been large purchasers of public bonds. The larger city banks have fairly extensive overseas branch networks of average size 10 offices, and some overseas subsidiaries and affiliates. In contrast, the 63 regional banks are domestic, locally-oriented banks with branch networks of average size 85 in 1981 and little overseas representation. They meet the credit needs of their regional business community and local municipal authorities, and are important suppliers of funds to the money markets. The relationship between Japanese regional and city banks is similar in nature to that between US regional and large money-centre banks. All the ordinary banks have extensive correspondent relationships with each other for payments purposes. The city banks and some regional banks are authorised to deal in foreign exchange, but the Bank of Tokyo plays a special role in government transactions. It has the most extensive overseas branch network of all the Japanese banks.

Both city and regional banks are ordinary commercial banks for legal purposes, deriving their powers initially from the Banking Law of 1927, which has now been replaced by the Banking Law of 1981. They issue their shares on the Tokyo stock exchange. Bank of Tokyo was given its special status under the Foreign Exchange Bank Law of 1954.

At the end of 1981 there were 71 foreign banks represented in Japan with a total of 96 branches, of which 23 were from the US, 8 from the UK, 19 from Continental Europe and 22 from elsewhere. They are required to obtain a licence from the Ministry of Finance in order to operate a branch. These banks engage in wholesale banking — interbank foreign currency deposit trading, short-term yen lending, and foreign currency lending to Japanese companies and local offshoots of foreign companies, trade financing and foreign exchange.

Specialist financial institutions are an important feature of the Japanese system, although it should be noted that in Japan as in other countries some of the differences between these institutions and commercial banks are progressively disappearing.

The trust banks are closely linked to the commercial banks, and the major city banks all have a trust bank partner. They are classified as ordinary banks under the Banking Law and undertake ordinary commercial banking business, but they are also privileged to engage in trust business under the Law concerning Ordinary Bank's Concurrent Management of Savings Bank or Trust Bank Operations of 1943. They are encouraged to concentrate on trust business by the Ministry of Finance, and only about one quarter of their accounts are banking accounts as opposed to trust accounts.

There are seven trust banks, and three other banks also undertake trust business. They provide long-term finance to industry through loan trusts and money trusts; and they provide financial management services through equipment, real estate, monetary claims and securities in trust, and through real estate business,

Figure 4.1: Financial Institutions in Japan

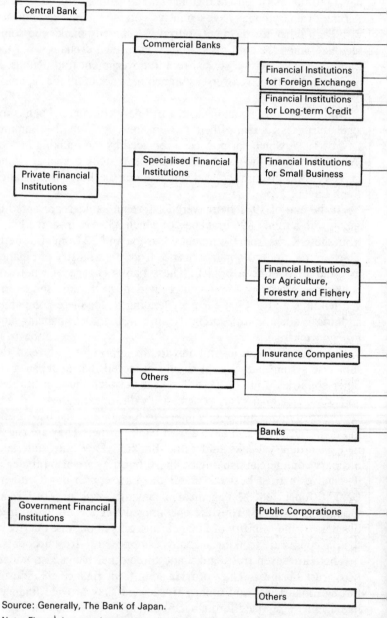

Source: Generally, The Bank of Japan.

Note: Figures in parentheses generally denote the number at the end of December 1981.

— The Bank of Japan

- City banks (12)
- Local banks (63)
- Foreign banks (71)

— Specialised foreign exchange bank (1)

- Long-term credit banks (3)
- Trust banks (7)

- Mutual banks (71)
- The National Federation of Credit Associations
  └ Credit Associations (456)
- The National Federation of Credit Cooperatives
  └ Credit cooperatives (473)
- The National Federation of Labor Credit Associations
  └ Labor credit associations (47)
- The Central Bank for Commercial and Industrial Cooperatives

- The Central Cooperative Bank for Agriculture and Forestry
  └ Credit federations of agricultural cooperatives (47)
      └ Agricultural cooperatives (4,501)
    └ Credit federations of fishery cooperatives (35)
        └ Fishery cooperatives (1,755)
    └ Federations of forestry cooperatives (47)
        └ Forestry cooperatives (2,256)
- National Cooperative Insurance Federation of Agricultural Cooperatives
  └ Cooperative insurance federations of agricultural cooperatives (47)

- Life insurance companies (21)
- Non-life insurance companies (22)

- Money-market dealers (6)
- Securities finance corporations (3)
- Securities companies (230)

- The Export-Import Bank of Japan
- The Japan Development Bank

- The People's Finance Corporation
- The Small Business Finance Corporation
- The Small Business Credit Insurance Corporation
- The Medical Care Facilities Finance Corporation
- The Environmental Sanitation Business Finance Corporation
- The Agriculture, Forestry and Fishery Finance Corporation
- The Housing Loan Corporation
- The Hokkaido and Tohoku Development Corporation
- The Local Public Enterprise Finance Corporation
- The Okinawa Development Finance Corporation

- The Overseas Economic Cooperation Fund
- Post offices (approximately 22,000)
- Special accounts (4)

securities agency business and so forth. They also engage in pension fund investment management.

The three long-term credit banks were created by a special law of 1952, principally to provide long-term equipment and working capital funds for manufacturing industries. Since then they have also begun to provide some shorter-term funds, to lend to other industries, and to enter the field of international finance. They now have significant overseas representation, especially the Industrial Bank of Japan (IBJ) with five branches, eleven representative offices and eleven affiliates worldwide in 1981. They are funded through the issue of debentures, wholesale deposits and recently negotiable certificates of deposit (CDs). The long-term credit banks are also allowed to engage to a limited extent in securities business.

Financial institutions for small and medium-sized business include Sogo or mutual savings banks, credit associations and credit cooperatives. The *Sogo banks* were established under a special law of 1951 and their origins go back to the 'mujin' mutual loan companies. They accept savings deposits and instalment savings, and they provide loans and bill discounting facilities. They now operate in effect as ordinary commercial banks, specialising in lending to the middle market, at the top end of which they compete with regional and even city banks. The *credit associations* have a long history but their present enabling legislation also came in 1951. They are associations of small and medium-sized businesses and their employees, who subscribe the capital. They take savings deposits and instalments savings, and offer loans and bill discounting facilities to members, to non-members with savings accounts, and to public bodies, banks and financial institutions. Their prime responsibility is to members in the local community. The associations' member and non-member business has grown quickly in recent years. The *credit cooperatives* are similar to credit associations but they are non-profit bodies whose activities are mainly limited to providing financial services to subscribing members.

The Shokochukin Bank acts as a kind of central bank to ensure the smooth functioning of financing to these financial institutions. Various government finance agencies and guarantee corporations are also active in this field.

Financial institutions for agriculture, forestry and fisheries are coordinated at national level by the Norinchukin Bank or Central

Cooperative Bank of Agriculture and Forestry, and at regional level by their local credit federations. The credit cooperatives themselves, of which there are many thousands, accept deposits as only part of their general trading business. Although they are empowered to make loans, they on-lend most of their funds to the credit federations, which are merely financial institutions.

There are 21 *life-insurance* and 22 *general insurance companies.* Life insurance companies are important suppliers of long-term loans for equipment to industry, and significant investors on the stock market. Some of the leading insurance companies are associates of the city banks and carry the same name (eg, Sumitomo). It is expected that these institutions will in future increase the level of their overseas investment.

There are six *money market dealers* who specialise in short-term deposit broking in the call money and foreign exchange markets. There are over 200 *securities companies,* the largest of which engage in dealing for customers, trading on their own account, underwriting and subscription to issues. The major companies have actively entered the area of international finance, at first raising money abroad for Japanese companies, but now also dealing on behalf of Japanese investors in foreign bonds, or foreign investors in local bonds, and participating in syndicated loans.

It is not necessary to elaborate here on the activities of the 12 government financial institutions which have special sectoral responsibilities. The Japan Development Bank has a general brief to provide long-term finance, orginally in the post-War reconstruction of the economy but since then in a variety of strategic areas. The Export Import Bank provides extensive financial backing to Japanese exporters, on a par with that offered by the equivalent US, UK and French institutions. We should also stress once more the importance of the postal savings system in the retail banking market. Its total deposits in 1980 were a full two-thirds of the total deposits of all types held by the city banks, and its share of the market for retail deposits has been steadily increasing as it has been able to offer consistently better rates of interest than commercial banks. The broad picture of financial institutions is shown in Table 4.1.

In order to gain a fuller picture of the workings of the Japanese financial system it is useful to review briefly the history of its development. In 1868 the Meiji government included as part of its modernisation programme the renovation of the insulated Japan-

Table 4.1: Banks and Financial Institutions in Japan – Number of Type, Number of Domestic Branches, Share of Deposits and Loans, December 1980

	No. of institutions	No. of branches	Deposits, billion yen	Loan, billion yen
All banks	86	8,759	207,921	153,999
City banks	13	2,714	87,875	71,342
Local banks	63	5,675	59,162	43,764
Long-term credit banks	3	54	21,844	16,524
Trust banks	7	316	39,040	22,369
Foreign banks	64	86	1,319	4,449
Medium & small financial institutions	1,088	12,145	76,167	61,971
Sogo banks	71	3,846	27,476	21,432
Credit Associations	461	5,637	34,499	26,347
Credit Cooperatives	476	2,569	8,647	6,905
Shokochukin Bank	1	93	5,545	5,372
Labour credit cooperatives	47	495	2,981	1,915
Financial institutions for agriculture, forestry and fishery	6,264	(19,563)	(39,669)*	(18,228)
Norinchukin Bank	1	38	10,974	6,088
Credit federations of agriculture cooperatives	47	323	16,856	3,679
Agricultural cooperatives	4,530	(17,094)	27,511	11,128
Credit federations of fishery cooperatives	35	—	1,111	810
Fishery cooperatives	1,686	(2,301)	1,184	1,012
Insurance companies	43	(1,982)	—	16,803
Life insurance companies	21	1,537	—	15,213
Fire and marine insurance companies	22	(443)	—	1,590
Sub-total	7,513	(42,191)	—	—
Government financial institutions	12	257	—	41,958
Postal savings	1	22,287	59,550	187
Securities companies	255	2,081	—	—
Total	—	—	386,288*	295,061*

Notes: Deposits include outstanding amount of bank debentures, loan trust, money trust and pension trust. Figures shown *adjusted by deducting duplication. Figures in parentheses include estimates.

Source: The Bank of Japan.

ese financial structure. In 1882 the Bank of Japan was established and laws were passed to set up various types of institution — commercial and savings banks, long-term credit institutions, and institutions specialising in trade finance. The trust companies, insurance companies and cooperative bodies also emerged as Japan became increasingly involved in trade with the West and began to transform itself from a feudal society into a more open, modern industrial society. The development process was continued with the passing of the Banking Law of 1927, defining the business of commercial banks and preventing them from engaging in investment banking. In 1929 there were several failures as a consequence of the depression, but the system survived and was harnessed to assist the war effort. In 1942 the powers of the Bank of Japan were considerably strengthened to assist in this process. During their period of occupation the Allies took several steps designed to prevent the resurgence of the Japanese industrial/ military machine. Various types of special financial institutions were abolished and transformed into the present commerical or long-term credit banks. Trust companies became trust banks and were allowed to perform normal banking functions. Certain special institutions were created to improve the financing of smaller businesses, and agribusiness, and to promote international trade and economic development.

The Bank of Japan has remained the presiding body with normal central banking responsibilities. Supervision and guidance of financial institutions, however, have been delegated to the Ministry of Finance under the Banking Law of 1927, and the Ministry of Finance has remained the body responsible for licensing businesses, vetting amalgamations, approving branches, overseeing bank accounting, supervision and inspection.

From 1955 to 1970 the Japanese economy experienced rapid growth. In the absence of a stock market of any depth or breadth the major Japanese corporations relied almost entirely on banks and financial institutions to finance their cumulative investment. Industry was very heavily borrowed and in accommodating their needs the city banks had continual recourse to support from the Bank of Japan, because of their drastically overloaned positions. The city banks' negative reserve position had to be financed by other banks lending to the short-term money market. Fortunately, the personal sector maintained a very high savings ratio during this period, and still does, partly because of the relative inadequacy of pension provisions in Japan. Throughout the period, the Bank of Japan has acted to keep interest rates down in the face of a perpetual over-demand for funds, and recognises that this has impaired the growth of efficient short-term financial markets and securities markets.

In the latter part of the 1970s the rate of growth in the economy slackened and some of the pressures on the financial system have eased. The authorities are now prepared to countenance the progressive liberalisation and internationalisation of the financial markets. As far back as 1965 steps were taken to deepen the markets by issuing public bonds and creating a National Debt, and since the oil shock of 1973/4 the public sector deficit has exceeded the corporate sector deficit as the government has taken measures to cope with rising oil prices. Since a large part of these bond sales were covered by the city banks, the pressures on them have not been reduced as much as they would have hoped. Consequently, these banks are still overloaned by comparison with most Western banks and suffer from funding difficulties. These difficulties have been exacerbated by the fact that they have not been completely free in the past to raise foreign currency deposits or to accept non-resident yen deposits to boost their deposit base, although they now derive a good quarter of their total deposits in foreign currencies.

The Ministry of Finance (MoF) has a standing Committee on Financial System Research which in the post-War period made several recommendations, some of which formed the basis of legislation — Reserve Requirements Law (1957), Merger and Conversion of Financial Institutions Law (1968), Deposit Insurance Law (1971). The simple framework of the 1927 Law could not possibly cope with the rapid evolution of the system, and the MoF's powers of administrative guidance were frequently invoked. In 1979 the Committee presented a report on 'The Future Course of Ordinary Banks and Revision of the Banking System' which was the foundation for the reforming and consolidating Banking Law of 1981.

According to this new law, the scope of banking business is the taking of deposits, extending of loans, discounting of bills, and domestic exchange business (as in the 1927 law), and also ten forms of ancillary business, namely: guarantees and acceptances; buying and selling of securities on a customer's behalf or on own account; lending securities; underwriting public sector debt and offering it for subscription; sale and purchase of negotiable CDs and similar instruments; acting as subscription agent for the sale of all types of securities; acting as agent for financial institutions; money transmission services; safe custody services; money changing; gold dealing.

The banks now have considerably increased powers to deal in

securities, especially the sale of public bonds at branches. In return the securities companies will be allowed to underwrite commercial paper and to issue CDs in the international market.

The 1981 law also codifies:

1. Limitations on credit facilities to any one person, and to directors, to 20 per cent of capital and reserves.
2. Bank holidays.
3. Business terms.
4. Disclosure of financial statements and certain business situations.
5. Rules concerning foreign bank representation.
6. Liberalisation of bank administration in, for example, authorisation and issue of capital, and establishment of offices.

Liberalisation of domestic banking has been accompanied by action on the international front by means of the Foreign Exchange and Foreign Trade Control Law of 1980, which consolidated many orders and ordinances made in the post-War period. Its fundamental principles were:

1. External transactions concerning capital, services and others are free in principle.
2. Current transactions are almost entirely liberalised, and capital transactions are free in ordinary cases.
3. Foreign direct investment in Japan is free in principle.
4. Licensing of capital transactions has been replaced by a reporting system.

The important shift was in the rules for capital transactions, including, for example: foreign direct investment by Japanese investors, inward and outward portfolio investment via the securities companies, foreign currency deposits, impact loans to residents and loan-guarantees by residents. The last three measures are particularly important to foreign banks operating in Japan. However, the legislation also contains provisions which allow transactions to be brought back under control if the foreign exchange markets are disorderly, or if there is a deteriorating balance of payments, or if there is financial confusion. These conditions have been deemed to apply since 1980, so that the authorities still exercise exchange controls in fact.

The powers of the Ministry of Finance are extensive, since it is responsible for the supervisory administration of all financial institutions and for the coordination of the relevant legislation. It operates through a banking bureau (coordination, commercial banks, special banks, small business finance, general research), a securities bureau, international finance bureau and local finance bureaux. Important aspects of administrative guidance affecting banks include:

1. Bank management, eg. loan/deposit ratios (max. 80 %), liquidity ratios (min. 30 %), dividend rates (max. 15 %), capital ratios (min. 10 %) and ratios of fixed assets to net worth (max. 40 %).
2. Concentration of loans, ie, max. 20 % of net worth to any one person.
3. Establishment of offices.
4. Diversification into areas other than those ancillary activities permitted by the Banking Law of 1981. Banks themselves may engage in certain other activities through wholly-owned subsidiaries, including managing bank buildings, credit guarantees and mortgage administration. Certain other 'peripheral' activities have been permitted to bank affiliates, including leasing, credit cards, housing finance, management consultancy, computer services; but the degree of involvement of the bank is limited. Similar rules apply to overseas subsidiaries. Disallowed 'peripheral' activities have included golf course management, real estate brokerage, retailing and travel agencies.
5. Self-restraint in requiring compensating credit balances from borrowing business customers. Compensating balances are still common practice in Japan, although discouraged.

The Bank of Japan is relieved of much of the burden of active supervision and can concentrate on key central banking issues, including:

1. Issue of bank notes.
2. Banking for commercial banks.
3. Banking for government.
4. Monetary policy — administered through the normal instruments of discount window lending, open market operations, reserve deposit requirements, and window guidance.

In its efforts to promote economic development the Bank has worked to keep down interest rates, to minimise reserve requirements, and it has frequently given window guidance in order to ensure the orderly growth of domestic credit. This guidance is quantitative, not qualitative.

The Bank of Japan controls interest rates through the Temporary Interest Rates Control Law, which gives the Policy Board of the Bank power to establish maximum limits of deposit and loan interest rates after consultation with the Interest Adjustment Council. Typical rates are shown in Table 4.2.

Through the Law on the Reserve Deposit System of 1957 the Bank of Japan requires banks to maintain non-interest bearing deposits with the Bank.

Finally we should mention the important role of the Ministry for International Trade and Industry (MITI), which coordinates Japanese policy and efforts in export and foreign markets. MITI has close links with the Export-Import Bank in particular and has an important say in many international projects and their financing.

4.2 Strategic Development of Multinational Banks

The city banks are the largest commercial banks in Japan and have played a vital role in financing Japan's industrial development. Their influence is even more powerful than it appears at first sight because they invest on behalf of client firms in marketed debt and equity, because Japanese corporations have a main bank rather than multiple banking relationships, and because the heavy reliance of corporations on bank finance means that the banks have some sway with heavy borrowers, especially if the borrower is in difficulties. Moreover, some banks are at the centre of industrial groupings based on the pre-War 'zaibatsus' or financial combines.

Of the 13 city banks (see Table 4.3) the six leading Tokyo and Osaka banks are the major multinationals. These all have assets over yen 13 trillion and are among the largest banks in the world. They have fairly extensive representation overseas, and are diversified commercial banks within the constraints on banking business imposed by the Banking Law of 1981. Table 4.4 shows that the profile of the leading banks is remarkably similar, with the exception of Bank of Tokyo which is a bank with specialised functions

Table 4.2: Japanese Interest Rates on Deposits and Savings (End of September, 1981)

		Guide-line rates provided by the Bank of Japan	Maximum limits under Temporary Interest Rates Adjustment Law
1 Bank deposits			
Time deposits	3 months	4.25%	
	6 months	5.50%	
	1 year	6.25%	7.25%
	2 years	6.50%	
Instalment deposits		4.10%	
Deposits for tax payment		3.00%	3.50%
Ordinary deposits		2.25%	
Deposits at notice		2.50%	3.00%
Special deposits and other deposits		2.25%	
2 Bank debentures			
Discount debentures (1 year)			6.42%
Debentures with coupon (3 years)			7.40%
Debentures with coupon (5 years)			7.60%
3 Postal savings			
Ordinary savings			3.60%
Instalment savings			4.44%
Time savings (1 year)			6.25%
Savings certificates (over 3 years)			6.50%
4 Dividend rates of trusts (5 years)			
Anticipated dividend rate of designated money in trust			7.43%
Anticipated dividend rate of loan trust			7.62%

Notes: All interest rates represent their maximum limits. Postal savings interest rates are those specified in the Cabinet order based on the Postal Savings Law. Dividend rates of trust are voluntarily decided by each trust bank. Current deposits bear no interest.

Source: Federation of Bankers Association of Japan.

and has a very extensive overseas network. It should be noted that Industrial Bank of Japan and Long-Term Credit Bank of Japan also have extensive overseas representation, but again these are specialist banks. The profile of the commercial banks shows a small number of domestic affiliates (with the exception of Dai-Ichi

Kangyo) typically including a leasing company, factoring and commercial credit, and housing loans; a number of international subsidiaries, typically including a bank in Brazil and a bank in California, and various international finance corporations in the main financial centres such as Hong Kong, London, Zurich, New York, Luxembourg; and finally a rather larger number of international affiliates, typically including merchant banks in key Pacific centres, various operations in Australia, and merchant bank participations in other places. A hypothetical structure of operations is shown in Figure 4.2.

It is important to understand the nature of the bank-centred industrial groups. In the pre-War period the zaibatsus represented

Table 4.3: Japanese City Banks, 1981

Name	Head office	Assets (yen billions)
Dai-Ichi Kangyo	Tokyo	21,741
Fuji	Tokyo	18,699
Sumitomo	Osaka	19,401
Mitsubishi	Tokyo	18,798
Sanwa	Osaka	17,032
Mitsui	Tokyo	13,256
Tokai	Nagoya	12,789
Taiyo Kobe	Kobe	11,042
Bank of Tokyo	Tokyo	13,749
Kyowa	Tokyo	6,955
Daiwa	Osaka	6,669
Saitama	Saitama	6,027
Hokkaido Takushoku	Sapporo	4,969

Japanese Trust Banks, 1981			Deposits, including trust accounts
Mitsubishi Trust & Banking Corp.	Tokyo	4,651	9,906
Sumitomo Trust & Banking Corp.		3,806	8,367
Mitsui Trust & Banking Corp.	Tokyo	3,680	8,739
Yasuda Trust & Banking Corp.		2,764	6,623
Toyo Trust & Banking Corp.		1,903	6,011
Chuo Trust & Banking Corp.		1,094	3,685
Nippon Trust & Banking Corp.		668	1,496

Table 4.4: Japanese Multinational Banks, 1979

	Domestic affiliates	International subsidiaries	International affiliates	Overseas branches	Other overseas offices
Tokyo Banks, 1979					
Dai-Ichi Kangyo	—	5	13	7	13
Fuji	4	6	12	6	12
Mitsubishi	5	4	14	6	12
Mitsui	4	3	16	8	12
(+ 1 subsidiary)					
Osaka Banks, 1979					
Sumitomo	6	4	8	8	10
Sanwa	4	3	15	8	10
Specialised Banks, 1979					
Bank of Tokyo	—	15	20	42	25
Industrial Bank of Japan	—	7	28	3	11
Long-Term Credit Bank of Japan	—	3	9	—	—

Figure 4.2: Japan Bank, Typical Structure

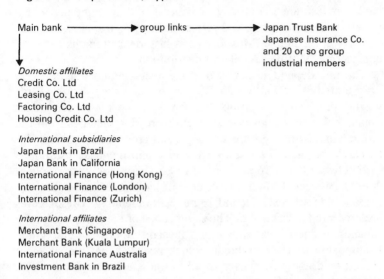

Main bank ⟶ group links ⟶ Japan Trust Bank
Japanese Insurance Co.
and 20 or so group
industrial members

Domestic affiliates
Credit Co. Ltd
Leasing Co. Ltd
Factoring Co. Ltd
Housing Credit Co. Ltd

International subsidiaries
Japan Bank in Brazil
Japan Bank in California
International Finance (Hong Kong)
International Finance (London)
International Finance (Zurich)

International affiliates
Merchant Bank (Singapore)
Merchant Bank (Kuala Lumpur)
International Finance Australia
Investment Bank in Brazil

an enormous concentration of power and wealth. They were holding companies controlled by wealthy families or clans, and the group bank played a subservient role. After the Second World War the zaibatsus were dissolved and various laws enacted to prevent the re-emergence of such power blocs again, by limiting the level of permissible cross-holdings.[1]

In the post-War period some of the leaders of old zaibatsu companies began to meet with each other on a regular basis, with the bankers acting as instigators. There have now developed a number of fairly loose groupings in Japan, mostly centred round leading banks, whose members have significant cross-holdings and who have a regular policy forum for the bosses of member companies. The four leading groups which still carry the old zaibatsu family names are Mitsubishi, Sumitomo, Fuji (group name Yasuda or Fuyo) and Mitsui. The Mitsui Group's relative importance has declined a little in recent years. Dai-Ichi Kangyo Bank and Sanwa Bank also have groupings, although these are not based on old zaibatsu links and are looser and more heterogeneous in character. There are also non-bank groups such as those led by Toyota, Hitachi and Matsushita, where the member companies tend to have a more homogeneous range of products, viz. automotive, electrical, and so on.

A typical bank-centred group will include a city bank, a trust bank, an insurance company, a general trading company and a variety of manufacturing and service industries. The industrial mix varies — for example, Mitsubishi has historical strengths in heavy engineering, Mitsui in retail and distribution.

The interdependence of group members should not be over-exaggerated — only about 20–30 per cent of a group bank's lending normally goes to group companies, while group companies obtain less than 20 per cent of their borrowing facilities from the group bank. Within groups the degree of cross-holding varies significantly but in 1979 a study showed group financial institutions held between 8 and 16 per cent of group shares and were responsible for between 12 and 28 per cent of lending. Main banks were responsible for between 9 and 13 per cent of lending. These figures are presented in Table 4.5. The significance of the groupings in the Japanese economy was shown in a special study by the Fair Trade Commission in 1977 in Japan, which revealed that the six main groups held about a quarter of all business assets in Japan, took about a quarter of net profits, held about one-fifth of all issued capital, and accounted for some 15 per cent of total sales.

The group system was found to have certain financial benefits for all concerned, in terms of the close and flexible relationships it

Table 4.5: Concentration of Share Holding and Lending in Six Japanese Large Enterprise Groups, 1979

Group	Percentage of share holding		Percentage of lending	
	By members	By financial institutions	By financial institutions	By bank
Mitsui	16.3	10.7	18.3	9.2
Mitsubishi	26.1	16.2	24.9	11.7
Sumitomo	27.4	15.9	27.3	12.8
Fuji	16.3	10.6	21.0	10.1
Sanwa	16.9	9.4	19.1	12.8
Dai-Ichi Kangyo	14.0	8.1	12.8	10.5

Percentage share of the six large enterprises in national economy	
Total assets	24.99
Paid-up capital	19.13
Sales	15.66
Net profits	26.60

Sources: Shukan Toyo-Keizai special issue; Fair Trade Commission, quoted in Banker Research Unit (1981).

engendered. The bank's credit risk is reduced because it has exceptionally close knowledge of its borrowers, and because of the degree of mutual support and aid between group companies. The bank can act to coordinate the financing of group companies, especially where there are seasonal or cyclical fluctuations in members' borrowing demands. The trust bank and insurance company can provide other financial services. The general trading company is financed to an extent by the group bank, and in its turn it provides trade finance to smaller group companies and to suppliers. Its intimate knowledge of these small companies again helps to reduce credit risk. The main bank also gains a considerable volume of stable retail deposits from group employees, and large current account balances from group companies.

When a group company encounters difficulty the bank will usually manage any rescue operation, for example by seconding senior staff. At all times the bank is prepared to act as financial adviser to the group, and as coordinator of group policy.

The role of the trust bank in the group complements that of the main bank, since the trust bank can offer longer-term lending. The city banks specialise in short-term lending for working capital, although in practice short-term facilities are renewed and made available permanently to successful companies. Furthermore, according to the Bank of Japan about one quarter of total commercial bank lending is technically of maturity greater than one year. The commerical banks also purchase bank debentures of long-term credit institutions, buy corporate bonds, and make loans and direct investments towards capital increase of corporations. However, the city banks have in general followed the classical pattern of commercial banks specialising in short-term finance, particularly as specialist institutions have been charged with the task of providing long-term credit.

Loans account for about 60 per cent of commercial bank assets. They have traditionally been to the business sector, although the proportion of lending to consumers for consumer credit and house purchase has increased recently. About 60 per cent of the city banks' lending goes to large enterprises, capitalised at more than ¥ 100 million. The city banks' loan/deposit ratios were as high as 80 per cent in the late-1970s but have since declined to about 70 per cent.

The typical lending arrangements in Japan are discounting of commercial bills or short-term advances against bills. Dishonour of bills is a serious matter, and banks will not normally continue business relationships with a customer who has twice defaulted. Arrangements are usually fairly informal in character, merely subject to the lending bank's General Business Conditions. These, however, give the bank considerable powers to intervene if a borrower has difficulty with repayments.[2] Banks require compensating balances from borrowers, and will also levy service charges. As in all Japanese business affairs the long-term relationship between borrower and lender is the most important factor affecting terms and conditions of financing.

In recent years, the city banks have also channelled a considerable volume of funds into the purchase of national bonds in accordance with the wishes of the authorities. For example, in 1980 city banks purchased 30 per cent of all bonds issued, and this represented one third of the total increase in bank deposits during the year.[3]

The city banks obtain most of their funds in the form of deposits, including demand deposits, interest-bearing passbook demand accounts, deposits at notice, and time deposits of varying maturities (three months, six months, one year, two years). Rates on deposits are regulated by the Temporary Interest Rates Adjustment Law, and are so set in relation to lending rates as to allow the banks a reasonable profit on the turn.[4] Since the authorities also keep a watchful eye on lending rates it is evident that the very profitability of the banks is to a large extent dependent on the views of the authorities, since they can determine the banks' spread. However, the Japanese authorities are increasingly trying to liberalise financial markets and where possible to allow flexible adjustments to interest rates in accordance with market forces.

The city banks obtain their deposits through their branch networks, from individuals and corporate customers. Overall, about 40 per cent of funds come from the personal sector, mostly in the form of passbook demand deposits and time deposits. The rest comes from the corporate sector, government agencies and financial institutions, but mainly the corporate sector. The majority of time deposits is of maturity greater than one year. Because of their overloaned position the city banks have also had to rely on call money, borrowing from the Bank of Japan, proceeds of rediscounting bills, capital and reserves to fund their lending.

With their relatively small branch networks the city banks do not play a dominant role in the market for money transmission services. The banks' ability to extend their networks is strictly controlled, and they are only allowed to open a couple of branches a year. The largest of the city banks has just over 300 branches, concentrated inevitably in the major centres, and particularly in Tokyo and Osaka.

Tokyo is, of course, the Japanese financial centre, where the money and foreign exchange markets are situated, so that banks who do not have their head office in Tokyo are nevertheless obliged to maintain a significant presence there. Tokyo's emergence as an international finance centre has been deliberately retarded by the Japanese authorities. The Japanese have been quite content to see the Asian dollar market and all types of off-shore financial services for the Pacific Basin area become domiciled in Hong Kong and Singapore. The Japanese banks maintain presences in both centres. At present, Tokyo's growth in importance is inhibited by exchange controls, and by its under-developed money and capital markets. However, the markets are being progressively liberalised and it may well be that in the medium term Tokyo and the yen will emerge as powerful financial forces to rival New York and the US dollar. Its emergence as a Eurodollar financial centre will only occur if the present with-holding tax on bank interest paid to non-residents is removed, reserve requirements relaxed, and other regulations abolished.

For a considerable time the Japanese banks were content to serve the needs of their industrial customers by traditional means, providing trade financing of imports and exports. Since Japanese corporations preferred to remain exporters rather than undertake foreign direct investment and become multinational corporations, this caused few problems. However, since the late-1960s the pace of Japanese investment overseas, especially in the US and Europe, has increased, and the Japanese banks have had to improve their international capabilities to cope with these demands. The Japanese banks have also found themselves in direct competition with US and European multinational banks in the increasingly global financial markets, especially the Euromarkets, and have therefore been obliged to match their peers in response to a competitive threat in order to maintain equivalent status. This has meant steady expansion of overseas networks and representation, the development of merchant banking capabilities, and an assault on the key international banking markets — Eurodollar credits, Euro-bonds, foreign exchange. The major banks are now active in all these markets and have at times adopted aggressive pricing policies in order to increase their market share rapidly. Japanese banks also make use of their overseas branches to raise Eurocurrency funds to finance the overseas operations of the major Japanese corporations.

In all their international operations the banks are monitored by the authorities, who are determined to see safe and orderly growth towards the long-term objectives of establishing a US dollar deposit base, and using the yen as a trading and reserve currency. For the city banks as a group foreign currency accounts now represent about 30 per cent of total assets and liabilities, while foreign currency income and costs account for about 40 per cent of total income and costs.

Our analysis of the business of the Japanese multinational banks has shown how they have played a special part in Japan's unique post-War economic development. We have seen how close the links are between Japanese banks and industry, and how the authorities have supported and guided the banks at home and abroad, in the national interest. These are the factors which have determined the strategic development of the major Japanese banks.

In contrast to the US banks there has been less emphasis on overt profit objectives, less pressure to diversify and to innovate, and a more relaxed relationship with the monetary authorities and regulators. Japanese business is said to thrive on consensus in all decision-making, on a strong sense of national identity, and to be motivated by very long-term strategic objectives rather than shorter-term profit goals. It is not then surprising that the banks fit this pattern, since they are so deeply embedded in Japan's industrial system.

During the period of post-War reconstruction, the city banks devoted their resources to the financing of the rapidly growing large industrial corporations. The pressure of demand for funds was such that there was little chance to develop lending to the small and medium-sized business (SMB) sector, or to the personal sector. In any case, specialised institutions catered for SMBs, and the demand for consumer credit in Japan was not strong.[5] Moreover, the banks' ability to diversify activities beyond normal banking services has been curtailed by the anti-monopoly regulations (see note 1, p. 253). On the international front Japanese corporations favoured exports rather than foreign direct investment, and so required only traditional international banking facilities from their main banks. The result was that until the late-1960s and early-1970s the Japanese banks remained largely in the traditional commercial bank mould, performing mainstream services for their corporate customers.

The picture changed as the growth of the Japanese economy slowed down, and as trading and financial relationships with the West deepened. In their domestic markets the banks began to show more enthusiasm in lending to SMBs as demand from the large corporations fell off, and as the authorities began to encourage innovation and enterprise in smaller firms. They also turned to housing finance and consumer credit, and were able to benefit from some liberalisation in Japanese social attitudes towards credit. The biggest change however came on the international front. With the backing of the authorities the Japanese banks determined to become active participants in the international markets and fully-fledged competitors of the major US and European commercial banks. This was seen to be a policy of national importance, since the danger existed that Japan could become dependent for more sophisticated financial services on Western banks — an unacceptable position.

According to the Bank of Japan, the prime factors in the internationalisation of Japanese banking were Japan's accession to the OECD and IMF in 1964, and the subsequent liberalisation of current and capital transactions which occurred; and the overseas activities of Japanese industry especially in the early-1970s, both in international trade and overseas investment. The methods which the Japanese banks chose to extend their international capabilities included opening of branches and representative offices, establishment of wholly-owned subsidiaries, participation in consortium banks, and acquisition of foreign banks. The major banks had London branches before the War, and since the War these have been reopened, followed typically by branches in New York, Singapore, Düsseldorf, Chicago, Seoul, and perhaps in Brussels, Seattle and one or two other locations. These branches serve to raise funds in major financial centres, and also give the banks a platform for participation in syndicated lending. They are also points from which to service the local financial needs of Japanese corporations overseas. Representative offices have been spread more widely but in similar financial/industrial centres. The figures in Table 4.6 show that the expansion has been a gradual process,

Table 4.6: Development of Japanese Overseas Networks: New Overseas Branches, Representative Offices and Agencies, 1971–80

	1971	1972	1973	1974	1975	1976	1977	1978	1979	1980
Dai-Ichi Kangyo	—	3	3	1	1	1	4	—	1	2
Fuji	1	1	3	—	4	2	1	2	1	2
Mitsubishi	—	—	1	2	2	1	2	1	1	1
Mitsui	1	2	2	2	—	3	1	2	1	1
Sumitomo	1	3	2	4	2	2	1	2	1	2
Sanwa	0	1	3	4	1	1	1	1	1	1

New Establishments Overseas, 1950–80

	1950–55	1956–60	1961–5	1966–70	1971–5	1976–80	Total
Branch/Agency	13	15	19	8	46	38	139
Sub-branch	1	1	2	7	4	3	17
Affiliated	3	1	1	3	34	32	74
Rep. office	4	5	9	17	108	97	186
Total	26	22	31	35	192	170	416

Source: Banker Research Unit, *The Top 100* (Financial Times, London, 1981).

carefully regulated, dating from 1970.[6]

Key subsidiaries have been established in London, Hong Kong, Zurich and one or two other centres, with a merchant banking function. Most of the banks have also acquired a modest-sized US bank with the aim of acquiring a dollar deposit base and a foothold in US financial markets.

The Japanese raise their funds abroad by taking Euro-deposits, borrowing from other banks, and more recently by issuing certificates of deposit in an attempt to secure a more stable deposit base for their operations. The Japanese banks encountered some funding difficulties in 1974 when the interbank market for Eurodollar deposits froze up, and since then they have adopted a more cautious policy in their Eurocurrency maturity mismatching. They have issued CDs in London, New York and Hong Kong. The overseas offices employ their funds in trade financing, foreign loans and securities investment, but also place some funds in the interbank markets, although by and large they are takers from the interbank markets.[7]

In their early years the Japanese banks concentrated on short-term credits, mainly supplying the working capital needs of Japanese firms abroad and foreign traders with Japan, but also lending to foreign governments and agencies who could not accept medium-term credits or needed a bridging loan before medium-term finance became available. During the 1970s the volume of medium-term credit increased and in 1978 overtook the volume of short-term credit. In 1979 the Japanese banks took a 20 per cent share of all syndicated Eurocredits, but since then their share has dropped as they have adopted a more cautious stance in the markets, conscious of increasing risks and diminishing returns in the Euromarkets. They have however continued to press on with short-term loans, partly because these are not monitored by the Ministry of Finance in the same way as medium- and long-term loans, and are not subject to the restriction of 20 per cent of net worth for medium- and long-term loans to any one country. Between 1980 and 1982 they were major forces in the London syndicated credit markets.

The broad picture of Japanese foreign assets and liabilities is shown in Table 4.7. The figures show the limited amount of direct investment; the reliance on short-term deposits; and the growth of longer-term lending as against shorter-term lending.

The bulk of Japanese banks' foreign lending has been funded and

Table 4.7: Assets and Liabilities *vis-à-vis* Non-Residents of Japan (US $ million)

	Assets		Liabilities	
	Dec. 1975	Dec. 1979	Dec. 1975	Dec. 1979
Long-term assets/liabilities	32,357	83,663	13,603	36,355
Private sector	24,522	62,141	11,591	27,970
Direct investments	8,322	17,227	2,084	3,422
Trade credits on exports/imports	6,832	10,468	98	38
Loans extended/received	4,984	14,938	1,702	1,815
Securities investments	4,104	19,003	7,695	22,606
Others	280	505	12	89
Government sector	7,835	21,522	2,012	8,385
Trade credits on exports/imports	330	575	—	—
Loans extended/received	5,497	16,574	414	268
External bonds	—	—	509	8,117
Others	2,008	4,373	1,089	0
Short-term assets/liabilities	25,977	51,702	37,713	70,233
Private sector	13,162	31,087	36,395	64,408
Monetary movements	12,947	29,946	26,418	50,208
Others	215	1,141	9,977	14,200
Government sector	12,815	20,615	1,318	5,825
Monetary movements	12,815	20,614	712	3,852
Others	0	1	606	1,973
Total assets/liabilities	58,334	135,365	51,316	106,588

Source: The Ministry of Finance.

made in foreign currencies. Yen loans have been marketed from time to time but their availability has fluctuated according to the Japanese balance of payments position and domestic credit demands on the city banks — the authorities treat all yen lending in the same fashion and apply the same guidelines. With currency lending the banks are freer, since they are dealing in purely off-shore transactions which are funded from overseas deposits. Nevertheless, the Ministry of Finance has intervened to restrict maturity mismatching, to impose a country risk limit, and generally to guide the banks in their approach to the market. Although the market leaders in underwriting and placement activities are the main securities houses, especially the four largest (Nomura, Nikko, Daiwa, Yamaichi), the city banks play an important role in the bond markets too, acting usually through their strategically sited subsidiaries in world financial centres. The banks' overseas subsidiaries act as underwriters and place Japanese and foreign Euro-bonds in both primary and secondary markets. On the Tokyo market the banks act as commissioned banks in the placement of foreign bonds on the so-called Samurai Bond Market.

On the domestic front the Japanese banks have since the late-1960s begun to offer the wider range of financial services characteristic of the universal multinational bank. In order to achieve diversification beyond the core business of banking as defined in the Banking Law, the banks have had to work through the medium of associated and affiliated companies in which they can only have a limited stake. However, because of the strong group ties common in Japanese industry, and because other group companies can also participate as shareholders in affiliated organisations, the degree of cohesion and synergy achieved is greater than might appear on the surface. In this way the banks have been able to extend the range of services to their customers to offer management consultancy services, investment management, credit cards, leasing, factoring, venture capital, housing services and housing-land development, housing finance, consumer credit and credit guarantees, computer systems and software. Besides these 'peripheral' banking services, the Japanese banks also have limited diverse interests in purely commercial undertakings such as oil and energy development, travel agency, business information and so on.

The Japanese banks have proceeded swiftly with the computerisation of their banking operations. On-line branch terminal networks were installed during the late-1960s and early-1970s and since then they have been improved and extended. ATMs were introduced in the mid-1970s and are now heavily used for cash withdrawals in an extremely cash-oriented society. The banks have also recently offered telephone banking services and widened the facilities of ATMs to include payments and transfers and the acceptance of deposits.

Internally the banks have sought to improve their management information systems, and in the future foresee rapid advances in office automation as further steps are taken to improve productivity and customer service.

In organisational terms the Japanese banks have usually adopted a divisional system along classical lines, with a mixture of functional, market-based and geographical divisions. The hierarchy at the senior level is fairly simple, involving one or two executive committees to which divisional heads report and which in turn report directly to the board of directors. As in all things the Japanese banks have been prepared to learn from and make use of

Western practices (e.g. divisionalisation) when they are useful. A simplified typical organogram is shown in Figure 4.3

The Japanese banks have a highly developed sense of social responsibility and take seriously their duty to act as a good corporate citizen and to make contributions to Japan's social and cultural development, as well as its economic growth. Typical activities in this respect have included the endowment of educational institutions, provision of scholarships, funding of hospitals, funding of social welfare projects, and so on. The banks also practise the system of life-time employment and adopt a paternalistic attitude towards their staff.

The figures presented in Table 4.8 show the development of the

Figure 4.3: Structure of Japanese Banking

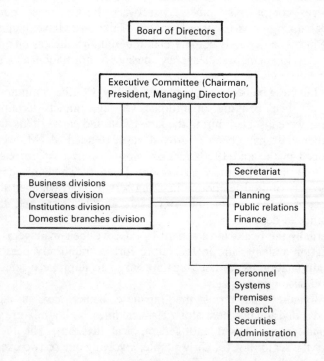

Note: Japanese banks conventionally present their organograms with horizontal lines of communication rather than vertical as above, which is the Western convention. This may reflect the Japanese dislike of overt management hierarchy.

Table 4.8: Development of Major Japanese City Banks, 1971–80
(per cent)

	1971	1980	Growth in advances 1971–80	Growth in deposits 1971–80
Dai-Ichi Kangyo			N/A	N/A
1. Profits/assets	0.8[a]	0.3		
2. Profits/shareholders' funds	16.4[a]	8.2		
3. Shareholders' funds/assets	4.8[a]	3.5		
4. Advances/assets	70.2[a]	59.0		
Fuji			227.4	289.5
1. Profits/assets	1.1	0.2		
2. Profits/shareholders' funds	27.5	8.2		
3. Shareholders funds/assets	4.0	2.5		
4. Advances/assets	66.5	56.5		
Mitsubishi			225.4	287.6
1. Profits/assets	1.0	0.4		
2. Profits/shareholders' funds	27.0	14.7		
3. Shareholders' funds/assets	3.9	2.5		
4. Advances/assets	67.0	57.2		
Sumitomo			232.9	286.5
1. Profits/assets	1.2	0.3		
2. Profits/shareholders' funds	18.7	7.4		
3. Shareholders' funds/assets	6.3	3.6		
4. Advances/assets	66.3	58.7		
Sanwa			224.3	292.5
1. Profits/assets	0.9	0.2		
2. Profits/shareholders' funds	16.2	6.3		
3. Shareholders' funds/assets	5.8	3.5		
4. Advances/assets	67.3	59.4		
Mitsui			241.9	284.8
1. Profits/assets	0.9	0.2		
2. Profits/shareholders' funds	16.9	7.0		
3. Shareholders' funds/assets	5.2	3.4		
4. Advances/assets	67.3	60.3		

Notes: Figures are derived from balance sheets and income statements of parent banks and do not include subsidiaries, although in the case of Japanese banks assets of subsidiaries are not large by comparison with the main bank.

a. 1973 figures. The growth of Dai-Ichi Kangyo over the period has been similar to that of other banks. Dai-Ichi Kangyo was the result of a merger. Earliest available figures are 1973.

Source: Banker Research Unit, *The Top 100* (Financial Times, London, 1981).

major city banks' balance sheets during the 1970s. The rate of growth of deposits and advances has been similar in all cases, since it has been strictly controlled. Deposits have grown more rapidly than advances as the banks have succeeded in normalising their ratio of advances to assets from about 70 per cent to about 60 per cent. The rate of growth over the period is similar to that achieved by the major US banks over the same period, although if the Japanese banks' figures are quoted in US dollars instead of yen they show a much faster rate of growth due to the appreciation of the yen against the dollar in recent years. The performance ratios show that profitability as measured by return on assets and equity has declined over the period, and there is some evidence that the Japanese banks have gone for growth at the expense of profit and have suffered pressure on their lending margins. Capital ratios have fallen significantly, and this is typical of all the major multi-national banks. Care must be taken in any assessment of the Japanese banks' true position, however, because their accounting policies allow for significant hidden reserves in property and other accounts.

It is worth noting that the progress of the Japanese banks has not always been smooth, and that they have encountered bad debt problems. One consequence of the group system is that the house bank may become very heavily committed in support of a large client corporation or a large single project. If the corporation or project fails then the bank may well have to absorb substantial losses. For example, in the early-1970s the large Ataka trading company extended massive trade credits to a Newfoundland oil-refinery for crude-oil purchases. These were unpaid and led to the bankruptcy of Ataka in 1974. In order to save the situation Ataka was merged into C. Itoh, another trading house, and the bad debts were absorbed by the group house banks, Sumitomo and Kyowa, especially Sumitomo which wrote off huge losses against hidden reserves and tax credits. The operation was conducted with full knowledge of the authorities, and foreign unsecured creditors lost nothing in the Ataka crash. Such is the relationship between the city banks and the authorities that foreign banks in effect regard the city banks as sovereign credit risks, since there is thought to be no possibility of the Japanese authorities allowing any of the major banks to fail or to cause loss to foreign creditors.

The Mitsui Bank has recently become heavily involved in support of Mitsui and Co., which has been engaged in constructing a massively expensive refinery in Iran. Mitsui and Co. has extended large supplier credits, although most of these are state-insured through MITI and the Eximbank.

In recent years the Japanese banks have become more heavily involved in syndicated credits to sovereign borrowers, and it is likely that they, like other international banks, will have to take their share of the burdens of rescheduling and bad debt provisions.

4.3 Case Study — Mitsubishi Bank

The Mitsubishi Bank had its origins in the Mitsubishi Exchange Office, established in 1880 to provide for the domestic and later foreign exchange of the Mitsubishi family zaibatsu. In 1895 the office was reorganised as the Banking Department of the Mitsubishi Company, the main trading company at the centre of the zaibatsu. The Banking Department was installed at the zaibatsu headquarters, providing money transmission, exchange and trade finance services. In 1919 the Mitsubishi Bank Ltd was set up in the aftermath of the First World War to take over the banking business of this Department and to offer a comprehensive range of commercial banking services. In the inter-war period the Bank opened a branch in London and agency in New York (1920), and a sub-branch in Dairen (1933).

During the Second World War the Bank was amalgamated with One Hundredth Bank Ltd, and its capital base augmented. It was by now the second largest commercial bank in Japan, with particular strengths in relation to the powerful Mitsubishi group and to manufacturing industry in general. The overseas offices were closed during the War, although in 1944 a sub-branch was opened in Shanghai.

In 1948 the Bank's name was changed to Chiyoda Bank Ltd. The Mitsubishi zaibatsu was dissolved by the special measures taken by the Allied occupation forces but in the early-1950s Mitsubishi group links were re-established through the medium of the Kiyokai (Friday Club) meetings of company executives. In 1953 the Mitsubishi name was resumed and during the 1950s and 1960s the Bank reverted to its role as a key provider of finance to Mitsubishi companies and other Japanese industrial corporations.

The Bank reopened its New York agency in 1952, and set up a London Representative Office in 1953, which became a branch in 1956. In the 1960s the Bank was one of the leaders in the process of internationalisation having acquired a subsidiary in Brazil in 1959 which later became Banco Mitsubishi Brazileiro S.A. in 1973 (80 per cent owned). The history of the Bank's overseas expansion in subsequent years is shown in Table 4.9[8]

Table 4.9: Overseas Expansion of Mitsubishi Bank, 1962–81

1962	Los Angeles agency
1967	Seoul branch
1969	Paris Representative Office
1970	Hong Kong Representative Office Participation in Japan International Bank, London Participation in Australian International Finance Corp., Melbourne
1971	Düsseldorf Representative Office
1972	Chicago Representative Office Mitsubishi Bank of California, Los Angeles (100%) (Commercial Bank) Participation in Libra Bank, London Participation in Thai-Mitsubishi Investment Corp., Bangkok
1973	Singapore branch Jakarta Representative Office São Paulo Representative Office Participation in PT Indonesian Investments International, Jakarta Participation in Liu Chong Hing Bank, Hong Kong
1974	Düsseldorf RO becomes full branch Mitsubishi Bank (Europe) SA, Brussels (100%) (Merchant bank) Participation in Amariah Chase Merchant Bank, Kuala Lumpur
1975	Toronto Representative Office
1976	Sydney Representative Office Mitsubishi Bank of California merged with Hacienda Bank Caracas Representative Office Participation in Ayala Investment and Development Corp., Manila
1977	New York agency becomes full branch Chicago RO becomes full branch Mitsubishi International Finance Ltd, Hong Kong (80%) (Merchant bank)
1978	Tehran Representative Office Houston Representative Office
1979	Mexico City Representative Office
1980	Madrid Representative Office
1981	Frankfurt Representative Office Zurich Representative Office Mitsubishi Bank of California merged with First National Bank of San Diego County Bahrain Representative Office Hong Kong Representative Office becomes full branch

Source: Annual reports.

Evidently the Bank's expansion has been gradual rather than explosive. Reliance was placed in the first instance on participation in joint ventures with leading international banks and/or local banks, and on the activities of representative offices (ROs) and agencies. In the later 1970s several ROs have been upgraded to branches as the importance of their contributions to the Bank has increased and as they have moved towards offering a fuller range of financial services. The Bank has also established key subsidiaries, including a Californian retail bank, a Brazilian bank, a Hong Kong merchant bank, and a European operation. In 1983 further investment in California was undertaken.

At the end of 1981 the Bank had 24 overseas offices — 8 branches, 12 ROs and 4 subsidiaries — spread across North America, Latin America, Europe, the Pacific Basin, and the Middle East. The Bank also had participations in 10 international consortia or local investment companies in 7 countries.

The Bank's confidence in its history and future progress was demonstrated by the opening of impressive new headquarters and head office buildings in Marunouchi, the financial district of Toyko, in 1980 in time to celebrate the centenary of the foundation of the Mitsubishi Exchange Office.

In 1981 the Bank undertook a formal analysis of its overall business and devised a strategy to cope with changing financial markets and the altering economic circumstances in Japan in the wake of two oil shocks:

> The Japanese banking industry is facing the urgent necessity of coping with such rapidly changing market conditions as the diversifying needs of customers, progress in the liberalisation of interest rate systems and foreign exchange transactions, and changing circumstances surrounding securities business. In addition, deposit growth is declining, and the spread between deposit and loan interest rates is narrowing in the recent low growth period in the Japanese economy. (*Annual Report*, 1981.)

The new strategy entailed rationalisation of the existing operating divisions, and their deployment in five major identified markets (see Figure 4.4). Three main operating headquarters have been established to service these markets: National Banking, covering consumer banking, small and medium-sized enterprises, and finan-

Figure 4.4: Mitsubishi Bank — New Organisation

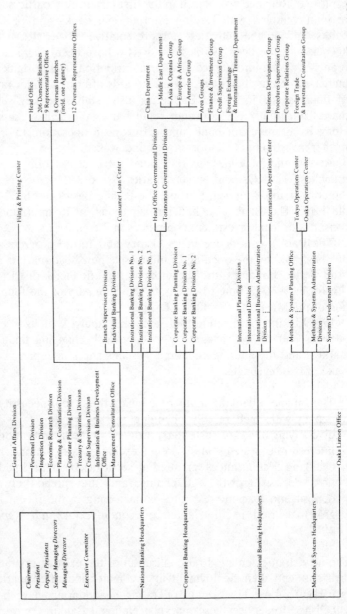

Source: *Annual Report* (1981).

cial/governmental institutions; Corporate Banking, covering large corporations; and International Banking, covering all international business and incorporating a planning division, administration division, banking division and also the Foreign Exchange and International Treasury Department. In addition to`the operating headquarters are the General Affairs Division covering the various support functions such as planning, research, personnel, inspection, credit analysis and so on, and Methods and Systems, responsible for the Tokyo and Osaka operations centres and for systems administration and development. The Bank has not pushed as far with market segmentation as some of the US banks, but it has basically shaped its organisation to fit the profile of its existing and desired customer base. In strategic terms, there is a new emphasis on the consumer and middle markets serviced through the domestic branch network of over 200 branches as key markets for the 1980s.

Besides its extensive branch network, the Bank also has interests in 21 regional banks, with participations ranging from 1.1 to 7.2 per cent, and interests in five mutual finance and savings banks, with participations ranging from 2 to 8 per cent.

The Bank occupies an important position within the Mitsubishi Group. Corporations with significant shareholdings in the Bank include the following major corporations:

	% Stake (1981)
Meiji Life	5.95
Tokyo Marine and Fire Insurance	4.7
Dai-Ichi Life Insurance	3.92
Mitsubishi Heavy Industries Ltd.	3.46
Nippon Life Insurance	3.29
Mitsubishi Corporation	2.20
Asahi Glass	1.81
Taiyo Life Insurance	1.78
Nippon Steel Corporation	1.77
Mitsubishi Electric Company	1.46

(Source: IBCA Banking Analysis.)

Many of these are merely institutional investors but there are evidently some group members with significant stakes. The involvement of the Bank with the group is more evident in its lending to large corporations, including the following:

	% of Bank equity lent (1981)
Mitsubishi Oil Company	21.2
Mitsubishi Corporation	17.9
Mitsubishi Heavy Industries Ltd	17.5
Nippon Steel Corporation	15.5
Mitsui and Company	14.2
Marubeni Corporation	13.2
Tokyo Electric Power Company Ltd	11.1
Mitsubishi Petrochemical Co. Ltd	10.6
Mitsubishi Chemical Co. Ltd	9.2
Mitsubishi Real Estate Co. Ltd	8.9
Mitsubishi Electric Co. Ltd	8.7
Nippon Kokon K K	7.6

(Source: IBCA Banking Analysis.)

The accounts published by Japanese banks do not permit a detailed analysis of spreads and margins. In fact, the aggregate figures for the city banks published by the Bank of Japan show more detail than the banks' individual annual reports. Since the profile of all the city banks is fairly similar this is not too grave a disadvantage, and we have used these figures.

Table 4.10 shows the sources of deposits of the City banks. It shows the heavy reliance on time deposits. The Japanese banks also rely on call money and bills but have not issued intermediate term debt or commercial paper. They still raise only a relatively small amount by means of CDs, although this is continually increasing. About one quarter of total deposits are in foreign currencies raised mainly through overseas branches especially in London and New York, and principally in US dollars.

Table 4.11 shows the heavily loaned position of the banks. It also shows the significant amounts of government bonds they have recently accumulated. Table 4.12 shows the breadown of lending by industry, stressing the importance of manufacturing and whole-sale/retail trade.

It is now possible to look a little more closely at the current operations of the Bank in order to assess strategic developments. In its overseas markets the Bank has been eager to participate in international banking markets, especially in view of the relaxed controls on foreign exchange enabling conversion of foreign currency funds to yen funds. The Bank has participated in many

Table 4.10: Japanese City Banks: Liabilities by Type of Source, November 1980 (yen 00,000 millions)

	Yen	%		Yen	%
Deposits					
Current	82	7.4	Private	746	87.8
Ordinary	109	9.9	Public	20	2.4
Notice	67	6.1	Financial	69	8.0
Special	18	1.6	Institutions		
Tax payment	1	—	Others (residual)	15	1.8
Time	505	45.7			
Instalment	—				
Free yen and foreign currency	68	6.2			
Sub-total	850	76.9		850	100.0
Certificates of deposit	11	1.0			
Bank debentures	14	1.3			
Call money	50	4.5			
Bills sold	38	3.4			
Borrowed money	14	1.3			
Foreign exchange	11	1.0			
Domestic exchange, etc.	20	1.8			
Other liabilities[a]	33	3.0			
Sub-total	191	17.3			
Loan loss reserves	9	0.8			
Reserves for retirement allowances	5	0.4			
Other reserves	2	0.2			
Sub-total	16	1.4			
Capital and reserves	48	4.4			
Total[b]	1,105	100.0			

Notes: Free yen deposits are now reclassified as yen deposits of non-residents.

a. Including borrowings from Overseas Banks' Credit and US Eximbank. b. Excluding acceptances and guarantees of 102.

Source: Bank of Japan.

major syndicated credits, and has begun to establish its position as a lead manager, managing twelve syndications in 1980. It has rapidly expanded its Eurocurrency lending to governments, government agencies and multinational corporations, and has also been involved in project financing of natural resources and manufacturing developments, and in making loans to Japanese firms investing abroad. These activities are in addition to its staple business of trade-related financing. In an effort to improve its

Table 4.11: Japanese City Banks: Assets by Category, November 1980 (yen 00.000 millions)

	¥	%
Cash	6	0.5
Cheques/bills	74	6.8
Deposits	25	2.3
Sub-total	105	9.6
Call money	18	1.6
SECURITIES		
Government bonds	64	5.9
Local government bonds	21	1.9
Public corporation bonds	17	1.6
Bank debentures	14	1.3
Industrial bonds	8	0.7
Stocks and shares	36	3.3
Foreign securities	6	0.5
Others	1	0.1
Sub-total	167	15.3
LOANS AND DISCOUNTS[a]		
Bills discounted	156	14.2
Loans on bills	298	27.3
Loans on deeds	23	21.5
Overdrafts	13	1.2
Sub-total	702	64.3
FOREIGN EXCHANGE		
Deposits with banks	6	0.5
Foreign exchange bought	23	2.2
Bills	28	2.6
Sub-total	58	5.3
Domestic exchange	18	1.6
Other assets	7	0.6
Fixed assets	16	1.5
Sub-total	41	3.8
Total	1,091	100.0

Notes: a. In 1980 Mitsubishi Bank made loans of ¥ 8,016 billion, of which ¥ 3,544 billion were to small and medium-sized enterprises, ¥ 641 billion for housing loans and ¥ 41 billion for consumer credit (*Annual Report*, 1980).

Source: Bank of Japan.

mismatch position the Bank has began to issue floating rate CDs of five-year maturity.

The Bank has been engaged in underwriting operations in the buoyant Eurobond markets, especially for large Japanese corporations issuing US dollar convertible bonds, but also for foreign

Table 4.12: Japanese City Banks: Loans and Discounts Outstanding and New Loans for Equipment Funds, by Industry, November 1980 (yen trillions) (00,000 millions)

	Outstanding		To small enterprises		New equipment loans, November 1980	
	¥	%	¥	%	¥	%
Manufacturing	227	32.9	80	35.1	0.682	19.5
Construction	38	5.5	18	7.9	0.52	1.5
Wholesale/retail trade	191	27.7	70	30.7	0.496	14.2
Real estate	33	4.8	29	12.7	0.191	5.4
Transport/ communications	20	2.9	7	3.1	0.517	14.8
Utilities	14	2.0	1	0.4	0.178	5.1
Services	43	6.2	23	10.1	0.439	12.5
Local government	5	0.7	—	—	0.18	0.5
Personal funds	78	11.3	—	—	0.841	24.0
Others (residual)	40	6.0	N/A		0.91	2.6
Total	689	100.0	228	100.0	3.505	100.0

Source: Bank of Japan.

enterprises. In the secondary market the Bank has been active in underwriting and issuing floating rate notes (FRNs), CDs and other securities. The Bank is the market leader in placements of yen bonds on the Tokyo market (Samurai bonds). By the end of 1980 it had acted as commissioned bank in 37 out of 100 issues made to date.

The Bank also engages in substantial foreign exchange transactions, and services the needs of foreign enterprises in Japan by providing assistance, advice and introductions as well as yen finance. The Bank is an important Japanese correspondent bank with over 1,000 correspondent links, and has been a member of SWIFT since its inception in Japan in 1981.

The Bank also engages in consultancy work in various areas, including the Japanese business and economy, project financing, overseas investment, export and import finance, foreign exchange, and so on.

In its domestic markets it has devoted more attention to the middle market, in spite of the difficulties of smaller firms in the recession, offering for example management consultancy services on business planning, budgeting and marketing. The Bank is also paying attention to the consumer market, where it had 10.7 million accounts in 1981, providiing 40 per cent of all domestic deposits for the Bank. It has introduced new annuity-type savings plans, and a variety of consumer and housing loans. The branch network is being gradually expanded, and the Bank has installed large numbers of multi-function ATMs. It has also introduced a telephone banking service where computers are programmed to recognise the customers' voice and respond to balance enquiries and other requests.

The Bank has entered the usual range of peripheral services through a number of affiliates under the 'Diamond' name (a diamond is the Mitsubishi group symbol) — Diamond Lease Co. Ltd, Diamond Computer Service Co. Ltd, Diamond Factors Ltd, Diamond Credit Co. Ltd (Credit Cards), and Diamond Seminar Ltd (Conferences). Its social responsibility policy has found expression in the establishment of the Mitsubishi Foundation in 1969. The Bank has identified six areas where it can help improve the quality of life, apart from its basic role of providing customer service and promoting economic development: participation in local events; conservation; education and culture; welfare projects; aid for the disabled; and cooperation with public bodies. The Bank contributes towards the Toyo Bunko centre for oriental studies, the Seika-do Museum, a Blood Donor Society, and it has established a sports centre. The Bank also makes special arrangements to employ disabled persons.

The Mitsubishi Trust and Banking Corporation is the largest trust bank in Japan. It was established as the Mitsubishi Trust Co. in 1927 to provide for the investment management needs of the Mitsubishi group of companies and families. After the Second World War it changed its name briefly to the Asahi Trust Bank, but in 1952 re-emerged as the Mitsubishi Trust Bank.

Like all Japanese trust banks it now provides a range of commercial banking services as well as trust banking, and also short-term as well as long-term lending. It has 52 branches in Japan and is a powerful force in the domestic savings market. It has also developed its international business and has overseas branches in New York, London, Los Angeles, and Panama, and representative offices in Hong Kong, Mexico, Singapore and Sydney.

The formal links between the trust and commercial banks are proscribed by law, but the trust bank is an important member of the Mitsubishi group.

Notes

1. By law a bank can only hold up to 5 per cent of a company's equity. This was reduced from 10 per cent in 1977, but banks were given a ten-year grace period to comply with the regulation. (Monopoly and Fair Trade Law 1947, amended in 1977.) Banks may not establish holding companies.

2. For details see Prindl (1981), pp. 59–60.

3. Federation of Bankers Association of Japan (1982), p. 26.

4. The Bank of Japan sets ceiling rates for various types of deposit. The commercial banks are free to set their rates within the guidelines, but in practice rates usually coincide with the upper limits of the guidelines. In setting guidelines, the Bank of Japan recognises the banks' legitimate profit needs, but also takes into account the banks' social responsibility and role in economic development, and the needs of small savers.

5. Much of the demand has been met by the loan companies (sarakin) who historically charged extremely high rates of interest. In the late-1970s US consumer finance operations such as Household Finance and Beneficial Financial have been permitted to establish branches, partly in order to stimulate competition among the banks.

6. The opening of branches and representative offices is controlled by the Ministry of Finance which now allows one full branch per bank every two years.

7. See, for example, the *Bank of England Quarterly Bulletin*, Tables 13 and 14, for their position in the London Euromarket.

8. An inside view on the internationalisation of Japanese banking was given by Kuranosuke Saito of Fuji Bank in 1972:

> Although the Japanese banks were late in enlarging their international activities, they have displayed an extraordinary eagerness for overseas expansion in the last 2 years. This development was facilitated by a certain relaxation of the restrictions that the authorities had placed on the overseas business of the Japanese banks. As a result of this policy change, conditions became favourable for global financial activities and the Japanese banks vied with one another in the establishment of overseas branches, the opening of representative offices and the foundation of a participation in international finance and investment companies. The main emphasis was on strengthening the network of branches or representative offices in the US, Europe and Asia and on the establishment of international finance and investment companies for development projects in Australia and Latin America ... the Japanese banks are clearly trailing the banks of the other advanced nations.
>
> At least partially responsible for this lag was the failure of the banks to perceive the necessity of adapting their foreign operations to the shift in emphasis from the foreign exchange business and the financing of foreign trade to capital transactions or bank-related activities such as consulting ... While the mobilisation of funds on a global scale will remain an important aspect of the internationalisation of banking, creative solutions to old and new problems will be the key to success in international banking. (Kuranosuke Saito, 'Banking Strategy in the Era of Internationalisation', *Fuji Bank Bulletin*, March 1972.)

Mitsubishi's view is similar:

> The expansion of our overseas network, however, has been accelerated since the beginning of the 1970s right along with the rapid development of international capital markets. In an effort to raise and manage funds efficiently and profitably in the most attractive markets and to meet the diversifying needs

of clients for global financial services, we have established a cohesive branch network, covering all business centres and organised subsidiaries in areas with good commercial and trade prospects. (*Annual Report*, 1981.)

References

Adams, T.F.M. and Hoshii, *A Financial History of the New Japan* (Kodansha International Ltd, Tokyo, 1972).

Bank of Japan, *Japanese Financial System* (Bank of Japan, Tokyo, 1978).

Elston, C.D., 'The Financing of Japanese Industry' (*Bank of England Quarterly Bulletin*, December 1981).

Federation of Bankers Associations of Japan, *Banking System in Japan* (Federation of Bankers Association of Japan, Tokyo, 1982).

Peat, Marwick, Mitchell & Co., *Banking in Japan* (Peat, Marwick, Mitchell & Co., Tokyo, 1982)

Prindl, A.R., *Japanese Finance* (Wiley, Chichester, 1981).

Vittas, D. (ed.) for Interbank Research Organisation, *Banking Systems Abroad* (London, Committee of London Clearing Bankers, 1978), ch. 8, 'Japan'.

Weston, R. *Domestic and Multinational Banking* (Croom Helm, London, 1980), Part 2, ch. 14, 'Banking Controls in Japan'.

Yonemura, T. for Banker Research Unit, *Japanese Banking* (Financial Times Business Publishing Ltd, London, 1981).

Data Sources

Annual Reports of City Banks.

Banker Research Unit, *The Top 100*, (Financial Times Publishing, London, 1981).

Bank of Japan, Monthly Economic Statistics.

5 BRITISH BANKS

5.1 Financial System

The British system is one of the least regulated systems in the developed countries. However, the high level of concentration in the banking industry and the historical influence of the Bank of England in the London money markets mean that it is in fact a quite tightly controlled system. Acting through the twelve discount houses and the clearing banks the Bank of England is able to assert its will to a considerable extent. On the other hand, the authorities have always recognised the legitimate freedoms of commercial banks and positively encouraged the actvities of UK and foreign banks in London, whether operating in domestic or international markets.

The Bank of England was founded in 1694 but was constituted in its present nationalised form in 1946 (Bank of England Act). Its main functions are typical of those of a central bank. It acts as banker to the government and has direct responsibility for maintenance of the currency and execution of monetary policy. The Bank is under the formal direction of the Treasury but in practice has a considerable degree of autonomy and much influence on policy-making. In operational matters it has complete autonomy, and intervenes virtually at will in capital, money and foreign exchange markets.

It maintains accounts for government departments and arranges short-term finance through the issue of Treasury bills, and long-term finance through the issue of government stock. It advises the government on stock issues and undertakes all administrative work. It administers Exchange Controls in force from time to time, and operates the Exchange Equalisation Account which holds the country's reserves of foreign currency.

The Bank also acts as a bankers' bank, providing settlement accounts and acting to ensure that daily liquidity needs of banks can be financed in the markets, by offsetting unusual cash flows.

The Bank attempts to ensure the continuing health of the UK system and of individual banks in a number of ways. Prior to 1979 there was no specific banking law in the UK. Banks were treated as

255

any other commercial company (although they were able to choose not to disclose profits) and informally guided by the Bank of England. However, the Banking Act of 1979 made statutory provisions. It firstly defined two classes of financial institution — recognised banks, and licensed deposit takers. Recognised banks must provide a full range of banking services, or maintain a particular specialisation (eg, discount houses) and fulfil certain other criteria — minimum net assets, suitable directors, high reputation. These banks may call themselves banks and advertise banking services, and take public deposits. Licensed deposit takers require a licence in order to accept public deposits, and still may not call themselves banks. They need not provide any specified services, but must have certain net assets, suitable directors and a good reputation. No other institution may accept public deposits, except for certain institutions operating under separate legislation, namely the building societies, the Trustee Savings Banks, the National Savings Bank and National Girobank, and Credit Unions.

The Bank has power to issue and revoke licences, to supervise and investigate institutions, and to wind them up if necessary. The Act also provided for the establishment of a Deposit Protection Fund to protect smaller deposits of banks and licensed deposit takers.

In formulating the Act the Bank had regard to the larger number of foreign banks operating in London, and they have been required to comply and seek recognition as banks or to obtain a licence.

The Bank has supervisory responsibility for all recognised banks and licensed deposit takers, although in the case of foreign banks it may rely on the supervision undertaken by the parent bank authorities. Indigenous banks are now increasingly closely monitored in certain key areas:

1. Capital adequacy — gearing ratios (adjusted capital base to deposits), and risk asset ratios (adjusted capital base to weighted risk assets).
2. Liquidity adequacy — mismatching of maturities, and management policies to maintain sufficient liquidity.
3. Foreign currency exposure — open positions in aggregate and in individual currencies.

The Bank also has responsibility for monetary and credit controls. Methods of monetary control were recently revised and new provisions came into force in 1981, with the aim of allowing market forces to work freely wherever possible, but at the same time to enable the Bank to influence them when necessary. The steps taken were:

1. Redefinition of the monetary sector as per Banking Act 1979 (see above).
2. Interest rates in wholesale markets to be maintained within four unpublished bands via dealings in bills with the discount houses. The Chancellor of the Exchequer must approve changes in bands.
3. In order to establish the necessary depth and breadth of bill market, the Bank extended the list of banks whose bills are eligible for discount at the Bank to include many foreign banks. Each bank with eligible status must however agree to maintain a certain percentage (now 5 per cent) of its eligible liabilities with discount houses, money brokers or gilt jobbers on average, and a daily minimum percentage of its eligible liabilities with discount houses.
4. Monetary sector institutions are required to keep ½ per cent of their eligible liabilities in non-interest earning balances at the Bank. In addition, the London Clearing Banks maintain ordinary current accounts for settlement purposes, which may not go overdrawn. These balances are the Banks' fulcrum for day-by-day management of cash flows in the money markets. The Bank may also call for Special Deposits to be placed with it by the monetary sector from time to time, if it wishes to withdraw cash from the money market.

The Bank is thus able to control short-term interest rates quite closely through operations in the bill market. It can also influence long-term rates through operations in the gilt market. It can make bank liquidity easy or tight in the sterling markets. In the currency markets, however, the Bank has little control. It does monitor foreign currency exposure of supervised banks, and in conjunction with the Bank for International Settlements, the Federal Reserve Board and other central banks, it attempts to monitor the Euromarkets in terms of size and maturity mismatchings. However, it has no control over Euromarket rates or Euromarket liquidity.

The *discount houses* are a unique feature of the British system and they cooperate closely with the central bank and the commercial banks. They make a market in secured call deposits, taking surplus liquid funds from the banks and using them to purchase bills, gilts and other money market instruments. There are only twelve houses and they are carefully supervised by the Bank. The houses have an important function in purchasing every week the total Treasury bill issue, and dealing in short-dated gilts and other stocks. It is here that the Bank and discount houses between them effectively determine short-term money market rates. The houses now also deal in the unsecured parallel money markets (interbank, local authority, CDs).

The *clearing banks* comprise the Big Four London clearing banks (Barclays, Lloyds, Midland, National Westminster), Coutts & Co (a NatWest subsidiary), Williams & Glyn's (a subsidiary of the Royal Bank of Scotland), the Scottish clearing banks and Northern Ireland Banks. The Cooperative Bank, Central Trustee Savings Bank and National Girobank are now also participants in the London Clearing which is the national settlement system.

The London clearers have nationwide networks comprising over 13,000 branches altogether. They are parent banks of financial service groups which offer universal banking facilities in the UK and also have significant international operations. As commercial banks, clearers have traditionally maintained 'arm's-length' relationships with business customers and have not taken participations in industry. They do now, however, engage in a substantial volume of medium-term lending to industry, and have merchant bank subsidiaries and equity investment arms.

In their domestic operations the clearers take retail and wholesale deposits, provide money transmission services, lend to personal and business customers and provide related banking services, usually through subsidiaries — finance houses offering commercial credit services, registrars, insurance broking, unit trusts, computer payroll services, credit cards and so on. In their international operations the clearers maintain overseas branches, own foreign subsidiaries, and engage in international financing from London and also other financial centres.

The clearers have foundations in eighteenth-century banking firms but a long history of mergers has produced the present high level of concentration in the industry. The last important merger occurred in 1968 when National Provincial and Westminster combined to form National Westminster Bank. Subsequent planned mergers or takeovers have been prevented by the authorities via the Monopolies Commission on the grounds that they would be against the public interest.

The *Cooperative Bank* is a subsidiary of the Cooperative Wholesale Society and part of the Cooperative movement in Britain. It has a network of about 70 branches and also offers banking services through the medium of Cooperative Retail Society supermarkets. It offers a full range of banking services in the UK and is expanding its international capabilities. The bank has strong links with the trades unions and with local authorities, but in most respects operates as a commercial bank.

The *Trustee Savings Banks* grew up as thrift institutions for working people in the nineteenth century. Regional banks were managed by unpaid trustees and invested deposits in government securities. However, they have gradually extended their range of services and are now in the process of transforming themselves into fully-fledged commercial banks with a public flotation in the near future. They already offer a full range of financial services to personal customers through an extensive branch network of 1,650 branches (all regions combined) and are starting to enter the business sector with commercial lending services. They have already acquired a finance house subsidiary.

The *National Savings Bank* was established in the nineteenth century (Post Office Savings Bank) and now offers savings accounts through the medium of the Post Office network of over 20,000 branches. The *National Girobank* is also part of the Post Office. It was established in 1968 to provide basic banking services through the Post Office network, but is now expanding its range of services to personal customers to cover personal loans, foreign services and so on, and has begun to offer business accounts. It is financially independent of the Post Office and part of the officially defined monetary sector.

The *merchant banks* are a small group of wholesale banks who had their origins in nineteenth-century merchant houses which undertook acceptance business. The 16 leading banks form the Accepting Houses Committee. They have expanded from this base to open a few provincial branches in industrial centres, and one of their specialisations is corporate finance, advisory services and issuing house facilities. In domestic markets they also provide investment management services. The merchant banks also have equity participation arms. They have substantial skill and expertise in international banking, operating in the Eurocredit and Eurobond markets, and offering trade finance services. Some banks are now parts of groups offering a wider range of financial services including commercial credit services, insurance and insurance broking, property development, and so on.

Finance houses provide commercial credit services to business customers (leasing, hire purchase, dealer finance, factoring) and consumer credit services. They take some public deposits but are basically funded from the money markets. Their most important market is vehicle finance. The 43 members of the Finance House Association account for 80 per cent of total business and the leading houses are all subsidiaries of large deposit banks.

Foreign banks are a powerful force in the UK financial system. There are over 400 foreign banks in London, mainly engaged in international banking. However, several US and Canadian banks have set up retail banking operations, and major international banks compete with indigenous banks in the provision of lending and related services to the corporate market. Some have established provincial offices in industrial centres for this purpose.

Building societies are not banks and are governed by separate legislation, namely the Building Societies Act 1962; and they are supervised by the Registrar of Friendly Societies. The societies are specialised, offering only deposit accounts and mortgage advances, viz. secured property finance. In the retail deposits market and housing finance markets they are more powerful than the banks and are market leaders on interest rates in those sectors. There is a number of large societies with branch networks of about 500, and a large number of smaller regional and local societies. The industry is, however, becoming increasingly concentrated as mergers take place. It is also possible that in the near future the societies will significantly expand the range of their services and develop as savings banks. Already several societies have combined with banks to offer chequing facilities and/or credit cards, and other financial services. At present building society depositors and borrowers receive tax benefits.

The government is an important financial intermediary, not only in the money markets through the issue of Treasury bills, but in the savings and investment markets. The National Savings Department offers various savings schemes which compete with those of banks and building societies. The goverment also sells bonds to banks and non-banks and there is a massive market in goverment gilt-edged stock.

Insurance companies are big collectors of funds through life policy premiums and general insurance premiums. *Pension funds* in the UK are large investment funds. These institutions have a dominant influence in the UK capital markets. Contractual savings through the media of life insurance and pension schemes carry signficant tax benefits for investors.

5.2 Strategic Development of Multinational Banks

Many British banks have a long tradition of international banking because of the previous importance of sterling in world trade and finance, the extensive activities of UK exporters and importers, colonial and Commonwealth links, and the importance of London as a banking centre.

However only a few of the largest banking groups have attempted to establish the sort of presence in world markets which is the hallmark of the multinational bank. These include the Big Four London clearing banks, and the overseas bank Standard Chartered Bank. Other smaller groups with significant international business are Royal Bank of Scotland Group (which includes the clearing bank Williams & Glyn's) and Grindlays, an overseas bank. Some merchant banks also have substantial international business and a few overseas offices.

Hong Kong and Shanghai Banking Corporation is not in fact a British bank. Its shares are issued in Hong Kong dollars and its head office is in Hong Kong where it has the status of central bank and note issuer for the Crown colony, working in close collaboration with the Ministry of Finance. However, its shares are quoted in London, it has many British staff and Hong Kong is closely tied to Britain, although maintaining a considerable degree of independence. The Bank also owns a London discount house, a small British overseas bank (British Bank of Middle East) and has various Channel Isles subsidiaries. It was prevented from further expanding its presence in the UK when both it and Standard Chartered were debarred from acquiring Royal Bank of Scotland Group.

These overseas banks are of course a legacy from the time of British colonial power. Standard Chartered is a merger between Standard Bank with substantial interests in Africa, and Chartered Bank with substantial interests in the Far East. Grindlays has interests in India and the Far East. Both Barclays and Lloyds have based their international operations on the foundations of traditional overseas banking organisations: Barclays Bank International, formerly Dominions, Colonies, Overseas (DCO), has interests in Africa; and Lloyds Bank International, formerly British Overseas Latin and South America (Bolsa), has interests in Latin America.

Since the late-1960s the British banks have also developed their international business in the Euromarkets, where they have the advantage of the London location, and in selected strategic foreign markets by opening foreign offices and acquiring foreign interests. Midland and National Westminster have had to start this operation virtually from scratch by building up in-house capabilities and by pursuing a strategy of acquisitions, although NatWest was able to build on the strength of International Westminster Bank in Europe and London.

All the British banks have attempted to establish a strong presence in the USA and have been major investors. Barclays made an early acquisition of a Californian bank, a policy imitated by Lloyds. Since then the other banks have made acquisitions and expanded their network of own branches. The subsidiaries owned by the major banks are:

Barclays:	Barclays Bank of California
	Barclays Bank of New York
	Barclays American Corporation
Lloyds:	Lloyds Bank California
Midland:	Crocker National
National Westminster:	National Bank of N. America (now
	National Westminster Bank USA)
Hong Kong & Shanghai:	Marine Midland

Both Barclays and National Westminster have now issued US dollar loan stocks on the US markets, requiring registration with the Securities and Exchange Commission (SEC) and Midland has now registered to do so. British banks have also opened offices in major financial centres in Europe, the Far East, and other important locations.

In their international business the British banks provide a full range of services, and with their London base have particular strength in the interbank markets. They are probably weakest in the Eurobond markets, since there is no significant sterling market. This weakness also reflects the clearers' limited role as merchant/

investment bankers for historical reasons. They are now expanding the activities of their various merchant banking subsidiaries and finance houses. The 1981 position is shown in Table 5.1.

In their first phase of development there were two main types of structural change — firstly interbank mergers and acquisitions, and secondly bank acquisition of related service subsidiaries. In a review of the banks' policy of 'expansion through subsidiaries and participation' in 1968 the then Chairman of the Midland Group Sir A. Forbes distinguished three methods of diversification employed by the Bank in the past: *the merger*, joining forces with an established organisation, as for example with Midland's merger with Clydesdale Bank and Northern Bank; *the establishment of an entirely new company* as a subsidiary, as for example Barclays did with Barclaycard (although using a licensed product, VISA); and *participation as a minority interest*, as Midland did with Standard Bank and Montagu Trust (although it has since divested). To these we might add outright acquisition of an established company, as with Midland's purchases of Forward Trust; and participation in consortium and clubs as with Midland and International Banks and EBIC. We shall see the various banks experimenting with all these methods in their pursuit of strategic aims.

The period to 1968 (when the Monopolies Commission prohibited the proposed Barclays-Lloyds-Martin's merger as against the public interest, since it would probably force Midland and Nat West to merge and thus leave a two-bank system), saw the present 'big four' pattern established, with the National Commercial Group (now the Royal Bank of Scotland Group) running alongside. In 1968 the National Westminster Group was formed out of National Provincial, District and Westminster to take its present form;

Table 5.1: UK Multinational Banks: Subsidiaries and Affiliates, 1981

	Domestic Subsidiaries	Domestic affiliates	International subsidiaries	International affiliates
Barclays	13	7	23	17
Lloyds	12	7	16	6
Midland	9	10	9	10
National Westminster	12	8	5	6
Standard Chartered	8	1	27	12
Hong Kong and Shanghai	26	—	41	11

Barclays failed to acquire Lloyds but took Martin's Bank and reached its present form; Lloyds and Midland maintained their independent growth; National and Commercial was formed from Royal Bank of Scotland and National Commercial Bank of Scotland, a further rationalisation taking place in 1970 on the creation of Williams & Glyn's out of Glyn Mills and Williams Deacon's.

The competitive balance between the five groups now seems fairly stable, and indeed the takeover of Royal Bank of Scotland by either Standard Chartered or Hong Kong and Shanghai was recently prevented by the Monopolies Commission. Each group has certain strengths, and unless the deepening recession puts excessive pressure on profit margins, or one group gains a major advantage in the new technologies, it seems likely that these five groups will continue to dominate the market for the foreseeable future. Whether the money shop chains operated by Citibank and others will establish a significant competitive presence remains to be seen. Threats are also posed by the Girobank, the Co-op bank, the Trustee Savings Banks and the building societies if they move into providing banking current account services.

During this first phase of development a process of concentration took place, as it did in many sectors of British industry. A similar concentration has also taken place in the insurance industry, and to a lesser extent amongst the building societies, although in both these industries it has proved possible for smaller retail companies to remain viable than in banking. Generally, however, the advantages of concentration for financial institutions are overwhelming in terms of increased capital strength, of standardisation of equipment and procedures, of corporate planning, training, promotion and advertising, and of group synergy. This is not to deny that there are possible disadvantages in size, in terms of maintaining close customer relations, of management control and staff motivation, of dysfunctional rivalries between departments or group companies. The LCB groups benefit here from the traditional branch system, with local managers given a fair degree of independence and discretion and encouraged to represent the bank in local affairs. However, a fully decentralised branch network is costly to run and modifications to the traditional structure will take place in future.

A process of diversification also took place. Sir A. Forbes referred to Midland's policy of *Diversification through Specialisation*, to be achieved through acquisitions, mergers, and so on.

There were two main types of diversification in this period — in banking services, and in so-called related services. Diversification of banking services came through such means as Personal Loans, launched in 1958, the Bank Giro Credit System (1960), and cheque cards, introduced in 1965. Related services expanded far more quickly. In 1958 most of the clearers made substantial investments in the finance house sector (eg, Midland and Forward Trust, National Provincial and North Central Wagon). In 1964 the clearers introduced industrial leasing facilities, mainly through their finance house subsidiaries. Later they were able to introduce factoring by the same route. In 1966 in-house Unit Trusts were established by clearing banks, new companies being set up for the purpose. In that year Barclays also introduced the Barclaycard scheme, a move to which the other banks finally responded in 1972 when Access was established.

An important strategic move was made when the clearers established subsidiaries or departments to deal in the newer money markets, thus enabling the banks quickly to mobilise wholesale deposits, a prerequisite of liability management techniques which were to become a feature of banking in the 1970s.

On the international front Lloyds acquired National Bank of New Zealand, thus expanding its overseas interests; while Midland Bank took part in the MAIBL consortium and EBIC club, pursuing its different foreign policy of association rather than acquisition. Barclays and NatWest banks made no international moves in this period, although the final links and mergers with Scottish and Northern Ireland banks were of course achieved.

One of the most significant changes in this period was computerisation and automation on an unprecedented scale. This had little effect on the banks' structure, since the computer networks were fitted to the branch networks, but it was another factor in favour of concentration and centralisation. The main computer centres were built in 1961 and the magnetic character method of reading cheques developed. Branch terminals were common by 1968 and the present semi-automated clearing system was well established.

The banks' development in the 1960s was fairly leisurely — a mixture of opportunism and defensive reaction, typified by the move into the finance house areas of business by acquiring subsidiaries, thus at once securing a large share of the profits and choking off any competitive threat to the banks' own lending business. In the next period the pace of change increased enormously; economic pressures increase; and the international markets and international competition become far more important, as they do for the UK economy as a whole.

In 1976 the *Chairman of Barclays* reviewed group changes over the previous five years and said:

> Until [1971] it would have been right for our stockholders to regard us as a major clearing bank with substantial investment overseas. During the last five years, however, we have assumed the role of an international bank, trading in some 70 countries, but still relying on our Clearing Bank as the mainstay of the Group.

In 1977 the *Chairman of Lloyds* discussed group development under his predecessor where:

> a coherent policy of international development was begun ... where our retail banking in the UK is going through a relatively less profitable phase, increased international earnings are there to take the strain.

In 1977 the *Chairman of Midland* referred to:

> advantages we are gaining from being a group which provides a wide range of financial services in an increasing number of world markets ... benefits of various acquisitions which took place in the early 1970s ... (eg) travel ... merchant banking ... insurance.

In 1978 the *Chairman of National Westminster* said it was:

> ten years since we defined the strategy to develop National Westminster as a diversified international banking organisation.

This last remark is of particular interest as it shows how the creation of the NatWest coalition led to a major review of bank policy and a redefinition of strategy. The same opportunity arose on a smaller scale when Williams & Glyn's was created; and it is reasonable to assume that after the failure of their merger plans in 1968 both Barclays and Lloyds must have reconsidered their strategies.

The evidence suggests that the banks' major strategic decisions were made before the introduction of Competition and Credit Control in 1971 and that these increases merely enabled the banks to pursue with greater freedom the policies they had already adopted.

This period also saw the steady growth of Euromarkets and the emergence of London as the major centre. Undoubtedly there was a simple defensive reaction on the part of the LCB groups — in order to compete in these new and profitable markets they had to develop their international business. The most powerful competitive stimulus came from the US banks, who were making important competitive inroads into the UK domestic corporate lending market, and it is in this area that the LCB groups made their other major thrust during the period — building up their term lending and making greater efforts to match their corporate customers' needs.

The American banks also provided excellent models of corporate structure and strategy. The most progressive US banks had for some years been practising the new business techniques of corporate planning, management by objectives, marketing and business development — and some of the beneficial results were revealed as they worked the Eurocurrency markets and took corporate business away from competitors. In this period the LCB groups began to match themselves against the major US banks and adopt some of the same management techniques. In developing an international strategy Lloyds and Barclays had the advantage of already owning substantial overseas interests. Barclays created Barclays Bank International (BBI) from Barclays DCO in 1972, while in 1971 Lloyds first acquired full ownership of Lloyds and Bolsa and then in 1973 created Lloyds Bank International (LBI) which became responsible for most of the group's international business (but the domestic bank retained its overseas branches). By 1973 both Barclays and Lloyds were involved in negotiations for the acquisition of branch networks in the USA and these acquisitions were completed in 1974, giving both banks a wide spread of overseas business.

The Midland adopted a different international strategy, concentrating on its existing correspondent network and maintaining its involvement in consortia and clubs. Barclays has also taken part in consortia but Lloyds has followed a policy of non-participation in this area. Midland also in 1972 acquired the Bland Payne international insurance broking firm, and an interest in Chartered Bank, but these were sold in 1979. Midland has never created a separate international bank, running its international business through an internal division.

NatWest was able to develop the old business of Westminster Foreign Bank with branches in Europe (now named International Westminster) and has expanded its international business by opening branches and representative offices.

Competition and Credit Control did give the banks some form of the freedom they required to expand their lending to industry as they were able to increase their advances/deposits ratios and practise liability management. Barclays set up Barclays Merchant Bank in 1971 to give a full presence in merchant banking activities; and in 1973 established its business advisory service to offer consultancy-type facilities to industrial and commercial customers. Lloyds made no specific moves in merchant banking and its medium term business was conducted through the parent bank, LBI and Lewis's Bank. They also established a Business Advisory Service on a smaller scale. Midland developed its merchant banking by acquiring Samuel Montagu in 1973 and Drayton Corporation in 1974. National Westminster developed the business of its subsidiary County Bank. The Nat. Comm. Group had Williams, Glyn & Co.

In this period the LCB groups also began to modify their organisational and management structures, a process which has also continued right through the 1970s. In 1972 after the establishment of BBI Ltd Barclays adopted a group board structure, with a central board overseeing three major areas of operations, each of which also had a full board. The areas were UK domestic banking, including Barclays Merchant Bank which also had an independent board; overseas and foreign business; and financial services, including the Trust Company and interests in finance house business. In 1973 Lloyds established a group headquarters and appointed a General Manager (Group Co-ordination) and a Group Chief Executive, but delayed changes to the board structure until 1978. The Midland made no major organisational changes, merely establishing domestic and international business as separate profit centres. National Westminster brought McKinsey in to advise on group organisation after the 1968 mergers, and was able to adopt a classical American multiple divisional structure. The Bank is split into functional divisions reporting to the main board, embracing both profit centres (such as international and domestic banking) and cost centres (such as management services and business development). Heads of the larger divisions sit on the main board. Williams & Glyn's also adopted a divisional structure.

Obviously an efficient and flexible top management structure with good communications between directors and executives, and between functional divisions of the bank, is essential if a group policy is to be created. It is vital too when that policy is translated into corporate strategies and plans that such communications continue to work right down to branch managers and clerical staff. Once again it is likely that the American banks will provide the model for future developments. John P. Rudy, Vice-President Corporate Planning for Citicorp, said in 1975:

> It is our thesis that a successful strategy in international finance is likely to be the product of a management system incorporating a heavy element of decentralised planning. Such a process should be driven by senior management leadership to induce a climate of flexibility of thought, expectancy of change, and freedom of expression, with the catalyst of institutional direction in terms of mission and growth.*

Many of the developments of the later 1970s carry forward from the major strategic rethinking of the late-1960s and early-1970s. However, the general worsening of economic conditions after 1973, and the chastening experience of the fringe banking collapse, had important influences on the banks. As the LCB groups struggled to maintain their profitability in the face of rising costs and narrowing margins during 1974–6 the need to operate effectively as an international group was brought home. This period also saw a rapid growth in the Eurocurrency markets business and made it obvious that an international strategy and presence was no longer an option but a *requirement* for any major bank. The period saw the further successful growth of the building societies and the establishment of full banking services by the TSB and Girobank and the rapid growth of the Co-operative Bank. Perhaps the 1970s will appear in retrospect as a sort of rearma-

---

*'Global Planning in Multinational Banking', *Columbia Journal of World Business*, Winter 1975.

ment period, a lull during which the groups had an opportunity to prepare themselves for the real battles of the 1980s.

In 1976 Barclays undertook further reorganisation, disbanding its Financial Services Division and operating a group structure based on two general boards (UK and overseas) and two specialised boards (Merchant Bank and Trust Company). In 1982 the Bank embarked on the process of fully integrating BBI and the parent bank into one organisation.

In 1978 Lloyds adopted a new board structure, with a group board overseeing separate boards responsible for UK banking and overseas banking — a set-up similar in principle to the Barclays arrangement. In his 1978 statement the Chairman stressed the importance of synergy, confirming remarks made in 1977 on the subject of group development:

> One of our aims now is to develop further the flow of business across the group, particularly between our British and overseas branches. At the same time we shall continue gradually, when we can profitably do so, to fill the remaining gaps in our range of services and in our geographical coverage.

Note that expansion now takes second place to improving internal efficiency. The Chief Executive talked in similar terms of:

> Welding together the member banks to create an increasingly powerful worldwide Group.
>
> Centralised systems to monitor levels of Group business by country, industry and customer have been further developed during 1977. These techniques are essential not only for risk evaluation purposes but also for the identification of further marketing opportunities.

Note the emergence of global management information and control systems at group level, and the stress on the need for centralised systems of an offensive nature (marketing) as well as merely defensive (risk evaluation). The banks have carried this policy further down the line by introducing marketing managers at regional level and also by implementing branch marketing plans.

In 1975 Midland reviewed its strategy with a view to making the best use of its recent acquisitions. It created a new International

Division to boost its correspondent banking business and began a programme of overseas investment which culminated in the acquisition of a controlling share in Crocker National Bank and the opening of several new overseas offices. In 1979 the Chairman was again concerned with group strategy, and considered the development of the business of Thomas Cook, Forward Trust, Griffin Factors, Bland Payne, the International division, MAIBL, EBIC, London American, Samuel Montagu, the new overseas representative offices and domestic changes such as the Corporate Finance Division and the new branch network in the context of the decisions of 1975:

> We decided that while our domestic banking, with its traditional blend of money transmission and lending services, must be and should remain the heart of the Group's business, faster growth and a greater proportion of Group profits should be looked for from operations outside the United Kingdom itself, and from activitives other than traditional banking — the related services of merchant banking, insurance, asset finance, including leasing, travel and specialised export finance, as well as personal and corporate financial advice.

The NatWest had completely redesigned its organisational structure subsequent to the 1968 merger, but further rationalisation and decentralisation took place in 1973 in the wake of a job evaluation review. In 1974 Area Marketing Managers were put in, and in 1978 further modifications were made with the introduction of Regional Marketing Managers and Group Relationship Executives. In the meantime the group continued its overseas expansion, opening offices in Singapore and New York, and investing in Holland, France, Germany, Canada, Switzerland and finally in 1978 in the USA with the acquisition of National Bank of North America. NatWest has a single main board and then a divisional and regional board hierarchy.

In this period we can observe the LCB groups consolidating their international positions and beginning the task of adapting to the new and highly competitive environment in which they will have to operate. Broad strategies were formulated in the early 1970s, but only now are the banks beginning to build the information systems and databases necessary to refine their strategies and to adopt truly active management policies based on knowledge of their markets. In similar fashion the broad advertising campaigns of the early-1970s are now being refined as specific products and services are aimed at specific target markets. But the biggest developments here lie in the future, as do the biggest developments in management structures, technology and related services.

It is possble that the main changes in banking as such, that is new techniques of borrowing and lending, new markets, shifts in flows of funds and economic trends, have now taken place. It also seems unlikely that there will be major changes in the status of individual banks. The spotlight in future will be on organisational and technological change, marketing and minimisation of costs — the improvement of internal efficiency, in other words.

We have seen how the LCB groups decided to go international in the 1970s; and how they have been developing as groups so that they are now, with their substantial overseas interests, in the process of becoming truly multinational. Barclays has advanced furthest along this road, with 60 per cent of its 1977 profits coming from Barclays Bank International; but all the groups now generate substantial profits from overseas. They are able to raise large amounts of loan capital in the Euromarkets and to transact business, by one means or another, in all the continents of the world. Such a process of multinationalisation entails certain other processes, the results of which can be observed in multinational giants such as IBM, ITT, BP and others — planning and control of activity at all levels in accordance with overall corporate objectives; strategic diversification; continuous reinvestment in the best available technology, resulting in a generally increased level of automation; intensive training and professionalisation of staff who are rewarded with increasing salary levels and fringe benefits; cultivation of corporate image. To quote John P. Rudy again on the planning function, it is a matter of:

> asking the right question about objectives and means ... assuring substantial effort to answer them ... establishing a quality fabric for resource allocation ... fostering flexibility, innovation and entrepreneurship that build productivity and progress. As part of the management process planning is a line rather than a staff duty that increases with the level of responsibility ... *planning must take place at the level of action if one is to cope successfully with uncertainty* ... The planning

function ... must fit the concepts and style of management in the organisation.

The LCB groups have until now planned from the top down. The far more complex and challenging process of planning from the bottom up is a task for the 1980s, a vital task if the LCBs are to thrive in the many marketplaces where they now compete. For in the marketplace it is the employee on the spot who represents the bank.

The typical organisation structure of a clearing bank is shown in Table 5.2. The outline balance sheet development is shown in Table 5.3. For all the groups there have been very rapid deposit and advances growth over the period, and the proportion of advances to deposits has increased markedly. Substantial profits have been retained but these have not been sufficient to prevent declines in the ratio of shareholders' funds to assets.

A more detailed picture of the asset portfolios of the big four banks is shown in Table 5.4. These figures confirm that each group has significantly increased its advances/deposits ratio over the period 1977–80, while maintaining fairly stable levels of liquid assets and investments. A more detailed breakdown of lending is shown in Table 5.5, which reveals a wide spread covering all sectors of the economy. The reduction in lending to the financial sector represents the winding down of commitments in that area after the secondary banking crisis.

Table 5.2: Typical London Clearing Bank Structure

Parent bank

International banking division/subsidiary
  — overseas branches
  — foreign subsidiaries/affiliates

Merchant bank
Finance house (loans, leasing, hire purchase, factoring)
Unit Trusts
Credit card company
Trust company/division
Channel Isles subsidiaries
Insurance broking subsidiary
Life assurance subsidiary
Venture capital subsidiary
Registrars
'Club' membership

Table 5.3: Development of UK Multinational Banks, 1971-9

	1971	1979	Deposit growth %
	%	%	1971-9
Barclays			
1. Profits/assets	1.2	1.7	
2. Profits/shareholders' funds	18.3	30.1	
3. Shareholders' funds/assets	6.8	5.8	
4. Advances/assets	54.6	67.6	
			355.2
Lloyds			
1. Profits/assets	1.3	1.6	
2. Profits/shareholders' funds	18.8	22.7	
3. Shareholders' funds/assets	7.0	7.0	
4. Advances/assets	57.5	71.9	
			456.4
Midland			
1. Profits/assets	1.2	1.7	
2. Profits/shareholders' funds	18.8	28.4	
3. Shareholders' funds/assets	6.3	6.0	
4. Advances/assets	51.9	65.3	
			443.1
NatWest			
1. Profits/assets	1.2	1.6	
2. Profits/shareholders' funds	20.7	30.3	
3. Shareholders' funds/assets	5.8	5.3	
4. Advances/assets	58.3	68.2	
			424.3
Standard Chartered			
1. Profits/assets	—	—	
2. Profits/shareholders' funds	—	—	
3. Shareholders' funds/assets	6.1	4.2	
4. Advances/assets	66.2	71.8	
			415.9
Hong Kong & Shanghai			
1. Profits/assets	—	—	
2. Profits/shareholders' funds	—	—	
3. Shareholders' funds/assets	3.7	3.4	
4. Advances/assets	49.8	39.3	
			399.4

Source: Banker Research Unit, *The Top 100* (Financial Times, London, 1981).

The significant changes in deposit structures of the LCB groups are shown in Table 5.6, namely the decline in the proportion of sterling current acounts and retail savings, and the increasing importance of sterling wholesale and currency wholesale funds. The currency funds are raised mainly to service matched currency lending arising from the increased international activities of the

Table 5.4: Categories of Assets as Percentage of Deposits for 4 LCB Groups and Parent Banks

BARCLAYS GROUP	1977		1978		1979		1980
Advances	72	(79)	78	(74)	76	(71)	79
Liquid assets	20	(27)	17	(18)	20	(21)	19
Investments	7	(10)	7	(9)	5	(8)	6
Special deposits	1		1		1		—
(BBI in brackets)	100	(116)	103	(101)	102	(100)	104

BARCLAYS BANK LTD.	1977	1978	1979	1980
Advances	69	72	72	67
Liquid assets	15	14	18	16
Investments	5	4	3	4
Special deposits	2	2	1	—
(BBI in brackets)	91	92	94	87

LLOYDS GROUP	1977		1978		1979		1980
Advances	71	(75)	74	(78)	78	(83)	82
Liquid assets	22	(26)	22	(23)	19	(20)	17
Investments	6	(1)	6	(1)	4	(1)	4
Special deposits	1		1		0		—
(LBI in brackets)	100	(102)	103	(102)	101	(104)	103

LLOYDS BANK LTD	1977	1978	1979	1980
Advances	64	70	72	70
Liquid assets	15	14	14	19
Investments	9	8	4	4
Special deposits	2	1	1	—
(LBI in brackets)	90	93	91	93

MIDLAND GROUP	1977	1978	1979	1980
Advances	69	71	71	73
Liquid assets	21	23	23	22
Investments	7	5	6	6
Special deposits	1	1	1	—
	98	100	101	101

MIDLAND BANK LTD	1977	1978	1979	1980
Advances	70	72	70	73
Liquid assets	20	22	24	21
Investments	7	4	5	6
Special deposits	2	1	1	—
	99	99	100	100

NATIONAL WESTMINSTER GROUP	1977	1978	1979	1980
Advances	71	73	73	76
Liquid assets	22	23	22	21
Investments	7	5	6	5
Special deposits	1	1	1	—
	101	102	103	102

NATIONAL WESTMINSTER LTD	1977	1978	1979	1980
Advances	64	62	62	61
Liquid assets	23	24	25	21
Investments	7	7	8	5
Special deposits	2	1	1	—
	96	94	96	87

Source: Report and Accounts.

Table 5.5: Classification of Advances of 4 LCB Groups, 1975-80

Per cent	1975	1976	1977	1978	1979	1980
Manufacturing	20.2	20.8	20.2	20.5	21.4	21.7
Other production	10.0	9.6	10.2	10.1	10.2	10.3
Financial	13.0	12.6	10.9	9.8	7.8	6.6
Services (inc. leasing co's)	22.5	22.7	23.5	22.4	22.5	23.0
Personal	14.5	13.6	14.3	15.1	16.4	16.3
Overseas residents	19.8	20.7	20.8	22.1	21.6	22.2
	100	100	100	100	100	100[a]
Other currency (£m) TOTAL	4,425 (22%)	5,636 (24%)	5,867 (23%)	6,492 (22%)	7,205 (20%)	9,219 (22%)
Sterling (£m) TOTAL	15,936 (78%)	17,647 (76%)	19,394 (77%)	23,036 (78%)	28,031 (80%)	33,510 (78%)
Other currency to overseas residents	11%	12%	11%	11%	13%	15%

		1971	1972	1973	1974
Other currency (£m) TOTAL		226 (4%)	800 (8%)	1,384 (10%)	2,150 (13%)
Sterling (£m) TOTAL	(1971-1974)	5,987 (96%)	9,357 (92%)	12,148 (90%)	13,898 (87%)
Other currency to overseas residents		3%	6%	8%	10%

Note: a. Percentages calculated as percentages of total advances, not as percentages of UK and overseas advances.

Sources: CLCB Statistical Unit.

banks, so that the significant change in terms of funds management has been in the shift to reliance on sterling wholesale funds to support domestic lending. This trend continues as the banks' deposit accounts remain unattractive savings vehicles, and as increasingly interest-rate-sensitive customers reduce their current account balances.

Behaviour of UK financial institutions during the 1970s is especially difficult to analyse because of the turbulent economic conditions causing high and fluctuating rates of inflation, high and fluctuating rates of interest, frequent governmental interference; because of the major changes in financial practices initiated in 1971; because of the increasing variety of competitors in the markets. However, it is unlikely that economic conditions will be any less turbulent in the 1980s, and during 1981 we have seen new

Table 5.6: Estimated Breakdown of Media of Deposits, LCB Groups, as Percentage of Total Deposits, 1960-80

	Sterling			Currency
	current accounts	retail deposit accounts	wholesale funds	(nearly all wholesale)
1960	57	34	5	4
1961	55	36	5	4
1962	55	35	6	4
1963	57	34	5	4
1964	55	34	7	4
1965	53	36	7	4
1966	52	38	6	4
1967	52	39	5	4
1968	51	40	5	4
1969	50	41	5	4
1970	53	43	—	4
1971	52	38	6	4
1972	44	30	18	8
1973	35	28	28	9
1974	29	32	25	14
1975	26	21	25	28
1976	25	18	24	33
1977	28	17	23	32
1978	28	16	23	33
1979	27	17	22	34
1980	22	18	24	36

Source: *Bank of England Quarterly Bulletin*, CLCB Statistical Unit, author's estimates.

controls and regulations brought into force which are at least as far-reaching in their effects as those of 1971. Meanwhile the variety of competitors continues to increase.

Bearing in mind all of these problems, what lessons for the 1980s can be drawn from the behaviour of the UK financial institutions during the 1970s?

1. It is unlikely that, after the lessons of 1972/3, any such spectacular growth in volume of business will ever again be achieved. This suggests that banks' volume of business will tend to grow in line with inflation and the economy as a whole, unless there is a major shift in their competitive standing in important markets.
2. It is unlikely that large new markets for deposits (viz. wholesale and foreign currency) will be found on the same scale as during the early-1970s. This will further reduce volatility of growth.

3. The banks are no longer in a position to countenance major shifts in their balance sheet structures as they did after 1971 when the advances/deposits ratio was increased substantially. This also tends to preclude erratic growth.

These three conditions will limit the growth of volume of business of the banks in the 1980s in absolute terms and also ensure that any growth will be gradual rather than explosive.

In the absence of major new markets (with the exception possibly of the market for the unbanked in the UK, and for housing finance) the banks' growth in volume of business will be a function of overall real growth in the economy, and additional inflationary growth. Real growth is expected to be slow during the 1980s, and inflation should also be at a lower level than in the 1970s, unless some international catastrophe occurs on a par with the oil price rises of 1974. The 'natural' growth of the LCB's volume of business will consequently be fairly slow and gradual in the 1980s. This will also apply to international business, since world economic growth is also expected to be slow during the period, and most governments and all international agencies are concerned to keep down national rates of inflation.

Since all financial institutions will be faced with the same sluggish development in most of their markets during the 1980s, it is to be expected that attention will be *refocused* on existing areas of business to explore:

— Possibilities of increasing market share by dint of competitive efforts.
— Possibilities of further exploiting existing market share by deepening and widening relations with customers.
— Improving profitability of existing operations to ensure that profits are maintained even if overall growth is limited.

... in other words, a much improved marketing effort aimed at achieving some new business and at making *all* business as profitable as possible. Costing information and pricing decisions will be of primary importance. The following areas offer potential future development:

Retail Market

Introduction of NOW and IBTA accounts, ie, interest paid on current accounts in some form or other. (NOW and IBTA accounts are now available in USA.)

Marketing and promotional efforts and greater degree of market segmentation.

Some unbundling of personal services.

Trend to higher-yielding consumer credit, eg, HP, credit cards.

Credit cards as basis for plastic-card-based banking.

Cross-selling of services.

Move into housing finance market on permanent basis.

Reorganisation and reduction of branch networks.

Wholesale Markets

Multiple banking relationships of corporate customers.

Reduced client loyality.

Corporate EFT services.

Specialisation by all but biggest banks.

Attempts to increase levels of fee income.

Use of account executives, business development teams, corporate branches.

This pattern of gradual growth over the next 5–10 years would be disturbed if the pace of technological change suddenly accelerates and new services are made possible. At present the introduction of new technology-based systems is predicted to be gradual and to follow market trends rather than to create new markets. But certainly by the 1990s, and possible earlier, it is likely that the whole basis of banking *operations* will have changed and become electronic rather than paper-based. This will inevitably have effects on customers and the financial markets in general, including for example the following:

1. Clearing banks will lose substantial interest earned on customers' funds in transit, as instant or same-day debiting and transfer of value take place.
2. Customers' cash management, especially corporate customers, will improve and levels of idle balances and transactions balances will decline.
3. Customers' cash requirements will decline and the cash distribution burden on the LCBs will be reduced.
4. Degree of personal contact between bank and customer will

decline as more and more money transmission services are available outside the bank building.

5. Banks will be required to develop their own EFT systems and will be able to exploit any competitive advantages they achieve in systems development.
6. Building societies and retailers may utilise new technology to compete effectively in the market for money transmission services.

The patterns of gradual growth may also be shattered by various other shocks and surprises affecting the world or national economies, international or domestic financial systems or individual banks and their subsidiaries. The incidence of such shocks is generally expected to increase in the near future and there are various possibilities:

1. Major defaults on international debts, especially of developing countries, leading to losses, and restrictions on lending policies.
2. International liquidity crisis, possibly triggered by 1. above.
3. International banking failures caused by 1. or 2. or by foreign exchange disasters.
4. Sharp decline in world trading conditions due to further rounds of inflation, higher political risks, wars, oil price changes, and so on.
5. Sharp decline in UK economy on exhaustion of oil reserves.
6. Loss of market dominance by London as financial centre.
7. Further sterling exchange rate problems caused by 5. above.

5.3 Case Study — Barclays Bank

Barclays can trace its activities back to the seventeenth century, but began to emerge in its form as a national commercial bank in 1896 with the creation of Barclay & Company Limited, an amalgamation of the banking partnership of Barclay, Bevan, Trilton, Ransome, Bouverie & Co with 20 private banks. Barclays Bank was the name adopted in 1917.

Barclays is unique amongst British deposit banks in the continued strength of representation of members of the original families. The present Chairman for example is a Bevan.

After the First World War Barclays began to expand its international business by investing in local banks in Africa, the Caribbean, the Mediterranean and the Near East. The bank selected countries which had political links with the UK stemming from British economic and imperial activities. In 1925 the foreign operations were organised as one unit, originally named Barclays DCO (Dominions, Colonial and Overseas), with the Bank as majority shareholder. In the late-1960s Barclays Bank International Ltd (BBI) became the vehicle for Barclays overseas enterprises, and in 1971 BBI became a wholly-owned subsidiary of Barclays Bank and the group's entire international business was transferred to BBI. However, the Bank has recently announced plans to merge the domestic bank and BBI to create a single multinational entity which will presumably be organised along divisional lines in a similar manner to the large US banks.

The domestic bank has steadily expanded its branch network to gain nationwide coverage, and broadened the range of its activities. It now has a network of about 3,000 branches, which is a little smaller than the NatWest's 3,200.

During the 1960s the Bank acquired a large finance house (Mercantile Credit) engaging in commercial and consumer credit. In 1966 it was the first UK bank to introduce a credit card, licensed under the VISA system. The Bank expanded the activities of its trust company, providing unit trusts and other investment management services. More recently it has begun to provide insurance broking and life assurance services through subsidiaries. In the early-1970s the Bank established a business advisory service designed to assist small and medium-sized businesses with financial and business planning; and a merchant bank to engage in investment banking.

During the 1970s BBI has made numerous important overseas investments, especially in North America where the Bank now has a significant presence. However, there was also a change of emphasis from local banking in ex-colonial territories to truly international banking, operating in financial centres in Europe, Australia, Asia and the USA, and engaging in wholesale banking in London, especially in the Eurocurrency markets.

For historical reasons Barclays has the most extensive foreign business of the London clearing banks, and now classifies 60 per cent of its assets under international banking:

	Total assets, 1982	
	£m	%
Domestic	23,775	40
International		
UK	12,026	20
USA	7,329	13
South Africa	6,116	10
Rest of the world	9,800	17
	59,046	100

The only British bank with comparable overseas representation is Lloyds Bank with significant investments in Latin America. Barclays' substantial presence in South Africa (Barclays National Bank Ltd) has caused it some public relations problems in the UK because of the controversy over South African racial policies.

Like Citicorp in the USA, Barclays has established a reputation as an innovator and market leader, not merely on the basis of size and range of services, but in strategic planning, marketing and business development. Barclays was the first British bank to embrace wholeheartedly management by objectives and business development targets. It has led with numerous new services, often forcing the other clearers to follow suit after a decent pause. Examples include the credit card, unit trusts, business advisory service, and large-scale investment in the USA.

The following comprehensive description of the group's current activities is taken from the Bank's 20-f report to the US Securities and Exchange Commission.

Domestic Operations

Domestic operations comprise operations of the Bank and its United Kingdom subsidiary and associated companies other than BBI.

Banking Activities. Through about 3,000 offices in the United Kingdom, the Bank provides a comprehensive range of banking services to corporate and personal customers. As a major UK clearing bank the Bank clears cheques and credits for all its branches and for banks for which it acts as a clearing agent, in the process providing services to many other banks in the United Kingdom. Deposits raised through the branch network and at head office comprise non-interest bearing current cheque accounts, interest bearing savings deposits from which withdrawals are subject to prior notice and other time deposits. Corporate lending activities cover the whole range of British industry and commerce and are mainly by overdraft facilities and short and medium-term loans. These lendings are generally at variable rates of interest linked to the Bank's published base lending rate (similar to prime rate) or to London money market rates. Lendings to personal customers are provided by all domestic branches, by overdraft facilities at variable interest rates, or personal loans, where the interest is charged at a fixed percentage rate. Home loans, which were introduced during 1981 and grew rapidly throughout 1982, are made at variable interest rates. In 1982 Barclays was the only UK clearing bank to re-open, after some 13 years, on Saturday mornings to provide personal customer service which is now available at over 400 branches throughout the United Kingdom.

Credit Card Operations. The Bank conducts its own credit card operation, Barclaycard, which has over 6.5 million cardholders and is honoured in the United Kingdom by some 190,000 merchant outlets. In 1982 a 'gold card' Barclays Premier Card was launched. Barclaycard is a member of the VISA international credit card network.

Merchant Banking. In 1967, the Bank established a subsidiary, now named Barclays Merchant Bank Limited (BMB), which constitutes one of the larger UK merchant banks and which contributed £818 million to the total assets of the Barclays Group at 31 December 1982. BMB's services include term lending in sterling and other currencies, acceptance credit facilities, loan syndications, corporate finance services including advice in connection with takeovers and mergers, capital issues and private placements and other investment banking activities including provision of capital for developing enterprises. BMB also has an industrial banking department serving the needs of certain specialist sectors.

Consumer and Industrial Finance. Mercantile Credit Company Limited ('Mercantile Credit'), in which the Bank acquired an initial 17.85 per cent interest in 1968 and full ownership in 1975, engages directly and through subsidiary companies in instalment credit and leasing (direct financing leases) in both the consumer and industrial fields throughout the United Kingdom and Eire. At 31 December 1982, Mercantile Credit contributed £3,042 million to the total assets of the Barclays Group.

Trust Activities. Barclays Bank Trust Company Limited (BBTC) was incorporated in 1969, in part as a successor to the trust department of the Bank. BBTC directly and through subsidiary companies engages in the business of asset management, particularly investment and property management, trust administration, pension fund advice and management, personal taxation, the management of unit trusts and managed funds, and the underwriting of life assurance and pension policies linked to these funds.

Other Services.   The Bank, through other subsidiary companies, provides additional related services, including insurance broking facilities. In 1982 a new service was introduced through involvement in the London International Financial Futures Exchange offering corporate customers the opportunity to deal in financial futures.

Associates. The Bank holds minority interests in Bank of Scotland (34.48%), Yorkshire Bank PLC (32%), and Finance for Industry plc (18.86%). Bank of Scotland has a network of approximately 500 Scottish banking branches, and subsidiary companies engaged in merchant banking and consumer and industrial finance. Yorkshire Bank PLC has approximately 200 banking branches located mainly in the Midlands and North of England as well as subsidiary companies engaged in industrial and consumer finance. Finance for Industry plc, which is a holding company owned by nine UK banks and the Bank of England, provides through its subsidiary companies capital and advice for small and medium-sized companies and medium-term finance for larger companies.

International Operations

International operations comprise operations of BBI and its worldwide subsidiary and associated companies (the 'BBI Group'). International operations are, in turn, subdivided into United Kingdom, United States and South Africa, being the principal areas of the BBI Group's international activities, and the Rest of the World.

United Kingdom. Through 30 branches in the United Kingdom, BBI provides a comprehensive range of banking services primarily for businesses engaged in international trade. It provides short and medium-term loans in sterling and other currencies and is active in foreign exchange, the management of syndicated loans, export credits, and international trade finance.

The major portion of BBI's lending and deposit activities in the United Kingdom is transacted through the Eurocurrency market. At 31 December 1982, approximately three-quarters of BBI's UK assets were in Eurocurrency.

United States. Banking activities in the United States are conducted through two subsidiary banks and the direct offices of BBI. The two subsidiary banks, Barclays Bank of New York National Association (BBNY) and Barclays Bank of California (Barcal) are principally engaged in retail and commercial banking. At 31 December 1982, BBNY and Barcal contributed £927 million and £488 million respectively to the total assets of the Barclays Group.

BBI has branches or agencies in New York, and in Atlanta, Boston, Chicago, Miami, New Orleans, Pittsburgh, San Francisco, Seattle and St Louis and an Edge Act Corporation, Barclays International Banking Corporation (BIBC), in Houston. The New York branch is the primary direct banking operation in the United States and as such clears dollar transactions on behalf of most of the Barclays Group worldwide and for other banking correspondents. It has specialised departments dealing with foreign exchange, letters of credit, collection of bills and securities transactions. At 31 December 1982, BBI's offices (including BIBC) in the United States contributed £4,396 million to the total assets of the Barclays Group.

Through its subsidiary company Barclays American Corporation (BAC) based in Charlotte, North Carolina, BBI engages in consumer and commercial finance activities in 37 states and has a total of 354 offices. At 31 December 1982, BAC contributed £1,518 million to the total assets of the Barclays Group.

At 31 December 1982, total operations in the United States contributed £7,329 million to the total assets of the Barclays Group.

South Africa. Barclays National Bank Limited (Barnat) is the largest bank in South Africa in terms of total consolidated assets and contributed £6,116 million to the total assets of the Barclays Group at 31 December 1982. Barnat and its subsidiary companies, with over 1,000 offices, provide full banking services, including corporate and consumer finance, leasing, merchant banking services and insurance broking.

BBI's interest in Barnat, 56.03 per cent at 31 December 1982 is now 55 per cent. It will be further reduced, within a period to be agreed, to a maximum of 50 per cent in compliance with South African legislation relating to the foreign ownership of banks.

Rest of the World. Outside the United Kingdom, the United States and South Africa, the BBI Group operates through offices of BBI, subsidiary and associated companies and through representative and business development offices in over 80 countries in Europe, Australasia, Asia, the Americas, the Caribbean and Africa. In terms of total assets the largest of these geographical segments is Europe (Western Europe excluding the UK) which at 31 December 1982 contributed £4,921 million (8.3 per cent) to the total assets of the Barclays Group. No single country in Europe or elsewhere in the Rest of the World contributed in excess of 5 per cent to the total assets of the Barclays Group.

While the BBI Group conducts deposit taking and commercial activities in most of the countries in which it operates and Eurocurrency business in some of them, the nature and extent of its bank related services vary, and include leasing, consumer finance, merchant banking, investment banking and foreign trade and development project financing. Additionally, BBI has shareholdings in a number of joint venture banking companies designed to advance trade and investment in specific geographic areas and business sectors.

The group balance sheet reveals the importance of international lending as the prime source of income (Table 5.7). The figure quoted includes interbank loans of maturity greater than 30 days, being mainly Eurocurrency business in London. The group has significant fixed assets, representing its extensive overseas interests. In funding the group relies heavily on Eurocurrency wholesale deposits and on domestic wholesale deposits (Table 5.8). Nevertheless, its retail operations in the UK, and also in South Africa, give it a useful base of core demand and savings deposits which are significantly cheaper than money market funds. These deposits

Table 5.7: Barclays Group: Average Balance Sheet and Net Interest Income, 1981

	Year ended 31 December (amounts in £ million)	
	Average balance	Average rate %
ASSETS:		
Cash and balances with central banks:		
Domestic	415	—
International	953	—
	1,368	—
Items in course of collection:		
Domestic	248	—
International	94	—
	342	—
Short-term funds:		
Domestic	1,589	13.8
International	3,766	14.8
	5,355	14.5
Securities:		
Domestic	719	13.0
International	1,193	9.6
	1,912	10.9
Lendings to customers, net of allowance, and placings with banks:		
Domestic	11,715	16.2
International	17,804	16.1
	29,519	16.1
Equipment leased to customers:		
Domestic	1,117	15.0
International	628	19.4
	1,745	16.6
Accrued interest and other accounts:		
Domestic	489	—
International	997	—
	1,486	—
Investments in associated companies and trade investments:		
Domestic	151	—
International	94	—
	245	—
Property and equipment:		
Domestic	530	—
International	332	—
	862	—
Total average assets and interest income	42,834	14.1
Percentage applicable to International operations	60.4%	

Table 5.7: continued

LIABILITIES AND STOCKHOLDERS' EQUITY

Demand deposits:		
Domestic	4,075	0.2
International	2,281	1.3
	6,356	0.6
Savings deposits:		
Domestic	5,118	10.5
International	1,337	6.1
	6.455	9.6
Other time deposits:		
Domestic	7,234	13.6
International	17,378	15.2
	24,612	14.8
Other liabilities:		
Domestic	626	—
International	1,887	—
	2,513	—
Long term borrowings:		
International	277	12.2
Loan capital:		
Domestic	59	8.3
International	332	13.5
	391	12.7
Minority interests:		
Domestic	5	—
International	114	—
	119	
Stockholders' equity:		
Domestic	1,421	—
International	690	—
	2,111	—
Total average liabilities and stockholders equity, and interest expense	42,834	10.2
Percentage applicable to International operations	58.0%	
Total average interest earning assets	38,531	
Relating to:		
Interest income		15.7
Interest expense		11.4
Net interest income		4.3
Total average interest bearing funds (excluding demand deposits) and interest expense	31,735	13.6

Table 5.7: continued

Notes: Lendings to customers include all doubtful lendings. Placings with banks repayable within 30 days are included with short term funds and those repayable beyond 30 days with lendings to customers. Intersegmental balances and transactions between the Domestic and International operations are excluded. The average balance due to the Domestic segment from the International segment for 1981 was £1,565 million and interest paid by International for that year was £245.3 million. The interest paid on demand deposits mainly relates to staff accounts.

Source: 20-f report, 1982.

Table 5.8: Barclays Group: Deposit Structures, 1980–2

	1980		1981		1982	
	£m	%	£m	%	£m	%
BARCLAYS						
Domestic						
Demand deposits	4,424	13.8	4,763	11.1	5,082	9.8
Savings deposits	5,018	15.7	5,723	13.3	5,742	11.0
Other time deposits	5,789	18.1	8,595	20.1	11,688	22.5
Total domestic	15,240	47.6	19,081	44.5	22,512	43.3
International						
Demand deposits	2,132	6.7	2,476	5.8	2,788	5.4
Savings deposits	1,213	3.8	1,401	3.3	1,449	2.8
Other time deposits	13,397	41.9	19,876	46.4	25,161	48.5
Total international	16,742	52.4	23,753	55.5	29,398	56.7
TOTAL DEPOSITS	31,982	100.0	42,834	100.0	51,910	100.0

Source: 20-f report, 1982.

mean that Barclays is like the other London clearers, exposed to a fall in domestic interest rates. However, the proportion of core deposits in the group's balance sheet is continually declining and the significance of the current account endowment effect is no longer so crucial to group profits. Nevertheless, the benefits of these deposits is reflected in the net interest margins the bank earns:

Interest margins

	1980	1981
Domestic	7.8	7.2
International	2.7	2.5
Group	5.0	4.3

The domestic margin is significantly better, although of course domestic retail operations involve high-cost branch networks which tend to equalise operating profit as against international wholesale business.

In recent years the group has considerably expanded its volume of loan capital, especially dollar denominated Euronotes and bonds.

Table 5. 9 shows the group's lending by geographical area, and shows the importance of South African and US operations to the group. Nevertheless, domestic and UK-based international lending account for over half of group lending. Closer analysis of domestic lending shows that about one third is to individuals, and the rest to the industrial and commercial sector.

Over half the total lending is of maturity less than one year because of the prevalence of overdraft lending in the UK, and over 90 per cent is at variable rates. This means that in its domestic operations the Bank's interest rate exposure is to falling rates, because of the portion of fixed rate non-interest bearing liabilities. UK based international lending goes mainly to non-UK residents, foreign companies and goverments, although there is also significant currency lending to UK industry. Again, this is mostly variable rate lending, including roll-over credits of ranging maturities as well as overdrafts. In its US lending the emphasis has been on commercial and industrial activity but a consumer book has been established, including some mortgage lending. Both in

Table 5.9: Barclays Group: Lendings by Geographical Area

	1982	1981	1980	1979	1978
			(£ million)		
Domestic	16,612	13,330	10,564	9,392	7,641
International:					
United Kingdom	4,794	3,844	2,508	1,834	1,325
United States	4,312	2,751	1,670	1,111	600
South Africa	3,796	2,635	1,470	1,199	1,147
	29,514	22,560	16,212	13,536	10,713
Rest of the World	5,755	5,113	2,896	2,027	1,726
Total	35,269	27,673	19,108	15,563	12,439

Note: Lendings in no single country in the Rest of the World exceed 5 per cent of the total lendings of the Barclays Group.

Source: 20-f report, 1982.

the USA and South Africa fixed rate lending is more common, accounting for about one half of total lending and resulting in an exposure to rising interest rates (see Table 5.10).

The Bank has responded to change in international and domestic markets by restructuring. The group proposes to reunite the domestic and international banks under one corporate umbrella. Meanwhile, the domestic bank has been reorganised with the help of McKinsey management consultants, emphasising product/market priorities as well as territorial factors, and provision for specialised services.

Senior executives of the Bank have openly discussed the threats and opportunities facing their own bank and other similar UMBs during the 1980s. Threats include:

1. International lending risk, and the need for cofinancing of LDC balance of payments deficits. Political and economic risks are also increasing.
2. Domestic lending risk, due to the UK recession. Political intervention is increasing, and there is increased competition for deposits. EFT will open up the prospect of competition in money transmission services too.
3. Fixed costs continue to rise as profits fall with lower interest rates, and heavy capital investment is required.
4. Margins on lending are forced down by competition, and cost of funding rises.
5. Competition to London as an international financial centre.
6. Competition in lending and related services from foreign, merchant and other clearing banks in the international corporate and middle markets.
7. Increasing burden of regulation and supervision.
8. Competition between banks, building societies, National Savings and others for domestic retail deposits, and need to rationalise branch networks. Need to surmount public relations problem in personal market with regard to bank profits and capital.

In this difficult environment several opportunities have nevertheless been identified:

— International lending and related services for commercial customers in selected growth areas, eg, USA, West Germany,

Table 5.10: Barclays Group: Analysis of Lendings by Type of Customer, Maturity, and Interest Sensitivity

The following tables analyse lendings at 31 December for the years indicated by type of customer and, at 31 December 1982, by maturity and interest sensitivity. The analyses by type of customer are based mainly on the requirements of the regulatory authorities in the respective countries and as they are not wholly comparable from one country's analysis to another, a consolidated analysis cannot be presented. In the maturity analyses, overdrafts are included in the less than one year category.

	1982	1981	1980	1979	1978
DOMESTIC			(£ million)		
Customers domiciled in the United Kingdom:					
Loans guaranteed by Export Credits Guarantee Department	637	630	710	935	968
Central and local government-owned utilities	244	345	259	323	241
Manufacturing, construction, financial and service industries	7,763	6,681	5,808	4,891	3,837
Agriculture, forestry and fishing	1,094	903	720	627	466
Property	695	570	437	410	421
Other businesses	191	88	112	14	32
Individuals	5,710	4,037	2,450	2,160	1,643
	16,334	13,254	10,496	9,360	7,608
Overseas customers	278	76	68	32	33
Total	16,612	13,330	10,564	9,392	7,641

	31 December 1982 (£ million)	%
Maturity:		
Less than one year	9,632	58
One year to five years	3,319	20
Over five years	3,661	22
	16,612	100
Interest sensitivity:		
Fixed rate	1,350	8
Variable rate	15,262	92
	16,612	100

	1982	1981	1980	1979	1978
INTERNATIONAL — UNITED KINGDOM			(£ million)		
Customers domiciled in the United Kingdom:					
Loans guaranteed by Export Credits Guarantee Department	380	162	184	73	—
Central and local government and government-owned utilities	393	260	315	229	253

Table 5.10: continued

Manufacturing, construction, financial and service industries	849	841	868	444	317
Property	12	28	29	27	16
Other business	254	262	152	203	193
	1,888	1,553	1,548	976	779
Overseas customers	2,906	2,291	960	858	546
Total	4,794	3,844	2,508	1,834	1,325

	31 December 1982 (£ million)	%
Maturity:		
Less than one year	1,470	31
One year to five years	1,709	35
Over five years	1,615	34
	4,794	100
Interest sensitivity:		
Fixed rate	426	9
Variable rate	4,368	91
	4,794	100

	1982	1981	1980	1979	1978
INTERNATIONAL — UNITED STATES			(£ million)		
Commercial and industrial	2,949	1,706	905	610	372
Mortgage and real estate:					
Secured by family residences	311	233	138	73	55
Other	321	203	137	46	34
Consumer instalment loans	628	479	363	315	77
All other loans	103	130	127	67	62
Total	4,312	2,751	1,670	1,111	600

The maturity and interest sensitivity of loans, excluding loans secured by family residences and consumer instalment loans are:

	31 December 1982 (£ million)	%
Maturity:		
Less than one year	2,253	67
One year to five years	711	21
Over five years	409	12
	3,373	100
Interest sensitivity:		
Fixed rate	1,783	53
Variable rate	1,590	47
	3,373	100

Table 5.10: continued

INTERNATIONAL — SOUTH AFRICA	1982	1981	1980	1979	1978
	(£ million)				
Manufacturing, construction, financial and services industries	2,094	1,525	622	690	665
Agriculture	342	255	183	123	171
Other businesses	317	138	90	78	49
Individuals	1,043	717	575	308	262
Total	3,796	2,635	1,470	1,199	1,147

	31 December 1982	
	(£ million)	%
Maturity:		
Less than one year	2,538	67
One year to five years	820	22
Over five years	438	11
	3,796	100
Interest sensitivity:		
Fixed rate	1,894	50
Variable rate	1,902	50
	3,796	100

Source: 20-f report, 1982.

Japan, Far East, China, Middle East, with particular emphasis on the growth economies of the Pacific Basin, and on the provision of specialised corporate financial services such as corporate advice, project finance, syndicated loan management, currency/ foreign exchange management, treasury/cash management, bond issues and trading, foreign investment advice.

— Growth in consumer credit, and in scope for pension fund management.

— Opportunity to deepen and widen relationships with corporate and middle market customers by closer involvement. In the corporate market industry specialists and account executives could help to provide more long-term and equity finance, possibly taking board seats to assist in control. In the middle market the branch manager will continue to provide staple services to business in the local community.

Management has concluded that these changes in the market place will result in changing skills requirements, resulting in a progressive specialisation of general managers and operational managers, with operational managers in turn specialising in corporate, treasury, consumer, middle market, marketing, planning and personnel functions. At the junior level progressive automation of procedures will release staff for more marketing and PR activities. The Bank sees a shortage of skills in one area only — systems development, increasingly important as banks automate both basic accounting and management information systems.

References

Boleat, M., *The Building Society Industry* (Heinemann, London, 1981).

Committee of London Clearing Bankers, *The London Clearing Banks* (Longman, London 1978).

Crossley, J. and Blandford, J., *The DCO Story 1925–1971* (Barclays Bank International, London, 1975).

National Westminster Bank, *The British Banking System* (National Westminster Bank, London, 1982).

Parliament, Committee to Review the Functioning of Financial Institutions. (Chairman, Sir Harold Wilson), Cmnd. 7937 (HMSO, London, 1980).

Reed, R., *National Westminster Bank: A Short History* (National Westminster Bank, London, 1983).

Revell, J., *The British Financial System* (Macmillan, London, 1975).

Tuke, A.W. and Gillman, R.J.H., *Barclays Bank Ltd 1876–1969* (Barclays Bank, London, 1972).

Winton, J.R., *The Story of Lloyds Bank 1910–1970* (OUP, Oxford, 1982).

Data Sources

Bank of England Quarterly Bulletin.

Financial Statistics (Central Statistical Office).

Economic Trends (Central Statistical Office).

Committee of London Clearing Bankers Statistical Unit.

Inter Bank Research Organisation.

Bank Annual Reports.

6 FRENCH BANKS

6.1 Financial System

As in West Germany and Japan, banks and other deposit-taking institutions play an important role in the French financial system, because of the relatively narrow capital markets and the minor role played by investing institutions since pensions are funded by social security and company pay-as-you-go schemes. Control and regulation of the system have been extensive, initially in the interests of post-War reconstruction and later in the interests of general economic expansion.

The most striking feature of French banking is the fact that since 1945 many major banks have been nationalised, although their management has operated autonomously and according to commercial criteria. In 1981 further nationalisations took place and at present there are proposals for sweeping structural reforms with a view to improving the overall efficiency of the system. Nevertheless, many of the previous rigidities in the financial system have been removed over the years, and the fact of public ownership has not prevented banks from developing their activities.

The first major category of bank is the *registered banks (banques inscrites)* who are on the official lists of the Conseil National du Crédit (CNC). According to the law of 1941 there are three categories of registered bank, although since the 1966/7 reforms the distinctions between the categories have been reduced.

Prior to the 1966/7 reforms *deposit banks* were not permitted to take deposits of maturity greater than two years, nor were they allowed to hold more than 10 per cent of the capital of private companies. These rules effectively prevented the deposit banks from doing very much term lending, from involvement in investment banking, and from diversification by means of acquisitions. *Investment banks*, on the other hand, were only permitted to take deposits of maturity greater than two years, and could not open branches. The same ruling on deposits also applied to the medium- and long-term credit banks. These rules prevented the investment and credit banks from engaging in commercial banking to any great extent.

The reforms had most impact on the investment banks, smaller than the deposit banks and privately owned. Some elected to become deposit banks, as did Banque Rothschild and Banque de l'Indochine, and started to open branches. Some, such as Paribas, chose to establish a holding company with two separate subsidiaries, a deposit bank and an investment bank. The new deposit banks frequently achieved branch network expansion through acquisition of small deposit banks, for example privately owned local banks. Nevertheless, these newer deposit banks still rely on interbank deposits for an element of their funding.

Deposit banks (banques de dépôts) are the largest category of registered banks, and the three nationalised banks account for about 60 per cent of all their deposits. Other types of bank in this category are the rediscount houses, the regional and local banks, various other banks with head offices in Paris, and foreign banks. These banks are permitted to engage in a wide range of banking activities in domestic and international markets, and since 1966 they have been allowed to purchase holdings in non-bank companies up to a limit of 20 per cent of that company's capital, and provided the total amount of such holdings does not exceed the bank's own net asset value. This gives the deposit banks some scope to engage in investment banking. As in West Germany, French deposit banks are important participants in the French capital markets, acting as issuing houses for equity and bond issues.

The three *national banks* (Banque Nationale de Paris, Crédit Lyonnais, Société Générale) with their extensive branch networks, powerful position in corporate markets, and international standing, play a vital role. They also have many diverse subsidiaries, including regional banks of significant size. There are also some large privately owned deposit banks, some of which are subsidiaries of bank holding groups.

Regional banks are still important in France, but the number of smaller local banks has been declining. The *rediscount houses* fulfil a special function as money market intermediaries. Paris has attracted a large number of *foreign banks* interested in wholesale banking, trade financing and the servicing of ethnic communities. In 1982 there were 120 subsidiaries or branches and over 50 representative offices in Paris, representing about 15 per cent of the total assets of all registered banks. There are very few provincial offices of foreign banks. The major countries represented are the United States, European countries, and the Middle East. Spanish and Portuguese banks service their respective immigrant populations.

Investment banks (banques d'affaires). The effect of the 1966/7 reforms was to reduce the number of investment banks considerably, since many were absorbed or converted into deposit banks. A number of mergers took place, affecting for example Lazard Frères, Banque Worms and others. The largest two banks — Compagnie Financière de Suez and Compagnie Financière de Paris et des Pays-Bas — transformed themselves into complex holding companies with interests in banking, finance and commerce. Suez Group, for example, controls Banque de l'Indochine and Crédit Industriel et Commercial; while Paribas Group controls Crédit du Nord and has a large stake in Compagnie Bancaire. The investment banks have been private banks but their specialisation in industrial banking has meant that they have always had close links with the nationalised banks and with government officials.

The medium- and long-term credit banks receive term deposits and grant credits for a minimum period of two years and are restricted in their ability to invest in industrial and commercial ventures in the same way as the deposit banks.

Finance companies (établissements financiers) must also register with CNC and are regulated in a similar fashion to banks. Most of them are subsidiaries of banks, engaged in leasing and instalment credit operations. They are not permitted to accept deposits from the public and must rely on money market funding to a large extent, or on lines of credit from their parent bank. Many credit banks (above) are registered as finance companies.

Under the Nationalisation Act of 1982 all registered banks with deposits in excess of FF 1 billion were nationalised, except for real estate companies and discount houses and banks with a majority of non-resident shareholders. Both quoted and non-quoted banks were nationalised, and those shares of the three national banks held by private investors were transferred to the State. Compensation is by means of government bonds. The existing chairmen and boards of directors were replaced by nominees cited by decree and including in each case:

five representatives of the State;
five representatives of staff;

five individuals, either experienced in the financial sector, or representing depositors or borrowers.

General management of the bank was handed over to a 'General Administrator', effectively a civil servant. A list of the banks affected is shown in Table 6.1. Basic profiles of the different categories of registered bank are shown in Table 6.2.

The National Savings Bank (Caisse Nationale d'Épargne) operates through the Post Office network of over 17,000 branches, in similar fashion to the British NSB and Girobank. The Bank is in fact a department of the Post and Telecommunications Administration. The traditional passbook savings accounts have been supplemented by current accounts since 1978, and the Bank also offers a range of savings schemes, term deposits, and shares in open-ended investment companies. Funds are deployed by the State trustee agency known as the Caisse des Dépôts et Consignations whose operations are subject to legal constraints, but an increasingly large part of funds is now channelled to the ordinary savings banks for lending to local communities or to individuals for housing scheme finance. The postal and telecommunications service (PTT) supplies the public, public sector bodies and banks with two important payment mechanisms — postal transfers and Post Office current accounts. Again this bears some resemblance to the British Girobank.

The Caisse des Dépôts also accepts deposits from solicitors, Social Security, mutual provident associations, consignations, and it administers pension and insurance schemes. It is one of the largest financial institutions in France with substantial holdings of securities, principally bonds, and it manages several open-ended investment companies whose shares are held by bank customers and institutional investors. In addition to its powerful role as an investing institution, the Caisse makes loans to local authorities, housing associations, and public or semi-public enterprises, especially in the communications and transport sector. With its enormous liquid resources, the Caisse is a leading supplier of funds to the short-term money markets.

The Treasury plays an important intermediary role in France. It receives funds collected from the PTT financial services network and also the deposits of public departments and local authorities. It issues savings certificates to the general public and Treasury bills to financial institutions. It approves loans granted by special credit

Table 6.1: French Banks Nationalised under Nationalisation Act, 11 February 1982

Under the Nationalisation Act of February 1982, all registered banks with deposits in excess of FF 1,000,000,000 were nationalised with the exception of: (1) banks with the status of real estate companies for commerce and industry, and discount houses; (2) banks with a majority of non-resident shareholders.

Banks nationalised were:

Quoted banks
Banque de Bretagne
Crédit Commercial de France
Crédit Industriel d'Alsace et de Lorraine (CIAL)
Crédit Industriel et Commercial
Crédit Industriel de Normandie
Crédit Industriel de l'Ouest
Crédit du Nord
Hervet (Banque)
Rothschild (Banque)
Scalbert Dupont (Banque)
Société Bordelaise de Crédit Industriel et Commercial
Société Centrale de Banque
Société Générale Alsacienne de Banque (Sogénal)
Société Lyonnaise de Dépôts et de Crédit Industriel
Société Marseillaise de Crédit
Société Nancéienne de Crédit Industriel et Varin-Bernier
Société Séquanaise de Banque
Worms (Banque)

Non-Quoted Banks
Banque Centrale de Coopératives et des Mutuelles
Banque Corporative du Bâtiment et des Travaux Publics
Banque Fédérative du Crédit Mutuel
Banque Française de Crédit Coopératif
Banque de La Hénin
Banque de l'Indochine et de Suez
Banque Industrielle et Mobilière Privée (BIMP)
Banque de Paris et des Pays-Bas
Banque Parisienne de Crédit au commerce et à l'industrie
Banque Régionale de l'Ain
Banque Régionale de l'Ouest
Banque de l'Union Européenne
Chaix (Banque)
Crédit Chimique
Laydernier (Banque)
Monod-Française de Banque
Odier Bungener Courvoisier (Banque)
Sofinco La Hénin
Tarneaud (Banque)
Vernes et Commerciale de Paris (Banque)
Union de Banques à Paris

In addition, shares of the three national banks in the hands of private investors were required to be transferred to the State.

Source: Peat, Marwick, Mitchell & Co., *Banking in France* (Peat, Marwick, Mitchell & Co., Paris, 1982).

Table 6.2: The French Registered Banks (Summarised Data), end 1981

Type of Bank	Number of institutions	Balance Sheet Total at end 1981 (millions FF)	%
DEPOSIT BANKS			
1) Deposit banks under French supervision			
Head office located in France			
National banks	3	1,235	57.0
Banks with head office in Paris	82	393	18.2
Regional banks	19	181	8.4
Local banks	50	17	0.8
Discount institutions	7	64	2.9
Banks with head office in overseas departments	6	3	0.1
Banks with head office in overseas territories	6	2	0.1
Total	173	1,895	87.5
2) Deposit banks under foreign supervision			
Foreign banks incorporated in France	49	119	5.5
Branches of foreign banks	53	149	6.9
Total	102	268	12.4
3) Deposit banks with head office in Monaco	4	2	0.1
Total Deposit Banks (1 + 2 + 3)	279	2,165	100.0
INVESTMENT BANKS			
Investment banks under French supervision with head office located in France	21	200	77.5
Foreign banks incorporated in France	13	56	21.7
Banks with head office located in Monaco	3	2	0.8
Total	37	258	100
LONG- AND MEDIUM-TERM CREDIT BANKS Banks			
Long- and medium-term credit banks under French supervision with head office located in France	59	83	90.2
Foreign banks incorporated in France	2	8	8.7
Long- and medium-term credit banks with head office located in Monaco	2	1	1.1
Total	63	92	100

Source: Commission de Controle des Banques, quoted in Peat, Marwick, Mitchell & Co., *Banking in France* (Peat, Marwick, Mitchell & Co., Paris, 1982).

institutions to the private sector in accordance with industrial development plans, and grants loans from the social and economic development fund to public enterprises. The development fund also gives subsidies, interest relief and provides State guarantees.

There are in addition a number of official and semi-official *specialised banks* with special legal status, providing mainly medium- and long-term credit to private and public enterprises. These include:

1. Crédit Foncier — mortgage bank specialising in construction finance.
2. Crédit National — formed to finance reconstruction after the Second World War, now a major source of long-term finance to the industrial public sector by means of refinancing commercial bank loans, by direct loans, and by loans in conjunction with the Fonds de Développement Economique et Social (FDES). The Crédit National funds its operations by issuing bonds and other securities which are mainly purchased by financial institutions.
3. Banque Française du Commerce Extérieur (BFCE) — nationalised in 1945, a State export-import bank which in conjunction with the French foreign trade insurance company Coface provides a comprehensive range of export credit and insurance, including various subsidised facilities.
4. Caisse Nationale des Marches de l'Etat (CNME) — specialises in providing guarantees to support applications to borrow from commercial banks by companies engaged on public works contracts, and in refinancing bank loans.
5. Crédit d'Equipement des Petites et Moyennes Enterprises (CEPME) — created in 1980 to provide finance for small and medium-sized businesses in conjunction with CNME.
6. Crédit Hôtelier — since 1945 placed under the control of the Banques Populaires, now provides finance to small and medium-sized businesses of all kinds as well as the hotel and catering industry.
7. Sociétés de Dévéloppement Régional — established in 1955 under the control of the Ministry of Finance in 16 regions to provide investment finance by means of equity participation and long-term loans for projects which will benefit the regional economy.
8. Institut de Dévéloppement Industriel — founded in 1970 to

supply capital to medium-sized firms in industries of national strategic importance, working in collaboration with financial institutions.

The *mutual and cooperative sector* is extremely important in the French system, and its size has grown in recent years. With the benefit of fiscal and other privileges these organisations have built up their deposit base and have begun to expand the range of their activities.

The largest of these banking institutions, and one of the largest deposit banks in the world, is the *Crédit Agricole* (CA). CA is in fact an amalgam of 3,000 local credit cooperatives organised in 94 regional banks under the overall control of the state-owned Caisse Nationale du Crédit Agricole (CNCA) in Paris. The local cooperatives grant loans of all maturities for agricultural projects, farming, equipment, and so on, and many types of loan are eligible for State subsidy. The CA operates through about 5,000 branches throughout France, and there are no restrictions on depositors. In 1981 the organisation was subjected to a full rate of corporation tax for the first time, but in return it was allowed to go into housing finance and consumer credit for household spending anywhere in France, and to lend to smaller businesses outside the agricultural sector, in towns of less than 65,000 inhabitants. The CNCA acts as a clearing house, a supervisory body, and also as a medium- and long-term credit institution for the mediation of State grants and subsidies.

Some credit cooperatives are not affiliated to CNCA but are part of a separate federation whose central institution is the Banque Française de l'Agriculture et du Crédit Mutuel.

The Crédit Mutuel (CM) is a grouping of over 3,000 local mutual associations which are not specialised in their lending to different sectors. Banking operations are conducted through 21 regional banks, and a central bank provides common banking services to the group as a whole.

Both CA and CM run passbook savings accounts which offer credit or tax advantages to the depositor.

The Crédit Populaire is a grouping of 38 banks whose origins lie in mutual savings banks and credit institutions formed in provincial towns. The banks now lend mainly to small and medium-sized companies, sole traders and professional people. Again there is a central bank, the Caisse Centrale des Banques Populaires, and a separate supervisory body, the Chambre Syndicale.

The *ordinary savings banks* are non-profit institutions, many of them established by local authorities to establish savings amongst lower-income groups. There are nearly 500 banks with extensive branch networks, although many smaller branches are run on a part-time basis.

The French system is highly regulated. The authoritative body is the Ministry of Finance, but the Ministry has delegated its powers to the Bank of France which is charged with supervising all aspects of credit and currency, and consequently the whole banking system. It achieves this by operating in the financial markets, and by working with or through the two supervisory bodies, the Conseil National du Crédit (CNC), and the Commission de Contrôle des Banques (CCB).

The Bank's functions are typical of a central bank in an advanced economy — issue of legal tender, acting as banker to the government and other financial institutions, responsibility for the national currency and reserve, elaboration and application of monetary policy, administration of refinancing schemes, credit restrictions on banks, certain Treasury functions, and so on.

The *CNC* has a membership of banks, finance houses and credit institutions, presided over by the Finance Minister or the Governor of the Bank of France. It vets applications for inscription on the list of registered banks and also monitors reserve ratios set by the Bank of France. It oversees mergers and attempts to promote healthy competition in the industry.

The *CCB* is presided over by the Governor and comprises various government and banking industry representatives. It monitors registered banks through receipt of regular reports, and also has powers to make special investigations. It sets maximum and minimum solvency ratios for individual banks. It can take punitive action against recalcitrant banks, but also acts as a court of appeal against certain regulatory decisions.

The Association Française des Banques (AFB) plays an important role in liaising between the CNC and the banks themselves, as a trade association. Figure 6.1 shows the French banking system in simplified form.

The systematic nature of French regulation is shown in the various balance sheet restrictions imposed by the CCB in accordance with numerous decrees. They include:

Figure 6.1: The French Banking System (a Simplified Presentation)

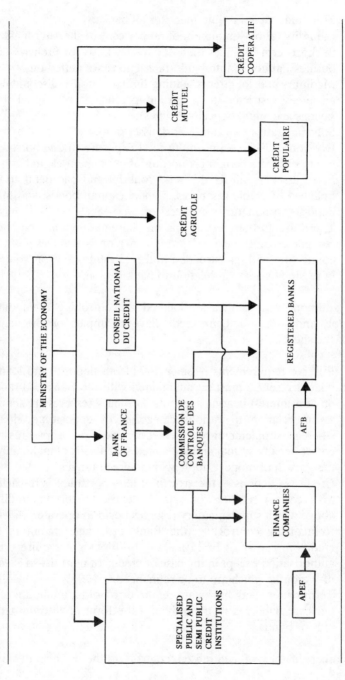

Source: Peat, Marwick, Mitchell & Co., *Banking in France* (Peat, Marwick, Mitchell & Co., Paris, 1982).

1. Minimum capital requirement for all banks.
2. Liquidity ratio — minimum of 60 per cent of short-term assets to short-term liabilities on a day-to-day basis for French franc business, although interbank transactions are netted out.
3. Medium- and long-term lending limits — non-rediscountable advances restricted to a certain coefficient of capital and savings accounts (basically 3 times).
4. Solvency ratios — a capital/risk asset ratio.
5. Division of risks — maximum total exposure to one borrower not to exceed a certain proportion of permanent capital.
6. Fixed assets — all fixed assets, doubtful and bad debts to be financed by stable resources, namely capital, bonds, and time deposits with maturity in excess of two years.
7. There are further restrictions on shareholdings in non-bank companies (not to exceed 20 per cent), on guarantees given in connection with construction and real estate, and on volume of leasing business in relation to bank capital.

In addition, various measures aimed at controlling the money supply and supply of bank credit have an impact on the banks balance sheets:

1. Reserve requirements — since 1971 both deposit- and loans-related reserves must be maintained with the Bank of France on non-interest bearing accounts. Ordinary reserves are simply set in relation to various categories of deposit and loan; whereas supplementary reserves operate on a progressive corset penalty system and are aimed specifically at maintaining the growth of money supply within agreed ranges.
2. Credit restrictions — the growth of loan portfolios is restricted to a certain multiple of capital ('encadrement du crédit'), above which supplementary reserves begin to operate.
3. Refinancing controls — the Bank of France monitors all credits in excess of FF25 million, but does not require prior authorisation except in the case of credits of maturity in excess of 3 months which are to be refinanced.
4. Term paper — all banks are required to hold a minimum of 5 per cent liabilities to the public in the form of medium-term bills or bonds.

Another feature of centralised control of the French banking system is the credit data bureau run by the Bank of France to which all loans in excess of FF450,000 must be reported. This enables credits to be monitored, and forms the basis of a statistical information service to banks.

Interest rates have now largely been deregulated since 1966 although there are still restrictions on the rates paid on demand deposits and retail time and savings deposits with maturities less than one year, administered through the CNC.

The present supervisory system is under review and proposals have been made by the Ministry of Finance for significant reforms. Important changes would be made to bring all banks including the mutuals and cooperatives under CNC control, to broaden representation on the CNC, and to give more formal powers to the Bank of France and the CCB to enable them to carry out their supervisory duties by creating a new Commission Bancaire. Moreover, the AFB would be amalgamated with the finance houses' trade association, the Association professionelle des établissements financières (APEF) to bring commercial and non-commercial banks still closer together.

The legislative background to French banking is much simpler and all measures are of recent date. The Banking Law of 1941 defined banks as 'firms or institutions professionally engaged in accepting from the public in the form of deposits or otherwise funds which they are using on their own account in discount, advances or financial operations' and established the banking register. Firms not registered are prohibited from taking deposits of less than two years' maturity from the public, and from describing themselves as banks. The Banking Law of 1945 provided for the nationalistion of the four largest banks, the creation of the CNC, and the categorisation of deposit banks, investment banks and long- and medium-term credit banks; although the reforms of 1966 and 1967, which have been previously discussed, eliminated some of the major differences for practical purposes.

Apart from regulatory provisions from time to time, the next major piece of legislation was the Nationalisation Act of 1982.

The Ministry of Economy is responsible for the French system of exchange controls designed to conserve foreign currency resources and to assist the balance of payments. Administration of the machinery is delegated to the Bank of France which relies on authorised banks to ensure observance of the rules for individual transactions. The following types of transaction are controlled:

1. Debits on non-resident accounts must be authorised by the Ministry of Finance which may also decide to control credits.
2. Imports and payments for imports.
3. Exports and payments for exports.
4. Capital transfers and investments with the exception of direct investment in the EEC and figures under FF1 million in any one year.
5. Foreign loans and borrowings.
6. Foreign exchange positions of bank dealers.

Broadly speaking, French and foreign banks are free to conduct operations in foreign currencies on the international money and capital markets from Paris.

6.2 Strategic Development of Multinational Banks

The largest French bank, the Crédit Agricole, has very limited international operations and very few overseas offices. The three national banks are among the largest 20 banks in the world and have traditionally had extensive overseas networks and undertaken a large volume of international business. As with the UK banks, some of these connections are based on old colonial political links.

However, other French banks have significant international representation, notably the former private banks Banque de Paris et des Pays-Bas, a subsidiary of Compagnie Financière de Paris et des Pays-Bas, and Banque de l'Indochine et de Suez.

Crédit Industriel et Commerciel also has some overseas branches and a good number of representative offices. BFCE has some branches and offices in major centres. Basic details are shown in Table 6.3

In their international business French banks have particular strengths in the Middle and Far East, Europe and the West Indies, but are less well placed in South America. This difference in bias reflects historical factors affecting the development of the colonial influence of European powers in the nineteenth century.

The overseas networks of the major French banks are compared in Table 6.4. For our purposes we shall concentrate on the activities of the three national banks, which are large deposit banks, have significant investment banking capabilities, and have tradi-

Table 6.3: French Multinational Banks, 1979

	Major Domestic subsidiaries & affiliates	Major International subsidiaries & affiliates	Overseas branches	Other overseas offices
Banque Nationale de Paris	6	21	24	33	23
Crédit Lyonnais	4	5	28	25	21
Société Générale	4	5	25	13	25
Compagnie Financière de Paris et des Pays-Bas	13	13	16	12[a]	15[a]
Crédit Industriel et Commercial	1	—	4	6	19
Banque de l'Indochine et de Suez	3	9	9	21	15
Banque Française du Commerce Extérieur (BFCE)	—	—	8	4	7
Crédit Agricole	N/A	N/A		1	2

Note: a. Banque de Paris et des Pays-Bas only.

Source: Banker Research Unit, *The Top 100* (Financial Times, London, 1981).

Table 6.4: French Multinational Bank Structure

100% State-owned bank (1982)	
Domestic subsidiaries	
Regional bank	Property leasing
Local banks	Equipment leasing
International bank	Instalment credit
Industrial bank	
Domestic affiliates	
Joint ventures with foreign banks	
Investment management	
International subsidiaries	
London international bank	
Swiss international bank	
Canadian international bank	
Other centres	
International affiliates	
Various participations in foreign banks	
Club membership	

tionally been involved in international banking, maintaining extensive overseas networks.

Of all the banks under study they are unique in the fact of public ownership. It is impossible to say whether this has in any way affected their overall development but certainly, as is the case with other nationalised French industries such as Renault in the motor industry, there are no restrictions on their activities applied by the State, and their stance in the markets does not differ greatly from that of competitors in other countries. Public ownership does mean that these banks have been able to maintain very low capital ratios by international standards, because the State stands behind them.

The banks are fairly monolithic in structure and in contrast to West German banks most of their activities are conducted through the parent bank rather than subsidiaries — for example, mortgage business, or international banking. The business of consolidated subsidiaries accounts for less than 10 per cent of total volume of business, although it is growing all the time. All three banks have interests in regional or local deposit banks, participations in investment banking and financial company subsidiaries, and also have stakes in credit institutions and finance companies. Through these media they have diversified their activities into leasing, factoring and instalment credit, property development and management, consumer and housing finance, investment banking and management of new issues, data processing and computer services. They also have become fully engaged in international money and capital markets through their foreign branches, offices and subsidiaries, and by participation in the three banking clubs — ABECOR, Europartners and EBIC (see Table 6.4).

They are similar to the West German Big Three banks in that, by comparison with UK banks, they have less involvement in money transmission, where the mutual banks and postal giro play an important role, but greater involvement in new issues and in mortgage banking. As in West Germany the big banks play a vital role in the capital markets because of the relative weakness of the stock exchange and investing institutions.

The relationship of the French banks to industry lies somewhere between that of the British and German banks. Their investment banking activities bring them closer to industrial management, and this relationship is fostered by the use of sectoral 'financial engineers' in the banks, by informal links among top French executives and civil servants many of whom graduate from the Haute École, and by mutual participation in the national and regional planning development process, with active collaboration in the financing of large projects.[1] Links with small and medium-sized businesses are less good, and the banks have been obliged to make special efforts to improve their penetration of the middle markets.

Differences between the individual banks are narrowing as diversification of activity leads to convergence, but there are some significant variations in emphasis. Banque Nationale de Paris (BNP) is very strong in commercial and industrial business, and has developed recently a leading role in international markets. Crédit Lyonnais has traditional strengths in consumer and housing finance, while Société Générale has strengths in financial services, property finance and the corporate sector.

The national banks have their origin in commercial banks founded in the nineteenth century to finance industrial development. This is still expressed in the full name of the Société Générale pour Favoriser le Développement du Commerce et de l'Industrie en France, and in the name of one of the two banks merged to form Banque Nationale de Paris in 1966, the Banque Nationale pour le Commerce et l'Industrie (BNCI). Crédit Lyonnais was not originally centred in Paris but has long been obliged to maintain its head office in the dominant domestic and international financial centre of France, although it still has a regional strength. The formerly very high degree of centralisation of these banks has however recently been reduced as they have given greater autonomy to regional administration.

Since the Second World War the banks have operated in a progressively liberalising environment and particularly since the reforms of 1966 and 1967 they have been free to develop their investment banking activities. Since the late-1960s they have all become involved in international banking and extended their overseas networks, as shown in Table 6.5. Table 6.6 shows the development of the banks' balance sheets. The low proportion of shareholders funds to assets and high proportion of advances to assets by comparison with other MNBs reflect the beneficial consequences for prudential bank management of nationalised status.

6.3 Case Study — Société Générale

The Société Générale pour Favoriser le Développement du Commerce et de l'Industrie en France, SA, which now describes itself as a French and international bank, was founded in 1864 by the steel magnate Joseph-Eugene Schneider. It originally evolved as an industrial bank with an extensive customer base in the new heavy manufacturing industries of this period of the European industrial revolution.

The Bank expanded rapidly and by 1870 had branches in all the

Table 6.5: French Multinational Banks: Foreign Network Expansion, 1970–9

	1970	1971	1972	1973	1974	1975	1976	1977	1978	1979
BNP										
Branches and other offices	—	—	—	—	6	5	4	—	3	12
CL										
Branches	3	3	3	4	7	1	2	5	6	5
Other offices	2	1	—	2	1	2	3	1	2	2
SG										
Branches	—	1	—	1	—	—	1	3	—	2

Source: Banker Research Unit, *The Top 100* (Financial Times, London, 1981).

Table 6.6: Development of French National Banks, 1970–9

	1970 %	1974 %	1979 %
BNP[a]			
1. Profits/assets	N/A[b]	0.1	0.2
2. Profits/shareholders' funds	N/A	9.1	19.1
3. Shareholders' funds/assets	N/A	0.9	0.8
4. Advances/assets	N/A	62.1	83.4
CL[a]			
1. Profits/assets	0.7		0.2
2. Profits/shareholders' funds	46.5		17.30
3. Shareholders' funds/assets	1.5		1.33
4. Advances/assets	91.5		86.0
SG[a]			
1. Profits/assets	0.2		0.2
2. Profits/shareholders' funds	11.1		14.3
3. Shareholders' funds/assets	1.6		1.7
4. Advances/assets	98.8		71.9

Notes: a. Consolidated for 1974 and 1979, unconsolidated for 1970. b. BNP accounting systems were changed in 1974 and previous years' figures are not comparable. Accounting standards for all banks were also changed in 1978, so that figures before 1978 are not strictly comparable. Therefore rates of growth have not been calculated.

Source: Banker Research Unit, *The Top 100* (Financial Times, London, 1981).

economically progressive regions of France. It engaged in international trade finance and in 1871 opened its first foreign office, in London. With its strengths in corporate and international finance the Société grew to be one of the largest universal banks in France and gained experience in managing a foreign network of subsidiaries and branches.

In 1945 the Société was one of the three large banques de dépôts chosen for nationalisation and the State remained sole shareholder until 1973. During this period the Bank played its part in the post-War reconstruction of the economy and the planned growth and development of regions and industrial sectors under the French system of economic management. The boards of directors of the nationalised banks have always enjoyed and still maintain autonomy in their operations, but they are expected to cooperate with the Bank of France and Ministry of Finance in the observation and enforcement of monetary policy and exchange controls, in restrictions on volume of credit, in guidance on priorities for lending, and on interest rates. The Société has also along with the others been expected to participate in French schemes to support exports in collaboration with BFCE and Coface.[2]

During the early-1970s the Bank expanded its foreign network by means of representative offices, branches in important financial or industrial centres, acquisition of foreign subsidiaries, and various participations (see Table 6.7). Having established a solid base in Europe during the early-1970s the Bank has since spread its wings and established a significant presence in all quarters, but notably in China and the Far East. The Bank also has important affiliated banks in many ex-colonial areas of Africa with which France still has special relationships.

This overseas network, extending representation from 15 countries in 1966 to 65 in 1980, has enabled the Bank to participate actively in the growth of the international money and capital markets and it has established itself as a major provider and manager of syndicated credits and Eurobonds, and as an active borrower and lender on the interbank markets in Paris and other centres. In 1982, for example, it managed 22 Eurobond issues for French and Canadian borrowers (12 in 1981 and 10 in 1980) and co-managed over 80. It managed or co-managed 68 Eurocredit deals (50 in 1981) to a total value of US$ 19.5 billion, giving priority to existing customers. The Bank also provides finance of foreign trade, foreign exchange, and engages in international leasing.

It is a member of the EBIC club of European banks. The Société is the smallest of the three national banks and has the least extensive overseas network but it is rapidly expanding its international activities. At present it has about 30 per cent of total assets in foreign currencies, and this is the same proportion as BNP and CL, but a larger part of this 30 per cent is in interbank lending. It derives about 40 per cent of total profit from overseas activities, but this is expected to increase as the newly established branches, especially those in the USA and Far East, begin to make larger contributions.

A senior executive of the Bank[3] has said that international profits are derived as follows:

Foreign branches and subsidiaries/affiliates	70%
Export credits	15%
Foreign exchange	10%
Other	5%

Table 6.7: Growth of Société Générale Group International Network, 1972–81

	1972 to 1976	1977	1978	1979	1980	1981
Representative offices	Caracas Berlin Teheran Beirut Jakarta Moscow Bangkok Warsaw	Cairo Manila Bucharest Stockholm Sydney São Paulo	Bogotá New Delhi Belgrade Athens Lagos	Buenos Aires Oslo	Nairobi Rome Hong Kong (China) Sofia Houston Edinburgh	Peking Canton Séoul Harare (Salisbury)
Branches	Tokyo Birmingham Manama	Hong Kong Amsterdam Frankfurt	Bristol New York	Leeds Singapore	Manila Taipei Athens Milan Rotterdam Bucharest	Los Angeles Panama
Subsidiaries		Sogeko (South Korea) S.G. S.A. (Canada) Inc.	Hudson Securities (USA)		S.G. Strauss Turnbull Ltd (Great Britain) S.G. Australia Ltd	
Affiliates	BEAL UAB EURAB BRADESCO EURAS EBC Union Congolaise de Banque Cominif (Iran) Coframex (Mexico) Al Bank Al Ahli Al Omani (Oman)	Sogefinance (Ivory Coast) S.G. (Nigeria Ltd)	Frab Bank (Middle East) (Bahrain)	Sudanese Investment Bank National S.G., Bank S.A. (Egypt)	Central European International Bank Ltd (Hungary) Trade Credits Ltd (Australia)	Banco Sogeral Brazil

Source: *Annual Report* (1981).

The Bank's Euroloan portfolio is concentrated on prime French borrowers and leading names from other OECD countries including Canada, with loans to Eastern Europe (10–12%), South America (12%) and Africa (8%) accounting for about one third of Eurolending.

In the immediate future the Bank foresees further expansion in the Far East.

In its domestic markets the Bank has diversified its activities to a considerable extent and has achieved the status of a universal bank. It is particularly strong in the areas of property investment, development, and leasing; and in the provision of leasing, factoring and hire purchase services to industry. The Bank also has subsidiaries engaged in export promotion, software development, and the usual range of unit/investment trusts (French SICAVs). It has an investment bank subsidiary, regional and local banks, medium- and long-term credit banks, and software companies.

The Société has a leading position in the domestic security market, including the primary bond market (74 issues managed in 1982), the secondary bond and equity market of the Bourse (10% market share), and new listings on the unlisted securities market which has recently been established in Paris.

The Bank's fiduciary services provide asset management for French and foreign investors by means of investment in property and securities in French and overseas markets. The Bank runs various mutual and commingled funds including offshore funds (see Table 6.8).

A comprehensive list of the principal French and international subsidiaries is provided in Table 6.9, with a note of the main activity of each unit.

The Société now has 2,600 domestic branches, comparable to the network of a UK clearing bank, dealing with 2.6 million personal accounts and 300,000 companies. It has 526 overseas offices in 65 foreign countries. It employs a total staff of 45,700 — 6,800 of whom work outside France. Since 1975 the Bank has been decentralising its domestic operations and has now established 13 Regional Delegations which have broad decision-making autonomy within policy guidelines laid down by the Bank. Regional management should be able to maintain close contact with industry, business and farming circles, and play an integral part in the local community. There are twice-yearly meetings with Regional Consultative Councillors.

Table 6.8: Various Types of Portfolio Management at Société Générale Group

---

At end of 1982, total assets of the security portfolios managed by Société Générale amounted to approximately FF 29,500 million, or US$ 4,370 million.

Four types of portfolio management service can be distinguished, with net asset value at end of 1982:

Mutual investment funds (SICAV)
The seven SICAV managed by Société Générale account for the largest part of the total assets managed: FF 13,207.4 million, or $1,957 million.

Offshore investment funds
Two offshore funds, Sogen International Fund and Bond Trust of the World, are managed respectively in New York and Luxembourg: together, $126 million.

In-house funds (commingled funds), a category which includes profit-sharing schemes and private mutual funds, it being mentioned that this latter investment instrument is meeting a distinct and growing success: together FF 7,300 million, or $1,081 million.

Individual portfolios, managed on behalf either of private persons or of financial institutions: FF 8,140 million or $1,206 million.

Source: *Annual Report* (1982).

The Bank has an ongoing programme of renovation of existing branches, new branch openings, and closures. It has made large-scale investments in computer facilities and now runs four major processing centres, two of which process customer account transactions, a cheque processing centre in Paris, and a securities processing centre in Nantes.

Table 6.10 shows consolidated balance sheets for the group in 1976 and 1981. On the liabilities side we can see that the Bank has a very low overall capital ratio, reflecting its privileged position as a national bank. It relies heavily on term deposits from banks and other financial institutions (about 30 per cent in 1976 and 1981) raised on the money markets. The major source of customer deposits is individuals through sight, term and savings deposits and savings bonds (29.8 per cent of total liabilities in 1976, declining to 19.9 per cent as sight and savings deposits and savings bonds were lost), followed by companies and private businesses. The Bank has not made significant use of medium-term bonds or commercial paper.

On the asset side we see again a significant volume of interbank dealing. Loans to customers are fairly evenly spread between short- and medium- or long-term lending and there have been no significant structural changes. The Annual Report for 1981 shows

Table 6.9: Société Générale Group: Principal French Subsidiaries and Holdings

SOCIETE GENERALE ALSACIENNE DE BANQUE 'SOGENAL' (42%): an important regional bank in eastern France, with six offices in West Germany, Switzerland, Belgium, Luxembourg and Austria.

SOCIETE CENTRALE DE BANQUE 'SCDB' (84%): general banking services, with five regional subsidiaries.

SOCIETE ANONYME DE CREDIT A L'INDUSTRIE FRANCAISE 'CALIF' (88%): medium- and long-term industrial credit.

SOCIETE FINANCIERE DE VALEURS INDUSTRIELLES ET DE VALEURS DE BANQUE 'VALORIND' (100%): investment banking.

SOGEBAIL (27%): the leading real estate leasing company in France, active as well in medium- and long-term credit.

SOGEFIM (100%): real estate leasing for smaller firms.

SOFINABAIL (100%): equipment leasing.

SOGEXPORT (90%): export promotion company.

SOCIETE AUXILIAIRE DE CREDIT (90%).

SOCIETE GENERALE DE GESTION DE PATRIMOINE 'SOGESERVICE' (100%): investment, legal and tax consultants, world-wide asset manager for residents and non-residents.

International

In addition to the activities handled by its international division in Paris, as well as its worldwide network of branches — with its important New York, London and Tokyo branches — and representatives, the Bank's major foreign subsidiaries and affiliates include:

Europe

SOCIETE GENERALE BANK LIMITED (100%): the group's investment bank in London.

SOCGEN LEASE LTD (100% through Valorind): equipment leasing subsidiary in London.

SOCIETE GENERALE STRAUSS TURNBULL (55%), based in London: secondary market operations in the dollar and sterling sectors of the Eurobond market.

SOCIETE GENERALE DE BANQUE EN ESPAGNE 'SOGEBANQUE' (100%): based in Madrid, with 19 branch offices throughout Spain.

SOGELEASING INDUSTRIAL S.A. (29%): equipment leasing in Spain. 3 branches in the country.

CENTRAL EUROPEAN INTERNATIONAL BANK LTD (11%), in Hungary.

SOGELEASE ITALIA (100% through Valorind): leasing.

Middle East

SOCIETE GENERALE LIBANO-EUROPEENNE DE BANQUE (25%): 10 branches in the Lebanon.

UNITED ARAB BANK (20%): five branches in the United Arab Emirates.

AL BANK AL AHLI AL OMANI (20%): two branches in the Sultanate of Oman.

NATIONAL SOCIETE GENERALE BANK SAE (49%): in partnership with the National Bank of Egypt.

Table 6.9: continued

Asia

KOREAN FRENCH BANKING CORPORATION SOGEKO (50%): merchant bank in South Korea.

SOGELEASE JAPAN (100% through Sofinabail): leasing.

North America

SOCIETE GENERALE NORTH-AMERICA, INC. (100%), in USA.

SOGELEASE CORPORATION (100%) through Valorind): leasing in the USA.

HUDSON SECURITIES INC. (100%): investment bank, based in New York.

CREDIT BAIL SOCIETE GENERALE CANADA (100%): leasing.

SOCIETE GENERALE (CANADA) (100%): six branches.

Pacific Basin

SOCIETE GENERALE AUSTRALIA LTD (65%): investment banking and leasing.

TRADE CREDITS LTD (30%): financing company in Australia.

Latin America

ARRENDADORA INTERNACIONAL SA (40%): leasing in Mexico.

BANCO SUPERVIELLE SOCIETE GENERALE SA (52%): 24 branches in Argentina.

BANCO BRADESCO DE INVESTIMENTO (3%): leasing Brazilian investment bank.

ARRENDADORA SOGECREDITO (20% through Valorind): leasing in Venezuela.

SOGEWIESE (20% through Valorind): leasing in Peru.

Africa

Subsidiaries or participations under Société Générale's name are located in Cameroon, Senegal, Nigeria, Morocco and Ivory Coast. Other subsidiaries or participations are: SOCIETE MAURITANIENNE DE BANQUE, BANQUE DE TUNISIE, SUDANESE INTERNATIONAL BANK, UNION CONGOLAISE DE BANQUES and UNION BANCAIRE EN AFRIQUE CENTRALE. The following companies specialise in leasing: SOGEFIBAIL in Ivory Coast (55%), SOGELEASE CAMEROUN (65% through Valorind) and SOGELEASE MAROC (40% through Valorind).

In addition to the above facilities worldwide, Société Générale is also a member of EBIC (European Banks International Company), a group of seven large independent European banks, which has technically and geographically orientated joint ventures:

BANQUE EUROPEENNE DE CREDIT (14%): short, medium and long-term Eurocurrency loans, in Brussels.

EUROPEAN BANKING COMPANY LTD (14%): international investment banking, in London.

EUROPEAN ARAB HOLDING (6%): head office in Luxembourg, 4 branches.

EUROPEAN ASIAN BANK (14%): head office in Germany, 18 branches in Asia.

EUROPEAN-AMERICAN BANCORP INC. (20%): based in New York: holding company for EUROPEAN AMERICAN BANK AND TRUST COMPANY, with 96 branches, and for EUROPEAN AMERICAN BANKING CORPORATION, which specialises in international financing.

EURO-PACIFIC FINANCE CORPORATION (8%): in Australia.

Source: *Annual Report* (1982).

Table 6.10: Société Générale Group: Consolidated Balance Sheets

	1976 FF million	%	1981 FF million	%
LIABILITIES				
Central banks, cash, etc.			24,238	4.8
Banks and financial institutions				
— ordinary accounts	14,040 ⎱	7.8	31,085	6.2
— fixed term deposits	53,095 ⎰	29.4	155,322	31.0
Securities			35,617	7.1
Customer accounts				
Companies & sundry accounts				
— sight	19,228	10.6	47,306	9.4
— term	18,425	10.2	48,481	9.7
Private individuals				
— sight	16,550	9.2	29,730	5.9
— term	5,431	3.0	11,920	2.4
Savings deposits	16,925	9.4	28,180	5.6
Total deposits	76,559	42.4	158,065	31.5
Fixed term savings bonds	14,838	8.2	30,259	6.0
Debtors	1,720	1.0	26,063	5.2
Other accounts	15,500	8.6	23,614	4.7
Securities transactions	596	0.3	2,454	0.5
Bonds	1,257	0.7	5,831	1.2
Capital and reserves				
Reserves from consolidation	274	0.1	1,157	0.2
Revaluation	—	—	1,174	0.2
Reserves	512	0.3	2,610	0.5
Capital	800	0.4	1,143	0.2
Extra-group holdings	1,040	0.6	1,288	0.3
Year's profit	519	0.3	1,131	0.2
Total capital and reserves	3,145	1.7	8,503	1.7
TOTAL LIABILITIES	180,750	100.0	501,052	100.0
ASSETS				
Central banks, cash, etc.	3,762	2.1	14,119	2.8
Banks and financial institutions				
— ordinary accounts	6,481	3.6	23,357	4.7
— term accounts	48,422	26.8	143,702	28.7
Bills and securities	16,688	9.2	38,643	7.7
Loans to customers				
— commercial loans			31,007	6.2
— other short loans	30,327	16.8	63,696	12.7
— medium-term loans	14,663	8.1	50,953	10.2
— long-term loans	15,393	8.5	39,664	7.9
Total loans to customers	60,383	33.4	185,320	37.0
Customer accounts	14,588	8.1	14,763	2.9
Collections	567	0.3	34,172	6.8
Other accounts	18,688	10.3	16,476	3.3
Securities transactions	901	0.5	2,561	0.5

Table 6.10: continued

Investment secutities	2,790	1.4	9,983	2.0
Participations	1,194	0.7	2,646	0.5
Non-consolidation subsidiaries	27	—	205	0.1
Goodwill	16	—	49	—
Revaluation surplus	—	—	178	0.1
Subordinated loans	—	—	60	—
Fixed assets	2,522	1.4	4,336	0.9
Leasing transactions	2,663	1.5	8,123	1.6
Capital assets leased	1,058	0.6	2,353	0.5
TOTAL ASSETS	180,750	100.0	501,052	100.0

that 82 per cent of lending was to companies and businesses and 18 per cent to individuals. The breakdown between maturities was as follows:

	Short-term	Medium- and long-term
Individuals	6.6%	93.4%
Companies and private businesses	55.2%	44.8%
All customers	47.6%	52.4%

Since 1976 there has been a general trend towards a greater volume of medium- and long-term lending, from 46.9 per cent of lending to all types of customer in 1976 to 52.4 per cent in 1981.

In February 1982 the Société reverted to 100 per cent State ownership and all private shareholders who had acquired shares between 1973 and 1982 were required to give up their shares in return for compensation. The new President appointed was M. Jacques Mayoux, formerly head of the steel group Sacilor. One of his major concerns has been the role of the national banks in the process of economic adjustment and corporate restructuring in the wake of the world recession and changes in world trading problems.[4]

Notes

1. See Bayliss and Butt Philip (1980).
2. This type of collaboration is no different in kind from that practised in other countries, notably the UK and Japan, although the French system of export credit

and insurance is undoubtedly one of the most comprehensive, and does include a substantial element of refinancing at fine rates.

3. *Financial Times*, 6 August 1982. Interview with M. Léopold Joerger, deputy general manager and director of international activities.

4. *Financial Times*, interview (1982).

References

Bayliss, B.T. and Butt Philip, A.A.S., *Capital Markets and Industrial Investment in Germany and France* (Saxon House, Farnborough, 1980).

Frazer, P. and Vittas, D., *The Retail Banking Revolution* (Michael Lafferty Publications, London, 1982), ch. 13.

Lab, R. for Banker Research Unit, *Banking Structures and Sources of Finance in the European Community* (*Financial Times*, London, 1981), ch. 2, 'France'.

Lees, F.A. and Eng. M., *International Financial Markets* (Praeger, New York, 1975), ch. 10, 'Financial Markets in France'.

Maycock, J., *European Banking: Structures and Prospects* (Graham and Trotman, London, 1977), ch. 1,, 'France'.

Morgan, E.V. *et al.* for EAG, *Banking Systems and Monetary Policy in the EEC* (*Financial Times*, London, 1974), ch. 3, 'France'.

Peat, Marwick, Mitchell & Co., *Banking in France* (Peat, Marwick, Mitchell & Co., Paris, 1982).

Vittas, D. (ed.) for IBRO, *Banking Systems Abroad* (Committee of London Clearing Bankers, London, 1978), ch. 3, 'France'.

Weston, R., *Domestic and Multinational Banking* (Croom Helm, London, 1980), Part 2, ch. 4.

Data Sources

Annual Reports of French banks.

Banker Research Unit, *The Top 100* (Financial Times, London, 1981).

Conseil National du Crédit, Annual Reports and Statistics.

7 WEST GERMAN BANKS

7.1 Financial System

The West German financial system is dominated by its deposit-taking institutions, especially banks, which are free to engage in all types of financial services, to participate in securities markets, and to invest in commercial and industrial companies. There are many different types of bank, the industry is not heavily concentrated, and most banks act as 'Universalbanken' offering the full range of services. There are a few specialist institutions. The banking sector is of course subject to overall regulation and control, especially in the area of international banking, but, in general, market forces and competition have been allowed to flourish.

There are three major categories of multi-purpose bank ('Universalbank') — commercial banks, savings institutions and cooperative banks. The savings institutions account for the largest volume of business, followed by the commercial banks and then the cooperatives (see Table 7.1). By far the largest specialist institutions are the mortgage banks, some of which are subsidiaries of the large commercial banks. Other specialist institutions are hire purchase houses, the Post Office, and various banks with particular functions.

Commercial banks include the *Big Three banks*, namely, Deutsche Bank AG, Dresdner Bank AG, and Commerzbank AG, together with their Berlin subsidiaries. These are archetypal commercial banks with their origins in private industrial banks founded in the middle of the nineteenth century. They have national branch networks of average size about 1,000 branches, and they also have wholly- or partly-owned subsidiaries among regional banks, private banks, specialist banks, and non-bank financial institutions. Although their share of total banking business has been declining since the War the Big Three banks are still a powerful force in the West German financial system, especially in the provision of short-term credit to industry. They are also the leading banks in the international field, with extensive overseas representation, and some foreign subsidiaries. They have close links with West German industry through shareholdings, representation on boards, and their activities in the securities markets. As Universalbanken

Table 7.1: West Germany: Selected Bank Statistics

	Bank offices			Business volume	
	No. of		Total	No. of	DM
	Banks	Branches	Banks	Banks	million
	as of 31 December 1981			as of 31 December 1981	
1. Commercial Banks					
"Big banks"[a]	6	3,125	3,131	6	228,149
Regional banks and other commercial banks	99	2,465	2,564	98	261,969
Branches of foreign banks	55	46	101	56	51,831
Private bankers	83	276	359	80	36,973
	243	5,912	6,155	240	578,922
2. Central Institutions of Savings Banks	12	312	324	12	418,490
3. Savings Banks	598	16,973	17,571	598	355,187
4. Central Institutions of Credit Cooperatives	10	47	57	10	103,218
5. Credit Cooperatives	3,933	15,799	19,732	2,268[b]	283,550
6. Mortgage Banks	38	31	69	38	358,375
7. Instalment Finance Institutions	104	654	758	117	29,755
8. Banks with special functions	16	74	90	16	169,189
9. Other (not covered by statistics	98	19	117	—	—
10. Postal Giro and Postal Savings Banks	15	(every post office)		15	41,726
Total	5,067	39,821	44,873	3,314	2,538,412

Notes: a. Deutsche Bank, Dresdner Bank, Commerzbank, and their Berlin affiliates.
b. Volume of cooperatives only reporting to the Deutsche Bundesbank.

Source: Monthly Report of the Deutsche Bundesbank, March 1982. Quoted in Peat, Marwick, Mitchell & Co., *Banking in Germany* (Peat, Marwick, Mitchell & Co., Frankfurt, 1982).

the Big Three undertake the full range of commercial and investment banking services and are active in all the significant domestic and international financial markets.

The regional commercial banks are less easily categorised. They tend to have particular strengths and emphases in their business mix, although they are in fact multi-purpose banks; and they have regional origins although many have national coverage. The most important banks are the Bank für Gemeinwirtschaft which is based in Frankfurt and has a national network of branches; the two large Bavarian deposit banks based in Munich — Bayerische Vereinsbank and Bayerische Hypotheken- und Wechsel-Bank —

which have great strength in their local savings markets through networks of over 300 branches largely concentrated in Southern Germany, and which are also privileged to undertake mortgage business on their own account; and the Berliner Handels- und Frankfurter Bank based in Berlin and Frankfurt which has a network of some 30 branches. There are also a number of smaller and more specialised banks which are really comparable to the private banks but are registered as companies rather than sole traders or partnerships. There are in addition a number of small West German overseas banks based in the old trading towns, notably the Ibero-American Bank AG (Bremen), Deutsch-Sudamerikanische Bank AG (Hamburg) and European Asian Bank AG (Hamburg).

Foreign banks have significant representation in West Germany through subsidiaries as well as branches. Most international banks have at least one branch in the country, engaging in wholesale banking, and usually sited in Frankfurt, Düsseldorf, or Hamburg, which are the major West German financial centres, although Frankfurt has in recent years come to play the most important role in international banking. In 1982, 273 foreign banks had offices in Germany — 190 representative offices, 58 branches, and 28 wholly-owned subsidiaries. Foreign banks also had stakes in about 30 West German-domiciled banks. The countries with the biggest input were France, Italy, Spain, Switzerland, UK, USA, Canada, Japan, Turkey and Yugoslavia. Spanish, Turkish and Yugoslav banks cater for immigrant workers, the others are interested in developing international banking business. These banks tend to concentrate on short- and medium-term lending to large West German companies and to West German subsidiaries of foreign companies; trade financing; solicitation of Eurocredit business for offices outside West Germany; interbank lending, foreign exchange and payment services. Some foreign banks have also established equipment leasing subsidiaries.

Private banks are still quite numerous in West Germany, constituted in the legal form of sole traders or partnerships. They have single offices or small local networks. They frequently specialise in activities such as bill discounting, securities trading and foreign exchange and in this respect are similar to British merchant banks. Nevertheless, they are Universalbanken and some have consumer and other commercial banking business.

The savings banks (Sparkassen) have their origins in the banks established in the late eighteenth century to provide savings and credit facilities to working people. Many of them have become linked with local or regional authorities which stand behind them by way of guarantee. They enjoy certain tax privileges as a consequence of their public status, but are also often restricted in their permissible activities by state rather than federal legislation, and prevented for example from trading in securities or dealing on the interbank deposit or foreign exchange markets. They are directed to use their savings deposits for long-term lending, especially mortgage lending or loans to their sponsoring town or country. There are about 600 Sparkassen and they occupy a strong position in the retail deposits market.

Crucial to the rapid development of the savings bank movement have been the *central institutions* which operate without restriction on activity. These Landesbanken/Girozentralen operate at the state level.[1] They collect surplus funds from local Sparkassen and on-lend these to other members, or on the short-term money markets, where they are powerful participants. They also issue bank bonds, a major source of funds to them. They also operate a giro system for cheques and money transfers between banks, and centralised services such as data processing, safe custody of securities, and so on. They all operate mortgage banks. The central institutions also deal in foreign exchange, and have begun to participate in international banking markets on a significant scale, especially in the short term Euromarkets. At the national level activities are coordinated by the Deutsche Girozentrale.

The cooperative banks have their origins in local self-help credit cooperatives founded in the middle of the nineteenth century, often combining trading and banking functions. The two distinct movements of Volksbanken and Raiffeisenbanken were merged in 1971 and the number of cooperatives has been decreasing rapidly, so that there are now fewer than 4,000 banks, some of them so small that they are run by part-time staff. There are regional cooperative banks, the Genossenschaftliche Zentralkassen, and a national bank, the Deutsche Genossenschaftsbank in Frankfurt. These banks act in similar fashion to the upper tiers of the Sparkassen, operating the giro system, dealing on the money markets and capital markets, and engaging in international banking activities. They also provide centralised services for members. The central institutions of the cooperative movement have not been as aggressive in entering commercial banking markets as the central savings bank institutions. The movement as a whole is not driven by profit objectives but is bound to serve the interests of its members. A large proportion of lending is still to individual members and small local businesses, although all restrictions on lending to non-members were removed in 1974.

The most important *specialist institutions* are the mortgage banks, which offer long-term housing loans and loans to local authorities. They take long-term time deposits but also issue mortgages or communal bonds. Some specialise in mortgages on agricultural property or shipping finance. There are 39 banks altogether, 14 publicly and 25 privately constituted. Most of the public banks are Landesbank/Girozentral subsidiaries, while most of the private banks are subsidiaries of the Big Three banks and regional commercial banks.

The commercial banks offer hire purchase facilities but there are also a number of specialist houses, the largest of which are bank subsidiaries, or closely linked to banks. Others are closely linked to manufacturers, especially car manufacturers.

There are a number of banks created to fulfil a special purpose. Briefly, the major institutions are:

1. Industriekreditbank — medium- and long-term loans for industry, especially small and medium-sized enterprises and industry in Berlin.
2. Ausfuhrkredit-Gesellschaft — medium- and long-term export finance (founded by commercial banks, 1952).
3. Privatdiskont — import and export trade financing by way of bill discount (1959).
4. Deutsche Wagnisfinanzierungs-Gesellschaft — founded as recently as 1975 by 27 commercial banks to provide risk capital and advice to small and medium-sized businesses, especially for the finance of innovations. It is supported by the government.
5. Kreditanstalt fur Wiederaufbau — long-term export credits and development finance (1948).
6. Lastenausgleichsbank — originally founded to assist refugees and war victims, but now also providing assistance to small and medium-sized businesses and to local environmental projects.

The West German *Post Office* offers money transfer, postal

cheque and savings services through a network of nearly 19,000 branches. It offers only minimal lending facilities, in the form of overdrafts to customers whose salaries are directly credited to their giro account. The Post Office does not have a large share of banking business.

The *building societies* (Bausparkassen) are mutual savings and mortgage associations whose sole purpose is to provide second mortgages to depositors. The largest are branches of the Landesbanken/Girozentralen, and others have links with banks or insurance companies. Their deposits receive favourable tax treatment.

Investment funds operate open funds in shares and bonds, and some real estate funds. They are closely regulated and are mostly subsidiaries of commercial banks.

Credit guarantee associations have been specially created by commercial and savings banks or local chambers of commerce to provide guarantees to members, especially smaller firms.

Securities depositories hold securities and operate a giro system for securities holdings of members, in the seven West German stock exchanges. The principal members are banks.

Investing institutions play a less important role in financial intermediation in the West German economy than in the UK and USA. The proportion of contractual savings to total savings is only about one third of the equivalent proportion in those countries, largely because state retirement benefits in West Germany are better, and because companies fund pensions from reserves created within their own balance sheets. The important institutions are the social security funds, which since 1972 have provided widespread benefits to contributors including the self-employed; and the life insurance companies, private pension funds, and general insurance companies.

The West German banking system has been governed by comprehensive legislation for some years, although banks are allowed a good deal of freedom to operate within the basic regulatory framework.

The fundamental statute is the Kreditwesengesetz (Banking Law), originally passed in 1934, revised in 1961 and elaborated in 1974. The Law provides a definition of banking activities for which permission must be obtained from the Federal Banking Supervisory Board[2]. This Board acts in cooperation with the central bank, on which it relies for support and guidance. Banking activities include deposit taking, loans, discounting, securities brokerage and custody, investment fund management, guarantees, and money transmission. Thus West German banks are able to provide commercial and investment banking services without hindrance.

The Supervisory Board requires banks to have at least two experienced owners or managers, to have sufficient capital resources and, in most cases, to be incorporated. The Board has the power to request information, order special audits, intervene in the conduct of business and to close the bank down.

The Banking Law also requires monthly reports from banks and annual accounts to be presented to the central bank. It requires banks to report loans in excess of DM 1 million to the central bank[3], loans to directors, managers and subsidiaries of the bank, and loans which exceed 15 per cent of the bank's equity. The Law establishes four governing principles of bank management:

1. Loans and investments (with the exception of certain low-risk loans) are not to exceed 18 times capital and reserves — risk assets ratio.
2. Long-term loans and investments must be funded on a long-term basis, for which purpose 60 per cent of savings deposits and 10 per cent of non-bank sight and time deposits are deemed to be long-term funds.
3. Certain short-term liabilities are not to exceed certain short-term assets.
4. The open position banks can maintain on foreign exchange markets and the markets for precious metals are strictly limited. In general these rules, which apply to all banks including foreign banks, are designed to ensure that all banks preserve adequate capital and sufficient liquidity for their own safety and the safety of the whole financial system.

In recent years West German banks have introduced deposit security schemes. These have been devised by the banking associations of the different types of bank, with official approval. The scheme run by the commercial banks provides limited safeguards for deposits of non-bank customers, up to 50 per cent of the banks' equity capital. These banks have also established a consortium liquidity bank to help banks in difficulties. These and other measures were brought in partly in response to the problems caused by the failure of one large private bank, Herstatt, in 1974, which was unable to meet its foreign exchange commitments.

The Deutsche Bundesbank was established by the Federal Bank Act of 1957. Its head office is in Frankfurt and it maintains regional offices known as Landeszentralbanken in each of the eleven states. These banks in turn operate 210 branches in provincial centres. Prior to 1957 the Landeszentralbanken were independent state banks. Their presidents now have seats on the Central Bank Council which is the main policy-making body of the central bank, particularly for monetary policy.

The Bundesbank performs the normal central banking functions including note issue, banker to commercial banks, banker to government. It is charged with regulation of the money supply and protection of the currency. It is an independent body but is bound to support the general economic policy of the federal government. In attaining its objectives the Bundesbank makes use of discount rate and money market rate policy, open market operations, and applies quantitative and qualitative credit controls. It also imposes minimum reserve requirements on banks, and may from time to time issue directives to the banking community.

The Bundesbank has acted firmly to maintain low levels of inflation and remarkably low interest rates by international standards. It has taken steps to restrict the use of the Deutschemark as a reserve currency and to insulate the West German financial markets from international capital flows as far as possible. For example, it has imposed very severe reserve requirements against liabilities to non-residents, sometimes as much as 100 per cent, to prevent the inflow of foreign capital.

In domestic monetary policy it has operated a system of monetary base control and maintains firm monetary targets. Although there are at present no exchange control restrictions in force, the Foreign Trade Act (Aussenwirtschaftsgesetz) of 1961 provides for the possibility of limiting inflows of foreign capital, outward investments, and the import and export of gold. The authorities do require extensive reporting of such transactions.

7.2 Strategic Development of Multinational Banks

A number of West German multi-purpose banks have now become active in international banking markets. Relatively few, however, have any significant overseas representation. The truly multinational banks for our purposes are the Big Three commercial banks, which have traditionally provided the full range of trade finance services to their corporate customers, and have been able to build on their experience in these areas. Other banks have more recently entered the field and have tended to specialise in certain markets.

The other banks which are significant presences in the international banking scene and which are among the world's 50 largest banks are the two Bavarian regional banks, Bayerische Vereinsbank and Bayerische Hypotheken- und Wechsel-Bank; the more progressive Landesbanken/Girozentralen, especially the Westdeutsche, but also the Bayerische; the central Deutsche Genossenschaftsbank; and the central Bank für Gemeinwirtschaft. The profiles presented in Table 7.2 show that only the Westdeutsche LG and Bayerische Vereinsbank have the same range of investments in overseas activities as the Big Three banks.

The overseas offices maintained by the West German Big Three banks reflect a similar selective policy of representation in major industrial and financial centres to that adopted by the Japanese city banks. Branches are typically opened in New York, London, Chicago, Hong Kong, Singapore, Tokyo and other centres. Representative offices are maintained in strategic locations around the world. The other banks maintain much less extensive networks, with branches perhaps in London, New York and Tokyo, and a few scattered representative offices. These banks do not have the same need to service the demands of West German industry in its multinational operations, and have only operated overseas offices since the early-1970s.

We shall now concentrate our attention on the Big Three banks, which are the money-centre deposit banks equivalent to those studied in other countries. The main banks engage in all types of permitted banking activity, taking deposits from individuals, corporations and other banks, and lending to all sectors of the economy, in domestic and foreign currencies, dealing with residents and non-residents. They deal in foreign exchange and precious metals; act as stockbrokers; make investments and engage in investment advice, analysis and management; issue and underwrite bonds; represent shareholders who have deposited securities; undertake trust business; and finance housing projects. They have extensive domestic branch networks, the largest being Deutsche Bank (1,300), then Dresdner Bank (1,100) and Commerzbank (800). The banks employ large numbers of staff, mainly in domestic operations — Deutsche Bank for example employs about

Table 7.2: West German Multinational Banking, 1979

	Domestic Subsidiaries	Domestic Affiliates	International Subsidiaries	International Offices	Overseas Branches	ROs
BIG THREE						
Deutsche Bank[a]	20	15	8	28	12	18
Dresdner Bank	13	13	4	15	8	14
Commerzbank	7	16	3	16	9	19
a. Plus some branches jointly run with Deutsche-Sudamerikanische Bank						
REGIONAL BANKS						
Bayerische Vereinsbank	7	7	3	18	6	10
Bayerische Hypotheken- und Wechsel-Bank	4	12	3	4	2	7
Bank für Gemeinwitschaft (BfG)	6	5	4	2	2	2
SAVINGS BANK CENTRAL INSTITUTIONS						
Westdeutsche Landesbank Girozentrale	5	6	2	10	3	7
Bayerische LG	7	8	1	—	1	4
COOPERATIVE BANK CENTRAL INSTITUTION						
Deutsche Genossenschaftsbank	4	17	4	5	5	3

Source: Banker Research Unit, *The Top 100* (Financial Times, London, 1981).

40,500 staff, some 35,000 at home and 5,500 overseas.

The typical structure of subsidiaries and affiliates is shown in Figure 7.1. The Berlin banks are subsidiaries for legal and technical reasons. The West German banks have diversified their retail banking activities and extended their representation by acquiring mortgage banks to provide long-term credit for house purchase and development. They have also acquired local savings banks and unit trust management companies. In order to provide comprehensive commercial credit facilities, they have acquired subsidiaries specialising in leasing, factoring, hire purchase and bill finance.

All the big banks have stakes in various commercial bank joint ventures such as the AKA, the liquidity and liquidation banks, the venture capital company and shipping banks. These participations show the West German banks' willingness to cooperate in the interests of economic development and to promote the welfare of West German industry.

On the international front the Luxembourg subsidiaries play a key role. They were established by the banks in order to conduct

Figure 7.1: Typical Structure of West German Multinational Bank

Domestic Subsidiaries
Berlin Bank
Mortgage banks
Private bank
Savings banks
Unit trust management
Leasing companies (equipment, property)
Factoring company
Hire purchase

Domestic Affiliates
AKA (export finance)
Liquidity bank
Venture capital
Shipping bank
Liquidation banks

International Subsidiaries[a]
Luxembourg finance company
Singapore subsidiary

International Affiliates
Investment bank (Middle East)
Investment bank (Far East)
Investment bank (South America)
Finance corporation (Australia)
'Club' participation

Note: a. Deutsche Bank also has capital corporation subsidiaries in New York, London, Hong Kong and elsewhere.

international banking operations outside the jurisdiction of the Bundesbank, and in particular to avoid the reserve requirements imposed by the authorities which have from time to time heavily penalised foreign currency and non-resident deposit-taking activities. In some respects these subsidiaries fulfil a similar role to that performed by the London and Caribbean branches of the US banks. Although they are subsidiaries, their activities are fully integrated with those of the parent bank. They account for about one half of all the banks' international lending. All the banks also have a Singapore subsidiary which gives access to the Asian dollar, as the Luxembourg subsidiary gives access to the Eurodollar market.

It is difficult to generalise about the extensive overseas participations of the West German banks. They have concentrated on making investments in investment development banks and finance corporations in key areas with prospects for economic growth — the Middle East, Far East, South America and Australia. The West German banks have shown little interest in establishing a presence in foreign retail markets, although there are still some old colonial links with banks in South America and Africa.

The banks have extensive correspondent relationships of long standing. They also showed in the early-1970s great enthusiasm for the idea of cooperation in international banking by means of the so-called banking clubs or consortium banks. Deutsche Bank has since 1963 been a member of European Banks International Company SA, Brussels (EBIC), along with Amsterdam-Rotterdam Bank, Banca Commerciale Italiana, Kreditanstalt Bankverein, Midland Bank, Société Générale de Banque, and Société Générale. EBIC itself has a number of subsidiaries and affiliates and is represented in all the major financial centres. Dresdner Bank has been involved since 1971 with Dutch, West German, Belgian, Italian, French and British banks in the ABECOR group. It also participates in the Euro-Latinamerican Bank (1974). Commerzbank has been involved since 1971 with the Europartners group together with Banco di Roma, Crédit Lyonnais, and Banco Hispanico Americano. ABECOR and Europartners have various investments and extensive overseas representation in similar fashion to EBIC, although EBIC remains the most important of these consortium banks.

Overall, the international business of the big banks accounts for over a third of total assets and net profits at present. The banks are major participants in the Eurocredit markets and are market leaders in the Eurobond markets. The West German banks are the major placers of Eurobond issues along with the Swiss banks. They play a unique role in Deutschemark Eurocredits, and enjoy a privileged position in Euromark bond issues since these must be placed by a West German bank. In the bond markets the Big Three meet intense competition from the state banks and central banking institutions.

In their domestic operations the parent banks rely on deposits, while the mortgage bank subsidiaries are largely funded by the issue of bonds. The deposits consist largely of time and savings deposits from the personal and business sector, and interbank deposits which account for as much as one third of total group deposits. The major uses of funds are in lending. Somewhat less than a third of total lending is in the form of mortgage advances, the rest consisting of short- and medium-term credits to the personal and business sector. The banks are required to maintain a considerable proportion of their assets in the form of liquid assets.

The banks' involvement in securities trading is not fully reflected in their balance sheets. They are dominant forces in placing of new issues and in trading in the secondary market. They frequently act as lead managers of placing consortia. They also frequently act as agents for the provision of long-term credits to industry, even though their own share of long-term lending is smaller than that of other banks.

There has been a considerable amount of comment on the West German banks' involvement in non-bank enterprises in industry, trade and insurance. West German banks are permitted to have investments in non-related businesses, although they are obliged to disclose long-term investments where they hold more than 25 per cent of the company's shares. It has been estimated that banks hold about 7.5 per cent of all quoted ordinary shares, and most of these are held by the big banks.[4] They tend to be in medium- to large-sized companies, and are mostly concentrated in construction, brewing, cement and retailing. The banks' involvement in industry has not been increasing, and recently there have been significant disposals by major banks. Some of the investments were acquired historically as a result of rescue operations conducted by the banks when borrowing companies failed.[5]

These investments carry voting rights, and when the investment exceeds 25 per cent of voting shares this effectively gives the bank a power of veto. Bank officials have extensive representation on company boards linked to voting rights. They also have seats on the supervisory (non-executive) boards of companies in which the bank has no stake. Many of the largest West German companies have bank representatives on the supervisory board.

In addition to their own voting rights the banks represent customers who have deposited shares with them, by way of proxy voting. Usually the customer leaves the bank free to exercise its own voting discretion. Banks can also take over the votes of other shareholders by mutual agreement. These bank voting rights, although significant in volume, are highly dispersed and do not represent a concentration of bank voting power.

There is no evidence that banks exert undue influence over West German industry. Nevertheless, their relation to industry is closer than the traditional 'arm's length' of British banking. This stems from the fact that the banks provide investment banking and stockbroking services and so maintain their position as the customer's closest financial adviser in all circumstances. Large West German companies also tend, like Japanese corporations, to turn to a house bank for the provision of the full range of financial services, even though they also maintain multiple banking relationships.

The role of the universal banks has been vigorously debated in West Germany. In 1979 the Gessler Commission reported its findings after a selective study of major problems in the banking industry. The Commission endorsed the present system and did not find that banks exerted great power over West German industry,[6] or that competition had been inhibited by the growth of the large bank groups. Nor did the Commission seek to impose any special controls over the rapidly growing international business of the banks.

In the extremely important capital markets the banks exercise self-regulation through the medium of the Capital Markets Sub-committee. Representatives of the major banks including all the Big Three banks sit on this committee and monitor the markets. They vet all proposed issues and administer the queuing system in the interests of orderly markets.

The Big Three banks have long histories as commercial banks. Before the First World War they maintained overseas branches to service the needs of German industry in its foreign trade activities. These activities were curtailed by the War and during the 1920s and 1930s Germany's economic and financial problems prevented the re-emergence of German banks on the international scene. There were numerous bank failures during the Depression and subsequently the industry was closely regulated. The large banks inevitably became closely involved with the financing of German industry in the war effort in the latter part of the 1930s.

Under Allied occupation the West German elements of the Big Three banks were broken up into 30 separate regional elements, with their activities confined to separate provinces. Opening of new branches was strictly controlled until 1958, and interest rates on deposits and loans were controlled until 1967. During the 1950s the Big Three banks regrouped and by 1957 had emerged once more as national banks with central organisations free to pursue commercial objectives. The separate constitution of the Berlin subsidiaries remains as a relic of the period of imposed dispersal.

During the 1960s the banks placed considerable emphasis on the development of a full range of domestic financial services. In particular, they sought to strengthen their position in the retail banking markets by offering small personal loans and instalment loans for specific purposes and by extending their branch networks. They acquired mortgage banks and in the late-1960s and early-1970s made efforts to provide an integrated housing finance service available through the branch network. Housing loans in West Germany are often packaged from more than one source and the banks have acquired the subsidiaries necessary to provide all types of finance, and made the service available through their own branches. They have also experimented with the provision of wider information services in the housing field. In the latter part of the 1970s the traditional fixed rate mortgages were supplemented with variable rate loans.

In the late-1960s the banks added to their share dealing and investment services by acquiring interests in investment funds of various types. They also developed during the 1970s new types of deposit/savings accounts and mixed deposit/investment plans to attract retail savings deposits. Here too, experiments have been made in the provision of information centres for investing customers.

Subsidiaries were also acquired to provide commercial credit services such as hire purchase, factoring and leasing to business customers. In the mid-1970s the banks in West Germany as in other countries turned their attention to the middle market, providing special small business credits, and better quality information and advice. They also participated in joint ventures set up with the purpose of providing risk capital to small and medium-sized companies.

During the early-1970s the banks made considerable efforts to upgrade and rationalise their data processing facilities. They devoted resources to corporate planning activities in an effort to determine clear strategic objectives, and to guide the process of acquisition, diversification and investment. The domestic branch networks were reorganised on a more decentralised basis.

In their domestic diversification the Big Three banks have been able to build on experience and reputation as universal national deposit banks. They correctly identified the retail market as one of growing importance in the period of rapidly rising disposable incomes of the West German 'economic miracle', and were prepared to provide a comprehensive range of high-quality services to customers with increasingly sophisticated requirements.

The banks' entry into international banking markets has been more rapid and spectacular. Prior to 1970 the West German banks had virtually no overseas representation, although they maintained considerable correspondent links reopened after the Second World War. They played a significant role in the finance of foreign trade for West German industry, providing trade financing, foreign exchange and payment services. However, the proliferating activities of West German, European and US multinational corporations made additional demands on the banks which could only be met by expanding the foreign networks. The operation of US and other foreign banks in the Euromarkets also provided a competitive threat to the West German banks in the provision of large credits to West German corporations, which increasingly needed finance for large investment projects in addition to trade financing. In addition, foreign investors were showing a great deal of interest in the West German capital market and this provided the banks with the opportunity to exploit a unique marketing opportunity.

In order to provide comprehensive services in the major industrial and financial centres, the banks promoted the activities of bank officers travelling to foreign cities, began to open representative offices in key centres, entered into cooperative ventures with other international banks, and participated in foreign investment and development banks. Their most important move, however, was to establish subsidiaries in Luxembourg in order to engage in the Euromarkets from an off-shore position. The West German banks have also shown considerable commitment to the consortium bank idea, and their activities in concert with other major international banks have given them the opportunity quickly to provide staff with the necessary international banking experience.[7]

By the middle of the 1970s the banks increasingly felt the need to conduct international operations in their own name rather than through joint ventures and affiliates. There was a switch in emphasis then to the progressive establishment of full branches and representative offices in major centres (see Table 7.3). Such a policy gives the bank closer control of activities, strengthens its name in the world markets, and opens up the possibility of global funds management. Deutsche Bank has shown itself the most ambitious in its drive to attain a fully multinational spread of activities, opening several new offices and branches, establishing wholly-owned subsidiaries, and also obtaining quotation of its shares on foreign stock exchanges.

Together with other international banks, the West German banks were increasingly driven to lending to sovereign borrowers over longer maturities during the later 1970s, and have incurred a share of the substantial troublesome debts to Latin American countries. They have also become for historical, geographical and other reasons major financiers of East-West trade and have provided substantial credits to East European governments. Here too levels of credit risk have increased in recent years.

The West German banks are now amongst the most prominent

Table 7.3: Overseas Expansion of the Big Three West German Banks, 1970–9

	1970	1971	1972	1973	1974	1975	1976	1977	1978	1979
Deutsche Bank										
New foreign branches	—	2	—	—	—	—	1	2	4	5
New representative offices and agencies	1	—	1	2	—	—	1	1	2	3
Dresdner Bank										
New foreign branches	—	—	2	2	2	—	—	—	—	2
New representative offices and agencies	—	1	1	2	1	—	2	1	2	2
Commerzbank										
New foreign branches	—	1	—	1	1	—	1	2	1	1
New representative offices and agencies	2	2	—	1	2	—	2	1	—	2

of international banks in the provision of syndicated Eurocredits and are lead managers in a significant number of cases. They are extremely powerful in the Eurobond markets where their skill and placing power are equalled only by the Swiss banks.

The development of the liabilities and assets of the banks can be seen in Table 7.4. The deposits of the banks have grown at an impressive rate during the last decade or so, and this growth would be even larger if denominated in US dollars since the Deutschemark has, like the Japanese yen, appreciated significantly over the period. The rate of growth of advances has been slightly slower, with the exception of Dresdner Bank which has shown very strong growth in both deposits and advances.

All three banks now maintain a ratio of advances to assets of about 70 per cent and the growth in Dresdner Bank's loan portfolio has in fact brought it up to this level from a significantly lower base. Commerzbank, on the other hand, has reduced its proportion of advances. Deutsche Bank has maintained its profitability, although the others have suffered some decline. In 1980 and 1981 Commerzbank in particular ran into further difficulties as a result of funds management problems, while Dresdner Bank has suffered from its exceptionally high exposure to Eastern European bor-

Table 7.4: Development of the Big Three West German Banks, 1970–9

	1970 %	1979 %	Growth in deposits 1970–9, %	Growth in advances 1970–9, %
Deutsche Bank			311.3	299.0
1. Profits/assets	0.7	0.7		
2. Profits/shareholders' funds	17.2	21.6		
3. Shareholders' funds/assets	3.8	3.2		
4. Advances/assets	71.7	69.9		
Dresdner Bank			340.6	380.4
1. Profits/assets	0.6	0.4		
2. Profits/shareholders' funds	14.7	15.5		
3. Shareholders' funds/assets	3.8	2.8		
4. Advances/assets	61.5	68.1		
Commerzbank			328.5	280.5
1. Profits/assets	0.3[a]	0.1		
2. Profits/shareholders' funds	7.8[a]	5.2		
3. Shareholders' funds/assets	3.8	2.7		
4. Advances/assets	75.7	68.4		

Note: a. Net profits rather than pre-tax profits.

Source: Banker Research Unit, *The Top 100* (Financial Times, London, 1981).

rowers. Deutsche Bank has maintained one of the most impressive records of consistent profits of any of the world's major banks.[8]

Capital ratios have shown some decline over the period, but regulations prevent the fall of shareholders' funds below certain levels. The banks have made repeated rights issues in order to maintain their capital base. The mortgage bank subsidiaries issue long-term bonds but the parent banks have not been obliged to issue intermediate term debt or commercial paper on any scale.

In their funding the banks have come increasingly to rely on time deposits, especially bank deposits, a substantial proportion of which is foreign currency or non-resident deposits, and savings deposits rather than demand deposits. This has inevitably put some pressure on interest margins and provided further stimulus to the development of fee-based services.

7.3 Case Study — Deutsche Bank AG

The Deutsche Bank (DB) was founded in Berlin in 1870 by a number of private bankers who saw the need for a centrally-located commercial German bank which specialised in the finance of international trade. Branches were quickly opened in major German trading towns and in important overseas centres, including an agency in London. In 1893 the Deutsche Überseeische Bank was founded to conduct operations in Latin America. The period up to 1914 was an offensive phase in the Bank's development as it became extensively involved in financing of foreign railroads and German international trade.

After the First World War considerable readjustment was necessary and the Bank was forced to adopt a much more defensive strategy in order to survive first the Depression and Great Inflation, and then the Third Reich and Second World War. By the time of the Allied occupation of Germany the Bank had long since lost its international representation, and its domestic operations had suffered considerably. The Bank was also broken down into 30 constituent provincial banks.

With the post-War currency reforms and remarkable resurgence of economic activity in West Germany the Bank was able to resume gradually its normal operations. In 1952 it was reorganised into three main parts, and in 1957 the Bank re-emerged as a national bank with its head office in Frankfurt and a Berlin subsidiary.

During the 1960s the Bank devoted considerable efforts to the strengthening of its position in domestic retail markets, recognising that in an affluent society retail deposits would be an important source of funds and that there was great potential for increased earnings from consumer credit and housing loans. The Bank approached the market by extending its branch network, so that it now has about 1,300 branches nationwide, and by broadening its range of services. Small personal loans and loans for specific purposes were introduced at an early stage. In the late-1960s and early-1970s the Bank took steps to improve and rationalise its provision of housing loans. It acquired various subsidiaries, and offered first personal mortgage loans, then personal building loans, and in 1975 tailor-made house finance packages, offering consumers the full range of its subsidiaries' services through its own network. In 1976 fixed rate mortgages were supplemented with variable rate mortgages. The Bank also opened property information centres in certain branches.

It was during this period that the Bank also elaborated its services to investors through the media of investment funds, savings plans, investment management services, and the provision of investment information.

Steps were also taken in the early- and mid-1970s to boost data processing capacity and to rationalise the new extensive branch network. There is a very high density of bank branches in West Germany and the Bank found stiff competition from the savings banks and other institutions, putting considerable pressure on branch profitability. The Bank responded by forming regional groups of branches to give marketing impetus, and by decentralising management control to regional offices to a far greater extent.

The small and medium-sized business sector was an important target market in the mid-1970s, with new types of loan, and supplementary advice and information offered by the Bank. Equity finance was also made available through subsidiaries. This is a long-term involvement in an area which the Bank may have neglected historically in favour of large corporate lending:

> Our business policy objectives of further extending and deepening business relations wth small and medium-sized business firms will be consistently pursued in the future. Our corporate advisors are devoting their attention particularly to such business. (*Annual Report*, 1976.)

The DB has expanded its international operations vigorously since the late-1960s. Policy decisions were taken at that time which have since been carried into action and later modified partly in view of changing circumstances. In the Annual Report for 1971 it was stated that:

> For efficiency in world wide transactions a modern all round bank must have above all adequate financial capacity, it needs broad placing possibilities in the issue business, it must be able to provide the facilities of all types of foreign exchange and payment transactions, it must offer a comprehensive advisory service and finally it must be present at all the important international business and financial centres.

Pursuing this policy, the Bank set up its Luxembourg subsidiary in 1970 to engage in Euromarket business.

> In view of the growing financing requirements of its customers and the steadily increasing activity of foreign institutions on the Eurodollar market the Deutsche Bank cannot and will not withdraw from the Eurobusiness. However, in founding this new company the bank will not alter its financing principles and remains fully conscious of the particular risks of this market. (*Annual Report,* 1970.)

It also collaborated with Amsterdam-Rotterdam Bank, Midland Bank, and Société Générale de Banque in the foundation of EBIC in Brussels, to coordinate the joint work of the member banks within the framework of aims agreed originally by the European Advisory Group established in 1963, and to commence a programme of overseas expansion by means of representative offices and subsidiaries. The major subsidiaries of EBIC were BEC (Banque Européenne de Crédit) in Brussels, the European American Banks in New York, and the Euro Pacific Finance Corporation in Melbourne. Since then, the number of EBIC members has grown to seven, and there are now additional subsidiaries in West Germany, one of which has a number of offices in the Far East (European Asian Bank), Brussels, Bahrain and London.

However, since 1974 the emphasis has shifted to the opening of branches or representative offices, and the establishment of subsidiaries in the Bank's own name, a practice which the bank had pursued only cautiously in the earlier period. It now describes its approach as a two-tier strategy based partly on cooperative ventures, and partly on its own expansion. Since 1974 the Bank has also sought quotations on the major European stock exchanges.

The Bank stated in 1976 that it had 'no ambition to be represented in all financial centres of the world', but, even though it may be pursuing a selective policy, it has nevertheless achieved widespread representation. The Bank in 1981 had branches in Buenos Aires, Antwerp (1978), Brussels (1978), São Paulo, Paris (1977), Hong Kong (1976), Milan (1978), Tokyo (1976), Asunción, Madrid (1978), London (1973), New York (1978) Barcelona (1981) and representative offices in Cairo, Sydney, Rio de Janeiro, Toronto, San José, Santiago, Beijing, Bogotà, Tehran, Nagoya, Osaka, Tokyo, Nairobi, Mexico City, Lagos, Johannesburg, Moscow, Istanbul, and Caracas. It had subsidiaries in New York, Hong Kong, Singapore, Toronto, Zurich, London and Luxembourg; associated companies in Brazil, Holland, Spain, and the UK; and further holdings in banks in Africa, Latin America, Asia, and Europe. The most important move in recent years has been to establish new branches to conduct corporate lending and trust business, and subsidiaries to engage in funding operations. A list of major subsidiaries and affiliates appears in Table 7.5.

In the recent past the Bank has encountered difficulties on both the domestic and international fronts. The rise in interest rates during 1979 and 1980 in West Germany led to reduced earnings for the commercial banks because of their substantial portfolio of fixed rate lending, and because of the effect on market values of their large holdings of securities. West German industry also suffered setbacks due to the worldwide recession, leading to increases in bad debt provisions. Like all major international banks, the DB also had to cope with the difficulties of sovereign borrowers suffering balance of payment problems. As a result, cautious lending and accounting policies have been adopted and the Bank has maintained earnings rather better than its competitors, who were also more dramatically affected by the changes in domestic interest margins. In 1981 the Bank benefited from reduced domestic interest rates, so that its overall interest margin improved from 2.59 per cent in 1980 to 2.93 per cent in 1981. It also recorded higher contributions from services business, and trading in securities on its own account. There was a smaller rise in

Table 7.5: Deutsche Bank Group: Subsidiaries and Affiliates, 1981

	%
EBIC Joint Banks	
Banque Européenne de Crédit, Brussels	14.30
European American Bank and Trust Co., New York	
European American Banking Corporation, New York	20.25
European Arab Holding SA, Luxembourg (with subsidiaries in Frankfurt and Brussels)	5.50
European Asian Bank, Hamburg	14.30
European Banking Co. Ltd, London	14.10
Euro-Pacific Finance Corporation Ltd, Melbourne	8.00
Deutsche Bank (Suisse), Geneva	100.00
D.B. Finance (Hong Kong) Ltd, Hong Kong	99.00
D.B. UK Finance Ltd	99.90
Other important West German participations	
AKA Ausfuhrkredit Gesellschaft mbH., Frankfurt	27.00
Deutsche Bank (Asia Credit) Ltd, Singapore	100.00
Deutsche Bank Berlin AG	100.00
Deutsche Bank Saar AG	69.20
Deutsche Centralbodenkredit, Berlin	80.05
Deutsche Gesellschaft Für Fondsverwaltung M.B.H., Frankfurt	100.00
DWS Deutsche Gesellschaft Für Wertpapiersparen M.B.H.	51.00
Deutsche Kreditbank Für Baufinzierung AG, Cologne	100.00
Frankfurter Hypothekenbank, Frankfurt	89.30
Gefa Gesellschaft für Absatzfinanzierung, Wuppertal	100.00
Handelsbank in Lübeck	55.50
Industrie Bank von Japan (Deutschland) AG, Frankfurt	25.00
Suddeutsche Bank G.m.b.H., Frankfurt	100.00
Other important overseas participations	
Atlantic Capital Corporation, New York	100.00
H. Albert de Bary & Co. NV, Amsterdam	50.00
Al-Bank Al-Saudi Al-Alami Ltd, London	5.00
Banco Bradesco de Investimento, São Paulo	5.00
Banco Commercial Transatlántico, Barcelona	29.50
Banco de Montevideo, Montevideo	43.60
Banco Español en Alemania SA, Madrid	15.00
Compagnie Financière de la Deutsche Bank, Luxembourg	100.00
European Brazilian Bank, London	13.70
Foreign Trade Bank of Iran, Teheran	10.00
Industrial & Mining Development Bank of Iran, Teheran	3.00
International Mexican Bank (Intermex Bank), London	12.00
Iran Overseas Investment Bank Ltd, London	6.30
Société de Gestion Fundeurope	33.30
Société Ivoirienne de Banque, Abidjan	12.00

Source: *Annual Report* (1981).

staff and operating expenses, and profits from foreign exchange dealing were improved.

Like all the major West German banks the DB has substantial direct investments in West German industry, although it does not hold a majority holding in any case. In 1981, DB held over 25 per cent of the following companies: Bergmann-Elektrizitäts-Werke AG, Berlin; Daimler-Benz AG, Stuttgart; Deutsche Dampfschiff-fahrts-Gesellschaft 'Hausa' AG i.L, Bremen; Hapag-Lloyd AG, Hamburg; Philipp Holzmann AG, Frankfurt; Karstadt AG, Essen; Pittler Maschinenfabrik AG, Langen; Suddeutsche Zucker-AG, Mannheim — a diverse range of companies including manufac-turers, shipping firms, and retailers. The DB also has stakes in various other industrial and commercial undertakings by way of holding companies in which it has an interest.

If we now turn to the group's balance sheet we can observe some significant structural changes over the past five years (see Table 7.6). The proportion of advances has increased, and within that there has been a marked increase in long-term lending and mortgages, now totalling 40 per cent of all assets. This has been matched on the liabilities side by a percentage increase in long-term mortgage bonds issued. Savings deposits have shown a dramatic fall from 18.5 per cent of total liabilities in 1976 to 12 per cent in 1981. Customer deposits as a whole have shown a smaller decline, because of the substantial increase in time depos-its. The increase in bank time deposits reflects the growing import-ance of international business in the group's activities. A slightly larger increase in claims on banks reflects the Bank's cautious policy on Eurocurrency credits to customers, and preference for interbank market loans:

> In 1981 we again exercised deliberate restraint in syndicated Eurobusiness, which we continue to handle largely through our subsidiary bank in Luxembourg. We participated only in a num-ber of selected large credits, mainly in the USA, Canada and Mexico ... The expansion of interbank business reflects our bank's growing importance as a 'bank for banks', especially for foreign banks in international payment business and in money dealing. (*Annual Report*, 1981.)

There are no detailed figures available on the breakdown of currency and other business, although the Bank states that it earns 40 per cent of income from international operations and 60 per cent from domestic. About 80 per cent of income is derived from the interest margin, and about 20 per cent from fees. The figures in Table 7.7 show that the Bank's lending is spread over industrial,

Table 7.6: Deutsche Bank Group: Consolidated Balance Sheet

ASSETS	1981 DM millions	%	1976 DM millions	%
Cash	7,138	3.7	4,845	4.6
Bills	2,620	1.4	6,952	6.6
Claims on banks	42,308	22.0	20,334	19.3
Treasury bills	615	0.3	275	0.3
Bonds and notes	6,890	3.6	3,860	3.7
Securities	2,265	1.2	1,881	1.8
Advances	79,768	41.5	39,802	37.8
Short- or medium-term	(44,674)	(23.2)	(21,729)	(20.6)
Long-term (more than four years)	(35,094)	(18.3)	(18,037)	(17.2)
Mortgage advances (long-term)	41,653	21.6	21,578	20.5
Recovery claims	350	0.2	475	0.5
Trust loans	1,924	1.0	947	0.9
Subsidiaries, associates, investments	602	0.3	435	0.4
Land, buildings, equipment	1,164	0.6	1,042	1.0
Leasing equipment	898	0.5	636	0.6
Bonds and notes issued by affiliates	1,809	0.9	583	0.5
Other assets	2,409	1.2	1,602	1.5
Total	192,413	100.0	105,247	100.0
LIABILITIES				
To banks	56,427	29.3	28,574	27.1
Including time deposits	(47,305)	(24.6)	(22,616)	(21.5)
To customers	73,671	38.3	44,073	41.9
Including time deposits	(34,730)	(18.0)	(12,064)	(11.5)
Savings deposits	(22,998)	(12.0)	(19,441)	(18.5)
Bank bonds	4,199	2.2	2,844	2.7
Mortgage bank liabilities	43,074	22.4	22.439	21.3
Provisions for pensions, etc.	3,417	1.8	1,629	1.5
Share capital	1,232	0.6	900	0.9
Disclosed reserves, profits, minority interests	4,659	2.4	2,622	2.5
Other liabilities	5,734	3.0	2,166	2.1
Total	192,413	100.0	105,247	100.0

Source: Annual Report (1981)

public sector and private borrowers in roughly equal proportions. In its purely domestic business 41 per cent of claims go to private borrowers for consumer credit and housing finance.

The Bank does not publish details of its organisational structure but appears to maintain a traditional functional and geographical system of control, operating in many cases through specialised subsidiaries such as the mortgage banks, foreign subsidiaries (especially in Luxembourg which accounts for about half of all international business), investment companies and so on. The Bank has adapted a corporate planning approach for some ten years now,

Table 7.7: Deutsche Bank Group: Domestic and Foreign Advances by Sector, 1981

	%
Steel, mechanical engineering, vehicles, office equipment	7.1
Electrical engineering and light industry	5.0
Metal production	3.9
Chemicals, nuclear, petroleum	3.7
Textiles, clothing, leather	2.7
Wood, paper, printing	2.6
Food, tobacco	1.8
Other	2.5
Manufacturing industry, total	29.3
Trade	13.8
Other business and public authorities	29.9
Private borrowers (not self-employed)	27.0
	100.0

Source: *Annual Report* (1981).

requiring submissions from subsidiaries, divisions and branches. This is a 'bottom-up' planning procedure designed mainly to provide clear corporate objectives and improve profitability through better strategic decision-making from management. Like other European banks, the Bank relies largely on managers with a background of general experience in the Bank, and stresses virtues of drive, ambition, staff management capability, loyalty and commitment rather than technical skills. Nevertheless, it is placing increasing emphasis on the planning function at all levels in the Bank. The high quality of its strategic decision-making in the past decade is shown by its current levels of earnings in extremely difficult circumstances.

Notes

1. 'Landesbank' means 'State bank', 'Girozentrale' means 'Central giro institution'. The cumbersome title reflects the geographical and functional roles of these institutions.
2. The general purpose of the Supervisory Board is that of 'containing abuses in the banking sector which endanger the security of the funds entrusted to banks, or which impede the orderly conduct of banking business, or which could lead to considerable disadvantages to the economy as a whole.'
3. This information is available to other banks via regular reports. It thus acts as a sort of credit information clearing house.
4. See Economists Advisory Group (1980), ch. 5.
5. The West German banks have shown their willingness to undertake this kind of assistance recently again in their rescue of the massive AEG manufacturing

Company. Twenty-four banks collaborated in 1980, injecting DM 1 billion in fresh capital and as a result taking 50 per cent ownership of the stricken company.

6. Gessler did recommend that banks should limit their holdings to a 25 per cent stake, just sufficient to give a veto power. Sterner critics of the banks have proposed lower limits. Defenders of the banks stress their beneficial effect as stable, long-term investors. The Gessler Commission was established by the Minister of Finance in 1978 to consider 'the fundamental problems of the credit sector.'

7. Dresdner Bank has actually helped to found a special joint training centre for ABECOR members, the International Bankers Institute in Bad Homburg.

8. Commerzbank passed dividends in 1980 and 1981, mainly because of the adverse effect of rising interest rates on a large mismatched portfolio. Dresdner Bank paid a reduced dividend in those years, as its mismatching was less extreme. Losses arose on fixed rate bond portfolios acquired before an unforeseen rise in the level of interest rates in the late-1970s, which also affected the returns on the largely fixed rate mortgage lending.

References

Economists Advisory Group, *The British and German Banking System: a Comparative Study* (Anglo-German Foundation, London, 1981).

Maycock, J. for Institute of European Finance, *European Banking: Structures and Prospects* (Graham and Trotman, London, 1977).

Morgan, V. *Banking Systems and Monetary Policy in the EEC* (Economists Advisory Group, London, 1974).

Peat, Marwick, Mitchell & Co., *Banking in Germany* (Peat, Marwick, Mitchell & Co., Frankfurt, 1982).

Scheidl, K. for Banker Research Unit, *Banking Structures and Sources of Finance in the European Community* (Financial Times Publishing, London, 1981), ch. 1, Germany.

Stein, J. for Bundesverband Deutscher Banken, *The Banking System of the Federal Republic of Germany* (Bank-Verlag GmbH, Köln, 1977).

Vittas, D. (ed.) for Inter Bank Research Organisation, *Banking Systems Abroad* (Committee of London Clearing Bankers, London, 1978), ch. 2, Germany.

Weston, R., *Domestic and Multinational Banking* (Croom Helm, London, 1980), Part 2, ch. 5, 'Banking Regulation in the FRG'.

Data Sources

Annual Reports of Commerzbank, Deutsche Bank, Dresdner Bank and other major banks.

Banker Research Unit, *The Top 100* (Financial Times Publishing, London, 1981).

Deutsche Bundesbank, *Monatsberichte* (Monthly Reports).

8 CANADIAN BANKS

8.1 Financial System

The Canadian financial system is similar to the British in as much as there is relatively little government intervention, and the banking industry is dominated by a small number of large deposit banks. Canadian regulations and supervisory practices are, however, quite detailed and extensive.

Chartered banks control about two-thirds of the assets of all financial institutions in Canada. There are eleven chartered banks, but the big five banks are much larger than the others and control over 90 per cent of all bank assets. They are multi-purpose commercial banks with extensive domestic branch networks, engaged in all aspects of retail and corporate sector banking. Canadian banks are restricted in their ability to invest in non-banking subsidiaries, nor are they allowed to engage in trust banking, or in securities underwriting. They are allowed to maintain investments in venture capital companies or investment banks, although the investment banking sector in Canada is not well developed.

The Banking Act of 1980 created two classes of bank: Schedule A domestically owned banks, and Schedule B foreign banks. Under Schedule A come the six nationwide universal banks:

Royal Bank of Canada (RBC)
Canadian Imperial Bank of Commerce (CIBC)
Bank of Montreal (BM)
Bank of Nova Scotia (BNS)
Toronto-Dominion Bank (TD)
Banque Nationale du Canada (BNC)

Banque Nationale du Canada, the smallest of these six banks, has a densely concentrated network of branches in Quebec. The Bank is of French origin and has less substantial international business than the other banks.

Then there are three wholesale banks:

350

Mercantile Bank of Canada
Continental Bank of Canada
Canadian Commercial Bank

and two regional banks:

Bank of British Columbia
Northland Bank

The six largest Canadian banks have a considerable volume of international business. In particular, they maintain offices, agencies and branches in the major US financial centres to conduct US dollar business; but they also have extensive worldwide networks, and are among the very few banks in the world to conduct foreign retail operations in host countries other than the USA.

Foreign banks were subject to severe restrictions prior to 1980 and could only operate as unregulated non-bank companies (financial corporations) offering wholesale financial services. The Banks and Banking Law Revision Act of November 1980 enables foreign banks to maintain subsidiaries, affiliates or representative offices, although specific permission is required from the Ministry of Finance for the opening of branches. Many major international banks have seized this opportunity to strengthen their presence in Canadian markets.

Trust and mortgage loan companies are the only institutions permitted to undertake fiduciary responsibilities in Canada. Historically they had another advantage over the chartered banks, since they were permitted to make real estate loans. Chartered banks are now permitted to make property loans, within limitations, but the trust companies maintain a strong market presence in this field of lending. The Federal Trust Companies Act or similar provincial legislation governs their activities. Federally approved institutions may operate nationwide but provincial companies must first obtain deposit insurance. The legislation effectively restricts their activities to mortgage lending, and mainstream trust business in the case of trust companies, although they do a little secured consumer and commercial business. They are funded by medium-term certificates of deposit ('guaranteed investment certificates') matched to the loan portfolio. Mortgage loan companies also issue debentures and have savings, time and demand deposits, but these are not chequing accounts. These institutions are not subject to reserve requirements.

Credit unions and caisses populaires are more significant consumer savings and loan institutions in Canada than in any of the other major developed countries, providing about a quarter of all consumer credit. They are cooperative associations financed by shares and deposits of members and traditionally organised around a group of employees or within a small community, supported by regional and central institutions. Their ability to offer personal service and fine rates has ensured their steady growth.

Sales finance and consumer loan companies finance instalment purchase of consumer durables and larger fixed assets. The sales finance companies provide dealer-based hire purchase facilities, and are often subsidiaries of manufacturers or banks. The loan companies make cash loans to consumers, frequently secured by way of chattel mortgage. These companies are largely funded by issue of debentures and commercial paper.

Finance leasing corporations operate in a similar fashion to sales finance companies, although their business is not so tied to dealers. Many leasing companies are bank subsidiaries.

Real estate investment trusts are mortgage financing intermediaries created under federal or provincial law and restricted to real estate investments.

Other types of financial institution such as investment funds (open and closed-end) and life and general insurance companies are also active in Canadian markets. Investment dealers perform broking and issuing house functions, and also participate in the money markets.

The Bank of Canada was established under the Bank of Canada Act, 1934 and nationalised by 1936 and 1938 legislations. Its general aims are specified by statute, but the Bank is free to achieve these aims according to its own judgement. The Bank fulfils all the usual central banking functions, including:

— Supply of notes and coin and control of money supply.
— Fiscal agent and banker to the federal government.
— Banker to commercial banks.
— Lender of last resort in money markets and effective control of interest rates through bank rate.
— Administration of reserve requirements.

The Bank cooperates with the Ministry of Finance in the area of monetary policy and the Minister has ultimate control by way of directives.

In 1967 the Canada Deposit Insurance Corporation was created to administer mandatory deposit insurance by all chartered banks and federally incorporated loan and trust companies which accept public deposits.

The major banking legislation in Canada dates back to the Dominion Bank Act of 1870, which provided for government supervision of chartered banks and limited charters to ten years, so that a decennial review of the Bank Act is required. The 1900 revisions elevated the status of the Canadian Bankers' Association to a public corporation. Later revisions have led to the following regulatory framework:

1. Minister of Finance oversees the banking system, receives copies of audited reports, and may request auditors to investigate further.
2. An Inspector General of Banks reporting to the Minister has powers to investigate all banks annually, to audit bank returns, to undertake ad hoc investigations of banks at the Minister's request, and to obtain any necessary written or spoken information.

The Act also delineates the activities of chartered banks. There are no restrictions on loan business and interest rates, except that mortgage lending is limited to 10 per cent of Canadian dollar liabilities for the parent bank; nor on deposits and rates. Primary reserves are required and secondary reserves can be demanded by the Bank of Canada. Banks can invest without restriction in all types of securities including corporate stock, and can take stakes in bank service corporations, export financing corporations, subsidiary mortgage loan corporations, or subsidiary venture capital corporations. The banks are now required to consolidate their subsidiaries and follow equity accounting of associates. Stakes in other companies are restricted to 10 per cent of voting shares. The banks can and do engage in underwriting as well as bond trading, but only act as agents for customers in stock and share transactions. Banks are not permitted to trade in goods, to engage in fiduciary activities in Canada, or in portfolio/investment management in Canada.

The Bank Act was last reviewed in 1977, and finally re-enacted in 1980 after long debate about the legislation concerning foreign banks. Since 1980 foreign banks can operate a Schedule B chartered bank in Canada engaged in full-service banking, subject to regular renewal of licence, a maximum of two offices, and an overall ceiling on foreign bank assets as a proportion of total Canadian bank assets.

8.2 Strategic Development of Multinational Banks

The five large chartered banks all have a significant volume of international business and extensive overseas representation, putting them in the multinational class even though they are smaller in total asset size than the US, French, West German and British banks, and do not operate from a financial centre in Canada which has the same status as New York, London, Paris, Frankfurt or Tokyo. Three of the banks have very extensive overseas networks, mainly in the Caribbean area. Their involvement in international banking dates back to the beginning of the century, although the most rapid period of expansion has been since the late-1960s.

Table 8.1 shows the extent of diversification and internationalisation of these banks, and Table 8.2 shows their rapid network extension in recent years. The banks have branches in the key financial centres and are active participants in the Eurocredit markets, and to a more limited extent in the Eurobond markets. They have some foreign retail operations, and have made strategic investments in various countries, often by means of joint ventures. The largest banks have established a presence in the Middle East, Far East, Australia, West Germany, Switzerland and Latin America in response to perceived market potential and available opportunities. The emphasis in these ventures is on wholesale financial services — merchant banking, Eurocurrency business, trade finance. The banks have also established offshore operations enabling them to engage in trust business from which they are debarred in Canada. These banks have now about one third of their assets in foreign currencies and derive about a third of their income from international operations.

In their domestic market the chartered banks are a powerful oligopoly, the only real competition coming in the retail banking area from mortgage companies and credit unions. The banks have

Table 8.1: Canadian Chartered Banks: Subsidiaries and Branches, 1979

	Domestic subsidiaries	Domestic affiliates	International subsidiaries	International affiliates
Royal Bank of Canada	1	7	23	11
Canadian Imperial Bank of Commerce	2	1	14	6
Bank of Montreal	2	3	9	5
Bank of Nova Scotia	1	4	19	12
Toronto-Dominion Bank	1	2	10	2

	Overseas branches	Overseas rep. offices	Domestic branches
Royal Bank of Canada	86	10	1,522
Canadian Imperial Bank of Commerce	46	15	1,715
Bank of Montreal	12	16	1,244
Bank of Nova Scotia	81	14	976
Toronto-Dominion Bank	10	16	1,021

Source: Banker Research Unit, *The Top 100* (Financial Times, London, 1981).

Table 8.2: Canadian Chartered Banks: Overseas Representation, Branches Opened (B) and Representative Offices (RO), 1971-9

		1971	1972	1973	1974	1975	1976	1977	1978	1979
RBC	B	N/A	N/A	N/A	N/A	N/A	N/A	N/A	N/A	N/A
	RO	—	—	1	—	1	—	—	3	7
CIBC	B	5	7	5	5	1	8	6	2	5
	RO	2	2	—	1	1	3	1	—	2
BM	B	—	—	—	2	1	—	—	2	—
	RO	—	—	4	2	—	—	1	1	—
BNS	B	4	4	5	4	2	6	4	8	2
	RO	—	1	2	2	—	3	3	2	—
TD	B	—	1	1	—	2	—	1	—	—
	RO	2	1	2	—	2	1	—	1	1

Source: Banker Research Unit, *The Top 100* (1981).

now created their own mortgage companies as subsidiaries and are thus coming to dominate retail markets too, with the exception of fiduciary business. In corporate markets the only real competition comes from foreign bank subsidiaries which may be expected to provide a stimulus in future. Oligopoly does not necessarily mean inefficiency and the chartered banks provide a comprehensive range of services nationwide. The banks have also taken seriously their role as national banks, providing financial services to small communities and developing business, often in coordination with government schemes.

The process of domestic diversification began with the formation of mortgage company subsidiaries which bought from the parent bank mortgages originated through the bank network, and enabled the bank group to take the volume of mortgage lending beyond the 10 per cent level permitted to the bank itself. The banks also went into credit cards, although these are promoted more as a means of payment than a credit instrument. Consumer credit is largely by way of personal loan. The dominant cards are VISA, Mastercard and American Express, but retailers also issue housecards. As in the USA, retailers are substantial providers of consumer credit. The banks have been fairly slow to develop ATM networks, relying perhaps on branches for customer service. Telephone banking has been developed. The banks have since the early-1970s provided commercial credit services (leasing, factoring) to supplement the traditional range of bank services to the sector, and have established merchant banking capabilities.

Table 8.3 gives a broad picture of balance sheet growth over the period, showing rapid expansion of deposits and even faster growth of advances which now account for between 60 per cent and 70 per cent of assets. Profits in relation to assets and equity have not been maintained and in consequence capital ratios have declined. This has been the case for nearly all UMNBs during the 1970s.

The typical business pattern of a chartered bank is shown in Table 8.4 although obviously each bank has its own peculiar features. In organisational terms, the banks are moving towards the US market-oriented pattern, from a previously geographical/ functional pattern.

The asset and liability structure is shown in Tables 8.5 and 8.6. Foreign currency assets and liabilities are over 40 per cent of total assets and liabilities, and much of this business is booked overseas in London or the Caribbean. Mortgage lending is an important part of assets (8 per cent of total). Non-mortgage lending goes to all sectors of the economy, but here too consumer credit is a significant element (9 per cent of total assets). On the liabilities side we can see the important part played by personal savings deposits (25 per cent of total liabilities).

Table 8.3: Development of Canadian Chartered Banks, 1971–9

	1971 %	1979 %	Deposit growth 1971–9 %	Advances growth 1971–9 %
RBC				
1. Profits/assets	1.1	0.6		
2. Profits/shareholders' funds	23.6	19.2		
3. Shareholders' funds/assets	4.8	3.4		
4. Advances/assets	55.9	63.7		
			350.2	404.7
CIBC				
1. Profits/assets	1.1	0.6		
2. Profits/shareholders' funds	28.5	25.8		
3. Shareholders' funds/assets	3.9	2.4		
4. Advances/assets	53.8	64.8		
			311.3	441.7
BM				
1. Profits/assets	1.0	0.8		
2. Profits/shareholders' funds	30.5	28.7		
3. Shareholders' funds/assets	3.2	2.8		
4. Advances/assets	59.2	69.6		
			320.8	397.7
BNS				
1. Profits/assets	1.3	0.7		
2. Profits/shareholders' funds	36.8	24.8		
3. Shareholders' funds/assets	3.7	2.9		
4. Advances/assets	N/A	N/A		
			443.6	N/A
TD				
1. Profits/assets	1.1	0.7		
2. Profits/shareholders' funds	34.6	25.5		
3. Shareholders' funds/assets	3.0	2.8		
4. Advances/assets	58.4	66.3		
			403.4	451.9

Source: Banker Research Unit, *The Top 100* (1981).

8.3 Case Study — Royal Bank of Canada (RBC)

RBC has its origins in the Merchants Bank of Halifax, chartered under the laws of Nova Scotia in 1869. In 1871 the Bank was chartered under the first of the Canadian Bank Acts. The Bank grew rapidly to obtain national importance and in 1901 assumed its present name. In 1907 the head office was transferred to Montreal which was already emerging as the prime financial centre of Canada.

Table 8.4: Typical Structure of Canadian Chartered Bank

Parent bank (chartered commercial bank quoted on Canadian and London Stock
  Exchanges).

Domestic subsidiaries
Real estate development company
Mortgage loan company
Commercial credit services
Leasing company

International subsidiaries
West Indian banks/trust companies
New York trust company
Channel Islands trust company
Finance company Hong Kong, Singapore, etc.

Strategic Investments
(eg)
Germany
Switzerland
France
Austria

Expansion continued at a rapid rate with the acquisition of
several smaller regional domestic banks in a typical pattern of
growth by amalgamation which we have observed in the development of large commercial banks in many countries. The Bank also
made some foreign investments in the Caribbean, such as Bank of
British Honduras Ltd (1912) and British Guiana Bank (1914).
Branches in London and New York had been established at a very
early stage to service Canada's trading flows and capital needs.
After the First World War the Bank continued its drive overseas
with the establishment of a subsidiary in France (1919) and acquisition of the Bank of Central and South America (1925), but with
the onset of the Depression and then the Second World War,
opportunities were limited for Canadian banks, as they were for
US, European and Japanese banks.

The next period of diversification came in the late-1960s. The
Bank had long been involved in property development through
Globe Realty Corporation, formed in 1912, but in 1969 it took
steps to expand its capacity for mortgage lending by forming Roy
Mor Ltd to purchase residential mortgages originated by the Bank.
In 1972 the Bank acquired interests in a leasing company and
mortgage insurance company, and in 1975 took a stake in a factor-
ing company. In 1977 it strengthened its position in the leasing

Table 8.5: Canadian Chartered Bank Assets and Liabilities, December 1981

ASSETS	C$m	%
Canadian Dollar Assets		
LIQUID ASSETS		
Notes, coin, central bank balances	7,341	2.1
Treasury bills	8,282	2.4
Government bonds	1,568	0.4
Call and short loans	2,445	0.7
Total	19,636	5.6
Securities, mainly corporate	10,178	2.9
LOANS		
Provinces	826	0.2
Municipalities	2,132	0.6
Canada bonds	916	0.3
General loans	120,095	34.3
Residential mortgages	28,535	8.2
Other mortgages	2,352	0.7
Leasing	2,112	0.6
Total Loans	156,969	44.9
Deposits with other banks	2,063	0.6
Items in transit	1,262	0.4
Acceptance liabilities	6,591	1.9
Other assets	5,656	1.6
TOTAL CANADIAN DOLLAR ASSETS	202,355	57.9
TOTAL FOREIGN CURRENCY ASSETS	147,387	42.1
TOTAL ASSETS	349,742	100.0
LIABILITIES		
Canadian Dollar Liabilities		
PERSONAL SAVINGS DEPOSITS		
Chequable	6,220	1.8
Non-chequable	43,206	12.4
Fixed term	43,086	12.3
Non-personal notice deposits	4,218	1.2
Non-personal term deposits	44,555	12.7
DEMAND DEPOSITS		
Personal	3,879	1.1
Other	16,026	4.6
Canadian Government	7,138	2.0
Other	38	—
Total	168,306	48.1
Bankers' acceptances	6,591	1.9
Subsidiaries	1,879	0.5
Other liabilities	5,522	1.6
Minority interests	103	—
Debentures	2,652	0.8

Table 8.5: continued

Taxation	1,077	0.3
Share Capital	2,342	0.7
Surplus	1,822	0.5
Reserve	1,059	0.3
Retained earnings	5,796	1.7
Total	197,148	56.4
TOTAL FOREIGN CURRENCY LIABILITIES	152,594	43.6
TOTAL LIABILITIES	349,742	100.0

Source: Bank of Canada.

business with the acquisitions of Roy Lease Ltd (previously Canpac Leasing) and Roy Marine Leasing. Roy Lease Ltd was subsequently merged with Canadian Acceptance Corporation, a finance company bought by the Bank in 1981. The Bank was also an early member of the VISA card scheme, originally in cooperation with three other major banks, but recently under its own name. The Bank also acquired a management consultancy in 1974.

The Bank's diversification of international activities since 1970 has been imaginative and rapid. Branches and representative offices have been established in all the major centres, and strategic investments have been made especially in the areas of merchant banking and fiduciary business. On the other hand, the level of investment in some of the West Indian retail banks was reduced. The Bank has made good use of joint ventures, although more recently has tended to go it alone when possible.

Some of the major ventures undertaken by the Bank have been:

1972   Interest in Libra Bank (London Eurobank).
1972   Interest in Canada International (Longman) Ltd.
1973   Interest in Inchcape Credit Corporation (Hong Kong finance/investment company, with Inchcape Group).
1973   Bishops International Bank (Joint Venture) and merchant banks in Africa, the Middle East and Far East.
1975   Interest in a West German private bank.
1977   Roy West Investments and Holdings (joint ventures with National Westminster).
1979   RBC (London) Ltd and (Asia) Ltd established as merchant banks.

Table 8.6: Canadian Chartered Banks — Non-mortgage Domestic Loans (C$m) 1981 (4th Qtr)

	C$m	%
Personal (Non-Business)		
Securities	1,665	1.3
Vehicles	6,091	4.7
Mobile homes	993	0.8
Home improvements	1,065	0.8
Other (personal loans)	18,501	14.4
Credit cards	3,549	2.8
Total consumer credit	31,865	24.8
Financial institutions	10,329	8.0
Agriculture	7,748	6.0
Forestry and fishing	1,436	1.1
Mining and energy	9,038	7.0
Manufacturing		
Food, etc.	1,753	1.4
Textiles	1,141	0.9
Metals	2,362	1.8
Transport	2,117	1.6
Chemicals	2,229	1.7
Other	7,364	5.7
Total Manufacturing	16,965	13.2
Construction	11,822	9.2
Transport	4,599	3.6
Wholesale trade	5,561	4.6
Retail trade	6,398	5.0
Services	8,252	6.4
Real estate	3,932	3.1
Conglomerates	514	0.4
Public enterprises	1,474	1.1
Institutions	1,711	1.3
Governments	2,982	2.3
Non-residents	1,458	1.1
Leasing	2,099	1.6
Others	152	0.1
TOTAL	128,633[a]	100.0

Note: a. Of which 2,178 under government guaranteed schemes.

Source: Bank of Canada.

Western Trust and Savings Ltd acquired (UK consumer finance house).

1980-1 West German investments increased, and wholly-owned subsidiary created in Switzerland. In 1981 RBC also bought out its partners in Orion Bank (London Consortium Eurobank) and merged it with RBC (London) Ltd to form Orion Royal Bank Ltd.

1981-2 Export finance subsidiary established and an international
trade finance network acquired from Consolidated Gold
Fields Ltd.

This has been a vigorous programme, which shows that the Bank is
determined to achieve multinational capabilities in the shortest
possible time by establishing branches and wholly-owned subsidiaries in all major centres. We can now briefly review its present
operations.

RBC is the largest of the chartered banks. It operates in all areas
of Canada and through branches, subsidiaries and agencies has
worldwide coverage. In 1982 it derived 57 per cent of income
from domestic business and 43 per cent from international. The
foreign proportion has been increasing steadily in recent years. It
employs about 39,000 staff, the vast majority in Canadian branch
banking.

Domestic Operations

The domestic network of some 1,500 branches covers the whole of
Canada's massive land area, and is organised into seven regions,
which report eventually to the head office in Montreal. The Bank
offers a full range of consumer banking services including a wide
variety of deposit/savings accounts and interest bearing cheque
accounts, together with investment certificates of Royal Bank
Mortgage Corporation, retirement savings plans and other tax efficient schemes. Customers now have multi-branch banking (access
to all services at any bank branch) and Personal Touch Banking
offers 24-hour ATM services facilitating cash withdrawal, transfers
between accounts, and so on. This is operated by a Client Card. In
addition, the VISA credit card is available. The Bank provides
consumer credit through fixed rate personal loans and VISA. It
also provides mortgage advances, and has recently introduced a
variable rate mortgage scheme.

The level of service and imaginative innovation make RBC a
world leader in retail branch banking.

The Bank provides a full range of services to small and
medium-sized businesses and participates in federal schemes such
as Small Business Development Bonds and the Small Business
Loan Programmes. Additional services include life insurance and
computer payroll services. Specialist managers are now installed at
district level to advise smaller firms. The Bank also employs agri-

cultural advisers and a comprehensive range of services to agri-business. Various publications are produced aimed at small firms and independent farmers.

In the corporate sector the Bank suffers increasing competition from foreign banks. It has now established Commercial Banking Centres in regions to provide expert management service of larger business accounts, and is putting emphasis on non-lending services such as payroll and cash management. A smaller number of some 500 national accounts is catered for separately in Toronto, Montreal, Calgary and Vancouver, and individual account executives coordinate bank services to these larger groups. In 1980 the Bank also established a special Global Energy and Minerals Group with bankers and technical experts in one operating unit. A similar move to market orientation of resources was the creation in 1979 of the World Trade and Merchant Banking Division, coordinating activities through seven international centres in Canada. The Division also includes the new Export Finance Company (international factoring) and Orion Royal Bank Ltd in London.

Table 8.7 shows the level of business in different segments of the domestic market. Clearly consumer and commercial/national accounts show a poor return on assets. The domestic treasury function and domestic foreign currency business show good returns as does the independent business/agriculture sector. Returns on consumer lending recently have been depressed because of the impact of rising rates of interest on a large portfolio of fixed rate lending funded from variable rate deposits.

International Operations

The Bank has over 200 operating units in 46 countries, and has correspondent relationships with over 4,000 banks worldwide in

Table 8.7: Royal Bank of Canada: Domestic Market Segments, 1982

	Assets, C$bn	%	Return on assets %
Consumer operations	13.3	26.4	.46
Independent business/agriculture	6.5	12.9	.83
Commercial and national accounts	14.0	27.8	.48
Canadian treasury	3.4	6.7	1.76
Foreign currency operations in Canada	9.4	18.7	.78
Other assets	3.8	7.5	—
Total domestic operations	50.4	100.0	.63

Source: *Annual Report.*

100 countries. The retail operations comprise 76 branches and 21 subsidiaries and affiliates, but their importance in the Bank's strategy is now reducing. The only recent major increase in retail investments was the acquisition of Western Trust and Savings in the UK, where RBC, like other North American financial institutions, see the opportunity to exploit a niche through the use of consumer money shops.

International operations are divided into six geographical areas, with recent emphasis on public sector and corporate banking. In the USA there is the Royal Bank and Trust Co. in New York with various branches, agencies and other representative offices in major cities. In Latin America and the Caribbean the Bank has a network of 68 branches in 16 countries as well as numerous representative offices, subsidiaries, and affiliates. In the UK, the bank has the centre of its international banking operations in London through its branch and through Orion Royal and its Eurocurrency, Eurobond and merchant banking business. In Continental Europe the Bank has a branch and a subsidiary in France, various subsidiaries in West Germany, and investments in the Netherlands, Switzerland and Belgium, along with various representative offices. In the Middle East and Africa the Bank has various offices which are controlled from London. In Asia Pacific the Bank's headquarters are in Hong Kong where there is a full banking branch and also a merchant banking subsidiary. Other offices have been set up in Japan, South Korea, China and Thailand.

The Bank has established two central objectives: 'the provision of high-quality banking services to all sectors of Canadian society, and a vigorous participation in international trade and world markets', which it will aim to achieve in an environment which will be difficult in the 1980s because of various factors:

— Continued inflation.
— Scarce energy resources.
— Redistribution of global economic and political power.
— Instabilities in the monetary system.
— Political tensions.
— Technological change.

In 1980 the Bank undertook a major strategic planning review as a consequence of which it established a divisional structure based on market segmentation which provided for greater decentralisation of decision-making. The Bank has attempted to increase responsiveness to changes in the marketplace by creating market-oriented operating units with considerable autonomy in customer-related affairs. The Bank also identified productivity and profitability as key areas for management effort in the 1980s, in an era when asset growth is expected to be slower than in the 1970s, but still rapid. Strategic and policy decisions have been concentrated with top management, setting guidelines for delegated decision-making by operating unit managers. Great stress is being placed on the continuous review of strategy, and continuous updating of professional skills.

In a recent discussion on bank profitability the Bank showed that its growth rate in total assets had been 20.2 per cent between 1971 and 1981, but its growth in equity had only been 14 per cent, resulting in a capital ratio of only about 3 per cent in 1981. This was attributed to inadequate return on assets. The Bank observed that the stock market rating of the banks in Canada had declined from 1974 onwards, reflecting investors' doubts about prospective bank profitability. During the 1970s international profits had grown faster than domestic profits, but by 1981 they were converging.

References

Blythe, L.N., *Banking in Canada* (MacDonald & Evans, Plymouth, 1978).

Canadian Bankers' Association, *Banking in Canada* (Canadian Bankers' Association, Toronto, 1982).

Frazer, P. and Vittas, D., *The Retail Banking Revolution* (Michael Lafferty, London, 1982), ch 12.

Galbraith, J.A., *Canadian Banking* (Ryerson, Toronto, 1970).

Green, D.W., *The Canadian Financial System Since 1965*, Bangor Occasional Papers in Economics No 3 (University of Wales Press, Cardiff, 1974).

Guenther, H. for BRU, *Banking and Finance in North America* (Financial Times Business Publishing, London 1981), chs 1–4.

Neave, E.H., *Canada's Financial System* (Wiley, Toronto, 1981).

Peat, Marwick, Mitchell & Co., *Banking in Canada* (Peat, Marwick, Mitchell & Co., Toronto, 1981).

Perry, J.H. (ed.), *Banking in Canada* (Canadian Bankers Association, Toronto, 1982).

Weston, R., *Domestic and Multinational Banking* (Croom Helm, London, 1980).

Data Sources

Bank of Canada Review, Bank of Canada.
Statistics Canada, *Financial Statistics*.
Annual Reports of chartered banks.

9 SWISS BANKS

Switzerland is one of the smallest countries in the world, with a minute population which enjoys a very high standard of living, and with a financial services industry which has come to play a key role in world financial markets. As a financial centre Switzerland's cities collectively rank with London, New York and Hong Kong. Switzerland's particular strength lies in its highly developed capital markets rather than in money markets, and in the investment management skills of its bankers, supported by the country's long tradition of neutrality, stability and the strength of its currency.

Swiss banks were financing European trade and governments from the eighteenth century onwards. The great commercial banks were established in the nineteenth century. After the First World War the country and its financial institutions became a safe haven for European money since its social fabric was strong, it was un-affected by inflation, and its banks were free from governmental interference. Since the Second World War Switzerland has once again emerged as an attractive investment centre for largely the same reasons, and because of the persistent savings power of Swiss residents. Its major banks have successfully exploited the unique position of Switzerland and contributed greatly to the promotion of that position by achieving a superb reputation for skill, discretion and prudence in world money and capital markets. The asset size of the Swiss banks does not reflect their true importance, since much of the business they conduct is of a fiduciary nature, managing the investments of an extensive range of customers from all parts of the world.

The largest Swiss banks are in fact the largest Swiss corporations, and the banking industry is the leading industry in Switzerland. Their position differs from that of all the other banks we have studied because of their bias towards capital markets rather than money markets. Nevertheless, they cannot be omitted from a study of multinational banks, and in many ways their activities provide a clue to the possible future development of the UMNBs of other countries which are increasingly turning away from deposit banking to fee-earning financial services. Our discussion will however be illustrative rather than detailed.

367

9.1 Financial System

The Swiss financial system is not strictly regulated. It is dominated by the three largest banks, but private banks and foreign banks are also important participants. Money markets are less highly developed than capital markets and some specialised markets such as gold and foreign exchange.

The Big Banks comprise the three UMNBs, Crédit Suisse, Swiss Bank Corporation, Union Bank of Switzerland, and two smaller banks, the Swiss Volksbank and Bank Leu. These are truly universal commercial banks performing a full range of services in domestic and international markets in Switzerland and through branches and subsidiaries in major financial centres of the world.

Cantonal banks comprise the 28 state banks of the cantons of the Swiss Confederation, orginally established to supplement the limited capabilities of private banks. They have about 1,250 offices throughout the country, but each bank is restricted to its own area and some are debarred from international banking. They are primarily regional savings banks and lenders to agriculture, small businesses and to the personal sector for housing finance. They have, however, expanded into business lending and securities, acting as issuing houses for public sector enterprises, and also managing foreign bond issues.

Regional banks, savings banks and mortgage banks also operate at a local level and have not become involved in international banking activities to a very great extent. Switzerland has about 240 of these small commercial banks taking retail savings and lending to local enterprise or on mortgages. Their share of total banking business in Switzerland has declined in recent years.

Credit cooperatives comprise mainly the 1,100 or so small members of the Raiffeisen Loan Association. They collect savings from the rural population and lend to cooperative members on a fully secured basis.

The 38 *private banks* in Switzerland are sited in the main financial centres and specialise in acting as portfolio managers and investment counsellors for a select number of wealthy clients on a worldwide scale. They are important participants in international stock exchange and securities business, and have considerable placing power with foreign and Eurobonds. They are not obliged to publish their balance sheets.

There is a large number of *foreign-controlled banks* in Switzerland, subsidiaries and affiliates of international banks eager to establish a presence in Switzerland's capital markets. They concentrate inevitably on business with foreign customers, and account for about a quarter of all foreign deposits and lending of Swiss-based banks; but they also compete in the field of Swiss domestic banking, servicing Swiss subsidiaries of foreign companies and Swiss-owned multinationals.

Other banks include a variety of finance houses, trust banks, money brokers, securities dealers and so on able to thrive in such an active financial centre. There are very few specialist financial institutions in Switzerland, although two institutions were created to refinance the lending of mortgage banks. The universal banks have pre-empted the need for a post office savings bank, an export credit institution, or long-term lending banks. The post office giro system is however the central payments system.

Switzerland has a thriving collection of mutual funds, and a successful insurance industry.

The *Swiss National Bank* was founded in 1906 as a joint-stock company and has never been nationalised, although its shareholders are largely cantons, cantonal banks and other public sector bodies. The federal government has statutory powers enabling it effectively to control the Bank if necessary, but in practice the Bank is accorded considerable autonomy. The Bank has headquarters in Berne and Zurich, and performs the usual central bank functions. However, its ability to regulate financial markets has always been hampered by the lack of depth of Swiss money markets and the absence of a large market in federal securities. It has therefore been obliged to resort to controls and decrees to achieve its objectives in the areas of monetary policy and currency management.

The governing legislation of the Swiss banking system is the Federal Banking Act of 1934, partially revised in 1971, and supplemented by the Ordinance of 1972. The law provides for:

— Definition of financial institutions.
— Banking licences.
— Rules on capital adequacy and liquidity.
— Credit controls.
— Rules on lending to related parties.
— Depositor protection.
— Reporting and auditing requirements.

— Supervision under the auspices of the Federal Banking Commission.

The 1972 Ordinance prescribes figures and ratios for prudential purposes. Banks in Switzerland must also comply with the commercial Code of Obligations. There is also an Ordinance governing the establishment of foreign bank branches.

9.2 Strategic Development of Multinational Banks

The Big Three Swiss banks have followed a similar process of development in their careful exploitation of the opportunites open to them in the Swiss and international banking markets. Free from legal restraints, they have become truly universal banks with comparable scope and range to the large West German banks.

Over half their assets are now in foreign currencies and they have extensive overseas representation (Tables 9.1 and 9.2). Their balance sheets have grown less rapidly than those of many multinational banks during the 1970s and they still have a very conservative ratio of advances to total assets. Their consistent quality of earnings has enabled them to improve their capital ratios over the period, in contrast to other multinational banks.

Table 9.1: Swiss National Banks: Subsidiaries and Branches, 1979

	Domestic subsidiaries	Domestic affiliates	International subsidiaries	International affiliates
Swiss Bank Corporation (SBC)	10	4	13	5
Union Bank of Switzerland (UBS)	8	—	5	11
Crédit Suisse (CS)	13	4	7	12

	Overseas branches	Overseas rep. offices	Domestic branches
Swiss Bank Corporation	13	24	189
Union Bank of Switzerland	6	20	227
Crédit Suisse	9	22	156

Source: Banker Research Unit, *The Top 100* (Financial Times, London, 1981).

Table 9.2: Development of Swiss National Banks, 1971–9

	1971 %	1979 %	Deposit growth 1971–9 %
Swiss Bank Corporation			
1. Profits/assets	0.6	0.5	
2. Profits/shareholders' funds	12.8	9.5	
3. Shareholders' funds/assets	4.5	5.7	
4. Advances/assets	29.2	46.1	
			115.1
Union Bank of Switzerland			
1. Profits/assets	0.6	0.7	
2. Profits/shareholders' funds	11.8	11.1	
3. Shareholders' funds/assets	4.7	6.0	
4. Advances/assets	32.1	47.3	
			144.9
Crédit Suisse			
1. Profits/assets	0.6	0.6	
2. Profits/shareholders' funds	14.5	8.9	
3. Shareholders' funds/assets	4.2	6.6	
4. Advances/assets	31.6	51.7	
			60.0

New branches and representative offices 1971–9

	1971	1972	1973	1974	1975	1976	1977	1978	1979
Swiss Bank Corporation									
Branches	1	1	—	1	1	1	2	—	1
ROs	1	—	1	—	1	2	1	1	—
Union Bank of Switzerland									
Branches	—	1	—	—	1	—	—	2	1
ROs	5	1	—	2	1	2	—	—	—
Crédit Suisse									
Branches	2	2	—	—	—	1	—	1	2
ROs	1	1	1	2	2	4	1	3	1

Source: Banker Research Unit, *The Top 100* (1981).

9.3 Case Study — Swiss Bank Corporation

The SBC had its origins in the Basler Bankverein founded in 1872 to provide credit to local industry. It assumed its present name in 1897, and now has head office functions split between Basle and Zurich, which has become the more dominant financial centre.

The Bank quickly extended its operations throughout Switzerland and played a major role as a financial intermediary in the industrialisation of the Swiss economy prior to the First World War. It also took an early interest in international business, taking stakes in financial concerns in London, New York and Paris. The First World War interrupted the Bank's progress, and Switzerland, like other creditor nations, lost substantial overseas investments in the economic chaos of the immediate post-War period. Between 1923 and 1929 some normality was restored and the Bank was able to assist in the restructuring of Swiss industry. It also took a leading position as an underwriter of Swiss and foreign bonds. During the Depression and Second World War the Bank had to adopt an extremely defensive position, liquidating foreign investments and repatriating all transferable balances. It did, however, open an American office in New York in 1939, an important indicator of developments to come.

In the post-War period the Bank established its position in domestic markets and developed into a fully-fledged international bank. In 1945 it took over the troubled Basler Handelsbank. It began to extend its network of Swiss branches and to promote its presence in retail banking. It now has a network of about 190 domestic offices and provides savings, consumer credit and mortgage finance, sometimes through subsidiaries. Its traditional commitment to industry has been reinforced by the addition of leasing, factoring and business advisory services to its range.

The Bank's involvement in asset management comes through private bank subsidiaries, and through its range of mutual funds. The Bank also engages actively in dealing in precious metals and coins, and handles fiduciary accounts for customers, mostly placed on fixed term deposit with foreign banks.

About 60 per cent of the Bank's total balance sheet assets is in foreign currencies. It has numerous overseas subsidiaries and branches in key financial centres. The Bank is the largest Swiss bank in terms of deposits and employs a staff of about 13,000, some 1,400 of whom work abroad.

Further Reading

Bär, H.J., *The Banking System of Switzerland* (Schulthess Polygraphischer Verlag, Zurich, 1973).
Bauer, H., *Swiss Bank Corporation 1872–1972* (Swiss Bank Corporation, Basle, 1972).

Iklé, M., *Switzerland: An International Banking and Finance Centre* (Dowden, Hutchinson & Ross, Stroudsburg, 1972).

Inter Bank Research Organisation, *Banking Systems Abroad*, (IBRO, London 1978), ch. 6 Switzerland.

Mast, H.J., *The Swiss Banking Industry* (Crédit Suisse, Zurich, 1978).

Mast, H.J., *The Swiss Banking System* (Crédit Suisse, Zurich, 1977).

Peat, Marwick, Mitchell & Co., *Banking in Switzerland* (Peat, Marwick, Mitchell & Co., Zurich, 1982).

Union Bank of Switzerland, *Swiss Stock Guide* (Union Bank of Switzerland, Zurich, 1982).

Data Sources

Swiss National Banks, *The Swiss Banks.*

Annual Reports of Swiss Banks.

10 REVIEW OF CURRENT ISSUES IN MULTINATIONAL BANKING

The development of multinational banks during the 1960s and 1970s may appear to have been smooth and successful, but it is now recognised that the industry faces significant problems in the future. A previous time of crisis occurred in 1974 when the operation of the international money markets was adversely affected by the failure of two banks and losses sustained by others. Since then the markets have thrived, banks' management skills have improved, and supervisory controls have been strengthened. But recently new problems have arisen.

The underlying problem is the increasing turbulence of the environment, in terms of:

structural balance of payments disequilibria
worldwide economic recession
volatile exchange rates
volatile interest rates
technological change

These obviously heavily influence banks' domestic and international operations.

In addition, the banking industry is now highly competitive. Traditional oligopolies and restricted markets are being opened wide to competition from banks and non-banks, domestic and foreign. It can be argued there is serious overcapacity in the world financial services industry, which will in time lead to a shake-out on a scale comparable with that experienced in the motor industry in recent years.

The real issue facing multinational banks in the future is simply survival; that is, long-term profitable growth. This means securing quality earnings from net interest income by intelligent asset and liability management, and by generating fee income from value-added services, while controlling costs rigorously. Achieving these aims in stressful and competitive conditions will be highly demanding. The poor relative performance of bank shares in many countries suggests that investors are sceptical of banks' abilities to attain the required rates of return in such a risky environment. On the other hand the financial services sector as a whole is generally thought to be a growth sector in the future. Business development and strategic planning then become the key management areas for the future, supplemented by adequate control through financial information systems. These controls must monitor profitability and returns, and cater for the major banking risks — credit risk, liquidity risk, interest and exchange rate exposure, and ultimately capital adequacy. External supervisors will also need to take a keen interest in these processes.

Credit risks obviously increase at a time of recession and in the past few years banks have been obliged to make heavy provisions against losses on domestic and international lending. Problems with sovereign lending to Eastern Europe and Latin America reached crisis proportions in 1981/2/3 but concerted action by banks, governments and official agencies has kept the situation within manageable limits. Undoubtedly extreme care will be needed over several years to sort out current problems and banks are now adopting more cautious lending policies in the Euromarkets. Asset quality and profitability have now become more important considerations than asset growth.

Increasing reliance on liability management means that banks must implement sound liquidity policies. The healthy operation of the key money markets becomes a matter of central concern, and here again banks and official agencies have cooperated to surmount temporary difficulties. Supervisors now monitor closely banks' liquidity management practices. In the event of unexpected losses banks rely first on current cash flows (earnings) as a defence, and finally on capital reserves. The declining capital ratios of the major banks in recent years is thus a cause for general concern, and is an issue continuously raised by supervisors. The maintenance of capital adequacy depends on the achievement of adequate rates of return, and here the banks face a significant communications problem. It is widely believed that banks make excessive profits, whereas the truth is that in recent years bank profits have been insufficient to maintain capital. A hidden question of deeper import to banks in future is whether their low profits are in fact attributable to excessive costs, as well as to the difficult environment.

The costs problem is also highlighted by the rapid change now taking place in information technology. As banking becomes more of a capital intensive industry unit costs can be reduced, but only if staffing is reduced as machines are introduced, and provided that the machines achieve their economic potential. Technological developments also enable non-banks to enter the banking industry at low cost, and possibly with superior skills in systems implementation.

Finally, it must be added that the regulatory environment continues to be a very important factor in development of banking, both in domestic and foreign markets. In many cases regulation is the biggest single constraint on banks' planned growth. As banks multinationalise the issue of reciprocity becomes important — the insistence by host countries that freedoms they allow to foreign banks are similarly allowed to their own banks operating abroad. Of course no body has legal powers in the international markets, but the concerted action of central banks and other agencies has persuasive effect.

Our country studies have shown that in many cases banks face the same problems in their business development. This is forcing them to look more closely at their activities, to define their product market scope more carefully and to assess their own distinctive competence. The drive to improve return on assets and boost return on equity encourages the same search worldwide for quality earnings from selected markets. Bank management worldwide confronts these same problems, and the small group of universal multinational banks will find itself locked in a long-term competitive struggle for survival in the future. The major uncertainty is the direction of development of the Japanese banks who could in time come to dominate the world banking industry in the same way they have come to dominate major manufacturing industries.

It has been shown that UMNBs have emerged in a number of countries and that they face identifiable common problems. An important forum for opinion on the current condition of these banks is the international bond market. It was observed in Chapter 1 that banks have not sought foreign stock market quotations as eagerly as some industrial giants, but many of the major banks have issued long-term loan stock in the Euromarkets, where they come under the scrutiny of the international investment community, and also, if bonds are issued in the USA as foreign bonds, under the eyes of the powerful rating agencies. Increasing numbers of banks are issuing bonds in the USA, and also short-term commercial paper.

To the international investor one international bank is essentially the same as another, each with its unique position in its domestic financial system due to the wide differences in the structure of the banking industry between countries, and each with its particular stance in international and foreign banking markets. The investor takes a broad view of each bank, focusing on its major markets and on its overall business structure and organisation. He assesses the resultant strengths and weaknesses of the bank in terms of:

Earnings record and margins, sources of income
Asset quality, domestic and international
Capital ratios and quality of capital
Management quality

Most importantly, the investor looks to the future, to the earnings prospects and business risks of each bank. It is fears for the future profitability of banks which have persuaded the investment community and rating agencies to take a more cautious view of bank bonds recently. Only a handful of major international banks are currently favoured with AAA (Triple A) ratings, and most of the US majors were downgraded in 1981. Leading banks still carry very good credit ratings (mostly Double A or above) but they are no longer regarded as undoubted credits. The following section discusses country by country the reasons for this sceptical view of the banks' future, from the perspective of the international investor.

US Banks

The Federal Reserve now classifies 17 money centre banks as multinational on the basis of their involvement in international and foreign banking markets. Concerned about sovereign risk exposure and declining capital strength, it has now insisted on a minimum 5% primary capital ratio (roughly, shareholders' funds to assets) for each of these banks. Of these 17 banks all but two have lost the Triple A, and six are ranked lower than Double A, a remarkably cool appraisal of some of the great names of US banking history.

The reason for this assessment is the conclusion that the risks and uncertainties facing banks now materially affect their prospective earnings in the medium- and long-term. Increased business risk is expected to become apparent through:

— lower returns on traditional banking business
— low returns on new areas of business
— greater exposure in less regulated, less protected and more competitive environments
— drive towards differentation and specialisation of services
— persistent pressure on capital ratios
— ongoing problems with credit quality of international lending and only slow improvement in quality of domestic lending to certain industrial sectors

Deposit deregulation, de facto breakdown of interstate barriers, competition, and technological advancement of delivery systems are causing the major banks to rethink their business strategies and adopt new postures in an attempt to improve earnings. This is often achieved through acquisition of both bank and non-bank enterprises, since this is quicker and cheaper than building up in-house operations. In order to finance acquisitions banks may issue more debt, or perhaps sell some existing assets. Debt issues increase business risk.

Whilst few commentators expect repudiation of sovereign debts, bank lending to LDCs has permanently deteriorated in quality, a fact disguised by rescheduling arrangements. The risk of partial losses remains high, and the assets have become illiquid, reducing the banks' flexibility at a time when they would wish to redeploy assets. In their domestic lending several US banks have experienced problems in certain sectors, notably real estate, energy, steel, mining and shipping. The expected recovery of the US economy will see many banks right, but exposure of certain less well-managed banks to problem industries remains.

The banks still derive the vast majority of their earnings from lending to the industrial and commercial sector, and to individuals. In commercial lending, there is intensified competition from foreign banks, finance houses and leasing companies, whilst larger corporate customers have easier access direct to the money markets through the issue of commercial paper. In retail lending, savings and loans offer an even wider range of services and compete with stockbrokers and others for retail deposits.

The US multinational banks remain powerful business organisations, whose access to diverse sources of capital and money market funding ensures their liquidity and enables them more than adequately to fulfil their economic functions. But doubts have been raised, not least about the evident quality of management in some institutions, where credit policy has been suspect and poor returns accepted. The possible future development of the industry is described in a final section.

Japanese Banks

Relaxation of regulations has led to more competition between City banks and long-term credit banks in the field of commercial lending, and between banks and securities firms in the field of merchant banking services. Nevertheless, the Japanese financial system remains tightly controlled, and bank profits are heavily influenced by interest rates managed by the government in the interests of industrial development and budgetary financing. The profitability and capital ratios of the City banks, the leading half dozen of which have multinational status, have declined because of commercial lending competition, and the forced purchase of low-yielding government bonds. The major city banks have pursued a growth policy in domestic and international business for several years now, accepting low margin business for the sake of market share. Their exposure to sovereign debt remains low, because of their relatively late and closely supervised entry to international lending markets. In their retail markets the City banks face tough competition from the Post Office and other savings institutions.

Undoubtedly Japanese banks will grow in stature as Japanese industry continues to extend its power in international markets. They have always been required to play a subservient role to industry, acting in a constrained environment, and this factor, which has resulted in limited and distorted financial markets in Japan, must affect their ability to develop in competition with Western banks in the near future. However, financial markets are slowly being liberated, and Tokyo still has the potential to emerge as the key Eastern financial centre, especially if the role of Hong Kong is diminished subsequent to its change in political status. The leading Japanese banks are gaining wide experience in international and foreign markets and the direction of their future strategic development is probably the most important factor affecting the future structure of the multinational banking industry.

British Banks

The leading British banks have a unique historical background in multinational banking, and London is still the pre-eminent financial centre. However, earnings of the four London clearing banks have suffered from low margins and increased risks in international markets, where they are quite significantly exposed to sovereign risk, as well as from tough competition and the effects of economic recession in domestic markets. The banks' low cost retail deposit base is being continually eroded by building societies, National Savings and other institutions, while commercial lending has become more competitive at the same time as credit quality has declined. The banks' ventures into fee-earning financial services have not significantly diversified sources of income and the recent commitment to increased mortgage lending to individuals has not resulted in high margin new business.

Nevertheless the clearing banks have a powerful established position in domestic markets and have become leading international banks, although stronger in commercial banking than in merchant/investment banking. Their earnings performance is expected to recover somewhat as the UK economy turns up, and as the international debt crisis is weathered; although there is still the possibility that the government will at some stage seek to tax banks more heavily.

Capital ratios in the clearing banks have declined recently, and questions have also been raised about the quality of capital since reserves include both property revaluations and unprovided deferred taxes, which US banks for example are not permitted to count as capital. However, it is now widely accepted that in the UK environment these items are quite properly credited to capital reserves, and on this basis the clearers' capital ratios remain fully adequate.[1]

French Banks

The Nationalisation Law of 1982 saw a material increase in state ownership of banks of all types and the reversion of the Big three banks to 100% state ownership. As a consequence of public ownership the Big Three French banks are able to maintain capital ratios far lower than those of their international competitors, and in theory need not achieve such high levels of profitability as the other multinational banks. However, it was observed in Chapter 6 that the major banks act as fully commercial enterprises. They have played a special role in support of French industry, but then the same could be said of banks espousing a doctrine of social responsibility in other countries. One consequence of extended public ownership of French banks and other industrial sectors is perceived to be a dilution of the strength of the relationship between the State and any particular institution. Paradoxically, wider state ownership in general means that each individual institution becomes more independent and needs to take greater responsibility for its own destiny. The French banks then, are regarded as less of an extraordinary case than previously, and this shift in perspective will no doubt persist as the banks affirm their multinational status and partial independence from the French economy.

In competitive terms, the French national banks occupy a powerful position in domestic markets with scope for expansion in the area of retail banking. They are also important participants in international lending, but have not been major forces in investment banking and have not made major foreign investments. Paris remains overshadowed by London as the major European financial centre, and shifts in the French political environment pose problems for international banks. Despite these drawbacks the French banks will prove a powerful force in future, and are able to draw on long historical experience of multinational banking.

German Banks

The Big Three German banks have suffered severe losses of earnings in recent years because of their exposure to rising rates of interest, and because of loan loss problems with regard to Eastern Europe and, subsequently, in the recession-hit domestic economy. The development of international financial markets in Germany has been hampered by regulation.

Nevertheless, as Germany comes out of recession, the German banks are well placed to take a leading role in multinational banking. Their earnings have already shown an improvement, and they are well able to conduct international operations from Luxembourg and other external financial centres. Their exposure to less developed countries is low by comparison with US banks, although they are more heavily lent to Eastern Europe. The quality of their asset portfolio should remain high now that doubtful debts have been adequately provided for.

The German banks have an important role to play in both domestic and international capital markets and have gained a powerful position in the international bond markets. As the scope of the international securities industry and the use of the Deutschemark as an investment currency are extended, the German banks will benefit accordingly.

Canadian Banks

The Canadian chartered banks have experienced difficulties in recent years because of their significant exposure to sovereign risk and their exposure to large troubled companies in the Canadian economy. Asset quality and profitability declined in consequence and this trend did nothing to help the traditionally low capital ratio maintained. Consequently Canadian banks, like the US majors, lost their top credit ratings in 1982.

Nevertheless the Canadian banks' position in their domestic markets remains strong, although competition for corporate business will increase now that foreign banks have been allowed better access to the markets. The branch banking operations are profitable, and the banks have long experience of international banking based in London and other key centres. As the Canadian economy improves the banks should see restoration of earnings once more.

Swiss Banks

The Big Three Swiss banks enjoy a unique and enviable position within a small but wealthy country which is also one of the world's key financial centres. Switzerland has extensive capital markets and is the recipient of large international money flows. The Swiss banks have extremely strong capital ratios further bolstered by hidden reserves, a long-term record of steady profitability (the true extent of which is masked by hidden transfers to reserves), and a low exposure to sovereign risk and domestic credit problems, covered by very full loan loss provisions. As international flows of funds increase and the turbulence of the surrounding environment persists, the attractiveness of the Swiss banks to investors can only be magnified. The mechanics of fiduciary business means that Swiss banks are able to expand their volume of managed funds without pressure on capital ratios and without exposure to interest rate, liquidity or exchange rate risks.

This brief survey of the current standing of multinational banks suggests that their strategic development will only be temporarily held back by the problems encountered in the wake of the post-1979 world recession. The reasons for this bullish view are:

— the international debt crisis is widely considered to have been contained by the concerted actions of governments, banks, the IMF and others. The danger of repudiation is receding, and it is more likely that banks will trudge through a series of reschedulings giving considerable concessions to borrowers and suffering losses on a discounted net present value of assets basis, but avoiding write-offs. The continued cooperation of the IMF and governments will be needed in order to surmount recurring liquidity crises and political problems; and banks will have to persist in their own efforts at collaboration. Provisions have already been made against losses, whilst considerable expertise has been gained in the procedures of rescheduling and greater caution adopted in new lending.

— domestic debt problems are likely to diminish as individual economies recover from the recession, following developments in the USA. Provisions have already been made for existing doubtful debts, and the process of rationalisation in many industries and companies has now run its course. New growth industries with substantial financial requirements are emerging.

— banks and other participants in the financial markets have now developed skills and methods designed to cope with the more difficult environments in which they now operate. They have learnt to measure and partially to protect themselves from the risks of exposure to rapidly changing interest rates and exchange rates; have developed new lending techniques such as project financing, leasing, forfaiting; and are continually improving their access to information.

— the process of diversification of services and geographical coverage will continue as the world's capital markets become increasingly international in character and as more countries liberalise their financial systems. Moreover, the provision of services based on advanced information technology will become increasingly important. At the same time, the structure of the multinational banking industry may well become consolidated as smaller or less successful banks recognise limits to the extent of their own diversification and to their ability to invest in new ventures, acquisitions or state-of-the-art technology.

This is not to say that the multinational banking industry has a comfortable future. Asset quality has significantly deteriorated, and this will reduce earnings and the liquidity of parts of the loan portfolio for several years. Competition in all the major markets remains extremely intense, so that margins everywhere are bound to be thin. The need for new investment is high, and many areas of operation particularly in domestic banking will require restructuring and rigorous cost control. Significant public relations problems remain in many countries.

Predictions are hazardous, a fact of life with which bankers are all too familiar, but it would be churlish to leave this review of the industry without giving some indication of the way in which the process of strategic development may continue in multinational banks. A recent extensive survey[2] of senior executives in a large number of US banks gives some indication of the approach being adopted to business development in future. The picture that emerges is broadly one of evolutionary growth in increasingly competitive markets. Large banks are expected to broaden the scope of their operations steadily, but without radical changes in their business mix, except that the largest will seize any opportunity offered by deregulation to achieve nationwide banking.

The main theme of the report, which echoes the theme of this book and could be extended to all multinational banks worldwide, is that the discipline of strategic planning will become increasingly important as the pressures of competition mount. Only well-planned and properly controlled operations will survive in the markets of the 1980s and beyond. The report stressed certain key strategic factors for the future — areas requiring particularly close attention from executive management:

General management

— Management quality, especially the encouragement of entre-

preneurial thinking by line management
— Management evaluation and motivation, with compensation linked to achievement of business objectives
— Risk and exposure management, notably the assessment of risk/ required return from different activities of the group
— Responsiveness to change, adapting to changes in regulations and markets by delivering new services to customers

Marketing

— Services, requiring overall decisions on the range to be offered, innovation, differentiation, bank image
— Customer service, meaning quality control at all levels, but also the ability to offer different levels of service suitable to different market segments
— Segmentation, enabling banks to identify profitable market segments by various systems of classification, for special attention
— Marketing skills, involving the development of more detailed and more rapid market intelligence, more effective education of customers, and better staff selling skills

Technology/Operations

— Technological readiness, the ability to take advantages of new systems to improve the delivery of services to customers and the internal efficiency of the bank
— Distribution, the exploitation of new methods of communication and delivery of services to supplement the traditional branch networks

Finance

— Capital access, identification of capital needs, tapping of available sources of capital, and investor relations to ensure the ability to finance new investments
— Pricing, the refinement of costing information to enable accurate pricing in highly competitive markets sufficient to maintain adequate profit margins, for different types of service and customer
— Asset/liability management, involving control of exposure to interest rate, liquidity and exchange rate risks, and the use of appropriate hedging techniques.

The report stresses that in general terms banks will need to monitor their environment more and more closely, and to measure their performance objectively against their peer group competitors in order to stay in touch.

This book has discussed universal multinational banks and our definition of UMNBs has embraced banks offering a wide range of retail and wholesale services, operating in domestic, international and foreign markets. It has been suggested that UMNBs will continue their existing process of strategic development, and that a small core of banks will emerge as the leaders of the industry. Commentators have now suggested that some of the world's leading multinational corporations in other industries have in effect become *global* corporations — the difference being that whereas a MNC operates in a number of countries and adjusts to the market in each, a global corporation treats the whole world as one market and adopts a similar stance in each country, selling the same product everywhere. The global corporation reduces costs by having fewer, more standardised products. Examples of this approach are:

Japanese MNCs, eg: Sony, Seiko, Toyota
US MNCs, eg: Coca-Cola, Procter & Gamble, Revlon, Mc-
   Donalds
The giant oil companies

This sample covers a wide selection of industries, and even a service industry in McDonald's. The question arises then, as to whether UMNBs will emerge as global corporations. It's evident that international wholesale banking is global in scope. International deposits and loans are the same in any financial centre, and indeed merchant and investment banking services are transferable worldwide to a certain extent, thanks in no small part to the emergence of English as a financial lingua franca and to the universality of accounting systems and computer languages. However, retail banking practices differ widely from country to country and no bank has as yet been able, like McDonald's, to offer the same service in different countries. The retail banking networks of the Californian subsidiaries of UK and Japanese banks are significantly different from their parents' retail operations, for example, although some cross-fertilisation of ideas is now taking place. As for the future, the introduction of cash management systems and the internationalisation of securities markets will see further standardisation of international wholesale services. In the retail markets, joint venture card systems and other examples of bank co-operation on a world-wide scale will see some standardisation, but banking habits in different countries appear so widely different that global retail banking remains a remote possibility.

It should also be observed that in this area bank regulators and supervisors are an important influence, since their requirements produce different environments in each country and favour the perpetuation of indigenous practices and institutions. This is one major reason why UMNBs tend to expand overseas by acquisition, a process that is likely to continue for the foreseeable future, wherever banks with free capital to invest see profitable opportunities.

Notes

1. Since the time of writing legislation has been passed which will lead to the removal of unprovided deferred tax from capital reserves.

2. *New Dimensions in Banking: Managing the Strategic Position* (Arthur Andersen & Co. and Bank Administration Institute, Illinois, 1983). The study took the form of a Delphi investigation, involving interviews with senior bank officials and other industry experts.

INDEX

Figures and Tables are indicated by (F) and (T) respectively, following the page number.

References to the countries which are the subject of whole chapters, in addition to those under the country concerned, will be found under: financial institutions, international banking, multinational banks, regulations, services, strategic development, structure, subsidiaries.

388